THE LEGACIES OF COMMUNISM
IN EASTERN EUROPE

THE LEGACIES

OF COMMUNISM

IN EASTERN EUROPE

■ ■ ■ ■

Edited by Zoltan Barany and Ivan Volgyes

THE JOHNS HOPKINS UNIVERSITY PRESS

Baltimore and London

All rights reserved. Published 1995
Printed in the United States of America on acid-free paper
04 03 02 01 00 99 98 97 96 95   5 4 3 2 1

The Johns Hopkins University Press
2715 North Charles Street
Baltimore, Maryland 21218-4319
The Johns Hopkins Press Ltd., London

Library of Congress Cataloging-in-Publication Data

The legacies of communism in Eastern Europe / edited by Zoltan Barany
and Ivan Volgyes.
    p.   cm.
    Includes bibliographical references and index.
    ISBN 0-8018-4997-7 (cloth : acid-free paper). —
ISBN 0-8018-4998-5 (pbk. : acid-free paper)
    1. Communism — Europe, Eastern.   2. Communism — Former Soviet
republics.   3. Post-communism — Europe, Eastern.   4. Post-
communism — Former Soviet republics.   5. Europe, Eastern — Social
conditions — 1989.   6. Former Soviet republics — Social conditions.
I. Barany, Zoltan D.   II. Völgyes, Iván, 1936-   .
HX240.7.A6L44   1995
335.43 — dc20   94-43245

A catalog record for this book is available from the British Library.

CONTENTS

PREFACE

Frankly speaking, until the late 1980s most students of Eastern Europe never thought that a book such as this would be written during our lifetime. Like most political scientists specializing in East European affairs, we merely dared to *dream* of the end of Communist rule in the region. In fact, as the 1980s wore on, only a very few of us who thought that the end of communism was near were bold enough to confide to anyone the conclusions we were forced to draw from events taking place in the Soviet Union and in Eastern Europe. Were we perhaps afraid of being labeled "hopeless optimists," or "congenitally anti-Communist cold warriors"? This may have played a part in our hesitation, but only a part. Our hesitation was in greater measure simply due to the fact that we were trained as observers and not as predictors of human events; although we saw the signs of the disintegration of the power of the USSR, and hence the rapidly approaching end of Communist rule in Eastern Europe, most of us instinctively shied away from prophesying.

And yet, when communism fell, most of us who have labored in the vineyards of Communist studies immediately sensed that we needed to place the system we had observed for several decades under the microscope of scientific observation one last time. We were all convinced that we had to take a slice in time and space of the remains of communism, before change altered Eastern Europe once and for all. It was not a professional autopsy that we wanted to perform; rather, we wanted to take a final glimpse of the legacies that communism left behind. It is this desire for that last, long look, a desire for an intellectual snapshot of the situation after the collapse, but before the people and the nations started to crawl out of their shelters, that brought us together to write a book on the legacies of communism.

The result is the volume you are now holding in your hands. It is not a book of "readings" in the traditional sense, for we tried to adhere rigorously to the analytic framework outlined in the introductory chapter. Nor is it a book of theoretical essays on the structural problems of the region, for we tried to examine the concrete legacies of the failed system. And finally, it is not a country-by-country litany of woes; although we deal with each formerly Communist East European state, the chapters provide the authors with an opportunity to discuss the legacies of Communism from a comparative perspective.

Accordingly, we arranged the book in two large parts, an introduction, and a conclusion. The introduction sets the theoretical framework for the volume. It details the bases for the subsequent analyses of the Communist legacies in the fields of politics, economics, society, the environment, and foreign and military policies — subjects that are then discussed with a regional and topical focus in part 1 of the book. Part 2 focuses on the peculiarities of the legacies in each of the former Communist states of Eastern Europe.

As these lines are written, the Eastern Europe we used to know no longer exists. Not only is "communism" as a system gone from the region, but so are several of the countries we discussed in this volume. East Germany disappeared from the map after an artificial existence of more than four decades. Czechoslovakia has disintegrated into two republics, ending a historical coexistence (interrupted only during the war years) of more than seventy years. And Yugoslavia, melded together between 1919 and 1926, has once again broken up into its constituent republics; symbolically, just as the bridge at Mostar has been destroyed, so has the dream of the integration of a "Yugoslav nation," perhaps forever.

Sadly, in the new Eastern Europe there is little domestic tranquility, civil society, civic culture, or — the greatest blessing of democracy — respect of different groups for one another. While crucial steps toward establishing democracy, such as the empowerment of the people to determine their own affairs, and to elect whomever they wish to represent them, have been realized in post-Communist Eastern Europe, the reemergence of traditional authoritarianism, national hatreds, and intolerance mar the political landscape. Nor can we say that the Communist legacies in economics have been quickly obliterated by the introduction of the market economy; though progress is under way in this respect, it will take a long time to integrate the East European economies with those of the West. All this, however, is the subject of another book. Yet the reader must understand that this volume was not based on the naïve expectation that once communism was gone, democracy would automatically "break out" in the region; we all knew that the lasting legacies of communism would be as difficult to erase as would the reemergent legacies of still earlier bygone ages.

Hence, as is befitting to social scientists, we have tried to separate those phenomena we may attribute to the impact of communism from those that were characteristic of the region before the emergence of communism as a system, and those that appeared since communism's fall. Admittedly, such a separation was not an easy task, and often the record is clouded at best. The extent to which we succeeded, of course, can best be left to the wisdom of the reader, who ultimately sits in judgment of our efforts.

■ ■ ■ ■

Finally, a few words about terminology, and sources. In this volume "East-Central Europe" denotes East Germany, Poland, the former Czechoslovakia, and Hungary, while "the Balkans" should be understood as the former Yugoslavia, Albania, Bulgaria, and Romania. When we talk about "the region," we mean all of Eastern Europe, that is, East-Central Europe and the Balkans.

Because of the nature of the research, the names of many of the interview subjects and other informants have had to be kept confidential.

ACKNOWLEDGMENTS

The origins of this book date back to the early spring of 1991, when, discussing the unfolding developments in Eastern Europe, we decided to organize an international meeting to examine and to argue about the profound and diverse legacies of communism. Months of preparation and planning culminated in a lively three-day conference held in Lincoln, Nebraska, in October 1992. Such an endeavor could only come to fruition through the help of people and institutions who believed in and actively supported the project.

We thank the Department of Political Science at the University of Nebraska–Lincoln, and particularly its then-chairman, John R. Hibbing, for considering ours a worthy project to be financed by the departmentally administered Hendricks Fund. We are also thankful for the active support and funding assistance of Graham Spanier, chancellor of the University of Nebraska, and John G. Peters, who was then dean of its College of Arts and Sciences. The following members of the Department of Political Science at the University of Nebraska–Lincoln, also deserve our gratitude: William P. Avery, David P. Forsythe, David P. Rapkin, and Raphael Zariski; as well as Edward L. Homze, from the Department of History, who moderated the conference panels. For the funding they provided, we also gratefully acknowledge the Cooper Foundation, the University of Nebraska Foundation, the Office of International Affairs of the University of Nebraska–Lincoln, and Martin Massengale, former president of the University of Nebraska.

We also thank Robert Blumstock, of McMaster University, Hamilton, Ontario; Richard I. Hofferbert and Otto Ulc, of the State University of New York at Binghamton; Volodymyr Khandogy, deputy permanent representative of Ukraine to the United Nations; Sergei V. Lavrov, deputy minister of foreign affairs of the Russian Federation; John Lukacs, of Chestnut Hill College, Philadelphia, Pennsylvania; John Spanier and Kenneth Wald, of the University of Florida, Gainesville, Florida; Laszlo Szegedi, of the Center for National Security and Defense Studies, Budapest; Toby Trister Gati, assistant secretary of state for research and intelligence in the U.S. Department of State; and Sergiu Verona, of the Library of Congress, for participating in the conference. Thomas A. Baylis, Jane L. Curry, Daniel N. Nelson, and Sharon L. Wolchik deserve our gratitude for agreeing to contribute to the volume on short notice. Affectionate thanks go also to DeDee Volgyes, who shouldered many of the planning and organizational tasks related to the conference.

A grant from the Research Institute of the University of Texas at Austin enabled us to hire Bruce Kellison, a doctoral student in the Department of Government at the University of Texas, to assist us with the coordinating and editing of the chapters. Without Mr. Kellison's exemplary work habits and many helpful suggestions this book would have been much more difficult to produce. Thanks also go to the department's Suzanne Colwell, whose computer skills and patience facilitated the completion of the manuscript.

Finally, our thanks go to Henry Y. K. Tom, executive editor at the Johns Hopkins University Press, who was the first to express interest in the manuscript and has overseen its metamorphosis to book form with great professionalism; and to Miriam L. Kleiger, our manuscript editor, whose insistence on clarity and consistency has made this a better book.

ABBREVIATIONS

ACP, Albanian Communist Party

AFD, Alliance of Free Democrats [Hungary]

APL, Albanian Party of Labor

BCP, Bulgarian Communist Party

BSP, Bulgarian Socialist Party

CDU, Christian Democratic Union [Germany]

CIS, Commonwealth of Independent States

CMEA, Council for Mutual Economic Assistance

CPSU, Communist Party of the Soviet Union

CSCE, Conference on Security and Cooperation in Europe

DBD, Democratic Farmers' Party [East Germany]

EC, European Community

EU, European Union

FDP, Free Democratic Party [West Germany]

FRG, Federal Republic of Germany

GDP, gross domestic product

GDR, German Democratic Republic

GMT, Greenwich mean time

GNP, gross national product

HDF, Hungarian Democratic Forum

HSP, Hungarian Socialist Party

HSWP, Hungarian Socialist Workers' Party

IM, "unofficial collaborator" (in German, *Inoffizielle Mitar-beiter*) [East Germany]

IMF, International Monetary Fund

JNA, Yugoslav armed forces

KGB, Committee of State Security (in Russian, Komitet Gosudarstvennoi Bezopasnosti) [USSR]

KOR, Workers' Defense Committee

LCY, League of Communists of Yugoslavia

LDPD, Liberal Democratic Party [East Germany]

MFN, most favored nation

MinEkologii, Ministry of Ecology and Natural Resources
of the Russian Federation

MPA, Main Political Administration [all East European
Communist countries]

MSzOSz, National Council of Hungarian Trade Unions

NAFTA, North American Free Trade Agreement

NATO, North Atlantic Treaty Organization

NDPD, National Democratic Party [East Germany]

NEM, New Economic Mechanism [Hungary]

NMP, net material product

NSWP, non-Soviet Warsaw Pact

OPZZ, All-Polish Association of Labor Unions

PDS, Party of Democratic Socialism [Germany]

PEC, Political Executive Committee [Romania]

PHARE, Poland/Hungary: Assistance to the Restructuring of the Economy

PZPR, Polish United Worker Party

RCP, Romanian Communist Party

RFE, Radio Free Europe

SD, Democratic Party [Poland]

SED, Socialist Unity Party of Germany (in German, Sozial-
istische Einheitspartei Deutschlands) [East Germany]

UDF, Union of Democratic Forces [Bulgaria]

W TO, Warsaw Treaty Organization

ZSL, United Peasant Party [Poland]

1

The Legacies of Communism: An Introductory Essay

Ivan Volgyes

It is no exaggeration to say that the birth and the demise of European communism were two of the most important political events of the twentieth century. The astounding, revolutionary character of communism's appearance was matched by the rapid disintegration of the system. Both were unexpected events that brought about great changes in the configuration of world politics. Near the end of this turbulent century it is perhaps appropriate to look back at the legacy of communism.

Since all of the former Communist countries in Europe have disappeared, the independent states that have taken their places seem to exist in a state of limbo. Within the political confines of the new state configurations, different varieties of social, political, and economic systems emerged, ranging from remnants of the old system that existed in these lands for nearly fifty years, through native authoritarianism, to partial democracy, in a curious coexistence of old and new cultures. As we have witnessed the reemergence of authoritarianism, chaos, intolerance, and even civil and religious wars, we are forced to ask, To what degree is the presence of these attitudes due to values and behavior patterns that were inculcated under the Communist system, rather than to those that were prevalent before the Communists took over?

Of course, we must keep in mind that the framework of this question isolates value formation from other powerful influences of the twentieth century. Shifts in behavior often accompany changing times, and this century has brought forth immense changes. The advancement of technology which has brought people and ideas together from all around the globe has had an enormous impact upon societies everywhere. Scientific and technological progress and its effects, some good and some not so good, cannot be discounted when one considers the shifting of values and changes in behavior not only in Eastern Europe but also in the West. Aside from technology, changes in economic situations and in the system

of alliances, as well as the impact of Western Europe's drive toward economic and monetary union, must likewise not be neglected when considering the question of value formation. While recognizing that other factors have affected society in Eastern Europe, can we nevertheless discern
whether it is the Communist value structure or the previously existing one
that can be regarded as the independent variable determining current
behavior?

Our examination, therefore, must look at the empirical data at hand:
what actually existed at the point of transformation in 1989–91 in the
lands with which we are concerned? For real evidence of the Communist
legacy, we must look, first, at the physical layout of the land; second, at the
prevailing economic structures; third, at the social system; and, fourth, at
the political patterns, both in the domestic and foreign policy realms.
Where possible, our examination must attempt to separate values from
behavior, for as we must note, political behavior does not necessarily
reflect ingrained political values.[1]

Our examination is also warranted by the fact that, in spite of the
general agreement among observers of the region that communism has
disappeared nearly without a trace, there exists a lingering suspicion in the
minds of the more thoughtful specialists of our profession that the impact
of communism was in fact greater than is generally assumed. Moreover, it
is also slowly becoming clear to many of us that a number of the values and
behaviors currently observed in the region have come into being, or at
least have come to light, as a direct, negative reaction to the decades of
Communist rule. For example, the long-suppressed values of nationalism
that were allowed to reemerge after the fall of communism have become
characterized by such an extreme negativism that they may threaten the
survival of the peoples of the region. It is worthwhile, therefore, to pose
the question, Would that nationalism be so extreme had nationalism been
allowed to exist in some form under the previous regime? While it is very
difficult to make this a testable hypothesis, we can at least ask the proper
questions. The examination below is the beginning of such a quest.

Physical and Environmental Legacies

The task of describing the physical and environmental legacies of communism is relatively simple. Geographers have already done an adequate job
of describing the "socialist landscape."[2] The legacy of the system is visible
and recognizable from Moscow to Prague, and from Warsaw to Sofia.

That physical legacy is traceable to urban space utilization programs derived from the concept of Communist urbanization. Communism was in part, of course, an urban affair; it regarded urban space as superior to rurality. In consequence, it developed an overall settlement strategy of herding people from the villages into urban areas, swelling the size of the cities and changing them in the process.

This strategy relied primarily on surrounding the historic kernels of the cities with newly built apartment house developments. The height of these buildings grew from four stories in the 1950s to ten stories or more, until the 1970s, when the housing industries in most of these countries came to a screeching halt. Looking down on these cities from a high vantage point, whether from the top of the Palac Kulturny, from Gellért Hill, or from an airplane, one is astounded to see that these modern housing structures define the outer edges of these historic cities just as fortresses and fortified walls encircled medieval towns and cities.

By contrast with the West European trend that began in the 1960s, however, relatively little emphasis was placed on the outside appearance of these structures. Made of prefabricated cement slabs, the East European structures differ only slightly from one another, depending on the decade of their construction. They are cheaply built and exude drabness, sameness, and emptiness. In apartment complexes in every East European state, there can be seen the same cluster and variety of shops and stores located on the first floor or in a central courtyard. In this respect, Bucharest or Budapest: what's the difference? The complexes were patterned after Soviet models, a patterning that extended even to the size of individual units. The factories that manufactured the prefab units of these apartments based their production on Soviet blueprints. Although adequate in the USSR, these "silos" provided only partial solutions to the problems of urban growth, and spawned new and perhaps more difficult problems in Eastern Europe.

Moreover, the small size of these apartments, which ranged from thirty-five to fifty-four square meters, soon became the source of serious dysfunctions. The apartments were originally planned for a lifetime of twenty years, perhaps for starter families, and at the time of their construction they appeared to be adequate; however, since most East European families either already were or rapidly became two- or three-generation units, the apartments quickly became inadequate and crowded. The behavioral dysfunctions resulting from overcrowding and the consequent claustrophobia are too well known to be detailed here. An unexpected result of the unsuitable housing was its negative impact on birth rates.

These "tenement" developments also became the sites of friction between residents more recently arrived from the villages, and the long-term city-dwellers. Stratification according to origin and time of arrival, and clashes between different ethnic groups or other minority groups, separated one housing development from another in terms of desirability and access. But even as urban in-migration ended, the patterns established earlier remained the same.

Finally, the urban landscape was also characterized by the sameness of the decorative elements of communism. The statues, the styles of functional buildings, ministries, and other governmental offices, and the use of "decorative" urban space — for instance, the large areas reserved for parades and reviewing stands — were truly similar to each other throughout the region. The thousands of statues of Lenin were completely interchangeable.

The similarities in the use of space were not restricted to the urban sphere; the rural environment also was affected. The Soviet doctrinal emphasis on collective production — collective and state farms and production systems — prevailed nearly everywhere, except in Poland and Yugoslavia. The unwillingness to invest in the rural sphere, the very antirurality of Communist ideology and practice, deemed that the areas outside urban control would remain backward. The large expanse of industrial farming, and the centralized function of marketing, not only discouraged private initiative, self-reliance, and motivation but also served to maintain control over the rural sphere by the urban center.

It is easy to recognize the legacy of communism in these respects; whereas the problems of lack of urbanization were there before the Communists took over, what exists now was clearly determined by the rulers in power during the Communist era. It is a different question whether — given the assigned priorities of the system — there were other alternatives available to the rulers; the fact is, however, that the situation existing today is the result of the choices made by these elites.

This latter statement is also true, however, in regard to two other areas intimately coupled with the physical sphere: the development of infrastructure, and the destruction of the environment. According to Marxist economic theory (see below), the development of infrastructure was a low priority; production became the central element of the system.

Hence, infrastructural development in Eastern Europe (e.g., the creation of first-rate communications and road networks) was low on the list of priorities. The fact that in 1990 there were on average only between eight and twenty-three telephones per one hundred families in the region illustrates this sad inheritance from the past. Desiring to limit the links of the population at large to the outside world, the Communist elite made a conscious decision to neglect the development of communications ties, and thus bequeathed a pathetic legacy to today's generation. With neglected and underdeveloped infrastructures, East European nations are struggling to become part of the Western world.

The Communist inheritance is also observable in regard to the deterioration of the environment. Again, the costs of environmental deterioration were not built into the costs of production; environmental concerns ranked far below production priorities. By their very emphasis on production, by making those industries that are especially harmful to the environment — steel, coal, and petrochemicals — the pillars of the economic system, and by their nearly total disregard for the health of the environment in these lands, the Communists left a legacy that will be more difficult to erase than practically any other. The result is a polluted environment that is observable everywhere in the region. Acid rain has killed most of Silesia's forests, the rivers of Poland are polluted nearly beyond salvation, the nuclear reactors are generally unsafe, and many of the large metropolises of the region are so choked with air pollution that the population is at risk every day. Perhaps the Communist elites did not have enough funds to create an environment that was at least reasonably safe; the fact, however, is that they chose to neglect the environment. Thus, today the people of the region must pay the price for both communism's sins of omission and its sins of commission. Whether the members of the Communist elite really wanted to harm the environment, the flora, the fauna, and the people is immaterial: intentions do not matter in the book of judgment, only facts. What is not immaterial is the legacy of harm they left behind.

Economic Legacies

It must be repeated that the Communist regimes in Eastern Europe did inherit an economically backward region, on the periphery of European development.[3] With industrial development concentrated in only a few selected production fields, the East European states in 1945–48 had a largely agrarian economic system. The road to the future clearly dictated adopting the model of rapid industrialization, and — aside from the fact that the model was to be imposed anyway — its adoption shortly after communism's rise to power seemed not only mandatory but also advisable.

The model included four major elements: the adoption of central planning controls, the dominance of the state sector, heavy industrialization, and the "closed circle" of trade. While central planning placed controls over all of the operations of the enterprises, it also alleviated individual responsibility; like the system as a whole, it always assigned the decision-making process to a higher level than was necessary. As a result, the basis of sound decision making at the proper level was eliminated.

When communism fell and the organs of central planning were closed down, individual decision making and responsibility began to be transferred back to the proper levels. Yet the basic tools of decision making — cost-benefit analysis, risk assessment, freedom of choice, financial choice, and the like, were unfamiliar to the new elites. Hence, very few well-qualified decision makers emerged who had the ability to transform the economic base rapidly and successfully toward a privatized economy. Clearly, therefore, one of the economic legacies of communism is the lack of well-qualified decision makers willing and able to assume fiscal and personal responsibility for enterprise behavior.

A second element of the Communist economic system was the heavy reliance of the economy on the state structure, and the consequent anti-entrepreneurial attitude both within the government and among the members of the polity. Since cooperative and state enterprises were the ideologically preferred form of production, and since private entrepreneurial activities were discouraged, prohibited, or proscribed, the state sector enjoyed an overwhelming advantage vis-à-vis the private entrepreneur. Hence, the caution adopted by members of the society in becoming entrepreneurs, and the aversion to risk taking on the part of a large number of the citizenry, are direct legacies of the system. While it is clear that risk aversion was also present in the pre-Communist period, and while it is noted that East European polities were not dominated by entrepreneurial attitudes and behavior even before the Communist takeover, the fact that the new generations, which have no familiarity with prewar societal attitudes, exhibit these behavior and value patterns indicates the overwhelming influence of the Communist legacy.

As far as heavy industrialization was concerned, the developmental model forced on Eastern Europe by the Soviet decision makers was derived from that which was adopted in the Soviet Union in the 1930s: the model of heavy industrialization coupled with the most incredible exploitation of labor. Gigantic, environmentally unsound but politically preferable steel mills and coal-fired smelters were created; the development of these states was to be fueled by the success of heavy industrial production. The Communist states would become the leading producers and exporters of heavy industrial products.

That the world's progressive economies were about to undergo a new industrial revolution driven by continuous technological advancement was not foreseen by Soviet and Communist planners. Even after it became obvious that the world was beginning to use far less steel and coal, the Communist planners continued to stick with their original assumptions. Consequently, the Communist states missed out on the fourth industrial revolution — the technological revolution — and their economies were doomed to remain largely technologically backward and outmoded. This, too, is a clear legacy of communism.

Finally, the network of trade among the nations of Eastern Europe, those nations' mutual reliance on each other's markets, and the fact that their products were not exportable for hard currency are also part of the inheritance from the recent past. It was, of course, advantageous for each East European economy to possess links and markets with the others; trade was a set of negotiations based on mutual interests decided in advance by a hegemonic power. The Council for Mutual Economic Assistance (CMEA) functioned in an acceptable manner as long as one could pay in barter and in transferable rubles for the items that all sides desired.

The collapse of the Soviet market — the Soviet Union's inability to pay for East European goods — doomed the system before it disintegrated. The autarkic pattern of trade which emerged stemmed from dual sources: the collapse of the markets of the East, and the inability to export satisfactorily to the West. The product mix suitable for the East was clearly not suitable for the West; this, too, can be attributed to the legacy of communism.

Societal Legacies

Our quest to discern the Communist part in the legacy of social development is made even more difficult by our inability to pinpoint what was peculiarly "socialist" in that process.[4] A skeptical observer may say that the societal development observable in Eastern Europe since 1945 has been simply a repetition of the urbanization and embourgeoisement trends established earlier in the ubiquitous, great West European centers. Such arguments cannot and should not simply be dismissed.

Yet societal development in the East had some peculiar characteristics that differentiated it from Western models of social modernization. In fact, the Communist model included the creation of several specific, interlinked social structures and processes: (1) the forging of an industrial working class; (2) the transformation of rural society from traditional peasant bases to "community-oriented" bases; (3) the creation of a loyal, white-collar *nomenklatura* class; and (4) the creation of a technical intelligentsia that overlapped or at least cooperated with the nomenklatura.

In addition, the Communist society was supposed to be characterized by several operational principles: a bloated, cradle-to-grave social welfare system; little differentiation between socioeconomic levels; and restricted social mobility, especially since the 1960s.

We are not suggesting, of course, that in all the states of the region these institutions and processes were developed to the same extent and at the same time, but in general they may be observed as the bases of social policy making everywhere. In order to briefly assess the legacies of the system, let us merely summarize the extent to which the regimes succeeded in implementing the Communist model of social structures described above.

The Working Class and the Peasantry

There can be no doubt that the Communist regimes of Eastern Europe did create an industrial working class everywhere in the region.[5] When the regimes came to power, all of the countries of the region were (to a greater or a lesser extent) largely rural and largely agrarian. Through the collectivization of the land and other measures, they forced the men to flee the countryside and to become workers in urban industries. Reasoning that the working class would be the leading force in society, the leadership lost no time in fostering the creation of a working class.

Yet, it quickly became very clear to thoughtful observers of the region that this was not to be the type of working class that was supposed to be class-conscious, educated, and technically and technologically advanced;

the Communist regimes clearly wanted to create a large *lumpenproletariat* as a substitute for an elite class of industrial laborers. Having already assimilated or co-opted into the Communist apparats the small industrial labor stratum they had inherited in the cities, the regimes were not anxious to create a class that would challenge their own right to rule. How right they were to fear the "real" working class was demonstrated by the rise of Solidarity as much as by the recurrent rebellions of the miners in Romania's Jiu Valley.

Though each of these governments planned to transform the masses torn from the rural sphere into urban citizens, these efforts were at best halfhearted and were characterized by doubts within the leadership concerning the very necessity of the process. It was easy to tear the masses from their rural roots by starving them out of agriculture and forcing them to commute to the cities. It was much harder, however, for the regimes to settle them down in the cities or towns, even in the newly created so-called socialist towns, for urban housing was precious and expensive even in the prefab settlements. It was cheaper, and politically less dangerous, to allow the vast numbers holding onto tenuous roots in rural life to maintain those roots by continuing to live outside the cities and commuting to work. Thus, the lumpenproletariat that was created was never really allowed near the sources and benefits of power. Its symbolic ruling role simply masked its powerlessness and the expropriation of its position in both the social and economic spheres by the regime.

■ ■ ■ ■

The introduction of industrial methods of production was the ostensible goal of these regimes' attempts to transform the rural sphere. Yet collectivization and the emphasis on the state farms were principally aimed at two divergent targets: the diminution of alternative sources of local power in the peasant community, and the abolition of agricultural work based on individual choice. While the first of these goals was uniform in the region, the second was only minimally implemented in Poland and Yugoslavia from the 1950s onward.

The policies of the Communist regimes were not merely aimed at attempting to abolish what Marx considered the "stupidity of the peasant way of life" but were clearly designed to ensure political control. In fact, in their various prewar economic forms — the dominance of large estates in

Hungary, for example, or the dominance of small peasant plots in Yugo-slavia — these states had been agriculturally self-sufficient, and many even had been able to export food. What the Communists really wanted in the rural sphere was not necessarily a successful agrarian economy, but politi-cal control over the village, and the dissolution of the strong peasant community that dominated the rural sphere.

Moreover, the introduction of the industrial production techniques of the large communal and state enterprises also meant the denigration of the individual worth of the "proper peasant." Shorn of his land, of his animals, of his right to make a decision about his life and schedule, the peasant became nonthreatening for the regime; he was relegated to an existence dependent upon the mercy of the state and its subsidiary organi-zations, which now dominated his life, both assigning his daily work and purchasing the fruits of his labor.

The Ruling Class and the Technical Intelligentsia

The real ruling class in the Communist state, of course, was its own white-collar nomenklatura. Populated by those deemed worthy by the Party, the nomenklatura included men and women in governmental, economic, and societal positions of responsibility. They moved easily from Party to government, from foreign policy directorates to economic directorates, their mobility only constrained by the desires of the higher-level Party authorities.[6]

The privileges of this class were vastly different from the conditions experienced by the rest of society. Though not uniform in the region — for instance, considerably less numerous in Hungary than in Romania — these privileges extended from the use and abuse of power to material wealth. Most significantly, the privilegentsia were able to make their priv-ileges transmittable, both to their offspring and to lateral relatives.

Some may argue that the members of the nomenklatura were, in fact, the "historical repository" of the revolutionary workers' power. While this may have been true for some of the older members of the elites — Zhivkov, Kádár, and so on — it did not hold for the vast majority of the no-menklatura in the 1980s. In fact, most members were second-generation white-collar workers whose parents, while perhaps born into the working class, had been moved into white-collar occupations by the Party in the 1950s or 1960s. Even for this first generation of the nomenklatura, the labor of the "worker" seemed to have become little but a distant memory rather quickly.

■ ■ ■ ■

A class that was to an extent coterminous with the nomenklatura, or at least coextensive with it, was the newly developed technical intelligentsia, which played a prominent role in society. Coming from diverse backgrounds, its members were the products of the 1970s and 1980s. They were interested in technological applications in every arena of public life, and used ideology only as a vocabulary of discourse and only when necessary; generally, they were technocrats trying to find practical solutions to daily problems.

Regardless of their social origins, they had in common a higher education, broader outside contacts than their seniors had, a greater comprehension of the Western world, and often a broad-based knowledge of Western languages. Better than any other stratum of society, they realized that the system was getting nowhere, though most were convinced that it could be simply reformed. And just like members of similar strata in other societies, they were convinced that they could do the reforming that had so far eluded their elders.

We should not forget, however, that even members of the technical intelligentsia failed to publicly verbalize their own conviction regarding the basically outmoded nature of communism. Moreover, very few of them gave any thought to a collapse of the system or to the consequences of such a collapse, especially with regard to their own future in a new system. The vast majority, in fact, felt that they had a right to assume the leadership of the country once the old-timers died out, and that they would continue to lead their respective lands toward a better, more rational Communist future.

Patterns of Society: The Bases of Societal Legacies

The stratified society, of course, was bound by institutional strait jackets that restricted and confined its every move. Yet the fact remains that to a greater or lesser extent, the Communists did create a cradle-to-grave welfare system and brought social benefits to a very large part of society. In this respect, the benefits of the Communist system were real. They ranged from free medical care, through paid maternity leave and child care provisions, all the way to payment for everyone who was employed, and employment for everyone who needed or wanted a job. Moreover, the very proclamation of gender equality bestowed upon women the chance (and the necessity!) to become a part of the labor force and to claim the associated benefits (and burdens). We may criticize the system and list its inadequacies, but it had some positive aspects among the negatives. The system's paternalism was one of its most important parameters.

Another parameter of the system was the extent to which social differentiation was permitted or accepted. Except with respect to the very powerful and the most privileged, social differentiation was considerably less marked in Eastern Europe than in Western Europe. Though it is fashionable today to describe social equality in Communist Eastern Europe in terms of merely relative deprivation, the ethos of a minimal "equality," and the relatively small distance between the rich and the poor, clearly found a responsive chord among the population of the region.[7]

A final parameter of the system was its relative social immobility. As noted briefly above, sometime between the mid-1960s and the 1970s, social mobility had come to a halt. The likelihood that a worker's son could compete on an equal footing with the son of a second-generation white-collar worker became more and more remote; thus the social demarcation lines that had developed over two to three decades were constantly reinforced. One more element affected the social system: the ever-present scarcity. Socialist systems, of course, were not meant to be characterized by shortages, but they were caught in a vicious circle of scarcity. In turn, society was involved in a never-ending struggle for scarce goods: a *bellum omnium contra omnis* that affected every element of daily life. When socialism fell, the social pillars of the system also crumbled, but left behind in the ruins was a social legacy not likely to be changed in the near future. It is not a proud legacy.

First, socialism left behind a working class largely unsuited for the modern age. The vast majority of the lumpenproletariat, the hordes of industrial semiskilled or unskilled laborers, were recruited to work in heavy industry, the steel mills and coal mines that were the staple of the socialist economy both in theory and in reality. Heavily subsidized, technologically backward, unable to compete in a world market already flooded with better-quality goods at lower prices, most of these industries eventually will have to be closed. When this is done, however, the successor regimes will have on their hands a remnant of the working class that will be undertrained and undereducated, with no convertible skills and no geographical mobility.

Second, the opportunity to create a production oriented, technologically advanced rural sphere will be severely hampered in those states (e.g., Hungary and Bulgaria) where the cooperative or state farms were relatively successful in providing adequately for internal or external consumption. The restitution of land to smallholders is likely to benefit mostly those members of the older generation who desired to reclaim their "shorn inheritance" and to begin to farm once again; it is hoped that they will be able to sell the products they produce on a wide-open, highly competitive market flooded by price-supported, cheaper West and South European goods. Yet the vast majority of the region's peasants will have minuscule strip lands that are not large enough to benefit from advanced agricultural technology. Moreover, they are all severely hampered by a lack of mechanized equipment suitable for small-scale farming; the huge Zetor tractors suitable for thousands of acres are practically useless for two-acre plots. And finally, the abolition of price support for agriculture — necessitated both by International Monetary Fund and World Bank demands and by the shrinking state budgets all over the region — will not allow the farmers to compete with Western Europe's heavily subsidized farm products, which are also protected by the regulations of the expanded European Union. The net result of the Communist legacy in the rural sphere is, perhaps, merely an indirect one: the Communist way of life and agricultural production has been rejected, although the East European states lack the possibility of becoming financially secure, modern agrarian producers.

In the rural sphere today, there are as yet few signs of the reemergence of the power of the local community. Throughout the last decades, in fact, the rural community also changed significantly; its social and political elites had become the holders of local power. Though many of these have been swept from power, the Communist legacy prevented the speedy emergence of a new community structure; the competing claims of the rural parties, the church, and the rural intelligentsia obscures the single path to a brighter future. Moreover, the very lack of community in the rural sphere — it was deliberately destroyed by the Communist regime during the last four decades — has rendered rural development an elusive promise rather than a reality.

Political Legacies

As noted above, some of the social legacies examined were direct legacies: the development of a closed society based on preferential stratification, the occupation of managerial positions by a technical intelligentsia, a bloated welfare system, and relatively little social inequality. Among the indirect legacies of the system is the need to increase social mobility and to make the welfare system more efficient, or at least to close the vast gap that must appear in strata differentiation. To put it differently, the necessity of undoing the harm — or at least attempting to remedy the dysfunctions — of the Communist system is an indirect legacy of communism.

In the political realm, moreover, our task is made all the more difficult when we consider the vast differences between proclaimed values and manifest behavior. Though recent surveys done in the region give us a good basis for the evaluation of the population's values,[8] it is very difficult to discern whether those values were formed by the experiences with Communist rule or were simply repressed values carried over from a previous era. Is it possible to determine whether and to what extent the values possessed by today's citizenry are the outcome of Communist political socialization efforts or are the results of decades of societal rejection of Communist political socialization efforts? I would suspect that definitive answers to such questions cannot yet be given, even with the use of available data sets.

We are at even a greater loss when we attempt to analyze behavior in the political realm. Even at the most superficial level, the questions that cannot be answered in any definite manner include the following:

1. Is low voter turnout the result of rejecting mandatory voting requirements during the Communist regime?
2. Is the resurgence of authoritarian political behavior the result of patterns learned under communism?
3. Is the citizenry's casual acceptance of most political decisions by otherwise unpopular legislatures or executives the direct result of habitual behavior under Communist rule?
4. Are the indications of the citizenry's low opinion of their own efficacy the direct results of the same habitual patterns?
5. Is the reemergence of acts of intolerance — ranging from open anti-Semitism to ethnonationalistic and religious civil war — a direct result of the suppression of such acts by the previous regimes?

Similar questions, of course, could be posed by the hundreds; let us simply try to postulate in general terms some of the legacies of communism — first, as they affect behavior, and second, as they affect values.

Once again, our evidence is largely contradictory in regard to political behavior. Participation rates in political activity are often low in the region. Generally, political parties are catch-all parties, mostly electoral rather than participatory organizations, which function well — if they function well! — only at election time.[9] Yet we cannot be certain whether the reason for such low involvement is the low sense of efficacy, the low regard for politics, the fear of backing the wrong horse, or some other aspect of daily life. And certainly, we cannot discern the extent to which such behavior is a legacy of communism, an imitation of political life in some Western states — for example, the United States — or a reemergence of the interwar pattern.

This uncertainty is especially notable in regard to political participation rates in the region. In Poland and Hungary, specifically, low voter turnout has become endemic; and especially in local elections, voter turnout is often simply pathetic. According to Polish sources, the absolute nadir was reached in 1992 in three county elections: not even the candidates running bothered to vote. In a local election to choose the mayor of a small town in northwestern Hungary, the necessary 25-percent participation ratio was not achieved, even after six tries.[10] Is the choice to exercise the freedom from compulsory voting a legacy of the Communist regime? Or is the manifest apathy a reflection of post-Communist disgust with the new politics—and the new freedom? At the same time we must also ask why voter turnout is consistently higher in some countries, such as, for example, the Czech Republic, Slovakia, and Romania. The issue of heightened national aspirations may hold a key to some of the answers, but the longitudinal series of observations today includes too few numbers to be the basis of definitive replies.

The tenuous link between governmental and/or administrative behavior and actual public values is another area of politics which merits examination. Habitual obedience to authority was the norm that always characterized public behavior during the Communist era. Though one really had no way to fathom the depth — or rather, the shallowness — of the legitimacy that was conceded to the authorities, there was a high correlation between public behavior and governmental desires. After the new democracies were established, however, the expected continuation of a high correlation between the two failed to materialize. In fact, severe cleavages between public values and governmental behavior were soon noted. The attempts by the governments to create strong new "party-states" or to adopt public policies that resulted in net losses for most of the citizenry — to wit: large-scale unemployment — were not matched by public support for the administrative programs. Whether such opposition to governmental measures was manifest in action (e.g., miners' protests in Bucharest, and the taxi strike in Budapest) or was latent and expressed mostly in the public opinion polls is immaterial from our perspective; we must, simply, question whether these behaviors are due to the Communist legacy or to a reaction to previous Communist practices.

Let me not dwell extensively on foreign policy ramifications of the Communist legacy, which extend all the way from the vacuum in security policies which was caused by the collapse of the Warsaw Treaty Organization, to the collapse of trade which resulted from the end of the Council for Mutual Economic Assistance and its pattern of mutual trade. These were, of course, all results of the end of communism, and hence were the very legacy of the system. The necessity of searching for new allies — who are not anxious to embrace the East European states as partners in risky ventures — in a world governed by different rules, for which the system in its heyday (or in its collapse) failed to prepare the nations of the region, is a most painful legacy of communism indeed.

Instead of a Conclusion

These thoughts are intended merely as a point of reference for all of us who are involved in the examination of the legacies of communism as they affect the political culture of post-Communist states. To be sure, there are good legacies as well: nearly universal literacy, electrification, and a far higher level of urbanization-*cum*-industrialization than existed before the Communists took over these lands.

Looking over these legacies then, can we judge what remains from these forty-some years that will be lasting, and of value? Definitive answers are hard to find, but we believe that in spite of the rapid disappearance of even the outward traces of the now-defunct system, certain social values and preferences will remain for a long time to come.

Foremost among the "permanent" values is the changed status of women in society: the transformation from women's traditional rural status as "chattel" has been enormous, and I believe it to be permanent.

Women in both white-collar and blue-collar occupations have discovered for themselves a life that affords them new rights and privileges, a new way of existence, access to the professions, and so on. Though owing to the growing unemployment necessitated by the economic restructuring of the region, as well as to the rather backward-looking employment and social policies of some of the regimes, efforts will be made to restrict the role of women and reverse some of their gains by sending them back to home and hearth, the net result is that the gains already made cannot be reversed. The mindset may still contain many values that are traditional with regard to the "proper" role of women as mothers and homemakers, but the advances made under the socialist system appear to be permanent, as do the double and triple burdens that women bear owing to the need to fill all the roles that they play.

Consistent with the general progress achieved in women's liberation during the Communist period is the changed value system of women in many countries of the region concerning family planning, birth control, and abortion. The previous practice of offering free choice in regard to these functions (a system generally prevalent in the region, except for some notable exceptions such as Albania and Romania), included ceding the right of such decisions largely to the women affected. As the regimes of today try to change these values, it appears certain that they will run into difficulties with electors long used to deciding these issues for themselves.

A second value that is likely to survive relates to the end of the traditional, rural way of life. While one may argue about the "fake" or "retarded" urbanization that took place in Eastern Europe during the last forty-some years, it is clear that most people were brought into an "urban" network made up of institutions, procedures, goals, and communications systems which did not exist before. While the villages — and for that matter the urban spaces of the region as well — remain backward by Western standards, they have been dramatically altered since World War II. And while one may argue that the "socialist silos" merely replicated closed village patterns within concrete walls, the fact remains that their inhabitants had already moved out of the strict confines of the rural existence that dominated a half century ago.

A third legacy that one may expect to be long lasting is the population's perception that society is divided into "them" and "us." It is true that the dichotomy existed before the Communists took over, but the gulf during the last five decades increased enormously. Moreover, while the "thems" before the war may have been feared, those developed under the Communist system were not only feared but also despised and held in contempt. The perception that the power holders are not "of us," that they have been imposed upon a people, is of course characteristic of polities where the civic culture has yet to emerge. The notion of legitimacy of rule — based not merely on elections but also on popular support — has not permeated societal perception.

In this regard, very few states of the region show signs of major improvement since 1989. In fact, the population continues to rate its efficacy as low with regard to political participation. The helplessness to affect and to impact meaningfully upon the course of events, when coupled with the sense that "people" must keep away from the "thems" is an enduring and endemic part of the legacy of communism. The acceptance of the paternalism-*cum*-authoritarianism of the previous regimes created a citizenry that often expects to be told what to do and channeled into compliance; peoples' taking responsibility for their own future has yet to be translated into "people's power" movements or processes.

A further legacy closely connected with the above is the constant need to find support in familiar patterns of existence, rather than relying upon the application of a new "Rechtsstaat," that is, the body of legal regulations adopted by the state. As in the past, laws are easy to make, but people seem to want to find ways of not complying with them. The fundamental conviction that the laws are always designed not for a national purpose in which the citizenry has a stake, but as a tool to enforce compliance with a cause that is not "their" own, forces people to seek the back doors of existence and progress.

Though the answers are not yet found, and the existing data provide us with a confusing pattern of responses, it is quite certain that a sense of equality will remain pervasive in the region. We are not referring here simply to the abolition of titles and privileges (such as those of the aristocracy) that took place at the end of World War II. Although in Poland and Hungary, the only two countries where the aristocracy played major roles before the war, one sees a small resurgence of a hankering for such values, the amazing thing is the survival of the "democratized equality" found in these countries during the last decades. While the economic transformation, the development of primitive capitalism with its nouveau riche parvenus and robber barons, does create a class of "haves" and one of "have-nots," the sense of social and societal equality remains pervasive. One could, of course, note the development of an antiegalitarian phenomenon, as well, in the sense that entire groups are losing their right to even a minimal livelihood, but the fact remains that the concept of egalitarianism remains deeply ingrained in the region.

Finally, perhaps most confusing is the sense of reliance on the state: the expectation that certain social benefits will be maintained for the entire population, including free health care, schooling, retirement, and even "full" employment. To be sure, there appears to be a sense of injustice among the people when these benefits slowly disappear, but I do not believe that these expectations will survive as a general demand in future generations. In fact, the data prove the value attached to such benefits, but they also show that people realize that these are indeed benefits, rather than rights attached to a particular system. What is likely to remain, however, is a sense of expectation that certain minimal benefits will be guaranteed. The expectation that people will not starve to death and that some opportunities for advancement will be guaranteed to everyone are ingrained in the citizenry, and the voters are likely to demand an accounting of any government as to its stewardship of these values.

It is true, of course, that some of the dysfunctions that we may observe are not the legacies of communism, or perhaps, put differently, are not the *direct* legacies of communism. Still, from a different perspective, communism also left behind a legacy that affects other states' politics concerning communism. Americans have had to take a long, hard look at the motivating sources of foreign and domestic policy behavior within the United States and toward allies and adversaries abroad. This, too, is an unintended legacy of communism, or more precisely, of the melting away of the system.

What a wonderful irony: it was not the state — as Marx prophesied — that dissolved itself, but communism itself that dissipated into thin air. As one travels the lands where communism used to rule, one is struck by the rapid disappearance of its everpresent trappings: the Lenin statues, the red flags, the red stars, and the slogans. They are gone nearly overnight, leaving behind very few visible reminders of a system that existed for the better part of the second half of this century. The invisible, intangible legacies left behind by communism, however, unfortunately will remain with the people of the region for a long time to come.

REGIONAL PERSPECTIVES

2

Marginality Reinforced

Bennett Kovrig

As East Europeans struggle to make up for lost time in their advance toward modernity, not the least of their handicaps is their image in the West.[1] That image is one of enduring marginality, of material and spiritual backwardness. To be sure, in their time the figures of the heroic Hungarian freedom fighter and of the self-immolated Jan Palach earned admiration and sympathy; Kossuth and Masaryk had aroused similar feelings — at least among liberals — a century earlier. But Communist domination, like earlier imperial rule, had the effect of retarding modernization and reinforcing the Western perception of East European marginality. This perception, regardless of the extent to which it coincides with objective reality, defines Western policies and actions at a time when East Europeans are in desperate need of aid and reassurance.

The fascist fallacy was buried in the rubble of Berlin in 1945; the Communist challenge collapsed with the Berlin Wall forty-four years later. The end of ideological civil war removed a gigantic obstacle to the reunion of the European family, but postideological Europe remains diversified and fragmented by the imprints of history. The West's euphoria over the implosion of the Soviet empire was soon tempered by apprehension at the political (not to speak of economic) "backwardness" of the survivors of communism. The prospects for the emergence of a pan-European political community are hostage as much to the notion of a historic East-West cleavage as to the variegated reality behind it.

Regional labels such as Eastern Europe, or East-Central Europe, have not only served geopolitical convenience but also encouraged facile generalizations where a less aggregative perspective might be more appropriate. Thus the region's societies are regarded collectively (at least in the West) as historical laggards on the path of economic, social, and political development. To be sure, the kingdoms of Bohemia, Hungary, and Poland were hardly backwaters of civilization in medieval Europe.

But while the devices of economic modernity were being forged and fructified in the culturally and politically favorable environment of north-western Europe, the eastern lands fell prey to absolutist empires.

Imperial rule, though typically exploitative, could, of course, induce modernization as well as stagnation. The areas closest to Western Europe, particularly Bohemia, developed more dynamically than the rest of the region; separated from the West by Ottoman rule and Orthodoxy, the Balkans stagnated. The causes of economic backwardness were more complex than simple dependency, but economic dependency also retarded the modernization of East European societies, and therefore of the region's political cultures.[2] Political dependency, meanwhile, provided its own justification, prolonging a certain backwardness that ostensibly legitimated imperial rule. "Bei Pressburg fängt Asien an," observed Metternich contemptuously; Asia, meaning barbarism, began at Austria's eastern border.

The new ideology of nationalism began to shake the imperial edifices in the nineteenth century. Ominously, it was more the German version of cultural and racial community than the French notion of civic allegiance that took root in this inextricably multiethnic region. And while in parts of Western Europe nationalism was wedded to liberalism in the ideology of the triumphant urban middle class, in the East political and economic liberalism found a less hospitable social base. The nation-building elites came more from the country gentry, possessed of traditional, agrarian values, than from the urban middle class, which was comparatively small and in large part of "foreign" (mainly German and Jewish) extraction. As these societies extricated themselves progressively and piecemeal from imperial rule, the entrenchment of national independence and the promotion of economic modernization seemed to require concentration of political will rather than divisive pluralism. The state — parliament and administration — thus became the tool of paternalistic government, the bulwark of cultural nationalism. The vote was reserved for a small minority, though it might be noted that on the eve of World War I the broadest franchise in a Western democracy, in France, extended to less than 30 percent of the population.

Modern Eastern Europe was born in the charnel house of World War I. In sweeping away old empires, the victors allowed their map making to be guided more by expediency than by Wilsonian principle. In consequence, Czechs, Serbs, and Romanians found their national aspirations largely satisfied. The Poles resorted to war to obtain more territory from Russia. The others were left nursing grievances. For all, nationalism became the state religion, marshaled to legitimize statehood and the new status quo or to amend the Versailles order.

At least superficially, the states of East-Central Europe and the Balkans came to resemble their western neighbors. In the early 1920s, the constitutional monarchies and republics of the region all possessed democratic institutions and multiparty systems, adhered to the League of Nations, and tried to promote economic growth as well as a degree of social welfare. That did not stop the West from regarding them with a mixture of derision and contempt, as shown by a learned observer's undiscriminating recommendation to the Council of Allied Ambassadors in 1920 not to take too seriously the new nations of Europe, whose affairs "belong to the sphere of farce."[3] Yet even if they fell short of the evolving standards of modernity set in the West, most of them had at least accepted in principle the conventions of pluralistic democracy.

The failure to fulfill this early promise is commonly blamed on their penchant for statism, on the weakness of the social strata — intellectuals, entrepreneurial bourgeoisie, and organized labor — that in the West sustained pluralistic politics, and on their susceptibility to radical nationalism.[4] The economic and social crisis of the Great Depression did impel regimes toward authoritarianism, as much to ward off more radical challenges from left and right as to impose remedial programs. Political liberalism, under assault worldwide from collectivist, corporatist, and sundry authoritarian alternatives, lost ground in the region before it had penetrated deeply.

The drift to authoritarianism was less an ideological phenomenon than the reflex of traditional elites seeking to preserve their power and national independence in an international environment dominated by German and Italian influence and the specter of bolshevism. That these elites felt driven to appease Hitler was as politically pragmatic and morally questionable as the performance of Chamberlain and Daladier at Munich. From distant London, the British prime minister could disparage the "quarrel in a far-away country between people of whom we know nothing." From nearer to Berlin, Germans claimed to know their eastern neighbors, and declared them racially inferior. The native epigones of Hitler, such as Stojadinovič in Yugoslavia, Codreanu and Goga in Romania, and Szálasi in Hungary, never won the allegiance of the majority, although, as in the rest of Europe, grass-roots support for the nationalist right grew at the expense of the nominally internationalist left.

Not to damn with faint praise, some liberal political values survived in much of Eastern Europe longer than in the politically more "experienced" countries of Germany and Italy, and the countries of the Iberian Peninsula; and the antiliberal virus ultimately incapacitated even such a bastion of democracy as France. It was not out of love for liberal democracy that Piłsudski invited the French in early 1933 to help crush Hitler before it was too late. But France's, or for that matter Britain's, love of liberal democracy was not strong enough to inspire timely action against its deadly enemy.

In short, it is reductionist to depict Eastern Europe as one dismal swamp of political primitivism on the periphery of European modernity. The several political cultures in the region stood at different stages in the transition from a traditional, parochial condition to a modern civil society, from *Gemeinschaft* (community) to *Gesellschaft* (society). They spanned a spectrum, ranging from Czech pluralism to Albanian tribalism, that encompassed most of the rest of Europe as well. The tradition of statism remained generally stronger, and the sense and expectation of individual political efficacy weaker, than in a few democracies of northwestern Europe.

■ ■ ■

Soviet Communist hegemony reinforced the region's marginality, its separation from liberal modernity. Yet the cleavage marked by the Iron Curtain and perceived by the cold war West as separating two political Europes, one modern and democratic, the other backward and totalitarian, was Procrustean in its time (modern and democratic Portugal?) and should not be arbitrarily projected back into history or, for that matter, into the future. As the U.S. State Department advised President Roosevelt, the political mood of East Europeans at war's end was "to the left and strongly in favor of far-reaching economic and social reforms, but not, however, in favor of a left-wing totalitarian regime to achieve these reforms."[5] This tendency reflected both the global ascendancy of liberal democracy — even Stalin nominally endorsed the prescriptions of the Yalta Declaration on Liberated Europe — over fascism, militarism, and colonialism, and the disgrace of those conservative elites and rightist radicals who had chosen to cohabit and collaborate with the Axis. The war did not erase the region's distinctive political cultures, certainly not the statist tendencies and national antipathies, but indirectly it had a leveling and democratizing effect on the region's societies.

Soviet patronage was a mixed blessing for Communists in quest of native roots and legitimacy, particularly among historically anti-Russian Poles, Hungarians, Romanians, and Germans. But in the early postwar period local Communist leaders disclaimed any intention of seizing monopoly power and eschewed talk of proletarian dictatorship, evoking instead a vague new form of popular democracy that encompassed other "progressive" political forces. Their inaugural platforms were consonant with the objective needs of modernization, including land reform, reconstruction, social mobility, and social welfare. They expanded their conspiratorial workers' vanguard into mass parties open to virtually all comers.

No social stratum was wholly immune to the appeal of a Communist reform program that soft-pedaled the Soviet totalitarian reality. Yet nowhere in the region did the Communists win a clear mandate to rule, and by 1947 their popularity was declining not only in Czechoslovakia but, in all probability, regionwide. For a growing majority of East Europeans, the Communists' threat to democracy and national autonomy outweighed their promise of egalitarian prosperity.

Meanwhile, in the liberated countries of Western Europe, Communists exploited their record of anti-Nazi resistance as well as the prevailing popular, reformist mood, which was similar to the mood farther east. Their Soviet patron had less leverage, but the destructive and disruptive effects of the war, penury, endemic shortages, and the calamitous winter of 1946–47 all contributed to social stresses that the growing Communist parties of Italy, France, and Belgium actively exploited. Communists were gaining in the Greek civil war, and that fact, as well as the prospect of freely elected Communist pluralities, if not majorities, galvanized democratic elites in Western Europe and the United States. The Truman Doctrine and the Marshall Plan were the first decisive steps toward the consolidation of liberal democracy in Europe. They also defined liberal democracy's boundaries, for Eastern Europe, including Czechoslovakia, was by Stalin's fiat made off-limits to Western aid.

Stalin's hopes for a comparatively peaceful extension of the Communist revolution and Soviet influence over the entire continent were thus dashed. The immediate victims of his tactical retrenchment were the East Europeans. At a secret conference in Poland in September 1947, European Communist parties received the Kremlin's new dogma. The world was, after all, divided into two irreconcilable camps; the capitalist-imperialist enemy had suborned social democrats and was taking the offensive; the popular front strategy (dating back to 1935) had lost its utility. The bemused French and Italian Communists were berated for foolish parliamentarism and ordered to go into active opposition. For their East European comrades, the end of popular front gradualism was the green light for seizure of monopoly power, the ideologically mandatory working-class unity to be achieved by forced merger with the social democrats.

From that point the two Europes evolved in some spiritual isolation from each other. In Eastern Europe, the hardships of Stalinism provoked alienation and revolt. An uprising flared briefly in East Germany in June 1953. The Communist Party in Poland contained mounting popular pressure in 1956 by promising reform and national autonomy, but delivered little of either. That same year, the Hungarians dramatically discarded communism and set course for liberal democracy, only to be crushed by Soviet arms. In 1968, reformers in Czechoslovakia's Communist Party more prudently offered what they called "socialism with a human face," with the same result. If most of the time East Europeans submitted to existential imperatives and learned to accommodate their masters, they also gave ample indication of where their political preferences lay.

The rest of Europe remained preoccupied with its own material concerns. Once the Marshall Plan had done its job, Europe's business leaders and governments felt liberated from America's reservations about trade with the enemy. West Germans insisted from the start on free economic intercourse with East Germany despite the unflagging repressiveness of the latter's Communist rulers. Western Europe's left-leaning intellectual elites deplored American talk of rolling back communism and rationalized East European Stalinism as a salutary tonic for backward societies. "Carried by history, the Communist party displays an extraordinary, objective intelligence: it rarely makes a mistake," opined Sartre in February 1956; although he deplored Soviet intervention in Hungary, five years later he was still insisting that "an anti-communist is a dog."[6]

As Stalinism faded and some of the East European dictators donned velvet gloves, even the term *totalitarianism* fell into disrepute in the West, victim to the illusion that Leninism was reformable. To be sure, the number of apologists for Soviet hegemony and Communist monopoly declined with each bloody repression. The majority of West Europeans remained anti-Communist and pitied their neighbors, but they were also more inclined than the Americans to appease the bear. Only in the late 1970s did they begin to show some zeal for the cause of human rights in the East, their consciousness raised by Sakharov, Solzhenitsyn, Charter 77, and the Helsinki process.

■ ■ ■ ■

The liberal West applauded East European nationalism when it challenged Soviet hegemony. In contrast, the post-Communist resurgence of both integrative and disintegrative nationalism has aroused deep ambivalence, and gloomy apprehensions about a return to a dark history of tribal strife. The revolutions of 1989 were undoubtedly nationalistic in throwing off the yoke of Soviet-Communist hegemony. Romania was thus atypical in its attenuation of the previous regime's national chauvinism, and the respite was of short duration. Conversion to liberal democracy did allow the airing and advocacy of multiple ethnic and national interests. But if liberal doctrine afforded unambiguous protection for the political and civil rights of individuals, including their freedom to form associations and parties, it gave less concrete guidance with regard to the collective rights of ethnic minorities.

The reemergent issues ranged from linguistic rights in culture and education, through local administrative autonomy, to outright secession.[7] The Czechoslovak parliament debated for months before agreeing on a new name for the state (the Czech and Slovak Federal Republic); the flames of Slovak nationalism and separatism burned on, and the federation's death warrant was signed after the mid-1992 elections. Predictably, the inflamed nationalism of one group tended to work to the detriment of the next minority, as in the case of the Hungarians of Slovakia and Vojvodina. Romania's National Salvation Front government soon reneged on many of its initial promises of cultural and educational facilities for the Hungarian minority, embittering both domestic interethnic relations and relations with Hungary. The minority had won political representation in what was the largest opposition party, but pluralism also allowed the resurgence of strident Romanian nationalism. Poland grumbled about discrimination against the Polish minority in independent Lithuania. And in Yugoslavia, nationalist tensions bordering on blood feuds intensified with a quasi-civil war in largely Albanian-inhabited Kosovo and an ultimately shattering civil war between Serbs, Croats, and Bosnian Muslims. At the limit, the unleashing of East European nationalism challenged the Versailles order — to the predictable horror of Western states doctrinally attached to the status quo (except in the case of the intra-German frontier). The Yugoslav outcome underscored the fundamental dilemma of the liberal approach to minority rights: Did these extend to freedom to choose independence or, in the case of trans-border minorities, annexation to a culturally more congenial state? International consideration of that question is, of course, a political minefield, particularly at a time when other old and young democracies are being tested by minority nationalisms and separatisms — Irish Catholic and Scots in the United Kingdom, Corsican in France, Walloon and Fleming in Belgium, Francophone Quebecois in Canada, and Catalan and Basque in Spain, to name a few. Liberal democracy is commonly linked to national self-determination and should in principle allow for peaceful divorce, but history, law, and political self-interest all militate against this logic.

International law enjoins peaceful settlement of disputes and regulates interstate relations but makes no allowance for self-determination directed against existing sovereignties, which are themselves the creators and ultimate arbiters of the law. This deficiency derives from the supreme interest of states in preserving themselves. Most sovereignties, nation-states, and frontiers have been the direct or indirect creations of war, a pedigree not propitious for future peaceful revision.

Language, culture, race, and religion, as well as political dictate and simple cohabitation, have all been catalysts of group cohesion and, since the late eighteenth century, of national sentiment. Self-determination works best when ethnicity coincides with a territorial base, hence the comparative readiness of Czechs and Slovaks to settle for divorce by mutual consent. On the other hand, once a complex ethnic mosaic such as Yugoslavia begins to disintegrate, whether an ethnic group emerges as a subordinate minority or a dominant majority is more likely to depend on the fortunes of war and peacemaking than on the simple principle of self-determination.

In such an environment, nationality problems multiply in descending scale like a traditional Russian doll. And perhaps least susceptible to peaceful resolution on the basis of full self-determination is the problem of a trans-border ethnic minority, for seldom are states prepared to cede territory for the aggrandizement of a neighbor. Thus, Romanians who might welcome the annexation of formerly Soviet Moldova regard Transylvania, with its concentrations of Hungarians, as inalienable in whole or in part from their state. Majoritarian nationalists prefer assimilation and even "ethnic cleansing" to granting minorities cultural autonomy and local self-government.

In a world without unclaimed territory, self-determination is necessarily destructive of existing sovereignties. International institutions based on the latter therefore have a bias in favor of the status quo and are not likely to facilitate the diminution or fragmentation of their members. Even liberal democrats tend to champion self-determination only when it is directed against imperial and tyrannical rule, and to prefer the building of integrative, democratic communities to fragmentation. "Real existing socialism" suppressed minority aspirations by claiming historically to have superseded the phenomenon of nationalism. Nationalism proved to be the more enduring of the two, and it is now the burden of the inheritors of liberalism, East and West, to steer their energies and demands by just and enforceable codes.

Eastern Europe was the source, and is once again the principal victim, of the phenomenon denoted by the pejorative term *balkanization*, which evokes all manner of deplorable consequences of ethnic claims to sovereignty, of feeble, chauvinistic, and fractious nation-statelets — in short, the stuff of diplomats' nightmares. There is, observed a U.S. State Department official against the background of the Yugoslav crisis, "a tremendous danger in accepting a principle that all ethnic groups would have the right to independent existence as a nation-state and that borders ought to be redefined in a way which would allow that to happen."[8] Still, in a world of more than 170 states, and in a Europe that seems at ease with Luxembourg, Liechtenstein, and several micro-states, Western liberal democrats' reservations about national self-determination in Eastern Europe bear the taint of expediency if not hypocrisy; and this particularly at a time when a tendency toward renationalization was emerging in the European Union. West Europeans' hostility to East European nationalism and their reluctance to confront the issue of ethnic minority rights and self-determination stem from several factors. Official caution is inspired by ambivalence about providing stimuli to minority consciousness and demands within their own borders; a reluctance to see supranational authority intrude into cultural policy and potentially into other, so far exclusively national, preserves; and apprehension at the implicit extension of collective responsibility for solving the tribal quarrels of others. Thus some major members of the Council of Europe, including France, the United Kingdom, and Spain, pursued a rather dilatory strategy in the matter of expanding or complementing the European Convention on Human Rights to cover protection of national minorities. The toothless Conference on Security and Cooperation in Europe (CSCE) recently instituted the post of high commissioner for minority problems, but Western diplomacy proved singularly unimaginative and ineffective in anticipating and preventing the Yugoslav disaster.

■ ■ ■ ■

Western governments and their collective institutions, notably the Council of Europe, have not shirked their duty to champion democratization. Obviously the success of democracy in Eastern Europe depends on more than the formal adoption of new institutions and processes, which at this point in history means assimilation of the West European–North American model. It is also contingent on modernization of the popular political culture, and on the emergence of a civil society in which individuals are confident of their rights, are tolerant of the plurality of opinions, and are participants rather than subjects in relation to the state.

This ideal condition is only approximated in even the most modern of polities. Dissident intellectuals in Communist times freely conjured up the image of an autonomous civil society as the antithesis of the depoliticized, dependent, and ineffectual socialist society. Not surprisingly, the post-Communist reality fell short of the mark, especially in the Balkans. Yet both internal and external critics have been perhaps too quick to detect undemocratic tendencies, in East-Central Europe at any rate, where the words "velvet revolution" could describe all three countries' emergence from communism.

To be sure, Poland's presidential election produced in the first round an unthinking protest vote, and the revised electoral law precipitated a fragmented parliament and unstable governments. The division of powers between president and parliamentary government proved contentious in all of the formerly Communist states (except, of course, Germany). In Hungary, for instance, the dispute revolved around the president's right to countermand the government's dismissal of the heads of state radio and television. The new rulers' sensitivity to criticism, as exemplified by the attempt in Poland to proscribe mockery and insult (as well as more li-

belous attacks) directed against them, is certainly unhealthy for democracy. Enthusiastic popular participation in the first acts of liberation and
democratic choice has given way to low voter turnouts, apparent political
apathy, and the enervation both of the new political classes and of the
population at large.

There were also rather inept attempts at historical justice, such as the
release of police informers' names in Poland and Czechoslovakia, the
exclusion of former Party officials from state posts in the Czechoslovakia
(such a measure is under consideration in Poland as well), the prosecution
of Bulgaria's former dictator for embezzlement, and legislation suspend-
ing the statute of limitations for certain crimes. The most sweeping and
vindictive purge was conducted in Germany. It is tempting to recall the
summary justice meted out at war's end to collaborators in, say, France or
Belgium, but perhaps four years of German occupation and forty-five
years of Soviet hegemony are not really comparable. Deepening economic misery may yet provoke a stronger backlash against the acolytes of
the old regime. So far, apart from the Germans, East Europeans have
been extraordinarily lenient with their deposed guardians. To put the
current weaknesses of East European democracy in some perspective, one
could cite the Perot phenomenon in the 1992 American election campaign, the regal presidency of France's Fifth Republic, unstable governments and rampant political patronage in Italy, wildly disproportional
representation in the British electoral system, and arrogant governing
parties, fragmented parliaments, and low voter turnout at various times in
most Western democracies. The strength of liberal democracy lies precisely in accommodating such variations while preserving the fundamental supremacy of law and the citizens' freedom to change governments.

The East Europeans should be measured not against Western ideals
but against Western reality. That reality, in the case of most West European countries, consists of a resilient civil society conditioned by at least
four decades of democracy and growing prosperity. Social justice and
harmony remain elusive goals, but the consensus on the rules of political
discourse encompasses Communist remnants as well as resurgent ultrana-
tionalists; the authoritarian temptation is dormant if not dead.

In contrast, the post-Communist societies suffer from the cumulative
shocks of war, revolutions and counterrevolutions, indoctrination, and
pauperization. Although abhorrence of Communist dictatorship remains
strong throughout the region, the body politic's defenses against undemo-

cratic tendencies are perceived to be comparatively weak. A sober observer noted in mid-1991 that the "combination of economic decline, political confusion, anxiety about the future, and the beginnings of disillusionment in the West forms the essential background to the appeal of populism, nationalism, the rise of ethnic strife, xenophobia, and anti-Semitism — of authoritarian solutions."[9]

There is a hint of historical determinism in the West's tendency, however benevolent, to apply double standards and underestimate the capacity of East Europeans to adopt and adapt liberal democracy. That system's legitimacy is not contested, and its processes are generally respected. The initial electoral strength of the former Communists in Romania, Bulgaria, Serbia, and Albania has waned. The reformed Communist parties that vie for electoral favor — and, in the cases of Poland in September 1993 and Hungary in May 1994, even manage to form governments — appear to be genuine converts to social democracy. The forces of radical nationalism in Czechoslovakia, Bulgaria, and Romania have seldom strayed beyond the guardrails of democracy; the remnants of Yugoslavia are a tragic exception. Slovakia and Romania have promised to abide by the Council of Europe's and the CSCE's guidelines for collective minority rights. If East Europeans were as politically backward as Western stereotypes would have it, then their recent acceptance of the conventions of liberal democracy is nothing short of miraculous.

■ ■ ■

To build democracy in the exceptional conditions of adversity that afflict the region in the early 1990s is certainly daunting. Deepening penury and a still-tiny propertied and entrepreneurial class do not make for a solid political foundation for capitalist democracy. On a visit to Warsaw on 4 February 1992, Foreign Minister Hans-Dietrich Genscher reiterated Germany's support for eventual Polish membership in the European Community, conditional of course on the "success" of the country's economic reforms.[10] That same day, on the podium of the Council of Europe in Strasbourg, Poland's president was ringing the alarm bells: "Nowadays our own people are not getting the feeling that they are any better off. The fruits of the victory have gone sour. Already one can hear some people wondering why we have ever done it. Democracy is losing its supporters. Some people even say: 'Let's go back to authoritarian rule.'"

Reality, said Lech Wałęsa, "has mocked all those who thought the over-throw of communism would move the Eastern world closer to its Western counterpart." The fault lay largely with the West, which "was supposed to help us in arranging the economy on new principles, but in fact . . . largely confined its effort to draining our domestic markets." Otherwise, com-plained Wałęsa, "the richer part of Europe has shut itself off from poorer part."[11]

Wałęsa's alarmism owed something to temperament and calculation, and Poland had some unique economic problems. Nevertheless, two years after the fall of the Wall, democracy was suffering from its failure to ful-fill the early and perhaps inflated expectations of the East Europeans. A public opinion poll commissioned by the European Community and con-ducted in October 1991 indicated that a majority in every country ex-cept Lithuania was dissatisfied with democracy. In Czechoslovakia, Hun-gary, and Poland, the three countries with the longest recent exposure to (and historical experience of) democracy, only 22 to 30 percent expressed satisfaction.[12]

These soundings did not necessarily signal a readiness to escape from freedom or a dislike of liberal democratic values. They do reflect an impa-tience with the slow pace of parliamentary government (the common complaint being that "all they do is argue"), a healthy distaste for incom-petence and corruption, and, at least in the case of Poland, an electoral system that militated against effective government. Then again, earlier surveys in Western Europe found barely half of the respondents satisfied with democracy, and as Irving Kristol observed in May 1992, there is even in today's affluent West a "profound and inchoate dissatisfaction . . . with democratic government itself."[13]

One chooses democracy not because it abounds in virtues, reflected the philosopher Karl Popper, but in order to avoid tyranny. That has not stopped people in the past from turning away in disillusionment from democracy and rushing into the waiting arms of tyrants-to-be. Liberal market democracy, although it may be the best mechanism so far devised for stimulating economic growth and legitimating the distribution of scarce resources, offers no magic shortcut for transforming socialist stag-nation into capitalist prosperity. Cautionary advice about the pace and discomfort of massive structural change was initially overshadowed by euphoria over regained freedom. Now, however unfairly, the new democracies are being judged on the basis of their capacity to deliver economic benefits; and the West, especially Western Europe, is being judged on the basis of its dedication to the economic recovery of its poor cousins.

Indeed, in the midst of the East European political revolutions it was a common article of faith that the Western cousins would rally round to facilitate structural change. Forty years of cold war rhetoric had left an imprint. The West would not risk its security to force a Soviet retreat, but it never ceased to dangle the lure of freedom and prosperity before Moscow's captives. The latter, declared Secretary of State Dulles during the Hungarian revolution of 1956, "must know that they can draw upon our abundance to tide themselves over the period of economic adjustment which is inevitable as they rededicate their productive efforts to the service of their own people, rather than of exploiting masters."[14] By the time Leninism collapsed, Western Europe had almost caught up to America in abundance, and deficit-conscious Washington was eager to pass the main burden of aid to its transatlantic partners.

That Western aid would carry political and economic conditions raised no objections in principle among potential recipients. All of them, including the Soviet Union, had saluted the flag of economic liberalism at the CSCE's Bonn meeting in April 1990. The extent of the socialist system's political disgrace and economic failure was such that few East Europeans entertained reservations about the necessity of change. The more talented members of the old *nomenklatura* were among the first to exploit the opportunities of the free market. This unanimity did not preclude debate over social justice and the optimal role of the state in a market economy any more than it did so in the West (though social justice got only passing mention at Bonn); it did reflect a popular grant of legitimacy to the liberal order that had eclipsed Leninism.

But if market democracy, or its embellished image, was the people's overwhelming choice in the moment of revolution, its consolidation and stability remained to an uncertain extent contingent on the material benefits of the new order. By virtue of living in the same neighborhood with West Europeans, East Europeans expect market democracy to deliver a standard of living closer to Western norms. The "welfare gap" separating them defies precise measure. In the World Bank's calculations of GDP per capita for 1990, the best-placed East European countries, Czechoslovakia ($3,140) and Hungary ($2,780), stood far behind the poorest European Community (EC) members, Greece ($6,000) and Portugal ($4,890).

However, using a more meaningful measure (particularly for consumers), purchasing-power parities, Greece's GDP per capita in 1990 was 58 percent of the EC average, and Portugal's 53 percent, while Czechoslovakia's was 66 percent and Hungary's 53 percent.[15]

Of greater immediate political relevance than such elusive comparisons was the contraction in the East European economies with the shift to market democracy. Symptoms of economic crisis were already in evidence in the final years of socialism. The subsequent systemic disruption, domestic and regional, had a devastating impact on output, trade, employment, and the standard of living, producing what was in fact a deep depression.

The decline in real GDP in 1990 and 1991 ranged from around 5 and 11 percent in Hungary to 12 and 23 percent in Bulgaria. Industrial production in the five countries of the Council for Mutual Economic Assistance (CMEA) aside from Germany and the USSR (Bulgaria, Czechoslovakia, Hungary, Poland, and Romania) fell by an average of 17 percent in 1990 and 11 percent in 1991. In the same period, the terms of trade of the East-Central European three with the Soviet Union and the rest of the former CMEA deteriorated sharply, and the volume of their exports to the area fell by an estimated 75 to 90 percent.[16] To be sure, these statistics were probably distorted by the overstatement of prereform output and by incomplete accounting of postreform private sector activity, but in most countries industrial production continues to decline. Privatization, restructuring, or liquidation of the largest and least productive state industries is still under way, and prospects are for further drops in output and higher unemployment.

After serving as a guinea pigs for state socialism, East Europeans must endure another historic experiment, the conversion of a bankrupt centrally planned economy into a prosperous market. The process began with much doctrinaire advocacy of free markets, partly in reflection of the Western fashion for denationalization and deregulation. Yet state involvement in the economy, along French dirigiste or German neocorporatist lines, remains the European norm, and most of the new regimes in the east, whatever their official label, are essentially social democratic. With no precedents to draw upon, politicians and economists are testing in practice the merits of "Big Bang" change versus incrementalism in relation to prices, subsidies, tariffs, and convertibility, and a wide variety of privatization strategies. By generally adopting the restrictive fiscal and monetary policies recommended by the International Monetary Fund, governments did rein in runaway inflation, but disappearing markets, collapsing industries, falling consumption, rising unemployment, and cutbacks in welfare state services are hardly conducive to the legitimation of market democracy.

By comparison with the backlash that is commonly provoked by far less distress in the West, parties and social organizations have shown great reluctance to exploit politically the severity of the depression. This restraint could be explained by the demoralization of the Communists and a certain consensus against rocking the fragile boat of market democracy. But as real incomes fall and enterprises close, even the democratic labor organizations, such as Solidarity in Poland and Bulgaria's Podkrepa, are rising to challenge the governments' economic reform tactics. Strikes were initially rare, but by 1992 they began to proliferate, notably in Poland. There, popular discontent propelled two formerly Communist parties to power in the September 1993 elections, signaling a potential shift elsewhere in the region to a more welfare-oriented version of social democracy.

Unless the East's democratically elected governments can offer some credible promise of economic recovery and an upturn in the standard of living, and can do so within a few years and not just a generation, the current mood of political apathy could turn vindictive and volatile. Democracy thrives on citizens' sense of both their own political efficacy and that of the system. Battered by prolonged material deprivation, the postsocialist permissive consensus is fraying, and not only the current governments but also democracy itself are engaged in a race against time.

Beleaguered democratic politicians are not alone in ringing the alarm bells. Warned the London *Economist* in early 1992: "Unless the economies of the East start to improve soon, three dangers will grow: threats to democracy, risks of ethnic conflict and unwanted pressure from easterners to settle in the West. For the foreseeable future, the keystone to Europe's security is economic recovery in the East."[17] That will require more than self-congratulatory celebrations of communism's collapse, and alms to keep the poor from the door.

The region's economic marginality was reinforced by the cold war, which brought not only a disastrous Stalinist experiment and (at least in the early phase) colonial exploitation but also the West's economic sanctions. So far, Western Europe's responses have not gone far to alleviate that marginality. A major, and unconcealed, liability bequeathed by the socialists was foreign indebtedness. The net hard-currency debt facing the post-Communist regimes in 1990 ranged from Poland's $43 billion to Romania's $1 billion. Poland, unable even to maintain service payments, was saved from formal default by the Paris Club with a partial write-off at a cost of $16.5 billion. And when Bulgaria slid into technical default on its $10-billion debt, the Paris Club rescheduled its share over ten years, with a six-year grace period. Hungary struggled hard to maintain its financial credibility by servicing a $20-billion debt, the highest per capita in the region, and owed mainly to private lenders. Even Romania's debt, impulsively slashed by Ceauşescu at terrible cost to consumers and producers, grew again to more than $3 billion by mid-1992.

This debt burden weighs heavily at a time of disappearing traditional export markets and shrinking industrial output — and at a time when the privatization and modernization of industry depend heavily on the confidence of foreign investors. Yet the bulk of the G-24 advanced industrial states' assistance (loosely coordinated by the European Commission in the Poland/Hungary: Assistance to the Restructuring of the Economy [PHARE] program) has taken the form of export credits and investment guarantees, and of interest-bearing loans that increase the immediate debt burden. Indeed, the current aid and commercial policies of the EC and the prolonged difficulty of economic conversion may well produce the unanticipated and unwelcome effect of a net transfer of resources from the poor to the rich.[18] That had been the fate of most East Europeans in their colonial past, in the Nazi era, and again in the early postwar period, when the Soviet Union extracted roughly as much wealth from its satellites as the Marshall Plan pumped into Western Europe.

Dependency and exploitation, abetted of course by indigenous profiteers and ideologues, had severely distorted and retarded the region's economic modernization. Today, as in the past, a weak state and a pauperized society are a poor formula for political stability and democratic legitimacy. The West may find it easiest in the short run to simply insulate itself from the political vicissitudes of economic stagnation in the region, much as it has coped with the Yugoslav civil war, but only at the cost of burying the promise of a politically coherent Europe. Alternatively, it could devote greater resources to the East's economic rehabilitation, in the form of more grants, debt relief, and market access. A doubling of EC aid to the East (to 0.2% of the EC's GNP), funded by a "solidarity tax," and market access for Eastern Europe's most competitive exports were among the recommendations submitted in 1991 by six foreign policy research institutes from EC member states. But one of the authors conceded in another publication that as the euphoria over the East's emancipation dissipated, so did the prospects for such generosity.[19]

Given its own protectionist and interventionist practices, the West's professions of faith in the curative and creative powers of the free market sound a little disingenuous, like a justification for parsimonious aid. Economic conditionality remains desirable, but not if it renders democratically elected governments incapable of preserving social peace and ultimately the democratic process itself. East Europeans emerged from their revolutions with a touching faith in the promise of Europe, and they heard many an encouraging word. The PHARE program is one attempt to fulfill that promise. A bigger test is their knock on the door of the European Union.

The association agreements concluded in late 1991 between the European Community and the three East-Central European countries granted only token market access for the latter's most competitive exports (agriculture, textiles, and steel), and no promise of membership. Seeing little alteration of their peripheral status, East Europeans are rapidly losing their illusions about the West. Speaking at a colloquium on "Europe and the tribes" at Paris in March 1992, Jacques Delors declared that the EC "does its utmost to assist the eastern countries; what is lacking is a clear signal to make them understand that they are truly part of Europe." The Polish scholar-politician Bronislaw Geremek seized the cue: "These signals would consist of a precise schedule leading to our accession to the European Community, complete with well-defined political, economic and social conditions."[20] There is little sign that the new "European Union" created by the Maastricht treaty is ready and able to rise to this challenge.

The region suffers from other insecurities in addition to the fear of continuing economic marginality. National animosities prompted by minority problems are on the rise, Russia and Ukraine are militarily powerful but politically unpredictable neighbors, and the Yugoslav civil war threatens stability in the rest of the Balkans. Regional linkages such as the Visegrád Four and the Central European Initiative have done little to alleviate insecurity, and East Europeans pin their hopes on Western institutions to guarantee a just and stable order. Here, too, their sense of marginality is reinforced by the West's palliative responses, such as NATO's North Atlantic Cooperation Council and "partnerships in peace," which fall well short of a commitment to collective security.

Indeed, the historic tendency to regard Eastern Europe as a separate region destined to remain backward and turbulent remains strong in Western Europe. The old patterns of neglect, isolation, and clientelism can reemerge, making such perceptions a self-fulfilling prophecy. A sense of marginality breeds disillusionment, and disillusionment feeds the politics of expediency and chauvinism. The Communists bear responsibility for forty — or rather, seventy — lost years in the quest of a morally united, politically and economically coherent continent. The democracies had prevailed in two world wars, only to let a lasting peace elude them. In both of these watersheds of history, the nations of Eastern Europe were potentially the greatest beneficiaries and actually the greatest losers. No wonder, then, if they regard themselves (in Milan Kundera's words) as representing the wrong side of history, its victims and outsiders. The West, emerging triumphant from the cold war, must learn from experience and adjust its perceptions and priorities in order to finally win the peace and bring East Europeans back from the periphery and into the mainstream of modernity.

The Economic Legacies
of Communism

Ivan Volgyes

It may be commonplace to say today that the Soviet-type economic system disappeared like the dinosaur, that it collapsed of its own weight and inefficiency, or that it had to surrender to the superiority of the market economy. It may be equally commonplace to attribute the collapse of the socialist, centrally planned economies to the successes of the capitalist system. And alternatively, it may be tempting to consider the disappearance of the Communist economic system as a revolutionary event, led by people who practically overnight wiped out the restrictive structures imposed upon them more than four decades earlier.

All these opinions are well founded, albeit a bit late; only a few of our economic analysts — most notably Gregory Grossman, Murray Feshbach, Morris Bornstein, and much of the CIA team — noted the process of collapse early in the game.[1] Of course, it was commonplace among analysts of the Soviet state to note that it was a "third world economy with a first world military," but drawing the necessary conclusion concerning its potential collapse was more difficult. It was much easier for all of us to accept East European wits' wonderfully cynical view that in the case of the economy — as in that of the system as a whole — the situation was hopeless but not bad, than to begin to examine the implications of that very hopelessness.

The reality was that the failures of the Communist economies of Europe did not "cause" the revolution; economies — contrary to Marx's view — are never substructures, but merely the superstructures that rest on the foundation of politics; and it was that political basis that was eroded, collapsed, and disintegrated practically overnight. The changes in the economic realm which we witness in the territory of the former USSR and in Eastern Europe, therefore, are, to a large extent, due to the changes that have taken place in the political system. What has happened in the economic life of the region, hence, are the results of political transformation that occurred since the collapse of communism in 1989–91.

The Inheritance of Ages Past

When Marx began to formulate his economic analysis of capitalism during the second half of the nineteenth century, he observed an economic production system in development, with all its dynamism, change, and innovation. The criticism he leveled at the negative aspects of capitalism became the static elements of the future Communist economic theories. Those theories ignored the changes that continued to occur in the much-criticized capitalist system, on the one hand, while also rigidly denying the potential for capitalism to reform itself into a market-oriented exchange system, on the other. Communism as an economic system thus came into being as a protest against a model that had already begun to cease to exist at the time when the Communist system came into existence in Russia. In short, Communist economic theory existed in contrast to a system that, historically, no longer existed. It counterposed a centrally directed and planned system, which Communists justified as a benevolent distributive organism, in contrast to the system (in fact already superseded) of monopoly capitalism. When added to the enforced isolation of the people living under the Communist system, however, the image of two contrasting systems — one depicted as exploiting the people, the other depicted as a paternalist distributor — provided a powerful propaganda stimulus to which often even the myth makers fell victim.

The rhetoric, however, masked an important reality: the Communist economic system established following the Soviet industrialization debates of 1924–28 was based on a theoretically rational economic model of development.[2] The Stalinist model of forced industrialization, with all that it implied, clearly was designed to subordinate "normal" economic developmental needs to the needs of a Soviet war economy, and it was this war-economic, centrally planned, and centrally directed economic system that became frozen into reality after the imposition of Communist rule in Eastern Europe. In short, the adoption of the model was flawed not only by a mistaken analysis of developmental trends in the market economies but also as a result of the adoption of the Soviet model, applied since the 1930s, in economies of different size, structure, culture, and level of development.[3]

The Domestic Bases of Communist Economies

The principal element of Communist economic systems was the primacy of heavy industrial development. Thus, members of Eastern Europe's new Communist elite, having inherited — with the exception of the Czech Lands — largely agrarian economies, believed that their very first priority was to develop heavy industry everywhere in the region. As we glance at the changes, we must note the alteration in the character of all of these states' economies during the period 1945–90. Whereas they had been largely agriculturally based, they became dominated by labor-intensive heavy industrial production. The region simply had to become the land of steel and coal, consuming ever larger amounts of labor, resources, and energy to produce more steel for more heavy industrial products.

A second pillar of the Communist economic system was the "sacred" principle of state (or "public") ownership. Ideologically justified as a higher principle, far above that of the value of property as owned by individuals, state ownership was extended to virtually every element of life. Only some of the activities of the region derived from the second (or unofficial and unregulated) economy which could be justified as not being a part of state ownership. The rewards reaped from the redistributive activities of the state, which was the owner of nearly everything, including private cars, apartments, dachas, and the like, were held up as the "unprecedented benefits of the socialist system." As long as there were no international bases for comparison, some of the people even believed in the "superior value of state ownership."

A third pillar of the Communist system was the creation of large-scale, mechanized agriculture. The giant collective and state farms, whether they were profitable or not, utilized huge machines, industrial production systems, and cheap labor. The system forced the upwardly mobile members of rural society to become the industrial laborers used to build the industrial bases of socialism, while it forced a large percentage of the rural population to remain bound to a centralized system of agro-industrial activity, receiving lower wages and fewer benefits than the urban industrial workforce.

The fourth pillar of the Communist economy in the domestic sphere was the principles and practices of planned production and central pricing. In theory everything was planned: the production targets that had to be met were laid down; everything had a price, and nearly everything had an artificial value. The fact that central planning simply meant merely having targets, often devoid of any element of realistic projection based on the balance of allocatable and needed resources, frequently made the system a mockery of reality. Reporting became based on wishful thinking, and the planned economy operated as a system based on the "constant recreation of scarcity," to use Janos Kornai's evocative phrase.[4]

A fifth characteristic of the Communist system was its theoretical denial of the value of infrastructural development. Infrastructure and the service sector, according to Marxian economic principles, were not a part of the value of a product, since they did not directly involve either productive labor or material. Consequently, the infrastructure — roads, railroads, telephones, sewer systems, the ecosphere — remained largely underdeveloped, and was allowed to deteriorate to a point at which it was practically impossible to refit it for the production needs of the twentieth century.

A sixth pillar of the system was its emphasis on vertical interest aggregation and articulation. The local needs of community became secondary in importance; what mattered was the approval or support of the hierarchically organized, vertical casts of characters. The future of a district employee was tied not to his local network but to his superior, located at the county level; in the economic realm, decisions made at the local level always had to be taken with an eye toward meeting the needs of the immediately higher sectoral units. The vertical system of allegiances and interest aggregation thus resulted in the effective destruction of the local community as an economic unit.

A seventh pillar of the Communist economic system was the concept of full employment, coupled with the obligation to work.[5] The irrational arrangement of the labor market created an artificial system in which minimal amounts of remuneration were offered to everyone for variegated amounts of labor, but the socially necessary minimal benefits were available to everyone. Full employment was easily achieved, while often the tasks accomplished needed only a fraction of the labor assigned to the job. An underqualified, huge labor force was born, whose members' personal goal was the avoidance of undue risk and the minimizing of individual decision making.

A final element of the system was the provision of acceptable living standards. In reality, of course, the living standards that existed in all of these states were far below those of the West European economies, but the propaganda that was a part of the daily routine attempted to mask this by a constant emphasis on the benefits of the system in the East — full employment, social insurance, constant progress — in contrast to the negative aspects of European and North American capitalism — unemployment, "no benefits," and constant crises. This false comparison worked well until the opportunities for international comparison became widely available to the population of the region, either through personal travel opportunities or through the visual stimulus of the news media.

In short, the domestic economic systems of communism operated on premises of economic development which were no longer valid toward the end of the twentieth century; whether they were ever valid as the bases of a viable and dynamic economic system remains a matter of speculation. Determined by politicians with a particular world view and a particular goal in mind — the creation of a gestalt socioeconomic and political system they called communism or socialism — the economic superstructure had to serve the interest of the political base. It became clear by the end of the 1980s that neither the economic nor the political goals of the system could be achieved any longer.

The External Bases of Communist Economies

The establishment of Communist political systems in Eastern Europe resulted in the immediate creation of Communist economies, but it did not include the simultaneous integration of external economic relations for the region. In fact, one of the principal objectives of Communist economic strategies was the imposition of autarkic development patterns for each state, forcing each state to rely on its own resources for national development. Following the initial stripping of economic resources from all of the states by the Soviet forces in the 1940s, no real integration took place in the region for a long time.

Even after the establishment of the Council for Mutual Economic Assistance (CMEA) in January 1949, autarkic practices assumed a curious duality.[6] On the one hand, each state, while theoretically a part of a joint economic system, was forced to continue its autarkic development pattern. As a result, throughout its existence the CMEA never became a multilaterally organized mini–Common Market, but remained a collection of states whose trade with one another was regulated by bilateral treaties of every possible source. And throughout the existence of the organization, there was the perception, and sometimes the fact, that the East European states were being exploited by the USSR.

On the other hand, the CMEA also served to guarantee the existence of an "internationally autarkic development pattern" by enforcing the East European states' reliance upon the USSR and upon each other, and hence institutionalizing an enforced isolation from the West.[7] This isolation, and mutual reliance based on the dictated specialization of production, meant that these states were unable to participate in the technological revolution that was sweeping the West during the 1970s and 1980s. In terms of actual external trade patterns, in the CMEA states the ratio of the influx of modern goods and technology from the West to the outflux of less modern goods (either to each other or to even more underdeveloped states) was no more than one to thirty, with the actual ratio depending, of course, upon the country in question.

All of these aspects contributed first to stagnation, followed by a growing separation from the West in terms of the quality of goods produced and their technical advancement, innovation, the percentage of investment devoted to research and development, and the incorporation of modern technology. While having to rely on each other for basic goods and services, these states, often correctly, perceived the products emanating from their Communist trading partners as inferior, and were either unwilling or unable to create an integrated system of modern economies based on continuous mutual cooperation as a sine qua non for advancement. Not only was the USSR itself, fearing a potential unified bloc of states that might be difficult to manage, opposed to the development of real integrative processes among the East European states of the CMEA, but the Soviet satraps continued to perceive trade with their socialist "brethren" as having secondary importance.[8] It is natural, then, that when the collapse came, neither the physical nor the attitudinal elements necessary for international integration were present in the external economic relations of the East European states.

Allow me to reflect at this stage on a question often posed as a nagging concern among people wrestling with the question of the inheritance of communism. It is, indeed, a fact that during the forty-some years of Communist rule the economies of the Soviet bloc countries all developed from agrarian to industrial production systems, that industries were built and developed in abundance, that agriculture became mechanized, that electricity was brought everywhere, that people became educated and literate, that cities and urban housing were built in profusion, and that social advances undreamed of in the 1930s occurred. Would these events have taken place to the same extent under a different system? I think that the answer, overwhelmingly, is yes; under a different system, in fact, the economic and social development patterns would not have stopped at the point of creating an industrial base but would have taken that base to a higher level of technological innovation, to a higher level of success and of integration with modern industrial technologies. But it was precisely the real integration with modernity that the Communist authorities did not want, for to attain that would have meant having open societies, freely engaged in international commerce. By imposing a certain pattern of economic activity and limiting economic growth, they could control the population and best exercise their rule. Power and control over Eastern Europe became far more important for the rulers than development, change, and progress.

After the Fall: Economic Legacies

As in other chapters of this book, it is not easy to determine the actual legacies of the Communist system; we really do not know whether, and to what extent, what exists today in the East European economies was caused by the operations or the failures of that system. What we do know is that what was inherited from the past, and thus from the Communist system, is insufficient for the operation of modern economies, economies that since the 1960s have been driven by the fourth industrial revolution, the technological revolution. In order to operate on the technologically advanced level required by modern global integrative processes, the East European economies must overcome that insufficiency.

The first legacy of the Communist economic system is the disadvantage with which East European economies, with their heavy industrial bases, operate in the global marketplace. The "rust belt" industries spew out heavy industrial products, steel or iron, for which there is no worldwide demand. "Socialist cities," such as Nowa Huta or Diósgyőr have suddenly become repositories of the unemployed; factories produce goods that have no market without subsidized state orders. After a while, the deficits derived from the fact that production costs are higher than sales revenues can no longer be covered. Hence, most of these inefficient, polluting industrial giants will have to be shut down, which in turn will cause staggering unemployment and little or no hope for new industries to replace those engaged in heavy machinery production.

A second legacy of communism is the necessity of recreating the private sector. Privatization, however, is a cumbersome process, as local or native capital is extremely scarce. As a result, the states of the region must resort to imaginative ways to re-privatize. Among them is the voucher scheme followed by the Czech Lands and Russia, in which every person can become a shareholder in a given venture. Another scheme is followed in Hungary, where managers and others can openly bid for the ownership of hitherto state-owned stores or enterprises; this works well with firms, stores, or other economic entities that are small, but does not work for large enterprises. In fact, the tendency of the Antall government in 1992 was actually to increase state ownership shares of the new economy. Still another way is to allow foreign firms to purchase minority or majority shares of ownership of the large-scale industries. The trouble is that people resent such sales, believing that foreign firms acquire such enterprises cheaply.[9] In short, the legacy of communism includes the enormous and unsolved problem of re-privatization of ownership, a problem that will continue to haunt the economic actors of these states for many years to come.

A third legacy of communism is the "mess" in the agricultural sector. The desire of the successor governments was to do away with the Communist system of collective farms by attempting to return, or sell, the land of the collective and state farms to their former owners and to others wishing to farm the land. Hence, the collective and state farms were abolished and dissolved in many places, and the ideal of a small peasant economy began to take place in practice. But small-scale agriculture demands different mechanical bases than does the large-scale agriculture favored by the Communists: it requires small-scale machinery instead of huge combines, small-scale capital investment, and an infusion of capital into processing and packaging technology; and none of these factors are plentiful in the region. Significantly, the shift from large-scale to small-scale agriculture also results in an enormous drop in industrial agricultural crops, forcing these states to import large quantities of scarce goods from the outside.

The end of the centrally planned economy may have been very beneficial, but the fact is that for more than forty years the Communist system destroyed or distorted the concept of the market. The abolition of the planned economy thus did not mean a rapid return to the free market. Rather, all of the East European states now exist in a state of limbo, with a semimarket system dominating daily existence. This is because markets, and hence market economies, cannot be created by edicts from above; rather, their development takes place very slowly. In the meanwhile, an irrational price structure, often dictated by practically unrestricted and unfettered imports, exists coupled with an undercapitalized, underdeveloped, and underutilized system of banking. The nations of the region, at the same time, are forced to choose either a national model of development without a large-scale capital infusion, or a model of development prescribed by the IMF and based on low deficits, high debt-repayment ratios, and permanent relegation to a secondary role in the world economy.[10]

It should, of course, not be surprising that the negative legacies of communism also include the deplorable state of the banking industry and of the financial institutions in general. Ideologically, it can easily be understood that Marxist theory abhorred money and longed for primitive communism, with its barter-based system that was deemed superior to the "dirty" concept of money. Economically, however, Communist systems had to exist in a semimarket situation. On the one hand, they had to trade with the West and were dependent on such trade, which meant that they had to offer value in monetary terms. On the other hand, they found themselves in the situation of engaging in commodity barter in which the goods exchanged were valued according to some sort of monetary yardstick. For this reason they developed a dual system of finances; while their national currencies were nonconvertible on the international financial markets, they possessed, for accounting purposes, first a convertible ruble rate, and later a convertible dollar-to-ruble ratio. The system of financial accounting, therefore, ignored the real movement of moneys based on the international valuation of currencies, on available gold, and on other financial resources, and neglected the development of a sound national currency that could be accepted in the West. Clearly, when the Berlin Wall fell, the emerging democracies would find the transition to a currency convertible in the international markets one of the most difficult and painful tasks to accomplish.

I do not mean to imply that in all instances the real values of the national currencies were extremely far from those that were set artificially by the state; in the case of Hungary, for instance, the real and the official value of the forint often differed by no more than 25 percent, and the Yugoslav dinar has been "semiconvertible" for a long time. The point that is worth making, however, is that the value of the national currencies was set arbitrarily, generally without regard to the laws of supply and demand on the international market; since these currencies were never intended to be used on these markets, their valuation by nations other than the "socialist brethren" was, in a sense, immaterial. And among the socialist brethren the value of each produced good, like that of each national currency, was always determined by bartering and allocating tasks within the complex international Communist system.

Given these ideological and international constraints, it is not surprising that the banking sphere remained backward, especially when viewed in light of the developments in banking which have taken place during the last thirty years in the West. In the West, banks have fueled economic development, serving as sources of funds for advancement and growth, and providers of risk and venture capital. By 1990 they were interlinked by electronic fund transfer networks, and they have provided the needed steam for the engines of economic change. In the East, however, the banks have been used for little more than to safeguard deposited savings, provide interest at given, centrally set percentage rates, and channel payments from private sources to public institutions. With their ownership, basically, in the hands of the state, and without any public control or responsibility exercised by overseers concerned with profits or losses, the banks were to be the weakest partners of the West in the necessary transformation process. Although in some instances, notably in Poland, Hungary, and the Czech Republic, efforts would be made to bring the banks up to the level needed for the economic takeoff, even these efforts would be little more than half-hearted attempts at creating modern, economically sound, and Western-oriented banking systems.

One of the saddest legacies left behind by the Communist system is the incredible backwardness in the infrastructure. As noted above, infrastructural development was not seen as a part of the production hierarchy under communism; hence little or no effort was made to invest in it during the last forty years. Yet, precisely during this period, the West has undergone an infrastructural revolution involving transport, communication, and telecommunication. Western Europe is beribboned today with multilane superhighways, its railroad system is swift and efficient, and its computer-driven telecommunications system is light years ahead of Eastern Europe's infrastructure. By contrast, the roads in Eastern Europe are mostly pothole-marked single lanes that fail to connect any but the largest urban centers to the outside world, the railroad lines are so old that the trains must often creep along with their loads, and the telephone systems are overloaded, jammed, and ancient. In Hungary, for example, out of three thousand settlements of urban status, fully one-third still had manual telephone centers in 1991! Moreover, adapting to the computer revolution is not merely a matter of having the expensive hardware — learning to use it will be natural for the next generation but will be an enormously hard task for the present elites of the region. It must be noted that infrastructural investment is difficult to obtain as long as the government seeking such investment wants to maintain the state monopoly on telecommunication, for no investor is likely to put his money in a field where governmental interference is likely to be permanent. And statist attitudes prevail among all but a handful of the region's political and/or governmental leaders; perhaps the most important exception is the Czech prime minister, Václav Klaus.

One of the principal criteria for speedy and successful development is that development be supported and "owned" by the community in which it is to take place. Yet, as noted earlier, the Communist emphasis on vertical allegiances — stemming from the government's fear of the strength of localism — managed to purposefully destroy the local community. The concept of empowerment, of individual responsibility, has been largely destroyed as well. Nearly five decades of Communist rule in Eastern Europe created a dual mind-set in the people: on the one hand, they expect someone in authority to tell them what to do; on the other, they have become atomized and have withdrawn from their role as participants in the local community, content to be left alone. Finding the courage and the wisdom to take control of and assume responsibility for their own fate would take as much of an effort as would rebuilding their shattered local communities.

One of the legacies of the Communist economic system is the skewed structure of employment, specifically derived from the heavy reliance of the Communist system on labor-intensive methods of development. Under the system, it was believed that economic growth could be generated by allocating ever-increasing numbers of laborers to industrial tasks. The trouble, however, was that most of these laborers essentially performed unskilled and semiskilled tasks; they largely commuted from the villages, and often lived in workers' dormitories provided by their employers. While the number of such commuters varied from country to country, they ranged from 15 to 30 percent of the workforce.[11] When the change from a centralized system of economic management to a market-driven system occurred, many of these unskilled and semiskilled workers were to find themselves the real losers in the transformation.

Instead of a Conclusion

Communism dissipated, imploded, drifted away; in short, it is gone "not with a bang, but with a whimper." It left behind very little which is visible, except for the negative legacies that must be overcome. In the economic sphere, it seems to me, overcoming the backwardness left behind will be easier for some of the former Communist states than for others.

For those states in which a significant private economy, by whatever name, was a working part of the previous system, revitalizing small, private trade and manufacturing activities will be easier than elsewhere. Hungary, Slovenia, Poland, and the Czech Republic are likely to be the states in which the retail sector will rapidly become successful. In other states, geographical isolation may hinder the development of this sector, as well as that of others.

In terms of industrial restructuring, the Czech Republic and Slovenia are likely to lead the way, with Hungary and Poland following behind. While joint ventures will help greatly, notably in Hungary, what appears to be most likely to drive the process most quickly is a successful and speedy privatization process and the removal of state control over market forces. The use of statist techniques as a cushioning device, however well intentioned, will only slow down development and the achievement of an industrial equilibrium beneficial to integration with the West.

A special note must be made of a potential bright spot for the near future, however ironic or inconsistent it appears to be: the efforts to "reestablish the CMEA," or to reinvent trade with the East — of course, in vastly different form than it existed before. In spite of the negative political perception that such a relationship implied in the past, the fact is that the closest and most obvious trading partners of the East European states are their former partners in the CMEA: their fellow East European states and the former republics of the USSR. Groups, such as the Association of Centers of Industrial Production Regions, that attempt to form regional trade compacts should be encouraged. While trade with the West is essential, a balance of continuous trade with the East is just as necessary if the East European states intend to survive the transition to market economies.

All of these tasks will be exceedingly difficult for the nascent democracies of Eastern Europe to manage. Given the prevalent protectionist attitudes and practices of the European Union, even under the most enlightened leadership the current transitory governments would find the job of managing them more than daunting. Coupled with the need to decide the proper course of future development, however, that job is even more difficult. Yet overcoming these economic legacies of communism must remain the primary task for the emerging democracies of the region.

4

The Sociological Legacies
of Communism

Jane L. Curry

Since 1989, democratic institutions have come to Eastern Europe. By standard definitions, based largely on the West European experience, *democracy* has been achieved. According to such definitions democracy has, basically, three essential, interdependent elements. One is the presence of institutions and procedures through which citizens can effectively express preferences about alternative policies and leaders. The second is the existence of institutionalized constraints on the exercise of power by the executive branch of government. The third is the guarantee of civil liberties to all citizens in their daily lives and in acts of political participation.[1]

In the years since the East European revolutions, new constitutions and new legislation have been passed providing for new, democratic institutions and/or democratic-style restraints on old institutions. There is no doubt that the elections in the region have been overwhelmingly free and competitive. More than at any time during the Communist era, a variety of views are expressed and a variety of voices are heard in the policy-making process. Power has changed hands and policy has been criticized in ways that were not even conceivable in the past. And nations, groups, and economic interests have been able, in large part, to go their own way.

Yet, in these new democracies, there is an increasing absence of the *demos*, the population, in the political process. Public opinion polling has shown that most people in Eastern Europe are disappointed and even disillusioned (and growing more so) with the transformation (tables 1 and 2).

Now, even when individuals do participate, their desires are all too often not reflected in political debates and policy decisions, or their votes reflect little real understanding of the positions of parties and candidates. In effect, in country after country, having been in power is the "kiss of

TABLE 1. Survey Respondents' Satisfaction
and Dissatisfaction with the Development
of Democracy, Fall 1991

Country	Satisfied (%)	Dissatisfied (%)
Albania	42	55
Bulgaria	39	45
Czechoslovakia	28	66
Hungary	30	60
Poland	27	50
Romania	41	55

Source: Eurobarometer/Gallup.

Note: The percentages do not add up to 100% because some respondents "could not say" or didn't answer.

death": ruling parties and coalitions have not been able to keep from
being rejected by the voters. When they are in power, the leaders of these
newly democratized countries have been, as often as not, openly con-
temptuous of those they rule.

In other spheres of life, economics and culture for instance, much has
changed as the controls have been removed, but much has remained the
same as before. This is a reflection, in part, of the short time that has
elapsed since the end of Communist rule. In large part, it is also a reflection of the strength of the social ties, attitudes, and traditions forged
under communism.

The reality is that what scholars and citizens alike thought was a
"second society" comprising black market trade, opposition media, and
fiercely held, old traditions was really the formative force in Eastern Europe. Communism, its rules and institutions, provided increasingly flexible boundaries for this second society, but at the end of communism's
forty years, what appeared to us to be, at best, a repressive system caught
"muddling through" had really worn down to a veneer over the stronger
and more penetrating second society.

Communism did teach its citizens lessons in the decades of its rule. It
did not create the model "socialist men" it set out to create, nor did it
create the homogeneity that was its goal. It did create a population that
was highly educated and mobilized with a sense of "rightful power." In
doing this, it created citizens with values, expectations, and behavior patterns quite different from those of their peers in the West or from the bulk

TABLE 2. Survey Respondents' Responses to the Question
"Will the New Year 1993 Be Better or Worse Than 1992?"

Country	Better (%)	Worse (%)	The Same (%)	Don't Know (%)
Czech Republic	18	64	14	4
Slovakia	14	64	14	8
Hungary	11	23	62	4
Poland	14	67	12	7

Source: Data from Gallup International/PENTOR, December 1992, cited in Eugeniusz Smialowski, "From Bad to Worse," *Warsaw Voice*, 17 Jan. 1993, 5.

of the population in other states (e.g., states in Latin America and Southern Europe) that have gone from being authoritarian to being democratic. The lessons and results of communism allowed East Europeans to force the Communists from power, however inadvertently this was done. But those lessons and results have also made creating and running functioning democracies, as we have known them in Western Europe, Latin America, and Southern Europe, more difficult. Grafting models for the transition and its outcome from these other societies requires taking the risk of overlooking the special social base created by communism.[2]

All of this poses a theoretical conundrum and an uncomfortable political reality: what are the sociological legacies of communism? Why is it that societies that fulfill the institutional requirements for democracy are stable even when there have been dramatic decreases in popular participation; in people's faith in the system and in their own futures; and in their trust of institutions, new political leaders, and political processes? Why have these conditions come about at a time when, on the whole, people's expectations — for immediate gains and for the direction of overall change — are being violated as frequently as they are being heard? And why, in societies such as Poland, where unfulfilled promises brought people to the streets during the Communist era, has this not been the case in the period of transition? Why has the dashing of the high hopes for democracy brought apathy and not upheaval?

The answer to these questions does not really lie in the remains of Communist-era institutions or even in the problematic economic transformation process with which these societies are dealing. The old, Communist-era institutions of control have been disbanded, given other roles, or declared transformed. Even when economic conditions stabilize or begin to improve, public opinion has grown increasingly negative, and domination by the political leadership has remained a fact of life.

Instead, the answer to these questions must come from the characteristics of the population that communism crafted and from the less quantifiable and more subjective realm of social attitudes, learned behavior, and patterns of interaction and expectation. None of these are the same as those that underlay and underlie the birth and survival of democracies elsewhere. Their significance and impact not only color the nature of political reconstruction in present-day Eastern Europe but will also have a long-term effect on the nature of the region's polities and societies.

The Population Base

The very nature of the social base that communism created for East European societies through universal and free education and massive industrialization is significantly different than the social base for democracy or even for development elsewhere.

Educational Legacies

All of the populations of Eastern Europe, with the exception of Albania, are highly educated. Not only is literacy virtually universal, but higher education and technical education are much more widespread throughout the population than they are in most of Western Europe and in the newly democratizing states in Latin America and Southern Europe which are so often used as models (table 3).[3]

At the very least, Western theories of development and political participation would indicate that highly educated populations are likely to be more politically conscious and participatory than those with lower educational levels.

Education in East European societies carried messages that were even more politically pregnant than the standard messages of Western-based education. What was conveyed, deliberately or inadvertently, in that education was far different from the messages in standard educational programs elsewhere. Rather than focusing primarily on literacy and technical education, Communist societies tried to use their educational systems to remake their people. So important was this that Marxism and political economy were part of the curricula at every level and in every area. In addition, the curricula attempted to teach cooperation and commitment to community, the "glories" of communism as a "workers' state" in which

TABLE 3. Educational Levels and Expenditures
in Selected Countries, 1992

Country	% of GNP for Education	Literacy Level (%)	% of University Graduates in Population
Eastern Europe			
Albania	—	99	—
Bulgaria	5.2	96	5.2
Czechoslovakia	5.5	99	4.1
German Democratic Republic	5.3	99	8.5
Hungary	5.7	99	5.1
Poland	3.8	99	5.7
Romania	2.1	96	4.6
Latin America			
Argentina	1.8	95	4.0
Bolivia	.5	66	5.0
Brazil	3.3	79	4.3
Peru	2.9	87	4.5
Southern Europe			
Greece	2.6	94	2.5
Portugal	4.4	84	1.0
Spain	3.6	93	3.7

Source: PC Globe, software (Novato, Calif.: Broderbund Corp., 1992).

workers were mobilized to lead, and the importance of politics and political leaders. Students were pushed to be involved in groups and activities from an early age.[4]

The messages that were heard clearly were not always those in the texts and in media-based adult socialization. They were, however, no less effective. Students and adults heard that they were important and that "their" state owed them support because it was their state. They also heard messages about their own importance as professionals and as workers. True, the messages were not always consistent: workers were told that it was their state but then given little voice in it; professionals were told both to be competent and to be the servants of the Communist Party even as they were isolated into full-time professional education programs at the university; and images of the glories of socialism were tarnished in the light of the daily grind of survival. Students did some rethinking when these messages did not bear up to the reality of shortages. But the sense of individuals' right to be served and of individuals' competence, even if it was ignored, was a constant. In short, education did far more than create a literate population. It created a mobilized, if disillusioned, population, divided into groups with special skills and interests.

Industrialization Legacies

The populations of Eastern Europe are highly industrialized populations that shifted from a rural social base to an industrial one in the great industrialization drive of the 1950s. Whether or not the industrialization was successful in economic terms, it was successful in transforming the largely peasant societies of Eastern Europe. Over the course of forty years, individuals were integrated into urban societies; even those who remained "on the farm" were involved in market economies and lost their children to the city (table 4).

Once industrialization slowed in the 1960s, upward movement from the working class into the intelligentsia stopped, and class lines formed between the working class, white-collar workers, and intellectuals. Peasants and their values were left virtually outside the polity and society. But within each social group, this limited mobility and the relative job stability of most workers meant that strong ties, forged by years of living and working together, formed among individuals in a given class and place.

In spite of the limits on the real political voice of any group or class, this industrialization created a class society in which individuals had a clear sense of competence, tempered by frustration at not being heard. Workers' calls for the "rationalization" of economic production were a reflection of their sense that they knew what should happen. White-collar workers called for "depoliticization" as a way for their interests and voices to be powerful.

At the same time, a state-controlled economy that employed virtually every working person brought with it a heightened sense of the relationship between politics and economics: economic difficulties were seen not as the fault of a firm or its management but as the fault of the state. In this light, too, individuals lost the sense of personal responsibility that industrialization usually creates. Instead of individual gains or losses being seen as results of individuals' work or failures, such gains or losses came to be seen as the product of the government's bad policy or poor management. After all, orders were given from the top, and only infrequently was there any attempt to attribute blame to factories or to reward them for good work. There was a structural deformation as well. A society was created in which the service sector of professionals and lower-level, individual ser-

TABLE 4. Urban-Rural Division of Population
in Selected Countries

Country	Urban Dwellers (%)	Agricultural Sector (%)	Industrial Sector (%)	Service Sector (%)
Eastern Europe				
Albania	34.8	34	51	15
Bulgaria	66.7	15	72	13
Czechoslovakia	74.1	8	71	21
East Germany	76.8	11	71	18
Hungary	59.5	16	58	24
Poland	61.2	16	61	23
Romania	54.3		71	13
Latin America				
Argentina	84.7	15	35	50
Bolivia	49.1	28	22	50
Brazil	73.9	9	36	55
Peru	68.8	15	37	48
Southern Europe				
Greece	58.1	17	29	54
Portugal	29.7	9	39	52
Spain	91.4	6	37	57

Source: PC Globe.

Note: The high level of urbanization reflected in these statistics on Latin America is not a figure truly comparable to statistics on European societies, since it includes a large percentage of peasants who have come to cities either to work in traditional servant jobs or to search for work and live in shanty towns on the outskirts of the cities. In this same way, the proportion of agricultural to industrial jobs in Latin America, Southern Europe, and Eastern Europe is more comparable because the service sector in Latin America is dominated by marginal employees doing nonproductive service jobs rather than doing the jobs most often connected with the service sector in European societies: professional and bureaucratic professions requiring educations and earning high incomes.

vice personnel (sales personnel, servants, and clerks) was much smaller than in the rest of the industrial or industrializing world.

Because of the ties this sort of state-society interaction created, improvement in one's living standard came to be seen not as a matter of individuals working harder but as a matter of the system changing. Now that the system has changed, workers are reluctant to buy into it by changing jobs and leaving what they perceive as "safe work" in the state sector. Life without a guaranteed job is hard for them to imagine. Their answer to potential unemployment or underemployment is to look for work in

TABLE 5. Ethnic Divisions
in Selected Countries

Country	Majority (%)	Minorities (%)	No. of Minorities[a]
Albania	92	2, 3	2
Bulgaria	85	8, 3, 4	3
Czechoslovakia	63	32, 4, 1	3
East Germany	99	1	1
Hungary	97	2, 1	2
Poland	99	1	1
Romania	88	8, 4	2
Yugoslavia	36	28, 9, 8, 8, 6, 3, 10 (other)	6

Source: PC Globe.
[a]Includes only minorities comprising more than 1
percent of total population.

the new trade and service sector, or to try to hold on to their old jobs and rely on political pressure to counter government desires to rationalize the economy.

What the dramatic industrialization of Eastern Europe did not do was create an entrepreneurial class comparable to the ones that were the backbone of Western democracies. The initiator and builder of industry in Eastern Europe was the state. Individuals played roles only as servants of the state, and learned some of the skills of entrepreneurship only because they had to meet state goals in a system that did not work as it should. The shortages, central planning, and vagueness in policy that were part of Communist rule did not teach the value of saving or of innovation. If anything, they gave people a deformed experience of entrepreneurship, focusing their attention on trading and on working around the system even if they were in it. This has made for an initial capitalism in Eastern Europe based on import-export and avoiding responsibility to the law.

The power of the state and the stress on higher education have had another crucial impact on the nature of East European societies. They created a disproportionately large bureaucratic class whose members were employed in Party and state institutions as managers and simple bureaucrats. More often than not, individuals stayed in one bureaucratic path. Their incomes and personal status were dependent not only on the state but on the survival of their part of the state as the major institution in the society.

So, while bureaucrats have been put in the middle by their positions and have been made aware of the failings of the system, they have also developed into a class that was entrepreneurial in its behavior but devoted to having a strong state sector. After all, the irrationality and bottlenecks they faced forced them to work through problems and think of solutions that "worked the system" even when the system did not work. Whether or not they were Marxist in their ideology, their positions were sinecures dependent on the state sector's remaining dominant. At the end of Communist rule, some used their positions and their ad hoc training to become "*nomenklatura* entrepreneurs" who began private enterprises. Others have remained in their posts throughout the transition. For these people, the system's failures were and remain very clear. The possibility that the new reforms will leave them unemployed and without ways to use their skills, however, is a greater threat to them than the old system's failures were.

Ethnic Legacies

Historically, Eastern Europe was always characterized by its ethnic mix, divisions, and conflicts. Two of the eight states (Czechoslovakia and Yugoslavia) in the old Eastern Europe were made up of very separate nationalities patched together, by outside forces, into states. Two of the eight (Romania and Bulgaria) were made up of one majority nationality and one large minority nationality, in addition to some smaller ones. Even the other states (Poland, Hungary, Albania, and East Germany), were not free of the legacy of ethnic divisiveness (see table 5).

All of the nation-states in Eastern Europe are further troubled by having part of their ethnic base living just across the border in another Communist nation. Finally, in all of these nations but Albania, old ethnic conflicts over the role of Jews and Gypsies have been left as festering sores in the national political life.

This complex of ethnic divisions anywhere would spell trouble. For these post-Communist states, this complex of potential and real conflicts is even more of a major issue. It was, after all, an issue that, for reasons of ideology and power, was papered over and not dealt with in the Communist period. Karl Marx, the ideological father of the Communist states, had declared that ethnic and national conflicts were merely tools of the capitalist class to divide and control workers. Without that class interest, he said, nationalism would fade away. In the early years, this made communism a particularly appealing ideology for members of ethnic groups who were marginalized where they lived. For the majority who felt disenfranchised by Communist rule, this fact was easily translated into the perception that communism was something dominated by Jews or members of other minorities. Beyond this, Soviet leaders enhanced their control when East Europeans did not and could not form, even in one nation, a united front. The result was that, although the regime censors barred nationalism and national histories from public discussion, little was done to rationalize borders of, or the position of nationalities within, individual countries.

Denying the problems, though, did not dissolve them: it made them more unresolvable. Old legacies of past conflicts were worsened by new issues growing out of Communist rule. During the process of taking over and industrializing these societies in the 1940s and 1950s, the decisions that were made about who would rule and where industry would be built worsened the differential between national groups. So the old splits of culture, religion, history, and language were exacerbated by economic and power inequities between groups.

The end of Communist rule took the lid off these problems. People were desperate to get "their equal share" and were all the more sure that the members of other groups had denied it to them. The freed media, in their competition for readers and for shocking new stories, played on these nationalist interests. For this reason, the conflicts in Yugoslavia and elsewhere overrode the ties of friendship between individuals which had formed during years of working against the Communists. The cleavages are so well etched that separation has been for many groups the only way to protect their interests.

Europeanization

From 1948 until the mid-1970s, the goal of most East European rulers was to get their people to look eastward to the Soviet Union rather than toward the democratic states of Western Europe and the United States. The rulers were no more successful at this than they were at making ethnic differences go away by refusing to acknowledge them. In effect, people wanted and admired the forbidden fruits of the West more than they might have if they had had normal contact with it.

Three factors in East European societies made the policy of turning eastward virtually impossible from the beginning. Much of the political, economic, and cultural history of Eastern Europe was not tied with Russia, and the history that did involve Russia was far from positive. Furthermore, the poverty and repression in most of Eastern Europe in the nineteenth and early twentieth centuries triggered waves of emigration to a better life in Western Europe and the United States. Whether or not these émigrés kept their ties with their families, their departure to better lives created an overriding social myth of the superiority of the West. Finally, the demonization of the West in Communist propaganda, and the options that the West offered in the Communist period through free radio stations, promises of political liberation, the import of better-quality Western goods and technology, and even charity shipments, reinforced this historical notion. Western society seemed all the more attractive in light of the failed promises of the systems that the Soviet Union imposed.

Since the East European nations had been under foreign domination for most of their histories, their histories were decidedly tied with the empires that had ruled them. Only a small sector of what became the Soviet bloc had been under Russian domination (it was the eastern part of Poland), and that experience had been mostly negative. Other regions had been tied to the Prussian, Austro-Hungarian, or Ottoman empires. Of these, the Austro-Hungarian Empire was the one that had left the most positive legacy. The Prussians had not been benevolent rulers, but they did instill German cultural traditions and a sense of superiority to the East which could not be easily replaced by Russian traditions or claims of superiority. The Ottoman Empire had also been repressive before it crumbled in the face of Western pressure, leaving behind the memories of Western liberation.

Historical memories of Russian and Soviet foreign policy did little to encourage a turn to the east. After the Russian Revolution, for instance, the Red Army tried to impose a revolution in Poland, Romania, and Hungary. These attempts were defeated, and left a sour taste. When the West was involved in Eastern Europe, however, it was in much more positive events. Communist-era history tried to erase both sides of this history, and in so doing made it seem all the more exciting. So the history was preserved and glorified by family retelling and by proscribed literature.

The large-scale emigration from East European countries to England, France, Germany, Canada, and the United States in the nineteenth and twentieth centuries, coupled with the treatment of the West as "forbidden fruit," never gave East Europeans a clear view of the West. Instead, the pieces of information and the material goods that East Europeans got from their contacts with those who had built a life in the West, as well as the time that individuals spent in the West as visitors, guest workers, and cultural exchangees led them to equate democracy with the wealthy capitalism of these societies. Successful émigrés became national heroes. Emigrés, particularly those who had escaped from communism, supported dissident movements, or at least, provided the material for an alternate economy with the presents and money they sent to their families and friends. For those who lived in Eastern Europe, reading between the lines of censored media while coping with the daily problems created by their countries' failed economies only made the West seem more glorious.

As a result, with the end of communism East Europeans initially thought that they were ready to abandon much for a full-scale shift to Western ways. Many of their peers in the third world and even in Southern Europe had developed a healthy distrust of "Western cultural imperialism" and "intervention" from their experience with the West. Few East Europeans had any of this. Their distrust focused on the Soviet Union and the other Soviet bloc states.

Three years after the end of Communist domination, the West is losing some of its aura as its perceived promises ring hollow. The revelations of Soviet crimes against untold numbers of innocent people have allowed the West to maintain more of that aura than it might have done if East Europeans judged the West only from their post-Communist contacts with it and its promises of aid to make the transition easy.

The Communist Legacy of Values

If East European states differ in their demography and history from the other states that have moved from authoritarian systems to democratic ones, the values of their populations are also different. True, these are not values that Marx would recognize as his own, but they are the values that people have taken away from more than forty years of living in Communist societies. Within Eastern Europe, different groups had different enough experiences that their expression of these values is not homogeneous, but these basic values have given political life all over Eastern Europe its particular character.

Seeing the World in Terms of "Them" versus "Us"

The critical distinction that communism taught people was the distinction between "them" and "us." It is a distinction that is played out on all levels.

On the most personal level, the use of the secret police in Eastern Europe created a situation in which individuals' initial reaction to each other was distrust. Only when individuals proved their trustworthiness by their actions did the distrust abate. As a result, ties of friendship and professional groupings played an inordinate role in determining social circles and even political groupings during the Communist era. If the shortage of housing, and the Communist policy of building standard housing units that housed people of all classes (except for the elite), might have tended to bring members of the various classes together in neighborhoods and communities, this learned distrust of others succeeded in splitting them up.

On a national level, the split between "them" and "us" took on far greater significance. The political elite was perceived as imposed by the outside. The relative secretiveness and insularity of the leaders' lives, and the revelations of their privileged positions, set them apart from the population. From the perspective of those at the bottom of the hierarchy, it seemed that the power wielded by "them" (e.g., the power to issue decrees and to act) made it impossible for "us" to be responsible or to act. This perception was magnified by the sense that "they" were not just an untouchable elite but a system imposed from the outside, by the Soviet Union. This perception also allowed East Europeans to avoid taking responsibility for their society and its problems by using "them" as a scapegoat.

Ironically, the split between "them" and "us" was powerful enough to bring Poles of all classes together under Solidarity for fifteen months. Once the Communist regimes looked weak there as elsewhere, and it was clear that the Soviet Union no longer was in control, the split was enough to band people together all over Eastern Europe against Communist rule. It has not been enough to keep them together once the "enemy," Communist rule, was gone.

After the end of Communist rule, a deeper level of social divisions surfaced. Individuals now distrust those who seem to gain more from the system. Workers distrust managers.[5] Ethnic groups distrust each other. The old religious opposition distrusts the secular opposition. Dissidents who fought communism and suffered for their dissent distrust those who did nothing to support them and now have benefited from their work. Adding to this has been the popular distrust of the secret police and its agents. This has been even more divisive since decommunization policies revealed how many people were involved in internal intelligence.

This perception of a world made of networks of "them" and "us" has been a paralyzing one in post-Communist societies. It has been difficult to form interest groups or even parties that are permanent. The gain of any one group makes them an enemy, a separate group. Thus, in the frequent elections since 1989, voters have tended to oppose whatever group is in power.

Governance in Eastern Europe has been marked by a never-ending shift from one victorious coalition or party to another. With this has come a personalization of politics: past splits and personal conflicts, rather than policy options, have become the stuff of politics. This is evidenced by the fact that parties do not have distinct platforms, they have distinct leaders who campaign against "them." The heroes of the revolution against the Communists lost their heroic stature once they became rulers. They became a new "them."

Cynicism

Accompanying this "them-versus-us" dichotomy has been a learned cynicism about politics. For all the claims that East European states were workers' states in which the working class built their countries, the citizenry learned early on that its voice mattered little. Voting was something to be done because it was required, not something done to affect politics. In Poland, where popular upheavals in 1956, 1970, and 1980 brought down Communist governments and resulted in promises of improvements, and in Hungary in 1956 and Czechoslovakia in 1968, where there were moments of relative freedom, the lesson was equally stark. Even if these popular movements were not brutally suppressed, months after promises of change were made it was again politics as usual.

In addition to all of this, for those who lived through the Stalinist period, allowing oneself to be a "true believer" rather than being cynical seems dangerous at best. East European Communists of that generation initially believed that they were building a better, new, industrialized society. Then many were drawn into condemning others, at least for their inaction. Finally, after Stalin's death, most saw the entire system attack itself. For those who experienced Stalinism and the repressive Communist rule that hit parts of these societies in the next decades, the message is equally clear. They have read and heard revelations about the horrors of Communist rule. The fact that so much could be hidden for so long implies that politics is not what it seems. The lesson of this and their symbolic participation under the Communists only serve to reinforce the notion that politics is a dirty business.

With this cynicism came a disrespect for the law. Fear bred obedience, not support or respect. Survival as a successful factory manager, a citizen with a well-stocked larder, or someone who had to make things happen required working around and bending the law. For the Communist rulers, the law was not something that regulated them. International law was seldom a force in their decisions, even when they signed treaties. In the end, the survival of the Communist system itself required compromising the law: in the 1970s and 1980s, an increasingly large number of people were allowed to live outside the laws against corruption, private trading, and even criticism of the system. By the end of the 1980s, the systems themselves broke their own canons when they made their final, desperate attempts to obtain popular support. All of this weakened their hold even as it taught people that leaders and systems, no matter how ideologically strict they claimed to be, could not be trusted to be consistent.

The result of this in Eastern Europe has been complex. Initially, the hope was that new, freely elected parliaments would provide a new, legitimate legal structure. The overwhelming pressure for change in nearly every part of economic, political, and social policy made this an impossible expectation. Attempts to rewrite constitutions and restructure the law have only reduced support for East European parliaments, because the changes have not brought the gains that the populations expected.[6]

Whether a law is new or old, many East Europeans continue to see it as something to circumvent. Crime has skyrocketed. Capitalism has been built by businesses that keep themselves one step ahead of the tax collector. Some new leaders have used their positions to bend the law and further their own interests, as the old Communist leaders did. Battles for power focus around the legalities of political maneuvers and the relationship between parliament and the executive. Leaders make use of vagaries in the law, or rail against it in their political battles.

East Europeans also take less notice of legal changes that go against their interests than do the citizenries of traditional democracies. The most striking case of this is the Polish population's original attitude toward the parliamentary bill to bar abortion. A large number of Poles said that even if a bill were passed subjecting all abortions to criminal penalties, it would make no real difference. They were sure that they would continue to be able to arrange for abortions in Poland.

The overall result of this cynicism is that, since the end of Communist rule, elections have been marked by enough nonparticipation that some elections have had to be rescheduled repeatedly just to get enough voters to make them legal.[7] Attempts at transforming the economic and political system have been complicated by people's refusal to obey the law, which prevents the changes from happening as planned. As a result, tax systems, inflation controls, and privatization programs remain more legal fiction than reality. Finally, support of or opposition to laws has been hard to rally because few think that laws will matter.

Egalitarianism

The value that was most at risk in the transformation from communism to capitalism was egalitarianism. The East European presentation of Marxism put great stress on the development of egalitarian societies out of state socialism. Until the Solidarity period in Poland, the myth was expressed in the official insistence that members of the elite lived no differently than did average members of the society. Few truly believed this, but there was never a clear picture of the extent of the differential.

While there were never societies in which material goods did not matter, the difficulty of getting even basic goods created a general sense that all had equal difficulty. The shortages of high-quality consumer goods had a leveling effect: until communism fell and Western interests entered in full force, the selection of consumer goods was limited enough that people looked much the same.

Where there were differences — when individuals received special honors, trips, or grants, or when they were able to get some hard-to-get good — the looming questions were, where? and why did that individual get something so special? In light of the Communist Party's control over elite jobs, travel, and access to privileges, the suspicion was often that individuals received special things because of secret connections to the Party or the police, or because of other personal ties. As a result, individuals involved in trade and those with special privileges were not generally respected.

At the same time, individuals were not willing to deny themselves opportunities in order to be equal. Survival and self-advancement meant making themselves special, people with skills and talents that the system could use. Until the change from communism, their focus was not on increasing their material wealth but on developing skills and contacts.

With the beginning of the transformation, the supply of material goods grew dramatically; prices went up; and expensive luxury items were available. Formerly blacklisted individuals were suddenly in positions of power, able to travel. Material possessions and ownership took on a new importance. Those who had power or resources were suddenly able to buy. Those who did not had to deal more directly than ever before with the experience of seeing stores that were open but stocked with goods priced so high that they were inaccessible. The new and unavoidable contrast between rich and poor certainly contributed to people's uneasiness about the level of conflict in their societies. It also contributed to a sense that their own economic situations were difficult or were growing worse.

In the end, East Europeans as individuals adapted to materialism easily. However, this resulted in the appearance of societal contradiction. Those who had been heroes for their suffering suddenly were well dressed and visible in their consumption. That was, at best, a shock. In addition to this, material gains did not parallel the hierarchy of social status: academics, physicians, and other professionals high in status suffered losses materially, while traders, whose occupation had the lowest status, gained dramatically.

Politicians as Leaders

Under the Communists, top leaders amassed power for themselves. Lesser members of the elite were "gray men" who were seldom seen and were heard from only when they spoke for the main leader. Because policy seldom was put into effect through parliamentary decrees, and more often was the result of party directives or of statements by leaders, the leader and his personal predilections were seen as the critical force in politics. East Europeans defined policies and eras in their politics according to who had been first secretary of the party: there was the Gierek era, the Kádár era, and the Ceauşescu dynasty.

Because laws were often less significant in setting out policy than were Party statements or internal guidance by top leaders, East Europeans expended a great deal of effort to divine what the leaders were doing and where they were going. They did this while possessing little real evidence about what was happening in the corridors of power. As a result, those "in the know," as well as the rest of the society, made judgments about what was happening by watching how individual leaders behaved and when they appeared. Gossip about individual leaders was not only entertaining; it was also a valuable currency in Eastern Europe, since individual leaders, rather than political or legal structures, were the focus for people's perception of politics.

In the post-Communist era, the top leaders, whether or not their powers have been limited by legal restrictions or international economic bodies, remain the focus of politics. The media focus on their activities, their statements, and their arguments as the stuff of politics. Individual politicians play on this interest and stress themselves rather than their policies. Given how quickly leaders have moved in and out of politics, the shift of leadership has created a sense of the instability of politics rather than a sense of the growth of new systems.

"Ignorance Is Bliss"

In an ironic way, East Europeans have moved from demanding freedom of the press to feeling a real discomfort with the free press. As the East European media have played on their desire for pornography, investigative reporting about society's problems, and real information about politicians, the media have become a battleground.

Virtually all of the new East European leaders have struggled against the press's freedom to attack them and their policies. Parties fight to own their own newspapers and to bar the broadcast media from covering them negatively. In doing this, they reflect the old traditions (both those of the Communist press and those of the underground press) to which they have grown accustomed. In both types of publication, there was a sense that leaders were sacrosanct, and also that they could not meet popular demands. The new leaders fear that any negative information in the press will reduce their already weak standing.[8]

The populations that initially wanted a free press are less than comfortable with what it shows. Revelations about what is wrong in society are interpreted far more negatively than similar reports would be in the West, because this negativism is a new phenomenon in Eastern Europe. People were accustomed to a positive picture of their societies. Revelations in the press have not brought support for democracy; they have instead contributed to the discomfort that people feel with their political system. Religious institutions and the right have pushed to "clean up" the media. Political parties and their leaders have railed against the state-owned broadcast media for misrepresenting them, and have insisted on actually owning their own newspapers rather than allowing commercial presses to handle their news. The press, far from being liberated and seen as a proof of the freedom of the new Eastern Europe, has been the target of battles for control, and proof to many that things are dangerously out of control.[9]

Key Groups in the New Societies

East European politics has been torn by the unresolved divisions of class, nationalism, and history. These divisions have been reinforced and even exacerbated by the new divisions that have emerged in the behavior of both the ruling elite and the population at large. Although the longstanding divisions are based on the different experiences of groups during the Communist era, they are now more unresolvable because of the hard times that have come with the transition from communism to capitalism and democracy. Gains by one leadership group are seen as losses for other groups.[10]

Former Opposition Leaders

In all but the most repressive states in Communist Eastern Europe (Bulgaria, Romania, and Albania), the group that emerged to lead the first stages of the transition out of communism consisted of opposition intellectuals who had either been dissidents or belonged to the silent opposition in the 1970s and 1980s. In the other states, many of these men and women were imprisoned, barred from the system, or at least marginalized for their independence and their criticism of the Communist system. Most survived repression by the regime thanks to the community they formed with other dissidents. Few felt much support from the population at large. Even fewer had any experience in management or government.

Their goal, as the Workers' Defense Committee (KOR) in Poland and the Charter 77 group in Czechoslovakia put it, was to keep information coming to the population so that it could live more civilly and be ready for the distant time when communism would begin to crumble.[11] Their focus was never on what should happen then. Rather, it was on what was wrong under communism. Even at what would prove to be the end of

Communist rule, virtually no one even claimed to have a program for handling the end of communism.[12]

Former dissident leaders came to power as a result of their ability to oppose the system. Their experience as managers came largely from their management of small underground press operations. Their experience of governing came, at best, from their having organized life in their tiny communities, and from their discussions of how to act in the underground and of what was wrong with the Communist system. These experiences put more emphasis on working around the system and on interpersonal relations, ideas, and talking than ruling ever would.

The former dissident leaders saw themselves as people who had sacrificed much in opposing communism. The limited support they had received from the "masses" convinced them that the masses needed to be led, to have their ideas formed, and to be shown how to live more ethically. These "anti-Communist democrats" were basically intellectuals, not men and women of the people, or individuals who had developed close ties with the populations. After all, when blacklisting dissidents and sanctioning them for their opposition, even the more liberal systems of Poland and Hungary not only kept their names out of the mass media but also often punished those who came in contact with them — or at least, open contact was made risky. Furthermore, dissidents' position made them see the world "in black and white" and focus their self-definition on being ideologically uncompromising. It was never their role to do the essential work of democratic politics: to mobilize the population, or to engage in compromise.

The "revolutions" in Eastern Europe occurred so quickly that there was no time to really form bonds between the populations and the leaders.[13] This was true even in Poland, where bonds between the intellectuals and the workers had begun to develop in the Solidarity period. These were largely broken down during martial law. Although the Solidarity leader and worker Lech Wałęsa was given the final say in all agreements,[14] the Roundtable negotiations that began and set the initial parameters for the transformation in Poland and elsewhere in Eastern Europe were dominated by the intellectual dissidents. So, rather than gaining legitimacy as the leaders of a historic battle against the "evil" of communism which had mobilized the masses, former opposition leaders took over because there was a leadership void. They were the only visible individuals not tainted by the system.

Lacking the potential to build charisma and legitimacy on the basis of their leadership of a successful revolution, these elites turned to elections. But holding competitive elections had a very different impact than leading a revolution would have had. Elections pushed former opposition members to run against each other and to define themselves in contrast to others. After the first elections, which focused on a theme of "us" against "them" (the Communists), the campaigns split the dissident community with negative and personal campaigning that reduced the dissident's status for the rest of the population.

The result of the power of dissidents and the use of elections as a vehicle for achieving legitimacy has been a virtual "anti-politics." The once relatively coherent opposition community has split into warring factions in every country in Eastern Europe. Politics has been marked not by compromise and coalition building but by increasingly sharp and radicalized ideological statements.

Day-to-day issues of economics and social policy which are of real concern to the population have been ignored as often as they have been dealt with in the politics of ideology. In effect, the public has not been the first priority of these once-dissident policy makers. And the heroes of the opposition, even when they have a long history of leadership, have dropped dramatically in their public approval ratings.

Professionals

In the Communist era, professionals and their organizations were treasured by the Communist authorities. The need that the regime felt for their expertise as scholars, journalists, scientists, and engineers served less to tie them to the regime than to give them some room for maneuver. It did not necessarily ensure that they got high base salaries, however. Because of this, many kept close ties with all of their colleagues so that they could involve themselves in a variety of institutions and projects to bring in extra money and keep up in their fields. More than any other group except the manual workers who went to the West as guest workers, they were able to travel and to bring back ideas and methods from the West. On the whole, though, this meant that they had less incentive to openly oppose the system than did intellectuals who had no technical skills the regime wanted to use. It did not prevent them from trying to keep some autonomy in their own work.

With the fall of communism, professionals saw the opportunities offered by the change less as a chance to institute democracy and more as an opportunity to right wrongs and put their professional affairs in order. The political world, though, was one they could only enter as generalists and popular local authorities. Moreover, what some found was that their standards of living and their power as professionals actually dropped precipitously.

The change to capitalism and to democracy was more uncertain for professionals in Eastern Europe than for former opposition leaders or for workers. Except for a few professionals in Poland and Hungary who had been able to set up private practices as physicians or lawyers, these professionals were very much a part of the state-owned system. They were employed by the state. And privatization in the public service sector was the last issue on the agenda of economic transformation. When privatization was possible, it worked to divide their communities as they fought over policy options and over jobs.

For some, such as journalists and physicians, the change offered the chance to expand the free-lance work they had done before, without worrying about the government's response. For others, such as academics in many fields, the change initially meant a dramatic expansion in Western support and travel opportunities. Professionals in all of these areas found themselves increasingly caught up in commercializing their work. Some were instant gainers. But most did not have the skills and resources required for independent commercialization. They were trapped in the old state structures or, in the case of journalists, in institutions that were still controlled by nonprofessionals. Their only other option was to take jobs as private traders or to set up other businesses. But these were careers that had traditionally had low status: to do this meant giving up their treasured positions as professionals.

Economists with experience in the West, and individuals in other professions who had criticized the Communist system as professionals, were sought after. They were the first to be taken into the new governments as policy makers. In this early stage, as the case of the former Polish minister of finance Leszek Balcerowicz illustrates, they functioned as professionals and not politicians. Their interest was in developing the professionally correct policy and not in what would be popular. Foreign advisers were more important to them than public opinion specialists. Decisions were made quickly so that information leaks would not interfere with the implementation.[15]

The last professional group to be drawn into the changes was the lawyers. After all, theirs had traditionally been a Party profession, although a few lawyers had risked defending dissidents. As a result, the legal profession was seen as defiled before its members were co-opted into the new system. After initially retreating, lawyers, particularly those who were young, found themselves drawn into the political process. They had much-needed expertise in writing laws. Ultimately, members of the legal profession came into political leadership as a second generation after opposition leaders had been rejected by voters. These men and women presented themselves as professionals who would make policy decisions on rational and legal grounds rather than political ones.

Members of the Former Establishment

The end of Communist rule in Eastern Europe did not do away with the Communist establishment; it merely dislodged the top Communist officials. In Romania and Bulgaria, where a dissident elite had been prevented from forming, establishment members who had fallen from favor with the old Communist powers or had dared to criticize them were the only candidates to represent an opposition to communism in the first elections. In Hungary, the Communist establishment fragmented before the transformation began so that some of its leaders could run as "alternatives" to communism in the first elections. In Poland, the Communist Party dissolved, and its younger generation started a new, Euro-Communist-style party, while in the Czech Republic the Communist Party resisted change and, as a result, has been relegated to the fringes of Czech politics. For all of the new, formerly Communist leaders, the two hopes for election have been their abilities to draw people with reminders of the social services and security that have been lost, and their use of nationalist slogans. In this, post-Communist leaders and parties became decidedly less Marxist than populist and nationalist.

The new systems could not replace these men and women of the bureaucracies who had achieved success by working in the system. In Poland and Hungary, a small but significant group of these officials — middle-level and even upper-level Party and state bureaucrats and managers — hedged their bets before the system fell. They used their connections and access to resources to open businesses and privatize parts of state enterprises. Others did not become "nomenklatura entrepreneurs" but remained in their jobs in the state bureaucracy, assuming that the state would remain and even that, without the Party, their services would be needed and their jobs would become more rational and less politicized.

These individuals were both targets of and anchors for the system. As the new leaders sought to explain why the "transformation" had failed to meet popular expectations, they vilified the old establishment. Yet, given how low the salaries of state employees were by comparison to salaries in the private sector, there was no pool of alternative bureaucrats and managers. As a result, the old Communist-approved bureaucracy remained more stable than the top leadership.

They were faced with virtually continual calls for "decommunization" from parliamentary deputies and the media. They also found themselves dealing with ministers and deputy ministers who had little or no experience in the state sector and little or no trust in the bureaucrats they were supposed to lead. For many, keeping their jobs was the only option they had: few of those who remained in the state bureaucracy had the resources or skills to succeed in private enterprise. Their overall response was to minimize their risks to an even greater extent than they had in the Communist period: rather than question policy, provide information for the ministers and other top ministry executives, or work on small changes in their own tiny fields, they simply go to work, do what is assigned, and leave.

These mid- and lower-level bureaucrats have constituted a swing group in post-Communist society. They were the first contact point many people had with the "transformation." Since the faces were the same, many walked away less sure of the transformation than they had been before. The bureaucrats were also the administrators and interpreters of policy. So, to the extent that they take the safest path, they tend to be conservative forces in the transformation. Finally, they are a ready, if not guaranteed, pool of voters for post-Communist parties. The harder the right and others pushed for decommunization regulations barring them from public service careers or investigating their pasts, the more supportive these individuals were of the "post-Communist" Communist parties, which had themselves gone far from the ideology of Marxism.

Voters

Except in the cases of Bulgaria and Hungary, the turnovers of power in Eastern Europe were forced by mass demonstrations. Only after the mass demonstrations in the streets of Dresden and the squares of Prague and

Bucharest, and the factory strikes in Poland, did leaders from both sides feel compelled to bargain together. After these demonstrations and the initial elections, though, mass power in politics essentially ended.

Those in the elite tended to see the voters as an undifferentiated group. But the masses that should have been the targets of political campaigns were even more differentiated than the electorate in Western societies. Their response to the "carousel at the top" tended to be the same both cross-nationally and within any given country: they gave up on politics and focused on protecting their day-to-day interests. What they needed from the system varied greatly depending on their age, their employment, and their resource base. As a result, although the masses were the ones most vulnerable in these times of economic failure, the crucial "missing pieces" in East European politics were the working-class parties, or mass parties, and powerful trade unions. So, for instance, while young workers may have wished to have a social safety net that would preserve their jobs in a shrinking job market, older workers and pensioners were concerned primarily with preserving and improving the benefits they had been promised for decades would be theirs at the end of their careers.

For blue-collar workers, there were no policies for economic reform that had favorable results for all. The workers who had done best in Communist societies were those who were in heavy industry. These were now the workers whose jobs were least convertible and most at risk. Not only were their products no longer needed but their factories and mines were so outdated that few wanted to buy them. Workers in smaller-scale industries producing consumer goods faced the prospect of either wage cuts in jobs that had always been the lowest-paying jobs in Communist societies, or unemployment when the factories that employed them were bankrupted because of the loss of the open markets of the rest of Eastern Europe and the Soviet Union, and the inability to compete in new markets. These workers, however, were in industries that were of interest to buyers from the West or even from within their own societies. Thus they had some clear potential to adapt, even if adaptation meant survival and not real gains.

The lessons that blue-collar workers learned during the Communist era neither fit with the new realities nor offered the frightening potential of worker-based instability for their societies. Workers in Poland had learned that strikes brought concessions from the Communists. When they had non-Communist governments pressed by Western financial interests, the strike was not as effective a weapon. Governments simply ignored them or forced major concessions. Elsewhere, workers had learned not that strikes were effective but that they could earn salaries without really working hard. The shift to production-based earnings required real sacrifices for them because it forced them to work harder at their jobs for less earning power, and it meant that they no longer had the free time to take on second and third jobs to supplement their incomes. It also has increased the stakes for strikes. The only lesson that has been retained is that workers are powerless to change their real position.

Only in Poland was the peasant class positioned to gain from the transformation. Yet this class of private farmers (more than 95% of Polish farmers were engaged in private farming during the Communist period) lost to foreign imports. Elsewhere in Eastern Europe, peasants were accustomed to state and collective farming. Economic transformation and the return of property to former landowners poses little but uncomfortable risks for them.

Certain groups whose special needs were provided for under communism — for example, pensioners and women, who got long maternity leaves — had come to expect those benefits. However, they had never been in a position to organize in Communist societies, and thus they did not have even skeletal organizations from which to push their demands. The result is that, in general, although women's organizations did develop in response to pressures against abortion, these groups became more marginalized than before. To the extent that it was possible, economic conditions have brought them back into the marketplace as individuals. Their struggles to use the marketplace, though, only alienated them further from the system.

The Sociology of a New East European System

East Europeans' attempts to emerge from communism and to forge democratic systems are dramatically affected by the social baggage they possess. They have to deconstruct industry, social groups, and social values before they can follow the paths of earlier, Western democracies. If this is not possible, they must live with new forms of democracy and even capitalism based not on the structures of traditional democracies but on the legacies of communism.

This transformation process was made all the more difficult because, however fast the shift to capitalism, the interlocking net of the Communist-era system forced economic change to go along with political change. The options for the development of East European democracy, then, reflect less the ways in which and the speed with which changes were made than the impact of these changes on their social base.

A "populist democracy" is one of the forms of government that may result from factors including the Communist experience, the transformation process, and the imposition of democratic institutions. Such a democracy is one that continues to avoid solutions and seeks to assign blame for the problems of the system. In this scenario, politicians would promise a generically better life and then would focus on attacking "legacies" or groups that kept improvements from being made. The worst-case model of this is Nazi Germany. The critical difference is that East Europeans have learned not to believe and not to get involved in politics. They want the systems that they think brought wealth to the West, but at the same time they do not want to be specifically involved in those systems as individuals. Thus the likelihood is that leaders will talk as populists and nationalists and even make structural changes. This was what the Slovak Communist-turned-populist leaders did in forcing the separation of Czechoslovakia.

The population, however, is likely neither to support nor to oppose these changes and calls for populism in any real way. Instead, individuals are likely to go on about their struggles to survive, and withdraw further and further from politics.

Another short-run option is a continuation of the current paralysis that characterizes most of East European politics. Since no government can meet its population's expectations regarding what democracy was to bring, periodic elections would be made more frequent by continual fragmentation within already divided parliaments. The result would be continual changes in government. Parties would form but would not have the time to develop roots from which they could mobilize stable cadres of voters. And policies would continue to be made on the basis of interpretations of the requirements for Western aid, and the apparent imperatives of surviving daily events.

The third and final alternative is the development of a new kind of authoritarian system in Eastern Europe. The legacy of communism serves as an obstacle to this scenario. Communism created societies that it could rule but that would not easily be mobilized by authoritarianism again. At the least, the people do not believe in politicians and their promises enough to be led.

None of these scenarios involves the emergence of the participatory democracies envisioned in Western democratic theory. Nor do these scenarios bode well for the development of adequately functioning pluralism in the near future.

They are not, however, necessarily hopeless scenarios for the future of Eastern Europe. Given the inability of East European economies to right themselves and improve rapidly, the apathy and values that were learned under communism and the social divisions that communism created may work to give the new polities a chance at remaining stable until popular expectations and reality are more congruent. The lack of real party platforms also means that no explicit promises are made, and no permanent constituencies are turned against each other. This gives these systems more time. It also allows them flexibility: coalitions can be experimented with, formed, and dissolved without disrupting the system further.

Clearly, ethnic bloodshed and fragmentation are still real possibilities. The disaster of the civil war in the former Yugoslavia is an indelible lesson. Positive inducements for the East European states to remain intact and to cooperate with each other also exist. In a competitive world economy, East Europeans can trade most easily with each other. Ultimately, given their Communist-era legacies of values and expectations, they can also talk with and understand each other more easily. As a result, it is possible that these societies will split apart and then find ways of cooperating, as the former states of Czechoslovakia are now doing.

What, then, is the social legacy of communism in the long term? Clearly, democracy will take time to build. Democracy built on others' values and rules will not work any more efficiently than communism did in Eastern Europe. But the admiration that East Europeans have had for the results of democracy and capitalism in the West, as well as their disillusionment with their other option, communism, make it likely that democracy will remain the general model. Communism may have taught strong but unintended lessons, but they are lessons nonetheless. In all, they are lessons that may remove the population from political action for long enough to allow new traditions to be learned and social divisions to be knitted together so that new bases can be found to redefine the societies and their systems.

A Final Question

Looking at Eastern Europe is a matter of looking at its special character. The social base, the values base, and the learned behaviors that came out of the Communist experience are indeed unique. The response of East Europeans to the stresses of "instant democracy building" is not what many expected. From this perspective, the very process of building democracy in Eastern Europe is a troubled one.

However, the population's resignation, its retreat into a preoccupation with survival, and the division between the leaders and the led are not unique to post-Communist societies. Western theories of democracy were written with an eye toward glorifying the democratic process in the United States and Western Europe. It assumed the best about those societies. If East Europeans can willingly copy our institutions, and then find themselves far from achieving a democratic process, without falling apart, this may also raise troubling questions for scholars and analysts: Are our old theories and analyses of democracy flawed? Is Eastern Europe proving that there are many roads and many foundations for democratic processes that are, at best, always faulty?

The Environmental Legacies of Communism

Barbara Jancar-Webster

In this chapter I examine the hypothesis that the environmental problems in Eastern Europe and the former Soviet Union may best be understood as the product of the fusion of the nineteenth-century Western industrial paradigm with Communist dogma. I address the hypothesis along three dimensions: the physical legacy, the economic-technological legacy, and the cultural-social legacy.

Physical Legacies

For reasons of space, I will not cite chapter and verse regarding the ecological disaster left by the decades of Communist rule in Eastern Europe and the former Soviet Union. Environmental degradation is the most serious physical legacy of the one-party regimes, and a legacy that will be handed down to the next generation and to the generation following. A veritable torrent of information on the scope and size of the catastrophe has been pouring from all the former Communist countries since the late 1980s. If today the torrent seems to have abated, we can only rejoice that no new news is good news, since every new piece of information seems to be worse than that which went before. I was a witness of the devastation caused by the giant smelters in the Kola Peninsula, and the tragedy of erosion in Tadzhikistan. The Aral Sea and Chernobyl are now household words in the West, as is *Waldsterben;* and the moonscape caused by coal mining in West Bohemia is well known. The list of environmental damage sounds like a litany: chemical pollution in Slovakia and Bulgaria; and water pollution in Poland, the Czech Lands, and Hungary — in the Danube, the Oder, the Vistula, and the Volga.[1] On top of damage caused by industrial production is the damage caused by the Soviet military in its long occupation of Eastern Europe; and that damage became much worse as a result of the pillage of bases by the departing troops and the on-site abandonment of everything that was not wanted at home.

So pervasive and visible was the damage to the environment perpetrated by the former regimes that it became the symbol for the arbitrariness that characterized life under communism, incited millions of people to challenge their governments, and effectively brought those governments down.

Environmental Implications of the Economic Legacies

With its centralized planning, extensive industrialization, and promotion of smokestack industries, Stalinism exemplified the values of what have been called the first and second industrial revolutions, which transformed Europe and the United States in the nineteenth century.[2]

In promoting the ideas of central planning, the dictatorship of the proletariat, and first-generation industrialization, Stalin was in fact writing in stone the system of technological monoculture that has characterized the development of technology in the Western capitalist countries. The paradox of technology is that its benefits often increase in proportion to its scale of application, whereas the environmental and social disjunctures resulting from the application of technology increase nonlinearly as the scale of application increases. Brooks has argued that as technology matures it tends to become more homogeneous, and less innovative and adaptive.[3] Success freezes the corporate enterprise into a mold dictated by the fear that departure from a successful formula might jeopardize the aggregate capital investment, the marketing structure, and the supporting bureaucracies. In the early stages of a technology, there are many options and choices. Competition dominates the market. Gradually one technological variation begins to win, as economies of scale, marketing, and production give it a competitive edge. The new technology and supporting systems now constitute an increasingly self-contained social system, unable to adapt to the changes necessitated by its success. "Thus, the technological activity may become strongly established with influential vested interests during the linear regime, before the disbenefits that increase non-linearly with scale, become apparent to the wider public."[4]

The results of Stalin's imposition of immediate technological monoculture are well known and require little elaboration. In the best tsarist autocratic style, Stalin attempted to force an economy ruined by world war and civil war into the middle of the twentieth century. In Czechoslovakia, Stalinism meant deindustrialization. An advanced technological program was forcibly replaced by first-generation industrial production.

In Poland and Hungary, a centrally planned economy and a monopolistic political system were employed to increase the industrial tempo and collapse the time between the first and second industrial revolutions. In Romania and Bulgaria, Stalinism effectively launched industrialization. The decision in favor of economic autarky in the fifties meant that each country had to produce its own iron, steel, and aluminum. The key to Romanian growth was Romania's refusal to follow a Council for Mutual Economic Assistance (CMEA) plan for agricultural development, and its channeling of investment into metallurgy, machine building, and energy and petrochemical production.[5]

Eastern Europe as a whole is not yet at the threshold of the third industrial revolution, the era of the microchip, biotechnology, and the information revolution. While the northern tier may be on the verge, the southern tier is just moving to the end of the second phase. However, the third phase is not yet stabilized anywhere in the world in permanent institutional form. At this stage of industrial development, the introduction of the technology that drives the third phase can only be achieved by innovation and competition. The quest for market control has driven the U.S.-Japanese relationship as it has molded the inner dynamics of Europe 1992, the North American Free Trade Agreement, and the Uruguay round. Brezhnev tried to jump-start the third phase with his Scientific-Technological Revolution. The attempt did not work. The technological monoculture inherited from the Stalinist system proved incapable of providing the necessary climate for innovation, and the system collapsed. Eastern Europe and the Commonwealth of Independent States (CIS) are now in what can euphemistically be called a phase of economic and political adaptation to social surprise.

The system also collapsed under the weight of environmental surprise. In the Communist system, information about the environment was considered a matter of national security and was kept secret, while the peoples of the East and the West were subjected to well-orchestrated propaganda claiming that the profit motive alone produced environmental degradation. During the 1970s, the nonlinear relation between pollution and technological development became increasingly visible. But while data were appearing in the scientific literature, the information had only restricted dissemination, and the public heard little about it. Widespread dissemination of environmental information started in Poland with the advent of Solidarity. The disaster at Chernobyl in 1986 increased public anxiety about and awareness of environmental problems, but the full force of information in Czechoslovakia, Bulgaria, East Germany, and Romania did not reach the general population until 1989. What East Europeans learned was that the damage done to the environment by technological monoculture under Communist systems was even worse in their countries than in the West. It took only thirty years for the discontinuity between technological application and environmental response to manifest itself, mainly because few effective steps were taken to control the negative effects of industrialization on the environment.

In effect, the social and environmental disadvantages accruing to the successful application of a technology in a free society were both intensified and hastened by a prior decision to freeze the whole system into a mold informed not by market success but by ideological principles. Because the economic system provided the security and control function that maintained the ruling group in power, the Communist leaders found themselves in a situation where they could not innovate within the system without bringing the whole system down. Economic restructuring was necessary for competitiveness on the world market and improvement of living standards at home, but regime stability demanded the maintenance of monopoly. By forced reduction in institutional variability and insistence on social and economic homogeneity, the Communist system interrupted any possibility of growth. Administrative paralysis set in, multiplying the negative impact of ecosystem surprise. The result: nowhere in the world is ecological degradation as proximate a reality as in the former Communist countries.

Environmental Implications of the
Social and Cultural Legacies

The transition to a new society has given rise to another phenomenon entrenched in the industrial paradigm: consumerism. The end of the twentieth century has seen all the peoples of the world reorient their expectations toward the achievement of Western standards. One of Eastern Europe's greatest dreams is to be reintegrated into the common European culture. Russia, Ukraine, the Baltic republics, Belarus, and Armenia share this dream. Reintegration means adopting the affluent life-style that the Communist regimes labeled decadent. More money equals more cars, more appliances, more convenient energy, more consumption. To argue with Milbraith that one does not need all these things, or that consumption is among the root causes of the destruction of the Western environment, is nonproductive, out of keeping with the zeitgeist.[6]

The legacies mentioned so far represent a fusion, a mixing, of the values inherent in the industrial paradigm and Marxist-Leninist dogma. In the transmittal of these legacies, communism was not an innocent or passive partner. Communist rule arguably intensified the physical legacy of technological monoculture and hastened the onset of social and environmental surprise. Chronic scarcity, official condemnation of the Western life-style, and a feeling of being isolated from the real world nourished and fed the popular dream of a world paved with gold and awash in comfort on the other side of the Iron Curtain. But it would be a gross error to assume that the Communist period left no legacies of its own making. These legacies, I submit, have more to do with practice than with values, and indeed provide instances in which practice in fact became value.

The first and most enduring sociocultural legacy is the continuation in power of the Communist bureaucracies. Under the Communist regime, the economy, as an extension of the state, shared in the political patronage game: the loyal were promoted, the politically unreliable were fired, and the emergence of enterprises or organizations that could acquire sufficient independent economic means to challenge the ruling hierarchy was not permitted. Virtually every individual in a position of administrative or managerial authority in Eastern Europe and the CIS today was at one time a member of a Communist party and/or a client of a powerful patron in the ruling group. This statement applies even to the leaders of some of the most prestigious grassroots environmental organizations, such as the Socioecological Union, the leader of which had the ear of none other than Mikhail Gorbachev himself. Although the nomenklatura system has formally been abolished, most of its former members still occupy important positions. Oligarchy and patron-client networks may have been broken up to some extent, but they are still functioning. What Elemér Hankiss forecast in 1989 has come to pass:[7] the former Communist vanguard has been transformed into a new *grande bourgeoisie*, as Party and state bureaucrats exchange their positions in the old bureaucratic hierarchy for positions in the managerial and entrepreneurial spheres. Bureaucratic power has become convertible, and is being converted, into economic assets that, in addition to providing more income, will ensure that power and status are transmitted to the next generation. Perhaps nowhere is this process proceeding faster than in Russia, as regionalization advances, central power diminishes, and privatization by the nomenklatura takes on a momentum of its own. The closest analogy to the transformed status of the old Communist bureaucratic class is the status of the French administrative elite. The renewal of the system thus risks perpetuating the old rigidities under new labels. The new East European and CIS bourgeoisie may shed their bureaucratic intransigence for an analogous concern for economic survival, and rather than encouraging innovation and experimentation with novel environmental solutions may opt for the "tried and true" technologies that open global markets.

János Vargha, the biologist who founded the Danube Circle to oppose dam construction, mistakenly puts scientists in a different category than bureaucrats. The partisanship of science politics in the West has long since undermined the myth of the objectivity of science. In Eastern Europe and the former Soviet Union, all scientists were state employees. Their function was to advise the leadership on matters pertaining to science, technology, and the environment, and the record shows that very few scientists ever openly dissented from the official position. True, scientists led the campaign to save Lake Baikal and were persistent in warning the regimes of the need to do something about environmental pollution. Western observers applauded the efforts of the informal environmental lobbies that once existed in the prestigious institutes of the national academies of science in the Communist bloc countries, and on some university campuses.[8] However, the fact remains that the special committee on Lake Baikal which was formed within the USSR Academy of Sciences twice revised its findings upon request from the government. Despite greater openness in Hungarian society, the committee within the Hungarian Academy of Sciences which was officially asked to evaluate the celebrated hydroelectric project on the Danube kept its negative opinion on the construction of the high dam at Nagymaros secret until after the fall of communism. The dissident environmental groups were composed of professors and students from many university faculties, but few scientists made their dissent public by demonstrating in the streets. Vargha was a maverick among his peers, and even he argued that the environment knew no politics. It was better to try to solve environmental problems from within than to oppose from without.

Today, with virtually no exceptions, the scientists and specialists who staffed the Communist environmental institutions and advised the Communist leaders have either been kept on or reappointed to renamed positions, as environmental scientists and administrators in the newly formed governments. While some have come under fire, most have continued to perform their old functions in their new jobs. Under the old regime, it was virtually impossible for non-Communists to advance in the administration. As a result, there are no other scientists to replace the former Communist officials. In interviews in such diverse places as Vilnius, Lvov, Smolensk, Alma-Ata, and Dushanbe, I found that in Russia and Ukraine, although in some instances the top personnel had changed, the middle-level personnel remain the same. In most cases, I was impressed with the competence of these people, and with their desire to improve the environmental situation. Many had been working on environmental issues for fifteen years or more. I also sensed their frustration as they felt that regional and local legislatures and executives were against them as they sought to implement a veritable flood of new environmental legislation. But while I would not underestimate their competence or their sincerity, the fact is that they all reflected, as was only natural, their education in Communist administrative attitudes and practices. In politics, a change in direction requires new people dedicated to the introduction of new policies. In Eastern Europe and the CIS, particularly in the environmental area, there simply are no new faces. The corps of environmental scientists trained in the 1970s has no understanding of how to make the new conditions work for the environment. The old hierarchical attitudes persist.

Managerial rigidity and unresponsiveness to change are not only characteristics of state-owned enterprise managers: they constitute an integral part of the habits and modus operandi of government administrators as well. These characteristics constitute the second major sociocultural legacy of communism. Most administrators have been accustomed to being given orders and obeying them. The concepts of strategic planning, risk taking, and assuming responsibility are unfamiliar to them. Many are at a loss now that they have to make their own decisions. Nowhere is there managerial expertise in environmental analysis. Few government administrators have any idea of the cost of pollution, whether that be calculated in terms of environmental deterioration, health effects, or industrial losses, because all those data were formerly the privileged information of ministerial higher-ups. Even fewer have any idea how to go about finding these data. The task at the local level had been to see that data was collected and forwarded, not to use that data to assess local environmental conditions. In Monchegorsk, in the Kola Peninsula, one of the ecological disaster areas of Russia, the chief of the local Sanitary-Epidemiological Service (SES) could not tell me the cost of one patient-hospital day, nor did his training permit him to estimate how much of the population's illness might be attributable to environmentally related causes. In his view, some people were more prone to sickness than others. Unless this factor was taken into account, he believed, it was useless to try to estimate the impact of the pollution in his town on public health. To change old habits will take time, education, and the willingness as well as the opportunity to learn.

A third sociocultural legacy is the presence of contradictory goals and values. There is ambivalence about the market economy, and little understanding of democracy. Privatization has not occurred on a wide scale in any of the East European countries, and in all of those countries environmental professionals warn that there would be dangers to the environment should large-scale privatization occur. In ongoing public opinion polls conducted all over Russia by Boris Yeltsin's party, the Democratic Front of Russia, environmental values have tended to be associated with the former Communist and leftist parties, while free-market and democratic values have been associated with the democratic parties. Consumerism and the market so far have proved incapable of motivating vibrant economic and political renewal. Every country in the area has been compelled to rein in the process of privatization and transition to a free market because of mounting widespread public opposition. A far more compelling value has been the traditional nationalism that only three years after the so-called democratic revolutions of 1989 has destroyed Yugoslavia, has dismembered Czechoslovakia, and is wreaking havoc in the Caucasus.

One problem is that the new values are being promulgated by the same people who propagated Marxist collectivist values earlier, and with the same enthusiasm. People are cynical about the oft-cited benefits of democratic elections. In the 1990 election in Czechoslovakia, Civic Forum behaved no differently from the unpopular Communist Party in the smear tactics it used to deter voters from voting for a leading political rival. Older people wept when they went to the polls, but young people observed by the author voted with little enthusiasm or show of conviction. Only 30 percent of the population participated in Hungary's local elections in September 1990, the tenth in the space of a year. The dissolution of Czechoslovakia has occurred with no consultation of the public at all, while war rather than election results is determining the future of Bosnia and Herzegovina. In Russia, the direction of the economy has been the product of intense infighting between the executive and the legislature, and the public so far has been a passive bystander.

Equally important, there has been only slow progress in the establishment of an environmental legal framework that would not only set standards but be capable of seeing that environmental regulations were implemented. While the road to Brussels is paved with the good intentions of East European environmental officials, and a great deal of work is being done on harmonizing standards and regulations, legal compliance is everywhere seen as a secondary, not the primary, priority. The history of environmental management in Russia from 1991 to 1992 is a case in point. After December 1991, the Russian Ministry of the Environment was renamed the Ministry of Ecology and Natural Resources of the Russian Federation (MinEkologii). Many of the committees dating from the Communist era which had to do with the environment were incorporated into its structure. These included the Committee for Hydrometeorology and Environmental Protection, the Committee on Water Resources, the Committee on Forestry, the Committee for Geology and Mineral Resources, and the Geodetic and Cartography Committee. The result of these incorporations was a huge new bureaucracy.

Coordination of this environmental leviathan is in principle provided by the regional departments of the ministry, which themselves contain four different subdivisions. But in practice, all questions pertaining to rational resource use, environmental protection, and public health continue to be handled at the federal level. Federal decisions were met with increasing resistance by the regional organs. During 1991, friction between the regional organs and the federal ministry was especially pronounced with regard to control of the Environmental Protection Fund established in March of that year using funds derived from penalties and taxes levied on industries having emissions in excess of a stated norm. The original act gave the central ministry control over the disposition of the funds. But in June 1991, the Supreme Soviet passed an act giving the right to self-administration to all towns and administrative regions. The acquisition of a degree of independence encouraged the towns to demand control over the funds. The Russian Environmental Protection Act passed by the Russian parliament in December 1991 strengthened the hand of the center, but not until more than 37 million old rubles had been lost to the regions and towns in the process.[9]

The fall of 1992 brought further reorganization. The ministry was renamed the Ministry of Environmental Protection and Natural Resources, with corresponding subordinate territorial agencies and fifteen departments. Changes were also made among environmental personnel at the top government levels. Seven members of the Supreme Soviet's Committee on Environmental Problems and the Rational Use of National Resources were relieved of their positions. Among the four new members was N. N. Voronstov, head of the Ministry of the Environment under Gorbachev. During a seminar at Moscow State University in October 1992, Minister Viktor Danilov-Danilyan emphasized that the seemingly large number of employees was not enough. There was a lack of inspectors, and this lack was being made up by the formation of interregional inspection teams. The former head of the old Soviet Ecological Committee, A. V. Yablokov, newly appointed as adviser to the president of the Russian Federation on ecological and public health problems, also addressed the seminar. Yablokov stressed that the efforts to reform the ministry and to take action at the federal level were not enough. Central planning in environmental regulation had been relegated to the past. If the laws now in force were to be implemented, strong regional agencies and active public participation were essential.[10]

Reports, reorganizations, and environmental seminars of this kind suggest that the new Russian government is aware of the importance of environmental problems and is trying to get environmental protection under its control. But the reality is not as positive. During 1991–92, pollution and pollution-related illness increased. A report from the State Committee on Public Health and Epidemiological Control indicated that in sixty-four industrial centers the ambient concentration of pollutants exceeds the permissible levels by a factor greater than ten; 4.3 million people currently work in conditions that do not satisfy hygienic standards, while the rate of job-related sickness doubled between 1987 and 1992. Drinking water and food supplies fail to meet standards in many areas. In 1991, there were forty epidemics resulting from violations of health norms in food sale and services. According to the report, one out of every two children in elementary school now is afflicted with a chronic disease, and only 20 percent were listed as being in good health.[11]

One major reason for the negative trend has been the lack of resolve with which the government has handled the monitoring and prosecution of above-norm emissions. For many enterprises, the extent to which emissions exceed the norm is so great that payment of the current mandated penalties would exceed the profits of the firm. During 1990–91, the Soviet government compromised by setting the maximum level of pollution penalties at 7 percent of net profit. This practice is being continued, and in effect is taking away any incentive to reduce emissions. New regulations passed in 1992 provide the government with a completely legal basis for not imposing penalties. The rules stipulate that when the sum of pollution penalties is equal to or larger than the net profit of a firm, the state authorities may "consider" closing the firm down. By law, then, pollution itself cannot drive an enterprise out of business. As under the previous regime, the state alone has the final say. If past history is any indication, more likely than not the government will decide to leave even badly polluting enterprises open.

"Waffling" with regard to enforcement has a long tradition in the Soviet legal system,[12] and while regulations such as those just described do not indicate a happy prognosis, there is also no reason to infer doom and gloom. An important case that strengthened the hand of the judicial system was settled in Moscow in May 1992. For reasons that are poorly understood, the Moscow Soviet apparently gave Russian State Television permission to build a corporate headquarters in Gorky Park. Valuable trees in the center of the park came under the axe as clearing of the land began. The Moscow Environmental Committee brought the Soviet into court on charges that because Gorky Park was a park, allocating land within it for construction purposes was against the law. The case dragged on through the winter of 1991–92, with the lawyer for the Soviet threatening to delay the proceedings indefinitely. The decision that was finally made indicates the problems faced by enforcement efforts in the environmental area. Significantly, the court ruled neither that building in Gorky Park was illegal nor that the Moscow Soviet was at fault. Rather, it ruled that construction had to stop, and that Russian State Television would have to take a fresh look at its permit. The roundabout decision, however, set a precedent, in that it did not support the government authorities but came down, albeit feebly, on the side of the law. This is only one case among many, however. Until legal compliance is perceived as the behavioral norm and not an aberration, sound environmental management will remain at the mercy of bureaucrats within the state-owned enterprise and the state administration.

What is particularly disturbing is that the public is not viewed as a positive source of change and that there is little conviction that democracy and the free market will solve the serious environmental problems confronting Eastern Europe and the former Soviet Union. Environmental professionals and activists alike point to a low level of public awareness of environmental issues and a highly individualistic leadership in those environmental groups that survived the immediate transition period. While environmental organizations played a decisive role in bringing down the old regime, they are now disoriented and disorganized. The East European environmental movements find themselves at a crossroads. One way leads to a green political party, with its postindustrial values and its fundamental rejection of the industrial paradigm. The other leads to nongovernmental organizations integrated into the existing international network, with their strong orientation toward legalism and regulation, and their basic acceptance of the current global economic status quo. In the resolution of these critical philosophical and structural problems, the movements can draw on their experience under the previous regime and on the support of a worldwide environmental network that seeks a democratic alternative to global corporate and high-tech interests. But the groups have yet to complete the transition from underground movements to responsible political actors. Until that is achieved, they are in a weak position to influence the new regimes' response to domestic environmental issues.

Civil society is even less developed in the CIS. While the past few years have seen the appearance of a plethora of new environmental groups, the credentials of those groups' leaders and the credibility of their commitment to an environmental agenda are questionable. Established environmental organizations such as the Socioecological Union maintain a visible and public presence primarily because of the political or scientific reputation of their leaders. In meetings with environmental activists in Moscow, I pressed them for numerical information about their membership, only to be told either that the membership could not be determined because there was no membership fee and people could come and go as they chose, or that "the people" supported the group's aims and would show their power when the proper time came.[13] In the newly independent republics, the former mass-based environmental organizations, such as Rukh, in Ukraine, and the environmental groups within Sajudis, in Lithuania, have become ghosts of their former selves, with one or two people constituting the entire active membership. As economic conditions worsen and ethnic conflicts persist, the public at large has neither time, nor energy, nor interest to invest in activities not directly related to personal survival. For the many, environmental activism has become a luxury. Fortunately or unfortunately, today it offers the few the possibility of short-term employment financed by Western foundations and academic institutions. However, real commitment demands job security and time, both of which are virtually nonexistent in the CIS today.

Finally, there is the risk of the return of the old Communist bogeyman, colonialism. The contribution of pollution-abatement costs to the total cost of obtaining raw materials or producing a product has been steadily rising in Western Europe, Japan, and the United States. Already the European Union has had to slow down its planned reduction of carbon dioxide emissions because of the enormous costs associated with implementation.[14] In the United States there is a growing group of economists arguing in favor of free-market environmentalism, in which business is allowed to seek a favorable cost-benefit ratio rather than regulated pollution controls, and the public ends its status as free-rider. The evidence is mounting that the multinationals are transferring polluting industries to less developed countries. It will be recalled that trans-border pollution from Romanian chemical plants producing for export sparked the first major environmental protest in Bulgaria. Representatives of the U.S. mining industry claim that the transfer had to occur in their business because restrictive environmental regulation had so raised the cost of mining in the United States as to forestall the opening of new sites and severely restrict the operation of existing ones. The North American Free Trade Agreement has become the butt of organized environmental displeasure because of its perceived encouragement of this transfer process from the United States to Mexico.[15] East Europeans and environmentalists in the successor states of the Soviet Union also fear that multinationals will see the area as a pollution haven. Public protest by the native peoples of the Yamal Peninsula forced the Soviet government to halt further exploitation of oil and natural gas resources there in 1990.[16] Today, the Yamal is once again threatened, this time by a signed agreement between a multinational oil consortium and the Russian government.[17] In St. Petersburg, there is much discussion about the potentially adverse environmental impact of a proposed gigantic new port to be built on the Gulf of Finland. The environmental authorities have given a negative assessment of the proposed construction. The opinion was given reluctantly because they are fully aware that in the interests of trade, Russia needs a modern port on a warm water sea. The Environmental Committee of the Leningrad region would prefer not to give any opinion at all, and particularly to be freed from having to make a decision. So far there has been only scattered opposition to the port, but when the project begins to receive more attention, the opposition will doubtless become more organized and more strident. Seeing the problems ahead, the committee insists that the port is of such national significance that the decision on its construction should be taken at the national level with full recognition of the environmental consequences.

Desperate to raise living standards, today's governments in the formerly Communist countries are being pushed to accept lax enforcement or lower standards to ensure employment and economic restructuring. My discussions with national professionals throughout Eastern Europe and the former Soviet Union were not encouraging. Most insisted that it was impossible to renovate the economy under conditions of strict environmental regulation. The first priority was to get the economy going.

Conclusion

In the face of this analysis, the prospects are not encouraging. All through the former Soviet Union and Eastern Europe there is a frantic effort to compensate for the damaging environmental legacies by seeing a deus ex machina in material, financial, and organizational aid from the West. The risks in counting on such a strategy are enormous, but quite clearly there is no money within the area to take on the huge task of clean-up and health care. Estimates of the amounts needed to rehabilitate the former USSR and Eastern Europe run into such huge sums that the Marshall Plan pales in comparison. Large-scale financing is not and will not be available. But some monies are forthcoming. In September 1992, Germany's Ministry of Environmental Protection provided 2 million DM to finance a project on environmental monitoring. The Group of Seven has promised to give Russia $600 million for the reconstruction of its nuclear power plants. Such monies are welcomed by the proponents of nuclear energy. Advocates of a nuclear moratorium, such as A. V. Yablokov, argue that with $2 billion, the turbines of the military-industrial complex could be refitted to run on natural gas, liberating Russia from any necessity to use nuclear power.[18] Until the West has made a careful study of the environmental needs and priorities in Eastern Europe and the CIS, there is the risk that aid may be given to remedy what the West may perceive as a salient problem, the mitigation of which in fact may only serve to aggravate the underlying environmental condition.

In its aid policy, the West has chosen to emphasize technical assistance and the encouragement of capital investment. However, technology and managerial skills are not transplanted in a vacuum, and the experience of one country cannot be transferred intact into another national setting. In the absence of a comprehensive and comparable environmental legal framework and an appropriate economic infrastructure, the West may prefer to export to Eastern Europe and the CIS republics those industries and technologies that are most polluting. We have already mentioned the precedents for such action. A mining company that anticipates having to secure 140 permits in order to open a mine in California might well consider transferring its operations to a comparable site in Eastern Europe, where only five permits might be required and where termination procedures are less rigorous. If such eventualities occur, the West could find itself a contributor to the worsening of the environmental problem, rather than the provider of its solution.

Again, in their rush to assist, international lending institutions could well lower their environmental criteria to facilitate priming the East European economic pump. While the European Bank for Reconstruction and Development and the World Bank have earmarked remedial environmental monies and have made loans dependent upon fulfilling environmental stipulations, past bank practice, coupled with the dismal record of past East European and CIS governments in implementing environmental programs, does not encourage confidence that current policies will be strictly enforced or implemented.

The new social systems of Eastern Europe and the Commonwealth are highly vulnerable to surprise. As fragile democratic governments face increasingly dissatisfied voters, they may decide that the better part of wisdom is to encourage Western investment and joint ventures no matter what the environmental cost. Moreover, Eastern Europe, the Baltics, Ukraine, and Russia share the same dream of a common European home. European integration in this context means adopting the affluent lifestyle of the parent culture. In the face of economic uncertainty, public pressure may combine with the transformed bureaucracies to force the choice of a prepackaged solution. The West German takeover of East Germany is a case in point. In the race for a place in the global markets and an immediate increase in living standard, East European and Commonwealth societies may opt to forgo any attempt to develop domestic solutions, and may pursue immediate economic gains in the form of "goulash capitalism." With the world on the threshold of a new phase in advanced technological development, the multinationals are anxious to push their products on the vast, virtually untouched East European and CIS market. Once the trappings of a consumer society are in place in the East, it may be even more difficult to transform the life-style to do without them than it is now in the West.

The conclusion that suggests itself is that deciding the course of environmental management solely on the basis of Western models and Western assistance may result in the mitigation of social frustration through continued and increasing environmental deterioration. At the end of the 1980s, vast numbers of people from the Oder to the Pacific became aware that they were living under the threat of environmental catastrophe. They were able to exploit that threat to change their political and economic system. The threat has not decreased in succeeding years. What has increased is the struggle for control of the way in which the industrial and natural resource spoils are divided among the economic and political elites of the former Communist societies. These elites are exploiting the danger of unemployment and lowered living standards to mobilize popular support for their interests. In so doing, they are deflecting public interest from the urgency of environmental remediation.

The predemocratic domestic environmental movements were able to develop their own individual philosophy, organization, and interaction with the international world. If they could succeed in a climate of censorship, oppression, and police brutality, there is reason to expect that they will find a way to use their experience to develop successful indigenous modes of operation in their newly open societies. Up to now, the new directions in environmental management in the former Communist countries have been largely passive. Social transformation and adaptation to new conditions require active learning. The longer East European governments put off dealing with their environmental problems, the harder it will be to address those problems. In the 1980s, public pressure that was

6

The Military and Security Legacies
of Communism

Zoltan Barany

The end of communism in Eastern Europe poses serious questions concerning the military and security future of this traditionally volatile region. From the global perspective at least, Soviet hegemony had achieved relative stability in Eastern Europe. Although occasional flare-ups did occur, the Kremlin and its soldiers, the Warsaw Pact, and the local Communist elites managed to extinguish them until 1989. The velvet and not-so-velvet revolutions of that year signaled not only the return of real sovereignty to these long-oppressed lands but also the reappearance of ethnic tensions and the reemergence of suppressed habitual antagonisms. With the abolition of the Warsaw Pact, a stabilizing and mediating influence departed from the region's politico-military stage.

Since the late 1940s Eastern Europe has been one of the most heavily militarized areas of the world. At the end of the 1980s the military manpower in this area, approximately the size of the upper Midwest of the United States, far exceeded 3 million active and reserve troops, not counting the occupying Soviet forces. What to do with such a large armed force and its equipment is only one of the many military and security dilemmas East European political and military leaders have had to face in the wake of communism. What guidelines and political arrangements will direct relations between the state and its soldiers? What to do with an officer corps educated, indoctrinated, and for the most part appeased by the Communist regimes? These and many other related considerations have kept local military and security experts, and their colleagues abroad, busy since 1989.

This chapter examines the problematic military and security legacies of East European communism through the looking glass of these quandaries. The first section portrays civil-military relations during the Communist era and concerns itself with the numerous problems the post-Communist states have faced in this area. The second section analyzes

Eastern Europe's regional security during the Communist era and the legacies left behind by the Warsaw Pact.

Civil-Military Relations

The relationship between the armed forces and the state is one of the most important political nexuses in the modern state, which needs a loyal military establishment that operates in accord with constitutional guidelines and provides effective defense of the nation from external aggression. In Communist systems, however, the military's external function is complemented by an internal defensive function, the task of defending the Communist Party–state from its internal enemies. Since Communist systems did not evolve through democratic processes but were imposed on society by force, the Party-state was in dire need of an effective armed establishment that was unconditionally loyal to the Party and to the principles of Marxism-Leninism. In order to ensure the military's reliability, Communist regimes built up a complex network of institutional controls and incentives.

The components of this control mechanism included the Administrative Department of the central committee of the Communist Party, which was charged with overseeing the military's politicization. A number of political bodies with names such as "Defense Council" and "Military Committee" were brought to life, staffed by the most powerful members of the Party and military elite. Civilian and military intelligence services kept a watchful eye on the armed forces to ensure the loyalty of the officer corps. In order to deter conflicts between the Party and the military, the Party co-opted some of the most influential high-ranking officers, who thus came to enjoy leading positions in the political realm as well. Since these individuals were indebted to the Party for their status and privileges, their allegiances were first to the Party and only secondarily to the armed forces. They became, as it were, the "Party in uniform."

In each of the Communist countries of Eastern Europe, the armed forces themselves maintained an organization, customarily called the Main Political Administration (MPA), that was to ensure the political and ideological indoctrination of professional and conscripted soldiers alike. The MPA employed a small army of "political officers" who were attached to all units down to the battalion or even to the company level and were in effect the foot soldiers of the military's political establishment. They were responsible for the political education and "ideological preparedness" of officers and soldiers alike. In practical terms, this meant that the essential task of political officers was to imbue officers and soldiers with Communist and internationalist values (such as the leading societal role of the Communist Party; and the moral, political, and economic superiority of the Communist system over capitalism). A network of Party organizations was also active within the armed forces; its importance was betrayed by the fact that it enjoyed the same administrative status as a county Party structure. In addition, the educational system (especially its military component) was heavily politicized on all levels in Communist societies. The Party and the military also maintained paramilitary organizations especially designed to popularize the military profession among the young. Membership in the Communist Party was a prerequisite for professional advancement in the armed forces.

Although in most Communist systems civil-military relations had shared a number of fundamental similarities, a major difference needs to be pointed out between the Party-army nexus of countries that were dominated by the Soviet Union (the non-Soviet Warsaw Pact [NSWP] states) and those that remained independent. The military establishments of the East European member states of the Warsaw Treaty Organization (WTO) were controlled not only by the local Communist Party but also by the Soviet Union. The Soviet Union, through its dominant role in the WTO, direct politico-military interference, intelligence organizations, and military advisers and other personnel (let alone the tens of thousands of Soviet troops stationed in the East European states)[1] exerted a strong influence on the Party-army affairs of the NSWP states, and in fact became a significant third actor in those states' civil-military relations.

Scholarly efforts at explaining civil-military relations in Communist Eastern Europe did not bring the desired results (i.e., empirically testable models) primarily because civil-military relations in the region's states and in different eras were so dissimilar that they simply could not be adequately served by an overarching model that was sufficiently flexible to accommodate all variations.[2] An examination of civil-military relations in the six former NSWP states is bound to demonstrate that, indeed, there were very few rules that were germane to all of them. The following six generalizations appear to be the only ones applicable to all six former NSWP states.

1. Throughout the four decades of East European communism, Moscow's influence on Party-army relations was pervasive, but Soviet control had slowly but perceptibly waned following the consolidation of Communist political power. In crisis situations, however, Moscow continued to reinforce its rule either directly (e.g., in Czechoslovakia in 1968) or indirectly (e.g., in Poland in 1980–81).

2. In all of these states, when the Communists gained power they inherited military establishments that were at least in part opposed to the new order. Therefore, initially, at least, the Party displayed a great deal of suspicion of the armed forces. Purges against the undesirable segments of the armed forces occurred in every NSWP state, especially during the period of Communist takeover and subsequent to uprisings.

3. In all six states, the Communist Party devised and operated several mechanisms to ensure the reliability of the armed forces (e.g., the MPA, political officers, Communist Party organizations in the army, the educational system, and politically based recruitment and promotion).

4. The extent of Party membership among the professional military cadres, particularly officers, was extremely high (at or above 75%) everywhere in Eastern Europe.

5. In every NSWP state, the Communist Party maintained special security forces and/or militias and generally relied on them to do the dirty job in crisis situations, thus indicating their lack of confidence in the regular forces' ability to repress internal uprisings.

6. The prestige of the military profession suffered in all NSWP states under communism, primarily because the peoples of the region considered the armed forces the defenders of foreign interests and/or of an unpopular political regime; as a result, all East European militaries encountered recruitment problems at one time or another.

Disparities, like similarities, are important to explore, as they can help us better appreciate the profound differences in the region's civil-military relations. Let us consider some of the most important areas in which Party-army relations in the region had diverged. For the sake of brevity, only the states occupying the opposing poles of the spectrum in question will be noted.

1. The participation of the armed forces in policy making was very important in Poland (1956–89, particularly after the declaration of martial law) and insignificant in Hungary.
2. The Party's co-optation of military personnel into the various levels of political administration was prevalent in East Germany but essentially nonexistent in Czechoslovakia.
3. Soviet influence on military policy and on the socialization of armed forces personnel was very important in East Germany and negligible in Romania (after 1965); this issue was closely related to affinities toward the alliance.
4. The influence of professionalization on the officer corps was great in Poland but substantially less in East Germany; this factor adversely affected the political control of the armed forces.

A brief examination of the military's role in the revolutions of 1989 can also lucidly demonstrate some of the major disparities in the civil-military relations of East European systems. The lessons of the revolutions suggest that the more gradual and the more carefully prepared the transitions, the smaller the role that the armed forces could play in them. This is not to say that sudden revolutions, by definition, would be accompanied by military interference in politics, but simply that such transitions offer soldiers better opportunities to play a determining role. Indeed, a brief look at the East European transitions, from Poland to Bulgaria, confirms this hypothesis. In Poland and Hungary the armed forces played no appreciable political role in the transition. It should be noted that the military leaders who governed Poland in the 1980s were Party officials who happened to be soldiers; in other words, they acted as "the Party in uniform." In East Germany and Czechoslovakia a very small minority of Party and military leaders made threats about potential military and/or militia suppression of the ongoing demonstrations. In the two Balkan members of the WTO, however, the situation was drastically different. In Bulgaria, Petar Mladenov's reform-Communist group hardly could have succeeded in deposing the Party leader Todor Zhivkov without the explicit support of Defense Minister Dobri Dzhurov. At the far end of the spectrum, the Romanian revolution probably could not have succeeded without the armed forces' active support.

What, then, were the legacies that this type of civil-military nexus left to the post-Communist era, and what were its implications? With regard to civil-military relations the legacies of East European communism are heavily politicized armed forces whose most important task was the defense not of the homeland but of the Communist regime. This general statement hides many important attributes of such a military establishment, however, and needs to be further examined. In the aftermath of the Communist regimes' collapse, the new political elites have had to confront several weighty matters concerning civil-military relations.

As we have seen, under communism the East European armed forces were supervised by the Communist Party, through a variety of control mechanisms. The task of the newly democratizing regimes is to minimize the armed forces' political power while maximizing their military professionalism. In order to attain that goal, the democratic state (the political master) has to ensure that the military establishment becomes and remains a political instrument; it can do so by defining the military establishment's functions and proper behavior, and the state's expectations.[3] The more professional the military, the less it is interested in or inclined to interfere in politics. The new professional armed forces should be prepared to "carry out the wishes of any civilian group which secures legitimate authority within the state."[4]

The new regimes have thus far concentrated on maximizing civilian control over the armed forces. In order to move toward a more comprehensive transformation of civil-military relations, the regimes would have to feel more comfortable with a highly professional army, and the ailing economies would have to turn around. It appears unlikely that these and other conditions necessary for the large-scale professionalization of the East European armed forces can soon be realized. There are several reasons, several legacies, that support this conclusion. What are they?

Perhaps one of the most important problems facing the new post-Communist regimes is the personnel management of the armed forces. Representatives in the new legislatures across the region have debated the "red or expert" issue — that is, the question of what to do with military officers, most of whom had been Communist Party members. It was clear that many of these officers had chosen to become Party members not because of any heartfelt loyalty to the Communist cause but owing to their accurate perception that without the Party card, advancement in the ranks was severely limited. To ascertain which of these officers were faithful Communists and which were merely opportunists would have been an impossible task. The new governments had come to the conclusion that it was impossible to dismiss the entire officer corps. All officers were given the choice of either leaving the armed forces or pledging their allegiance to the new constitution and the freely elected parliament. To be sure, some of the high-ranking officers who had been too intimately associated with the Communist regimes were dismissed, while others, mostly those who had reached pension age, were retired.

A related and by no means negligible issue is the attitudinal dimension of the Communist officer corps. Schooled and trained for decades in Communist dogma, its members are often unable to make independent decisions and cannot easily discard the legacies of communism that so profoundly affect their personal world views. These deeply entrenched mental and psychological rigidities are characteristic mostly of middle-aged officers ten to fifteen years before pension age, who cannot be relieved of duty but who often appear to be either reluctant to change their ways, or unable to do so. Owing to such officers' numerical preponderance in the East European militaries, it appears clear that it will take another generation until the region's officer corps will be made up entirely of "new" officers.

The system of military education left behind by the Communist era is in dire need of comprehensive reform. During the Communist period the prestige of the military occupation plummeted, and service academies became the strongholds of the academically incompetent. Even so, campaigns to recruit professional soldiers encountered serious problems in many of the region's states (particularly in East-Central Europe), as good prospects chose to pursue civilian occupations. The task of the new regimes is to convince their countries' "best and brightest" that a military career in the national army is not only a fine career choice but also a well-rewarded one. With the current economic problems and the shrinking military budgets this will not be an easy goal to accomplish.

In the Communist era as much as 30 percent of the instruction in military colleges was taken up by Marxism-Leninism and other politico-ideological subjects, although the dogmatism that had characterized these courses seems to have diminished in the late 1980s. Since 1989, ideological training generally has been replaced by courses on military and security policy, international military law, military history, and other similar subjects. Yet the labels must be somewhat misleading, as in most cases the same instructors who taught "Scientific Marxism and the Socialist Armed

Forces" are now lecturing on "The Military and the Democratic State," and it is scarcely possible that their values, attitudes, and teaching methods did an "about face" in the fall of 1989. It would seem that the comprehensive reform of military education will only be completed once the faculty of the military colleges is replaced.

A related negative legacy of the Communist era is that in all East European states there is a conspicuous shortage of civilian military experts owing to the fact that military affairs and related subjects were either not taught, or were taught only to trusted military cadres. The new governments and legislatures are in dire need of independent and objective experts to provide them with precise political analysis, information concerning the effects and implications of alternative decisions, and general advice regarding a wide array of military and security issues. In the absence of such individuals they must rely on military personnel whose views are often biased.

Some important steps leading toward a comprehensive democratization of civil-military relations have already been accomplished in much of the region. The most significant factors in the depoliticization of the East European military establishments were the abolition of Communist Party control over the armed forces and the legal regulation of the armed forces' role. All party organizations were forbidden to operate within the armed forces, the MPAs were abolished or restructured, and military oaths were rewritten to reflect loyalty to democratically elected governments and to national constitutions. With the end of Soviet political dominance and military occupation, the armies of Eastern Europe are becoming genuinely national armies once again, and the presence of an external influence in civil-military relations is no longer a valid concern. At the same time, the nationalization of the armed forces may be a mixed blessing to many officers who can no longer depend on their Soviet colleagues to protect them from their own political leaders and who will not be able to exert pressure on the East European governments for increased military spending or the selection of certain "recommended" weapons systems for purchase.[5]

There are several guidelines available to those attempting to democratize civil-military relations by curbing military power and promoting military professionalism. In his book *The Third Wave*, Samuel Huntington has offered such advice to East European democratizers. Some of the measures he recommends (e.g., the clarification of chains of command,

and the reduction of the size of armies) have already been completed, although others (for example, purging potentially disloyal officers, increasing the incomes of soldiers, and purchasing sophisticated weaponry for them) do not seem realistic in the current politico-economic situation.[6] Separating those officers who harbored genuine pro-Communist sympathies from those who joined the Party in order to further their careers would be well-nigh impossible. The economic cost of acquiring modern equipment and implementing major salary increases would be clearly prohibitive.

For a number of reasons, then, the new East European regimes have placed the emphasis on securing and expanding their political control over the armed forces and ensuring the loyalty of soldiers to the state through cost-effective means such as rhetoric (speeches and articles lauding the crucial protective role of the military in a sovereign state) and symbolic gestures (such as awarding medals, and standardizing uniforms in accord with national traditions). Considering the current political and economic conditions in the region, this may in fact be the wise strategy to follow, provided that once civilian control over the armed forces is firmly established such control is augmented by state-sponsored professionalization of the military.

The East European countries and their armed forces were in many respects different from each other during the Communist period. With the fall of communism, the collapse of the Warsaw Pact, and the retraction of Soviet influence, these states will be even more dissimilar in the future.[7] Their differences stem from disparities in their political, economic, and sociocultural development which often reach back to periods before communism. The legacies left behind specifically by the Communist era — for instance, the fact that democratic oppositions (of dissimilar size and political impact, of course) existed in all East-Central European states but not in the Balkans — also support different political trajectories among the region's states. Although there are some fundamental similarities in the democratization processes of all East European armed forces, the profound disparities between the armed forces of the East-Central European states and those of their former WTO partners in the Balkans may define the future stances of these military establishments as well.[8]

Although some steps still remain to be taken in the transformation of the Czech, Slovak, Hungarian, and Polish armed forces, these militaries have already undergone comprehensive reforms. While this process has had its ups and downs, the difficulties usually originated in a lack of political and legislative experience. Nonetheless, the depoliticization of the armed forces did not encounter any major problems in these states. In these countries the armed forces are led by civilian ministers, their officer corps have not been involved in politics, and their leaderships have experienced comprehensive changes in personnel. The political and structural changes and reforms affecting the militaries of the two Balkan members of the WTO thus far have been much less extensive and convincing. Some military leaders in Southeastern Europe have actively opposed the depoliticization of the armed forces; there have been recurrent rumors of impending military coups; and the military leadership did get involved in political debates on a number of occasions.[9] The Romanian Army is the only NSWP force to have seen action in the postrevolutionary era; this occurred when it was deployed or threatened to intervene in domestic crises in March and December 1990, and September 1991.[10] In stark contrast to East-Central Europe, shifts in personnel in Bulgaria and Romania customarily came after protracted infighting in political and military circles.

Regional Security and the Long Shadow of the Warsaw Pact

Throughout the Communist period the determining characteristic of Eastern Europe's security situation was the region's domination by the Soviet Union. Soviet domination of the East European militaries commenced in the wake of World War II, a decade before the Warsaw Pact was called to life in 1955. The East European satellites had to adopt the Soviet Union's offensive military doctrine without regard to their own national security concerns. Soviet-made armaments became standardized across the bloc, and Moscow's military advisers supervised the comprehensive sovietization of native military establishments. During the first few years of its existence, the Warsaw Pact added little organizationally to the bilateral agreements between the member states already in place. Still, the WTO had a great deal of political significance for the bloc, in that it provided a formal framework for binding the Communist states together, limited the sovereignty of the individual member states by forbidding their participation in other alliances, and served as a useful forum for the expression of Eastern Europe's support of various Soviet foreign policy positions and initiatives.[11] Furthermore, the Warsaw Pact also enabled the

Soviet Union to maintain Moscow's capability for rapid military intervention in the region and limited the capacity of East European armies to put up sustained resistance against the Soviet occupation forces.

From its inception, and even after its limited reorganization following the August 1968 invasion of Czechoslovakia, the Warsaw Pact remained an alliance thoroughly dominated by Soviet hegemony. Moscow had intended to create a well-integrated multinational military force befitting the image of the united socialist community. Real integration, however, had proved an elusive goal, as Soviet military policy and leadership remained synonymous with the WTO.[12] Romania, for instance, had only been a pro forma member of the WTO after the mid-1960s, owing to President Nicolae Ceauşescu's refusal to participate in joint military exercises and his prohibition of foreign troops on Romanian soil. In fact, the problems of the Warsaw Pact had been symptomatic of the entire "family of socialist nations." The blatant disregard of the East European states' national interests in decisions regarding military doctrine, strategy, expenditures, and armaments had been some of the most important complaints of dissidents and democratizers throughout the region's Communist period.

As a result of the strengthening democratization drive in the East European states, which culminated in the revolutions of 1989 and Moscow's increased willingness not to meddle in those states' internal affairs, by 1990 the WTO had become an essentially defunct military-political organization; it was unceremoniously abolished in the summer of 1991. Negotiations concerning the withdrawal of Soviet occupation troops were completed expeditiously, and the last of the troops left eastern Germany in 1994. Nonetheless, the departure of the Red Army troops presents further dilemmas to the successors of Communist leaders in the former Soviet bloc. The Soviet Army occupying these states had caused enormous environmental damage and left their former bases in catastrophic condition. The lack of proper restoration and repair of exercise grounds, shooting ranges, historic barracks, buildings, and other facilities had given rise to widespread public protests as well as to innumerable unsolved legal cases. Since 1990, the East European governments have been negotiating with their Russian counterpart concerning restitution payments without much success.

As happily as the fall of the WTO and the withdrawal of the occupying forces was received in the states of Eastern Europe, much of the region found itself in a precarious security situation in the wake of communism. The realization that the former NSWP states were unable to protect themselves from virtually any external attack came as a shock to the post-Communist politicians and their constituents. The occupying troops of the Soviet Union had provided adequate air defense for these states, but once they were gone the newly sovereign states were left incapable of guarding their airspace. The former NSWP states do not possess large caches of sophisticated weaponry, since in the Soviet-WTO doctrine of "coalition warfare" their forces were supposed to supplement those of their better-equipped Soviet brothers-in-arms. Owing to their strategically more sensitive location, the northern-tier NSWP states (Czechoslovakia, Poland, and East Germany) received priority consideration from Soviet arms producers, but their arsenals are remarkably antiquated and are insufficient to provide reassuring self-defense capabilities. Just how serious the situation is has been demonstrated by the repeated violation of Hungary's airspace by Yugoslav fighter jets as Hungarian forces helplessly looked on.

In the security domain, then, the most important legacy of communism is the power vacuum left behind the retreating Soviet forces. The East European states are no longer members of a Warsaw Pact that could guarantee the defense of their territories from external threats, and they are incapable of protecting themselves. Fortunately for the former East Germany, it became the beneficiary of NATO protection, but what of the rest of the former NSWP states? Starting in the late 1960s, Romania, where no Soviet troops had been stationed since 1958, had established an "entire people's war" doctrine similar to the military doctrine of neighboring Yugoslavia. As a result of that doctrine the poorly equipped and poorly trained Romanian armed forces were complemented by large numbers of reservists and "Patriotic Guards"; thus, Romanian security was less strongly affected by the demise of the WTO. To some extent, however, all of these states have had to face the loss of the security the Warsaw Pact had afforded them. Ironically, and perhaps most importantly, the WTO had saved the East Europeans from themselves, for the traditional enemies of the region's states had become their brothers-in-arms in the Warsaw Pact, and longstanding feuds had been prevented from surfacing within the alliance.

With the Warsaw Pact and Soviet hegemony gone, ethnic tensions, virulent nationalism, separatism, and thinly veiled revanchism — aptly characterized as the New Tribalism — once again could emerge unabated. Every country in the region has experienced nationalist or racist incidents, and most of the governments have been unable to address these incidents satisfyingly. Attempts to make a sober analysis of such threats and to manage them have often been frustrated by the turbulent political situation in individual states and in the region as a whole. Although Yugoslavia was never a Warsaw Pact member, the war in the former Yugoslavia serves as a timely reminder of what might happen between and within former WTO allies if solutions to their problems are not found.[13] Czechoslovakia fell apart in January 1993 with relative civility, but there are no guarantees that traditional antagonisms (Hungarian-Romanian, Polish-Russian, Slovak-Hungarian, and so on) will be settled or at least managed in a like manner.

In sum, then, although Eastern Europe has traditionally been a highly flammable region, the security legacies of communism are uniformly negative. Owing to the longstanding Soviet-Communist domination of Eastern Europe, the most important security legacies of the Communist era are (1) the lack of a comprehensive regional security structure; (2) military establishments that are numerically large but poorly equipped; (3) the absence of military-security doctrines reflecting the national interest; (4) human resources (officer corps) that have not been accustomed to intellectual independence and creativity; (5) inadequate professional contacts both within and outside of the region; and (6) armed forces whose personal and material components are unprepared for a post-Communist era.

The East European states, particularly those in East-Central Europe (the Czech Republic, Hungary, Poland, and Slovakia) are keenly aware of their security limbo and have looked at different solutions. All of the East European states would like to become members of NATO, which thus far has judged their membership premature. Although NATO has already granted several East European countries membership in its newly created Cooperation Council and in the Partnership for Peace program, both of these were established to give the post-Communist countries of the region an organizational affiliation without any binding commitment to their security. The fact is that as the New Tribalism began to take hold, the West, and more particularly, NATO, has grown more wary of East Europeans and the "bag of tricks" they might bring along to Brussels.[14] Still, perhaps it is not unreasonable to speculate that the East-Central

European states could gain full membership in NATO within the next decade.

In the meantime, politicians and soldiers have sought to enhance their countries' national security by establishing bilateral military cooperation agreements with former WTO neighbors, NATO members, and other European states. The East-Central European states, especially, have actively explored the possibilities of military cooperation since their first summit meeting in February 1991, in Visegrád, Hungary. Ukrainian leaders have suggested a Carpathian cooperation option that — while it would not replace a security structure like NATO — might assume a defensive position in light of the potential emergence of a xenophobic, anti-Ukrainian, and anti-Polish political force in Russia. In the Balkans, Bulgaria has improved its relations with its former adversaries Greece and Turkey. Clearly, however, every state of the region considers full-fledged NATO membership as the only true guarantor of its national security.

Another related task that the newly sovereign East European states have had to address has been the elaboration of entirely new defense doctrines. Although not all of the new doctrinal concepts have been worked out everywhere in the region, it appears that all of the former NSWP states desire to introduce entirely defensive doctrines based on the principle of sufficient defense capability. Realizing that fielding a military force capable of deterring large powers would be well-nigh impossible, those who devised the new doctrines intend to rely on international guarantees and emphasize relatively small but superbly trained and well-equipped forces that could hold off the potential enemy until help arrived either in the form of allied military assistance or international (especially United Nations) intervention.

The creation of such highly professionalized armed forces equipped with modern weaponry is of course an extremely expensive proposition even for prosperous states, let alone for the impoverished East Europeans. Inevitably, because of these governments' unstable economic circumstances the purchase of new armaments is low on their list of priorities and is likely to remain so in the foreseeable future. The Warsaw Pact had demanded ever-increasing defense outlays from its East European members, who generally acquiesced. While the quality of weapons purchased from the USSR had often been suspect, there were scarcely any qualms about quantity. Nonetheless, the arms these states have ended up with in the wake of communism are in many cases not what they need. Furthermore, while new weapons were regularly added to the arsenals, money for maintenance was often unavailable. Thus, a significant proportion of tanks, vehicles, large field guns, and the like are rusting away, while more sophisticated equipment is almost totally absent from the arsenal of these states.

The national armies of the NSWP states could operate only in cooperation with the Soviet forces; independently, they were unable to conduct offensive maneuvers. Military officers, heavily indoctrinated with Marxist-Leninist values but less well versed in the theories and practices of modern warfare, were not able to act independently and confidently without their superiors. Another legacy of communism, then, is the inability of these armies to carry out successful military missions in case of armed conflicts.

Owing to a multitude of economic problems and to the new defense doctrines, the military establishments of Eastern Europe have changed noticeably since 1989. Manpower and budgets have been cut substantially in all of the former NSWP states but Romania, where President Ceauşescu, fearing Bonapartist tendencies, deliberately emaciated the regular armed forces.[15] Because of declining budgets and the postponement of arsenal development, the technical and infrastructural conditions in these armed forces are rapidly deteriorating. The East-Central European armies have made successful bids for the discarded equipment of the former East German military. They and the armies of the other former NSWP states are also interested in acquiring surplus equipment that NATO armies may have to offer. It is clear, however, that the economic transition in Eastern Europe will take decades and there is no realistic hope for the substantial improvement of East European arsenals in the near future.

In the process of the East European states' economic transition, a major role has to be played by the defense industry, which is one of the most developed sectors in several of these economies. The reduction of conventional armed forces and armaments, as well as the rapid shrinking of the East European defense industries' international markets, have had a deleterious effect on arms production. The only solution appears to be the massive conversion of defense industries, which poses yet another challenge for these economies and societies, particularly in regions such as Silesia and Slovakia, where defense-related plants have been the main employers. The conversion has been initiated everywhere in the area, and has often been modeled on the experiences of more developed states. Not surprisingly, East Europeans have, with some success, attempted to recruit Western investors to finance the conversion of facilities. Still, much remains to be done in this respect as well, since the prospect of growing unemployment and the resultant social dissatisfaction makes politicians and managers apprehensive of dramatic changes.

Conclusion

Eastern Europe's Communist period left perhaps even more profound ingrained legacies in the military and security arena than it left in other areas, both because Moscow had permitted the smallest amount of latitude in defense matters and because the armed forces had been the traditional strongholds of conservative Communists. As a result, these legacies will be extremely difficult to overcome in the foreseeable future. Although the financial-economic aspects of the problems awaiting solution seem prohibitive enough, it would seem that the human dimension of Eastern Europe's security dilemma is even more serious. Politicians and even enterprise managers can be replaced with relative ease. But because the military personnel that the new regimes inherited from the past hold a monopoly on military-security knowledge and skills, replacement of the personnel at missile sites and air defense installations, or even in the lecture halls of military colleges, will have to wait for some time.

In the wake of the cold war, East-Central Europe and the Balkans have been left in a security limbo. Bilateral military cooperation treaties and intraregional agreements do offer some hope of stability. Still, this traditionally volatile region clearly needs some sort of Western oversight and assistance, whether it be under the aegis of NATO, the CSCE process, or some future security structure. The war in the former Yugoslavia and the rise of the New Tribalism across the region should serve as somber warnings to spur reluctant Western (especially West European) politicians and military planners to pay more attention to the East. The other alternative might well be an Eastern Europe embroiled in initially contained but progressively widening armed conflicts, one consequence of which would almost surely be a Western Europe overrun by millions of desperate refugees.

The situation seems more hopeful in the area of civil-military relations. Although problems have been encountered along the way, there are no signs of military coups on the horizon, and by early 1994 all of the former NSWP states had completed the depoliticization of their armed forces or made significant progress toward it. Owing to their different experiences and the variety of traditional political and social roles these armies have played in the past, their transition processes have been quite dissimilar. The record of the East European armed forces in the transitions underscores the profound disparities between the countries of the region. It appears that the countries of East-Central Europe are well on the way to completing the democratization of their armed forces. These armies seem to be depoliticized and loyal to the constitutional order that is taking shape in their respective societies. The situation in the Balkans has been somewhat different. The Bulgarian and Romanian armies have not made an unambiguous commitment to political democratization and seem to be ill prepared for a new democratic era. In sum, then, just as the political transformation of East-Central Europe is more convincing and comprehensive than that of the Balkans, the depoliticization process of the armed forces in the former region also has been more reassuring.

COUNTRY STUDIES

7

Eastern Germany

Thomas A. Baylis

Assessing the legacy of the four decades of Communist rule in what are now the five "new states" of the Federal Republic of Germany (FRG) and the eastern section of Berlin requires that we address two apparent puzzles. First, how did the state that in the 1980s was widely regarded as the most successful in the Communist camp in terms of economic well-being and political stability come to be the one that in several respects has been the most devastated by the transition to a market economy and political democracy — in spite of receiving a level of West German assistance dwarfing Western aid to all other former Communist states together? Second, why, after citizens of the German Democratic Republic (GDR) had surged into the streets in 1989 to bring down the old regime, and then had eagerly embraced unity with the FRG, have many of them come to look back on the days of Communist rule with a surprising degree of affection? This widely observed "GDR nostalgia" is documented by the strong showing of the post-Communist Party of Democratic Socialism (PDS) in borough and communal elections in east Berlin and Branden-burg;[1] the survival of the Communist ritual of *Jugendweihe* (youth dedica-tion), originally introduced as an ideological substitute for Christian con-firmation; the continuing attachment of former East Germans to their accustomed newspapers (now owned by Western firms, but retaining many of their former staff) in preference to West German publications; and responses to numerous opinion surveys.[2]

The two puzzles are not unrelated: the nostalgia for the GDR past reflects the fact that, in spite of their earlier, unambiguous rejection of the old order, many former East Germans believe in retrospect that in impor-tant ways — that is, in providing material security and in promoting cer-tain social values they find missing in their new, Western-dominated envi-ronment — the old order was a success. The second puzzle also reflects easterners' profound disappointment that their exaggerated expectations

of the benefits of joining the West have not been fulfilled. These expectations were, ironically, nourished for years by the regime of the Socialist
Unity Party of Germany (SED; the East German Communist Party). For
while the SED maintained a system of rule whose repressiveness and
resistance to reform were surpassed in Eastern Europe only in Romania, it
also cultivated a relationship with the capitalist FRG that brought with it a
growing dependency. From the beginning, the GDR had been forced to
define itself in relation to its formidable western neighbor. What began as
an intense ideological rivalry, with the GDR's leadership determined to
demonstrate the superiority of its socialist course to that of the capitalist
West, ended as a form of dependence that, if economically useful and
perhaps vital to the East German state, proved to be politically and psy-
chologically subversive of that state's authority. The regime's efforts to
insulate East German society, through the policies of *Abgrenzung* (demarcation), from the negative influences growing out of the web of economic
and political ties it had forged to the FRG proved a failure. It is especially
its dependence on the West which distinguished the GDR from its Communist neighbors and makes the legacies of its forty years of Communist
rule in many respects distinctive.

Political Legacies

Like its neighbors, East Germany developed its own political culture
under Communist rule, although it was not precisely the political culture the regime intended, influenced as it was by elements of the pre-
Communist past, defense mechanisms developed in response to the dictatorship, and exposure to the West German media.[3] Many of its surviving
components resemble those that have been observed in other formerly
Communist states. Residents of the former East Germany today, concludes Jürgen Kocka on the basis of recent surveys, "seem to expect more
from 'the state,' in terms of securing economic growth, stabilizing prices,
and guaranteeing employment." They hold to "old-fashioned virtues
such as obedience, orderliness, modesty, cleanliness, and duty," and are
less enamored of "hedonistic, postmaterialistic, and individualistic values"
than are West Germans.[4] The relationship of the individual to the state
under communism was (and to some extent still is) an ambivalent one;
citizens came to take much of the state's paternalism for granted, but at
the same time sought to shield themselves from its efforts to mobilize
popular enthusiasm and punish deviance, by withdrawing into their pri-

vate "niches."[5] The longing for harmony and consensus and the fear of political conflict and competition once identified by Ralf Dahrendorf as hallmarks of the German political character seem to have been reinforced in easterners by the Communist experience.[6]

■ ■ ■ ■

The institutions of Communist rule, which have now with few exceptions been abolished, have nevertheless left their own legacy. Politically the GDR was dominated by its Marxist-Leninist ruling party, the SED, to an even greater extent than most of its East European neighbors. Nearly one of every five adult citizens belonged to the SED, and almost all of those in the appropriate age bracket were members of its young people's auxiliary, the Free German Youth. The SED's effectiveness in suppressing dissent within its own ranks while penetrating and closely monitoring the rest of society probably exceeded that of other East European ruling parties. The Party was not immune to the forces that eroded the authority of its sister parties, however, or to the unusually strong influences of the West. In the 1970s and 1980s the regime became less overtly repressive than it earlier had been, granting more space to its citizens for apathy and routine grumbling, if not for open dissent. Even though this modest relaxation appears unimpressive in comparison with the liberalization of rule in Hungary and Poland in the same period, it had considerable value for many East German citizens and probably owes something to the FRG's policies of *Ostpolitik*.[7]

The SED survives today under a different name, the Party of Democratic Socialism (PDS). But it is hardly the same party it was, having lost not only its power but most of the property and financial resources it formerly commanded. While most of its members and many of its voters are holdovers from SED days, its old leadership is gone, replaced by ostensible reformers drawn largely from the middle ranks of the old Party.[8] Its policies are those of an opposition party of the democratic left. It benefits electorally from GDR nostalgia and from the frustrations that unity has produced, but for the present it is excluded by the other parties from government participation. While in danger of losing its federal Bundestag seats in the 1994 national elections, it remains a significant opposition force in the eastern German states, and it is not inconceivable that one day, like the Polish and Hungarian post-Communists, it could return to power in some of them.

The SED was aided in its exercise of social control by the Stasi, the intrusive and pervasive state security police. Using as many as seven hundred thousand informers ("unofficial collaborators," or IM, as they were referred to in the organization's files), as well as by eighty thousand full-time personnel,[9] the Stasi thoroughly penetrated church and other opposition circles. The vast files the Stasi left behind (including dossiers on 5 million East Germans and 2 million West Germans) have been a source of bitter controversy in the postunification period. Individuals examining their files have discovered that close friends, relatives, and on occasion even spouses had dutifully reported their activities to the police. While some identified as "IM" deny that they were even aware of this status, and many dispute the accuracy of the reports, others have viewed the files as an all-but-infallible instrument for separating the *Täter* (perpetrators) from the *Opfer* (victims) of the Communist period. Fear of the Stasi undoubtedly weakened the GDR's opposition and inhibited the emergence of a critical dialogue, either within the Party or in intellectual circles, that might conceivably have saved the regime from its gravest errors of policy. In the post-Communist period the Stasi legacy has sown continuing distrust and has aggravated the problem of finding competent easterners to fill important positions. The acrimony of the Stasi controversy, like that of similar controversies elsewhere in Eastern Europe, reflects in some measure an unhappy reality: that most East Germans felt obliged, or chose, to make greater or lesser compromises with the regime — compromises that many would now prefer to deny or repress.

There is irony in the fact that the former "satellite" parties of the GDR, most notably the Christian Democratic Union (CDU), have furnished many of the occupants of government and parliamentary positions in the new states. These parties — the CDU, the Liberal Democratic Party (LDPD), the Democratic Farmers' Party (DBD), and the National Democratic Party (NDPD) — prior to 1989 had all proclaimed their unqualified support of the policies of the SED and of its "leading role" in East German society. In practical terms, they served as outlets for those who wished to fulfill their political activism quota but preferred not to join the SED, or who were not wanted (mostly for reasons of social background or association with the Nazi regime) by that organization. In spite of initial misgivings, the West German CDU and Free Democratic Party (FDP) forged electoral alliances with the East German CDU and LDPD, respectively, in early 1990 and subsequently merged with them. The electoral success of the alliances then placed many of the former *Blockflöten* (as critics disparagingly labeled former satellite party officials)[10] in office; some subsequently had to leave because of awkward revelations about their pasts or simple incompetence. The NDPD later joined the liberals and the DBD the CDU.

Political dissent was never entirely crushed in the GDR, but even sympathetic Western commentators tended to minimize its significance, especially when comparing it to Poland's Solidarity movement and the extensive counterculture that movement helped inspire, or even to Czechoslovakia's well-publicized Charter 77. Yet in the fall of 1989 East German dissidents suddenly found themselves "swimming on the crest of the waves" of a largely spontaneous popular revolution that brought down the Communist regime and opened the way to unification with West Germany.[11] Within months of their rise to prominence, however, most of the dissidents found themselves again on the outside, rejected at the polls and ruefully observing the takeover of the revolution by West German elites. Instead of the democratic, reformed socialist order most of them had advocated, they witnessed the absorption of the former GDR into the Federal Republic, and the replacement of the laws, political structures, and economic system of the former with those of the latter.

Nearly all dissent in the GDR in its last years operated under the shelter of the Evangelical Church.[12] The regime's decision to seek a modus vivendi with the church in the hope of co-opting it, culminating in Erich Honecker's meeting with Bishop Albrecht Schönherr in 1978, made such a protective role possible. The survival of dissent even when church-state relations deteriorated in 1988 and 1989 was undoubtedly also due to the regime's reluctance to jeopardize its special economic arrangements with the West German government (which used the West and East German churches in pursuit of its policies, e.g., as a conduit for "buying free" East German political prisoners).

The church-state understanding, although interpreted differently by the two sides, opened up a limited space for the activities of independent groups devoted to peace, the environment, and other causes. These groups, which came to number in the hundreds, remained small and fragmented, and none of their leaders attained anything like the international prominence of a Havel or a Wałęsa.[13] While harassed by the authorities and subjected to intense surveillance, they were ultimately tolerated. Arguably, their very ability to make use of the church's facilities and infrastructure, along with the publicity afforded by the West German media, gave them greater access to ordinary East Germans than has commonly been assumed. The very fact that the thousands, then tens of thousands, and finally hundreds of thousands of demonstrators who brought down the regime began their marches following the regular Monday Protestant "peace services" in Leipzig suggests the catalytic function performed by church-protected dissent.

The organizations that formed during 1989 — New Forum, Democracy Now, and Democratic Awakening — and that sought to coordinate the mounting popular revolution appeared for a brief time to be the authentic spokespersons for a newly liberated people. They played a pivotal role in the government-opposition roundtable that managed the first weeks of transition and agreed on the terms of the March elections. But they saw their goal — the creation of a grass-roots democratic, reformed socialist, and still independent GDR — rapidly recede in the face of demands for quick unification; and politically they were overwhelmed by the entrance of the major West German parties into the election campaign. A number of their leaders, however, remain prominent figures in eastern German political life, as members of governments or parliaments (e.g., Rainer Eppelmann or Wolfgang Ullmann) and/or as independent voices speaking on behalf of a frustrated population (e.g., Jens Reich). Institutionally, the alliance between Bündnis-90 (the political party that grew out of the opposition movement of the GDR) and the Greens is the inheritor of the protest movement, and is represented in the Bundestag, the state parliaments of eastern Germany, and many local governments.[14]

Here, however, we need also to take note of the effects of the regime's policy of encouraging the most able and outspoken of its critics to leave the country — on occasion by expelling them outright, but more often by granting them permission to leave and applying economic or other pressures to persuade them to do so, or by arresting them and then releasing them to West Germany in exchange for a substantial payment. This policy, dissidents generally believe, weakened their ability to be effective;[15] it also deprived East Germany of many who might have assumed leadership positions once the old regime had fallen. However, the policy probably facilitated the formation of linkages between the dissidents and the outside world and encouraged ever-growing numbers of East Germans to seek exit permits for themselves, another catalytic element in the ultimate destabilization of the regime.

Economic Legacies

It is in the economic sphere that our first puzzle appears to be most demanding of an answer. Was the supposed "economic success" of the GDR, celebrated extravagantly by its own propaganda but also seemingly confirmed in the more measured appraisals of Western analysts (some of whom suggested that the GDR's per capita GNP exceeded that of Britain or Italy), nothing but smoke and mirrors?[16] The short answer appears to be that, although much of the GDR's economic reputation was based on the regime's faulty and falsified statistics, the country's technological level and standard of living were probably superior to those of all other Communist countries.[17] They were based, however, on crumbling economic foundations and almost certainly could not have been sustained. The GDR's decaying physical plant, inadequate infrastructure, and low productivity, and the sacrifice of the environment to production goals, would have proven heavy burdens for economic reformers to overcome even had the GDR remained independent. Forced, with almost no time permitted for adjustment, to compete in West Germany's advanced capitalist economy, even the fittest East German enterprises had little chance of surviving after unification.

The blame for the GDR's economic distress is normally assigned to the inherent infirmities of Communist central planning or to the GDR political leaders' reckless disregard for economic rationality. To these, however, must be added the GDR's unfavorable starting point, and international circumstances over which the country's leaders had little control. After World War II, heavy reparations deliveries to the Soviet Union delayed the beginning of economic recovery in the GDR at a time when Marshall Plan aid was helping to lay the groundwork for the West German "miracle." The Stalinist model of economic development imposed on the GDR forced it to build an industrial structure inappropriate to its limited resources; Soviet demands and economic isolation from the West required that it produce a range of goods far too wide for a small country. Cold war strategic trade restrictions denied the GDR access to advanced Western technology, while the obligations stemming from its membership in the Soviet-led Council for Mutual Economic Assistance (CMEA) also impeded technological advancement. By the 1980s, rising Soviet prices for oil (reflecting the 1973 and 1979 OPEC price increases) and reductions in oil deliveries forced the GDR to become still more reliant on its only significant domestic source of fuel, its dwindling supplies of highly polluting brown coal. The Polish crisis of 1980–81 led to a cutoff of Western credits and the threat of default. The GDR responded with desperate measures: slashing investments in order to maintain consumption, and selling whatever it could to the West even if only a fraction of production costs could be recovered.[18] A remarkable secret commercial and financial network led by Alexander Schalck-Golodowski raised desperately needed hard currency in the West through such means as arms sales, currency speculation, and the sale of East German art and antiques. The regime also negotiated with the conservative Bavarian leader Franz-Josef Strauss to obtain West German credits of DM 1 billion in 1983 and DM 950 million in 1984.

These credits supplemented more longstanding forms of de facto West German support for the GDR's economy. Special arrangements for "inter-German trade" (dating to the Berlin Agreement of 1951) permitted East German goods tariff-free access to West German markets and provided for an interest-free credit line (the "swing") to cover imbalances. In addition, the FRG paid the GDR subsidies (largely in hard currency) for the use of transit routes to Berlin, for entry fees for West German visitors to East Germany, for excess postal costs, and, as noted earlier, for the release of political prisoners. Private gifts and tourism expenditures by West Germans and support by the West German Evangelical Church for East German church projects added to the total. The combined value of these benefits was estimated in the mid-1980s to be some $1.5 billion annually.[19] While still only a fraction of the GDR's estimated GNP, they may well have been vital to the country's economic survival. In particular, they helped the GDR to maintain (or, after 1980, recover) its standing with Western creditors and allowed it to overcome many of the bottlenecks that plagued other Communist economies. They came at the cost of a level of Western cultural penetration, however, that ultimately helped lead to the regime's undoing.

Former Politburo members and economic officials have also put much of the blame for the GDR's economic difficulties on what they view as the economic ignorance of Erich Honecker and the reckless arrogance of his economic "czar" Günter Mittag. The critics point to the two men's alleged refusal to take the GDR's escalating foreign debt seriously, to Honecker's insistence on pursuing an expensive mass housing program, the centerpiece of his regime's repeatedly invoked "unity of social and economic policy," and to both men's preoccupation with the development of the GDR's microelectronics industry.[20] They charge that the emphasis on housing and microelectronics led to a grievous neglect of other vitally important sectors of the GDR economy and ultimately to economic crisis. In defense of Honecker and Mittag, however, it might be said that the stress on solving the housing problem (however overblown the claims for its success)[21] addressed an issue that had typically been a source of deep discontent in other Communist societies. The attention given to microelectronics also appears more rational if one recognizes its original premises: continuing East German membership in the CMEA, for which East Germany was the most advanced supplier of such goods, and continuing denial of access to advanced Western technology. Once Germany was united, however, the GDR's microelectronics industry was unable to compete with Western producers, and its massive investment lost nearly all its value. Moreover, the very fact that Honecker and Mittag effectively shut themselves off from criticism by their own economics experts probably hastened the regime's demise. The problem, in other words, may have been not simply the deficiencies of central planning per se, but those of planning that was devoid of any effective mechanisms of political accountability.[22]

The legacy of the GDR's economic policies — and, one must add, also of the haste with which, and the specific policies by which, German economic union was consummated — is a landscape littered with closed factories, dying forests, polluted waterways, and masses of unemployed workers. Industrial production in eastern Germany had fallen to one-third of its 1989 level by the end of 1991, and the region produced less than 7 percent of Germany's GNP in that year. When the number of people forced to retire early, doing "short-time" work, working in government "work-creation" projects, or enrolled in work-training programs is added to the number of those officially jobless, the total approaches 40 percent or more of the workforce. Most surviving industry in eastern Germany has been sold to western German firms; such firms also dominate the growing retail and service sectors. While there will be islands of advanced technology, such as the new Volkswagen and Opel plants, and the infrastructure is being rapidly modernized with the help of government funding, the economic future of the region seems to be as a poorer dependent of western Germany, where most ownership, capital, and research will remain concentrated.[23]

Societal Legacies

Even though eastern Germany, unlike most of Eastern Europe, was already industrialized when the Communists took power, the new rulers dramatically reshaped the country's social structure. The bourgeoisie was virtually eliminated, except for a small retail and artisan sector; the peasantry was collectivized; and the industrial working class—the ostensible new ruling class—was enlarged. The GDR claimed that the proportion of skilled workers in its population was twice that in the FRG.[24] Many, however, were employed in obsolescent or highly polluting industries or in industries that were greatly overstaffed, and had to face unemployment following unification.

Perhaps the most significant change in social structure which accompanied the Communist takeover was the creation of a sizable, educated white-collar stratum of Party and state functionaries (including educators and ideological officials; cadres and Party organizational specialists; the "technical intelligentsia"—scientists, managers, and economic administrators; and the security police). Either because their jobs became obsolete, because of complicity with the departed regime, or simply because of their excessive numbers, many in this group became unemployable after economic and political union. Others, however, joined the reemerging bourgeoisie by participating in "management buyouts" of smaller state firms, or by being hired by newly arrived Western companies.

Women in the GDR participated in the labor force in larger numbers than in any other country: in 1983, 47 percent of the workforce was female. To maintain this level of employment without jeopardizing the birth rate, the Communist state provided special benefits for mothers with children: shorter workweeks, generous provisions for maternity leave (up to eighteen months at some 80% of full pay), nearly universal kindergartens, and extensive pre-school and after-school care facilities. While East German women complained of the double burden of work and housekeeping (they continued to perform 87% of the latter), combining career and family came to be the normal state of affairs for them. Reunification brought unwelcome changes for many. Layoffs hit women disproportionately; nearly two-thirds of the unemployed are female. The availability of inexpensive kindergartens and other forms of child care declined sharply; most had been sponsored by economic enterprises, which (if they survived at all) hurried to shed these responsibilities in the new economic environment. The GDR's generous provisions for abortion gave way to a compromise with the more restrictive West German law passed by the Bundestag; the compromise was, in turn, struck down by the Federal Constitutional Court. Under its ruling, most abortions are formally illegal, although in practice they will not be prosecuted; they can no longer be funded by public insurance, however. In spite of these restrictive policies, the birth rate among women in eastern Germany has fallen to half its level under the old regime, and is substantially below that of western Germany — a striking indicator of women's altered status.[25]

Like other Communist regimes, the SED sought throughout its existence to cultivate the support of youth, not only through the educational system but also through a network of official youth organizations and the cultural and recreational facilities they maintained. Although youth alienation earlier had become serious enough to be a theme of GDR literature and film, notably in the writings of Ulrich Plenzdorf, the respected Institute for Youth Research in Leipzig consistently reported that a majority of East German young people felt "strongly tied" to the GDR — until 1985. Between that year and 1988 came a dramatic decline in support — from 51 percent to 18 percent in the case of apprentices, from 57 percent to 19 percent in the case of young workers, and from 70 percent to 34 percent in the case of students.[26] The timing of this disaffection (which probably mirrored that of other groups in the population) offers clues to some of the reasons for the regime's demise: the impact of Gorbachev and his proposed reforms, and the expansion of east-west travel opportunities during the period. A high proportion of those who left the GDR, legally or illegally, in the late 1980s were young skilled workers.[27]

On a different level, the punks, skinheads, and neo-Nazis whose activities have attracted international attention since unification were already a visible phenomenon in the waning days of Communist rule. However, the disappearance of the structures created by the regime for youth socialization, recreation, and entertainment (such as the paramilitary "Societies for Sport and Technology" and clubs and discos sponsored by the Free German Youth [FDJ; the Communist youth organization]), coupled with the fear or reality of unemployment, have left many young people in eastern Germany at loose ends.[28] Their susceptibility to the lures of the radical right becomes somewhat easier to understand in this context.

Another group that enjoyed special, albeit ambivalent, attention from the Communist regime was the intellectuals. On the one hand, promi-

nent filmmakers, actors, artists, musicians, and especially writers, such as
Christa Wolf and Heiner Müller, were the source of considerable prestige
for the GDR. The regime rewarded such intellectuals by allowing them
significantly greater scope for critical expression than it granted East German social scientists and journalists. It was often said that by far the most
perceptive analyses of the problems of East German society were to be
found in its literature;[29] accordingly, cultural figures acquired an importance for ordinary citizens which they normally do not enjoy in the West.
Predictably, many intellectuals sought to test the limits of East German
censorship and of the tolerance of the regime. Some, if they were refused
permission to publish their work in the GDR, had it published in West
Germany instead, from whence its contents could be transmitted back to
the GDR, either through smuggling or via the electronic media. The
result was a series of confrontations between the artists and the state, and
the departure, either forced or voluntary, of some of the country's most
talented writers and other intellectuals for the West.

It is my own view that the estrangement between the intellectuals and
the state was a significant element in the state's progressive loss of credibility. West German critics and some of the East German writers who
fled or were expelled from the GDR disagree, however, and argue that
figures such as Wolf and Müller in effect lent their prestige to the regime
by continuing to write under its auspices, however many conflicts they
may have had with it.[30] The acerbity of the controversy has undoubtedly
contributed to the decline in the attention given the arts and literature in
the new states, although similar declines have been reported throughout
the former Communist bloc. The writers concerned have continued to
publish, however, and remain significant voices speaking on behalf of
many of their former compatriots.

It needs to be emphasized how profoundly East German society was
influenced by West German society, even while continuing to be very
different from it. The East Germans' experience of the West was intense,
but largely vicarious. Much of it was transmitted by West German television and radio, which were watched or listened to by nearly all of the
country's population in preference to the GDR's own services. Some came
in the form of the millions of West German (and West Berlin) visitors, the
gift packages they brought or mailed, and the telephone calls that went
across the inter-German border. The East German retirees (men over
sixty-five, women over sixty) who were permitted to travel to the West

were joined in the GDR's last years by millions of younger East Germans. The growing number of sports, cultural, educational, and economic exchanges, and the "sister-city" arrangements that were among the fruits of Ostpolitik also left their mark.

The Communist regime, largely abandoning its Abgrenzung policies of the 1970s, if anything came to encourage and abet the spread of Western influence.[31] East German television programming was adapted to meet the Western competition — for example, by showing a greater number of Western crime dramas. The GDR developed its own, not untalented, rock bands. The regime sought vainly to respond to rising East German consumerism, fed by the West German media, and established Intershops for the sale of Western goods for West German Deutschmarks. The Deutschmark became, in some sectors, the country's "second currency," indispensable for obtaining certain scarce services. Even the regime's repeated insistence in its economic rhetoric on striving for "world standards" (read: Western standards) reinforced the image of the West as a measuring rod for success.

If the GDR was in fact pervaded by Western influence, why, one might justifiably ask, have former East Germans had such difficulty in adjusting to their country's actual accession to the FRG? In part, the difficulty lies in the fact that the vicarious experience that most had of the West was inevitably a distorted one; it could not be the same as the actual experience of becoming part of the West. Moreover, East Germans, while becoming immersed in many aspects of West German culture, continued to take for granted the paternalism of the socialist state: the absence of unemployment, the subsidized prices, and the various social services and protections the state offered. Once unification came, they also discovered that much of what the West seemed to offer, especially in material terms, would not be immediately available to them. Hence the continuing high rate of migration from east to west, which by the end of 1992 had reduced the population of eastern Germany to less than 16 million.

Environmental Legacies

By the last years of the Communist regime, protection of the environment had become an issue of growing political significance in the GDR. A rather inept raid conducted by the Stasi in November 1987 on the "Environmental Library" maintained by dissident groups in the Zion Church in East Berlin gave rise to a cause célèbre that was highly publicized in the

West and served as something of a catalyst for the further development of
the opposition. The library, which had opened in September 1986 with a
"few dozen" books (some of them smuggled in from the West by Green
Bundestag deputies), became the home of the *Umweltblätter* (a more-or-
less regular underground publication on environmental and other dissident themes) and a site for lectures and discussions.[32] In the course of the
following years, a number of similar libraries were established throughout
the GDR.

The regime looked upon the unofficial environmental movement
with undisguised suspicion but acknowledged the movement's appeal by
creating its own official "Society for Nature and the Environment," which
had some sixty thousand members in 1986.[33] Concrete data on the environment were regarded as state secrets to be protected against exposure
to the "class enemy"[34] — thus the emphasis placed by unofficial groups on
simply providing information — but the seriousness of the GDR's pollution problems could not be easily concealed from a public breathing the
foul air or living close to forests whose trees had been stripped of their
leaves. Public consciousness was heightened still more by the Chernobyl
accident; as in other spheres, the influence of Western media and the
example of Western environmental activism contributed importantly to
shaping popular awareness. Surprisingly, the GDR possessed an impressive body of environmental law, but in practice ecological considerations
nearly always gave way to the putative imperatives of production.[35]

According to Western experts, sulfur dioxide emissions in the GDR
were the highest in Europe, owing to the country's heavy reliance on its
primary domestic resource, brown coal, for electricity generation and
heating. Air pollution was the most serious in the industrial south of the
GDR, particularly the areas around Leipzig, Halle, Cottbus, and Bitter-
feld, the center of the chemical industry. Statistics on lowered life expec-
tancy and the frequency of heart disease and respiratory disease in these
areas suggested some of the human consequences of the problem. Other
human consequences followed from the scarring of the landscape and
the destruction of villages which resulted from attempts to reach the
dwindling reserves of coal.[36] The acid rain produced by air pollution was
largely responsible for the destruction of the country's forests; the damage
was said in a United Nations report to be the worst in the world.[37] For
some time the regime looked upon nuclear power as a way of escaping
its fateful dependence on brown coal, but the Chernobyl accident and

difficulties with Soviet equipment deliveries prevented any rapid conversion; shortly after unification the major East German reactor complex, at Greifswald, had to be closed for safety reasons.

The pollution of the GDR's rivers, especially the Elbe, the Werra, and the Saale, through the dumping of chemical wastes and other wastes was severe. Still more damage to rivers, streams, and groundwater resulted from the heavy utilization of chemicals, including DDT, in agriculture. Not surprisingly, there were many inadequately secured toxic waste dumps; waste was even imported from West Berlin and West Germany in exchange for hard currency, and deposited in such places as Schönberg, in the northern GDR. Open-pit uranium mining carried out under Soviet auspices in the south of the country is said to have "left many square miles of irradiated soil that would cost billions of marks to clean up."[38] Another, rather different, environmental problem that plagued East German workers was noise pollution. Noise at some six hundred thousand work sites was said to have exceeded permissible levels as of 1982; loss of hearing was a frequent consequence.[39]

Perhaps the single clear benefit that the deindustrialization of the former GDR since unification has brought has been the reduction of air and water pollution levels, since many of the "dirtiest" plants have been closed. New, cleaner power plants are under construction or planned, and others will be outfitted with emission-reduction equipment. The production of brown coal briquets with more than 1 percent sulfur is to be halted by the end of 1994. However, it is reported that some Western businessmen, in order to escape rigorous environmental restrictions in the West, have gone to the eastern states in the expectation that the desperate shortage of jobs will mean looser regulation.[40] As the relatively poor showing of the Greens in elections in the eastern states suggests, in the ongoing struggle for economic resources the repair of the environment in eastern Germany is unlikely to receive high priority.

Conclusions

Adapting the matrimonial metaphor that was popular in the Western press at the time of German unification, we can say that the formal ceremony by which the two Germanies were formally joined in October 1990, after a rather longstanding and sometimes difficult affair, was something of a shotgun wedding. As so often happens in these cases, neither partner proved to be well prepared for marriage, in spite of their lengthy experience together. More than three years after the ceremony, the two still face serious difficulties in understanding one another, and in spite of optimistic pronouncements from both sides the long-term prospects for marital bliss remain clouded.

Assessing the legacy of Communist rule in the GDR is correspondingly difficult. "Socialism in the colors of the GDR" (to use a slogan from the waning days of the regime) came to be an odd mixture of one-party rule, Marxist-Leninist rhetoric, and a panoply of concessions to Western consumerism and cultural values. In effect, the regime promised its people all the material comforts and cultural diversity of advanced capitalism without capitalism's insecurities and social injustices. The regime's inability to deliver on the promise became increasingly obvious in the late 1980s, and more and more East Germans voted — first figuratively (through mounting numbers of applications for exit visas and, in the summer of 1989, flight across the Hungarian border or into West German embassies) and then literally (in March 1990) — for advanced capitalism itself. Both "votes" were born of desperation, first individual and then collective, and were accompanied by unrealistic expectations and the temporary repression of many social attitudes and values that had been instilled by four decades of life under Communist rule.

The consequence has been a severe crisis of adjustment on both sides. Instead of "two states — one nation," a favored formula of the years of Ostpolitik, the new Germany must now be described as "one state — two societies." "Despite efforts to incorporate and integrate the East," writes Kocka, "a separate GDR identity seems to have been revived, defensively and obstinately documenting the present limits of Westernization."[41]

Of course, the pain of adjustment is distributed highly unevenly, as it has been throughout all of Eastern Europe, with women, the old (and the prematurely retired), and those in the most economically depressed regions suffering disproportionately. For others, especially those educated young people who managed to escape severe political encumbrances, there are opportunities unthinkable under the old order. Among the former intelligentsia of all ages, to be sure, a great majority belonged to the SED and/or had connections to the Stasi; in most cases, their often considerable talents have effectively been lost to the new states.

The legacy of East German communism for Germany as a whole and for post–cold war Europe also deserves attention. The economic decline and the social and political malaise of the enlarged Federal Republic of

Germany must be attributed in considerable measure to that nation's inability to integrate the old GDR into the new Germany. It is not at all clear how soon the country will emerge from its difficulties — whether resurgent rightist nationalism can be contained, the rise in unemployment in both parts of the country reversed, or the loss of credibility of the major political parties stemmed. For Western Europe, the uncertain reliability of the German state and of the Deutschmark as the anchors of the European Union is particularly worrisome. For Eastern Europe, whose leaders once feared German economic domination, the reduced German capacity to act as a source of economic stimulus and as an economic and political bridge to the West is unsettling.[42] As so often in the past, "the German problem" has again turned into a "European problem."

8

Poland

Andrzej Korbonski

One of the most frequently observed phenomena in twentieth-century Europe has been the need for new ruling elites in various political systems to deal with the legacy of the past. The history of the past eighty years or so is replete with examples showing the difficulty that political leaders in various national settings have had in coming to terms with the inheritance bequeathed to them by their predecessors. One needs only to mention the case of the Bolshevik leaders in the wake of the 1917 revolution, having to deal with the Tsarist past; the Weimar democratic politicians after 1918 trying to overcome the legacy of Prussian authoritarianism; and more recently, the leaders of the Federal Republic of Germany seeking to minimize the effects of twelve years of Nazi rule.

Needless to say, Eastern Europe has also provided an excellent example of a region struggling with its own past. In fact, one can distinguish three separate stages in the sociopolitical and economic development of the area, where the problem of overcoming the legacy of the past has become top priority for the rulers of the various East European countries.

The first stage began with the Treaty of Versailles, in 1919, which gave birth to a number of new states and changed the frontiers of several existing countries, thus redrawing radically the map of Eastern Europe for generations to come. The record shows that the new ruling elites, especially in such countries as Czechoslovakia, Poland, and Yugoslavia, which were created on the ruins of four historical empires destroyed in World War I — the Austro-Hungarian Empire, the German Empire, the Ottoman Empire, and the Russian Empire — labored mightily and only partly successfully to build new nations and states after centuries of subjugation. Poland, which is the object of this essay, provided a perfect example of a country in which the process of state- and nation-building simply could not be accomplished in the two decades that separated the two world wars.

The second stage covered the period after the end of World War II and coincided with the process of Communist seizure of power in the region. Here again, it can be shown that the new Polish Communist elites, imposed on the country by the incoming Red Army, had to face the difficult task of eliminating the effects of the legacy of the past. There is no need to go into details of this endeavor: the methods used by the Polish Communists are well known and have been ably discussed in the literature. However, the interesting conclusion is that, as in the case of the post–World War I failed attempts to eradicate the past, the Communist leaders quickly discovered that overcoming the historical past proved to be most difficult and frustrating.

The third stage began, of course, with the miracle year 1989 and has continued until today. It is the purpose of this essay to discuss, first of all, the legacy of more than forty years of Communist rule which is faced by the new elites in Poland, the ways and means of dealing with the different aspects of the inheritance, and the possible success or failure of these efforts.

For the purpose of this essay, I shall define the legacy as both a set of legal-institutional structures and a set of psychological and/or behavioral variables which emerged as a result of more than four decades of Communist rule. Both the institutional and the behavioral components will be examined under four broad headings: the political legacy, the societal legacy, the economic legacy, and the environmental legacy. It should be made clear at the outset that there is a considerable overlap between these categories and that they are being used here mainly to make the discussion more systematic. Another caveat concerns the impact of external or exogenous variables, such as, for example, the influence of the Soviet Union or, more recently, the influence exerted by Western Europe and the United States. Although a comprehensive examination of the Communist legacy would demand a consideration of Soviet influence, as illustrated by the impact of the Warsaw Pact (WTO) and the Council for Mutual Economic Assistance (CMEA), for reasons of space only the purely internal or domestic aspects of that legacy will be analyzed here.

Political Legacies

In discussing the political legacy of communism in Poland I focus on one of its aspects, the institutional structure, and leave the discussion of psychological and behavioral variables to the next section.

The sharp difference between the systemic change in Poland in 1919 and the change seventy years later was that in the former case the new Polish rulers were essentially faced with an institutional tabula rasa left behind by the three partitioning powers that had governed the country over the previous 123 years. This meant that in addition to building a nation, the new rulers had to start from scratch and write a constitution, organize a government and public administration, and hold parliamentary elections. Although in 1919 Poland could boast of having a fairly numerous political class and also a rather well-developed multiparty system that covered the conventional right-left spectrum, neither of them proved particularly helpful in propelling the country in the direction of political stabilization and institution building.

When the Communists arrived on the scene in 1945, they were faced with an easier task. The country was in shock following the nearly six years of German occupation, the political class was decimated, and the population at large was tired and demoralized, yearning for a return to normalcy, almost at any price. Using a combination of carrot and (mostly) stick, the new Communist rulers succeeded in accomplishing the process of institutional transformation in an impressively short time.

In contrast, the post-Communist elites in 1989 were saddled with a most difficult task. One could argue that their task would have been easier if the country they had inherited from the Communists had been in a state of institutional collapse. But this was far from being the case. The new leaders had to deal with an institutional structure that was highly developed and complex, and because of the suddenness of the Communist downfall essentially untouched, reflecting more than forty years of institution building. The key question was what to do with it.

Before discussing the institutional legacy in greater detail, one unique aspect of the Polish situation ought to be mentioned. As is well known, the first non-Communist government in Central and Eastern Europe was formed as a result of a compromise between the Communists and the opposition, reached during the so-called roundtable negotiations, held in early 1989. The agreement produced several key institutional changes, including the creation of the office of the presidency of the republic; the replacement of the Soviet-imposed council of state; the addition of an upper chamber, the senate, making the Polish parliament a bicameral one; and a change in the existing electoral law, guaranteeing the opposition 35 percent of the seats in the lower chamber, the Sejm. In other words, important institutional restructuring was accomplished while the Communists were still formally in power. Nonetheless, the standard Communist institutions remained largely in place and had to be dealt with by the new leaders.

Starting with the political parties, there was, first of all, the former ruling party, the Polish United Worker Party (PZPR), which only a short time earlier had enjoyed a virtual monopoly of power and which managed to attract an impressive percentage of the Polish population to its ranks. Through its *nomenklatura* the party controlled all the commanding heights of the state, including the government, the economy, the media, and the apparatus of coercion: the military and the police. In addition, there were two satellite political parties — the United Peasant Party (ZSL) and the Democratic Party (SD) — that acted as "transmission belts" for the Communists, together with a plethora of other organizations (labor unions, youth groups, and others) that were supposed to express the "pluralistic" character of the old political system.

But this was only a part of the institutional legacy in Poland. Unlike the other countries in the region, at the time of the Communist collapse Poland possessed an impressive anti-Communist opposition, which had been institutionalized since the mid-1970s. For example, there was the Workers' Defense Committee (KOR), and especially since 1980 there was Solidarity (Solidarność). Although by the end of the 1980s the opposition was outlawed and severely reduced in numbers, its hard core managed to survive, and it was expected to supply the political elite that was poised to take over from the Communists defeated in the elections of June 1989.

Our survey of the institutional legacy would not be complete without a mention, albeit a brief one, of two other powerful institutions, the labor unions and the Roman Catholic Church. On the eve of the Communist downfall, the labor movement was badly divided. On the one hand, there were the remnants of the once-powerful Solidarity, deeply hurt by the imposition of martial law in December 1981 and by internal conflicts. Outlawed and persecuted, Solidarity barely managed to survive underground, yet survive it did, helped undoubtedly by the symbolism and memories of its glorious past. Its capacity to organize two waves of strikes in 1988 which led directly to the roundtable negotiations of early 1989, was a good testimony of its ability to remain an important institutional actor on the Polish political scene. Solidarity was opposed by the All-Polish Association of Labor Unions (OPZZ), which included members of the old pro-Communist unions who refused to join Solidarity, reinforced by former Solidarity members looking for an institutional affiliation after the outlawing of their own union. Numerically stronger than its banned rival and closely identified with the ruling Communist Party, with its leader sitting on the latter's politburo, OPZZ refused to always follow the party line, and at the end of the 1980s it began to behave more as a traditional pressure group, articulating its members' interests, than as a "transmission belt" eager and willing to be at the Party's beck and call.

Throughout most of its post–World War II history, the Catholic Church could claim that it alone carried the onus of resistance against the Communists. However, the birth of Solidarity in 1980 deprived the church of that particular monopoly, marking the beginning of a subtle yet unmistakable competition between the two centers of anti-Communist opposition. The banning of Solidarity in the wake of martial law partly restored the church to its previous privileged position, but for various reasons (which owing to a lack of space cannot be discussed here), in 1989 the stature of the church was somewhat tarnished. Still, it remained a powerful institutional actor, and its strength was boosted by the election, in 1978, of a Polish pope, John Paul II.

Thus, the Communist political legacy in Poland in its institutional aspects presented a mixed picture. In contrast to what occurred in some of the other countries in the region, in Poland certain key institutional changes took place while the Communists were still in control. However, the leaders who took over the reins of the government from the Communists had little experience and precious few resources of their own, and had little choice but to approach the task of institutional restructuring most gingerly.

Societal Legacies

Here I want to examine the psychological and/or behavioral aspects of Communist legacy in Poland which may be subsumed under the heading "destruction of civil society."[1] Although the notion of civil society can in many respects be viewed as "highly unclear and contested," there seems to be a consensus that civil society represents a "web of autonomous associations, independent of the state, which [bind] citizens together in matters of common concern."[2] Other definitions emphasize the voluntary character of civil society and its ability to occupy public space between the state and the masses (or, as some prefer, the society at large).[3] Still other writers, in search of greater realism, simply tend to identify civil society with the opposition, with a "second society," with the market, or finally, with both "domestic" and "political" societies.[4]

The concept of civil society came into bloom in the wake of Solidarity and its demise following the imposition of martial law in December 1981.[5] From then on, Poland became an object of several studies extolling the virtues of civil society and its role in weakening the fabric of the Communist state.[6] Indeed, one may agree that at some point in early 1981, the situation in Poland easily fit the image of an embryonic civil society. Solidarity itself had quickly become a mass organization including more than one-third of the adult population. Other organizations representing peasants, students, intellectuals, and workers who for various reasons refused to join Solidarity further filled the space vacated by the state. They became authentic articulators of individual and group interests, acting also as intermediaries between the regime, their membership, and the masses. However, the ease with which the military rulers were able to assert themselves in December 1981 testified to the apparent fragility and impotence of Solidarity. The latter, which embodied the idea of civil society, disintegrated quickly when faced with pressure from the state.

Two questions that are integral to the concept of civil society and are also highly relevant to our discussion are the question of the notions of public and private virtues, and the question of citizenship.

In his brilliant analysis of the causes of the failure of democracy in Germany, Ralf Dahrendorf discussed at considerable length the crucial importance of public virtues as the dominant value orientation of the people and as a necessary condition for the existence of civil society and democracy.[7] According to him, public virtues or values aim at a "frictionless mastery of relations among men" and are supposed to serve as a "model of general intercourse between men" (300). In contrast, private virtues are seen as "unfilled spaces that imply a degree of resistance to anything public" and "provide the individual with standards for his own perfection, which is conceived as being devoid of society" (300). To carry the argument further, the predominant acceptance of private virtues cannot provide a social basis for civil society. Civil society, then, requires the existence of public virtues that commit individuals to getting along with others (327).

I think that there is considerable agreement that Poland in the 1970s and 1980s was characterized by the predominance of private values and virtues at the expense of public ones.[8] To a large extent this was a delayed

reaction to Stalinism, which two decades or so earlier had managed effectively to destroy and atomize the public sphere and even tried, albeit
unsuccessfully, to penetrate the private space. Faced with that danger,
many people in Poland and elsewhere in Central and Eastern Europe
sought refuge in their own limited private sphere, rediscovering the family and close circles of friends.

The public space and its institutions were regarded as adversaries:
they were mistrusted rather than trusted, and the same applied to groups
and individuals beyond the immediate affinity or friendship circles. The
public value of "getting along with others" was replaced by a feeling
of *homo homini lupus*. The idea of civil society, characterized by civility,
mutual trust, and understanding, and most importantly, tolerance in the
broadest sense of the word, never got off the ground; and its place was
taken by an uncivil society that featured rudeness, mistrust, and lack of
respect for other people's ideas or their national or ethnic origin, as well as
a lack of tolerance of different behavior patterns. The discrepancy between the private and public spheres appeared striking.

The other aspect of civil society, related to the previous one, is the
notion of citizenship. This is particularly relevant in the Polish case, since
the Polish equivalent of civil society is the "citizens' society" *(śpoleczenstwo
obywatelskie)*. To narrow down the discussion of an otherwise complex
concept of citizenship, I want to focus on only two of its attributes: civil
rights (respect for, and protection of, individual rights and freedoms), and
political rights (participation in political processes).

The record shows that in Poland, even at the height of Solidarity,
which was previously equated with an embryonic civil society, the idea of
respecting individual rights and freedoms was neither fully developed nor
broadly accepted by both elites and masses. Quite the opposite: intolerance rather than tolerance was the operating principle in social intercourse. The notion of compromise was never internalized. Individuals'
ethnic, national, and even religious origins were often viciously attacked,
and even the hallowed institution of the Catholic Church, frequently
cited as a charter member of Polish civil society, could hardly serve as a
paragon of tolerance. In such circumstances, "getting along" and conducting a rational discourse among different components of civil society
proved virtually impossible.

As to political rights, or the right to participate in politics, the pre-
sumption is that citizens, as members of civil society, will recognize their

rights and obligations and will actively participate in political activities by voting in the elections or by joining political parties or other organizations. Here again, however, the record is rather dismal. Some of it is due to the previously mentioned problem of underdeveloped public virtues. To paraphrase Dahrendorf, a person "who places the private virtues of withdrawal from others above the public virtue of contract and cooperation" certainly becomes unpolitical, or apolitical.[9] Even prior to the Communist collapse, the above description fitted an average Pole almost perfectly. Perhaps the best example is provided by the unimpressive turnouts of voters, first in the referendum of 1987 and then in the famous "contractual" elections of June 1989, when a sizable percentage of eligible voters stayed home.

There are two possible explanations of the apparent withdrawal from politics on the part of Polish voters. Thus, Kenneth Jowitt blames the "Leninist legacy" for creating a "ghetto" political culture in Eastern Europe, which implied that the population regarded the "political realm as something dangerous, something to avoid," with the result that "political involvement meant 'trouble.' "[10] The other explanation is in terms of a low level of political sophistication of the electorate, caused by a long-term policy of social infantilism propagated by successive Communist regimes.[11]

To sum up, it appears that whatever societal formation existed in Poland in the 1980s, it hardly resembled a society characterized by "civility [which] considers others as fellow citizens of equal dignity in their rights and obligations as members of civil society."[12] If anything, the opposite was true, and many visitors to Poland have regularly noticed the absence of civility both in the political arena and in interpersonal relations.

Economic Legacies

The new leaders who took over during 1989 were confronted with a heavy burden, the Communist economic legacy. That legacy included, among other things, such features as a declining rate of economic growth and industrial output, a distorted price system, decreasing productivity of labor and of capital, hyperinflationary pressures, a huge hard-currency debt, and a continuing heavy economic dependence on the Soviet Union, in addition to psychological-behavioral aspects.

The literature on the institutional aspects of the Communist economic legacy in Poland and the rest of the region is extensive, and there is no need to repeat the various arguments, except very briefly.

THE HEAVY BURDEN OF SUBSIDIES. The heavy burden of subsidies, an integral part of the policy of soft budget constraints, has for years affected a large part of the Polish economy. Subsidies were popular with the people, who enjoyed paying relatively low prices for food and other consumer goods, as well as for rent, transportation, medical services, and so on. They were also appreciated by workers in many inefficient factories that survived only because of subsidies. For the workers, these subsidies meant an almost iron-clad guarantee of security of employment, which encouraged absenteeism, theft, and overall low productivity.

THE HIGH DEGREE OF MONOPOLIZATION. Because the Polish economy was modeled after the Soviet system, many industries in Poland consisted of a single producer, which took advantage of the situation by charging monopoly prices and passing a portion of the benefits to the managers and workers in the form of various bonuses and premiums. Thus, competition was limited and inefficiency was encouraged.

THE DISTORTED PRICE SYSTEM. As in all Soviet-type economies, the prices in Poland, already affected by subsidies, reflected neither supply-and-demand conditions nor the cost of production. The major consequence of the distorted price system was the inability of both planners and producers to engage in rational economic calculation. Previous attempts to rationalize the price system met with fierce popular resistance in December 1970, June 1976, and August 1980, and it was only during the period of martial law that some reforms of retail prices were successfully accomplished.

THE ANTIQUATED INDUSTRIAL BASE. As is well known, during the so-called forced-draft industrialization, all the Soviet satellite countries had to emulate the Stalinist economic system, which, among other things, emphasized heavy industry at the expense of light industry, agriculture, and the service sector. As a result, all countries within the Council for Mutual Economic Assistance (CMEA) developed nearly identical industrial structures, stressing iron, steel, and other energy-consuming — and energy-wasting — industries.

THE HUGE HARD-CURRENCY DEBT. In the 1970s, Poland tried to modernize its industrial base with the help of generous Western credits, which were to be repaid by the export of goods to the West. Recession in the West, diversion of some of the credits to the import of consumer goods, and policy makers' unwillingness to abandon entirely the old Stalinist policy of central planning and autarky resulted in a rapid growth of hard-currency debt that began to absorb a rising share of the revenue from the exports to be used for servicing the debt.

These and other problems formed a part of the economic legacy which was bound to present great difficulties for the incoming new leaders. But there was one aspect of that legacy that was likely to help in the process of economic restructuring: the relatively vibrant and dynamic private sector. In addition to growth in agriculture and small-scale industry and handicraft, there was, especially during the 1980s, the growth of a private trading sector, illustrated by tens of thousands of Poles who regularly traveled abroad in search of Western consumer goods that could be resold at a hefty profit at home. They ended up not only controlling flea markets in Istanbul, Vienna, and West Berlin but also, more important, accumulating huge amounts of capital, billions of dollars, that was waiting for an opportunity to be invested. Thus, although at the end of the 1980s the state sector still occupied a dominant position in the economy, there appeared next to it an embryonic capitalist class that had no counterpart elsewhere in Eastern Europe.

What about the psychological aspects of the economic legacy? One of them clearly was a distorted popular attitude toward work. From a perspective of more than forty years of communism, one thing was certain: although the massive indoctrination and socialization effort failed in creating a new Polish Communist man or woman, it generally succeeded in eradicating many of the values and beliefs — such as honesty, commitment to hard work, respect for quality, ability to work with others, and so on — that tend to improve one's work performance. There is much anecdotal and empirical evidence to show that blue-collar workers in Poland, Solidarity's example notwithstanding, have become largely demoralized as a result of decades of Communist-inspired policies and propaganda.

Another psychological problem focused on the attitude toward the state and the idea of a "social contract." For a long time, the latter was used by the Communists as a political formula that, in return for a guarantee of some economic benefits, managed to secure social peace. Before the collapse of Communist rule, the social contract had already begun to show signs of wear and tear, but the memories of it appeared to be deeply rooted. In other words, large segments of the population continued to expect "them," or the government, to provide many goods and services either free of charge or at nominal cost. Simultaneously, the same groups generally welcomed the idea of marketization, which, they hoped, would provide them with generous amounts of consumer goods. Apparently, many Poles did not see the clear contradiction between a thoroughly paternalistic state, spreading the safety net far and wide, and a free-market economy. The new leaders will have to solve that contradiction, a task that is bound to be difficult and time consuming.

Environmental Legacies

The final aspect of the Communist legacy which deserves separate mention is the environmental, or ecological, legacy. The record shows that on the eve of the Communist downfall parts of Poland were among the most ecologically devastated areas in Europe. By far the most scarred was the Polish share of what was known as the "triangle of death," embracing Northern Bohemia, Southern Saxony, and parts of Upper and Lower Silesia.[13]

All of the available data show that Poland, together with the other countries in the region, has been a victim of great environmental damage in the three basic areas of ecological concern: air impurity, water pollution, and toxic waste. The only ecological threat that the country has been spared is that of nuclear pollution. Despite an early official commitment to develop nuclear energy, Poland did not complete a single nuclear power plant and relied instead on solid fuels, such as coal and lignite. However, Eastern Poland, in particular, was badly affected by the Chernobyl disaster, and the country remains sensitive to the widely reported problems with the Soviet-built nuclear plant in Lithuania.

Although I shall not go into detail here, it is clear that most of Poland's environmental problems were bequeathed to its new rulers by their Communist predecessors, although some of the problems can be traced to the interwar period, if not earlier. Among the latter problems was, in particular, the country's great dependence on coal as the main source of energy for industrial uses. Already a major coal producer between the two world wars, Poland acquired after World War II large coal fields in Upper and Lower Silesia, which had until 1945 belonged to Germany. During the forty-odd years of Communist rule, coal and lignite mining was significantly expanded, making Poland one of the leading producers in the world. This expansion continued even when the other Communist countries in the region began to switch to oil, natural gas, and nuclear power, and Polish leaders have been criticized for not following suit. As a result, however, the country suffered less from the effects of the worldwide energy crisis of the 1970s, especially after the major upward adjustment of oil prices by the Soviet Union, essentially the sole supplier of oil to East-Central Europe.

The major expansion of the metallurgical industry, particularly of iron and copper manufacturing, paralleled that of the coal and lignite industry, and metallurgy soon became the major source of air pollution and toxic waste in the country. The highly controversial decision in the 1970s to construct the Katowice steel plant, the largest and most costly investment project in Communist Poland, was a case in point: together with another steel plant and a power plant, the Katowice plant became responsible for 10 percent of Poland's total soot emission.[14]

The main water and soil polluter has been the chemical industry, which also underwent considerable expansion in the 1970s and 1980s. Finally, as elsewhere in the region, the ecological damage caused by the Soviet troops stationed in Poland from 1945 to 1993 completes the dismal picture.[15]

There is little doubt that it was the successive Communist governments that were largely responsible for the ecological devastation, although it is also clear that in many instances they had relatively little freedom of action in this respect. Such issues as the expansion of air- and water-polluting industries, the ignoring of the real economic cost of ecological damage, and the neglect of the environment by Soviet troops in Poland were mostly decided not in Warsaw but in Moscow, often under the aegis of the CMEA. Obviously, however, the Poles themselves were also guilty. Until the emergence of a widespread concern for the environment in the 1970s, and the beginning of economic reforms emphasizing rational economic calculations, the country's planners and enterprise managers tended to ignore ecological damage while concentrating on achieving maximum output regardless of cost. In Poland, as elsewhere in Eastern Europe, the incentive system for both managers and workers was largely based on maximum input, which, of course, meant encouraging the waste of resources, mainly fuel, thus aggravating the environmental cost.

Only during the late 1980s did things begin to change for the better. The early environmental consciousness-raising movement finally managed to gain national attention and began to act as an effective pressure group. The pre-1989 economic reforms succeeded in restructuring the price system, which ultimately penalized waste and encouraged more economical use of air-, water-, and soil-polluting resources. Finally, Western economic aid has increasingly been targeted at areas requiring ecological cleanup.

Still, it is clear that decades of environmental neglect have taken a heavy toll on Poland. Although it appears that today there is a strong popular consensus in favor of protecting the environment, the cost of the cleanup is bound to be staggering. Because of many other long-neglected areas of public concern (e.g., transportation, communication, education, and public health), few if any resources will be left to take care of the environment. Moreover, with the country embracing the idea of a reduced role for the government, there is a danger that the tough environmental rules and regulations enacted in the closing years of Communist rule will be either ignored or not properly administered. Ironically, the stringent environmental legislation may well prove to be a deterrent for foreign investors in Poland, who may be reluctant to incur the additional cost of environmental protection.[16] However, the policy of closing down the worst polluters, the rust-belt industries, a policy begun by the Communists, may have an opposite effect.

Conclusion

An examination of the political, societal, economic, and environmental legacies of more than forty years of Communist rule in Poland has indicated several difficulties that must be faced by the new democratic rulers committed to eradicating or minimizing the ill effects of the inheritance bequeathed to them by their predecessors.

The greatest problem in the political context is likely to be the difficulty of replacing the Communist nomenklatura. The new political elite itself is numerically weak and, on top of that, poorly equipped for the task of governing. Its leaders are former shipyard workers, journalists, and history professors; and although no one could doubt their sincerity and their commitment to the new democratic order, they are hardly ready for the task of running a complex state and a reasonably well developed economy. Thus, in Poland as elsewhere in Eastern Europe, there is a strong likelihood that the new non-Communist leaders will have little choice but to rely on the officials inherited from the Communist regime for the implementation of institutional transformation.

Insofar as the societal legacy is concerned, I would argue that the top priority for the new leaders in Warsaw should be to help to change the traditional Polish political culture in the direction of creating a true civil society as a necessary first step on the road to a stable democracy. This should be paralleled by an effort both to overcome the existing mistrust of politics which was inherited from the Communist period, and to achieve true legitimacy for the new democratic order.

The economic legacy is as complicated as the societal legacy, if not more so, and the problems encountered in the economic sphere appear harder to solve, at least in the short run, than do the difficulties in the sociopolitical arena, especially in the structural and environmental contexts. Thus the effort needed to rescue the economy from its difficulties may be daunting; yet such rescue is crucial in light of the close relationship between the level of economic well-being and the democratic order.

The Czech Republic and Slovakia

Sharon L. Wolchik

In Czechoslovakia and its successor states, as in other post-Communist states, the Communist era left an enduring legacy. Evident in the economic and political institutions of these societies, this legacy also continues to influence popular perceptions and values, and what the people expect of their government. Although the post-Communist leaders of Czechoslovakia, and after 1993, of the Czech Republic and Slovakia, have made a good deal of progress in restoring democratic government, recreating a market economy, and reorienting their countries' foreign policies, the impact of forty-odd years of Communist rule continues to affect these efforts.

In the Czech Republic and Slovakia as in other post-Communist countries, the local pre-Communist history and traditions have also had an important impact on developments since the end of Communist rule. As the remainder of this chapter illustrates, in some areas the Communist and pre-Communist legacies are congruent; in others, they are not. In Czechoslovakia as elsewhere in the region, the impact of Communist rule itself was conditioned in important ways by the country's pre-Communist history, political experiences and traditions, social structure, and level of development. In many respects, the legacies of communism in what was until 1993 Czechoslovakia are very similar to those found in other post-Communist states. These similarities reflect the fact that the basic structures of the Communist systems instituted in the various states were similar, despite differences in the way the systems operated in individual countries. However, the ways in which Czechoslovakia differed from many of the other states that became Communist after World War II have also been reflected to some extent in the impact of communism in that country.

This chapter examines several aspects of this legacy. After a brief overview of the main features of Communist rule in Czechoslovakia, it turns to an evaluation of the legacies of the Communist era in the economy, the polity, and society. It also examines the impact of living in a Communist system on popular attitudes and perceptions, as well as on relations among people.

The Communist System

In many of the other East European states that became Communist after World War II, a Communist system was clearly imposed by outside actors. Such factors also played an important role in Czechoslovakia, where the proximity of Soviet troops and the advantages the Communist Party derived from the country's special relationship with the Soviet Union and its association with the liberating Soviet troops clearly aided the imposition of the Communist system. However, the Communist Party also had a substantial degree of domestic support. In part, this support reflected the Party's strength during the interwar period, when Czech and Slovak Communist leaders were able to capitalize on generally progressive political traditions, particularly in the Czech Lands (Bohemia and Moravia). Winning from 10 to 13 percent of the vote, the Party sent deputies to the parliament and remained legal until democratic political life was ended by the annexation of the Sudetenland, German occupation of Bohemia and Moravia, and the break-up of the state. Support for the Party, which in the 1946 elections won 36.8 percent of the vote, the largest percentage gained by any political party, also reflected many Czechs' and Slovaks' awareness of the Party's advantages, as well as the opportunism of many who expected personal gain from supporting it.[1] Thus, whereas in Poland the Communist system had clearly been imposed by Soviet troops and was therefore perceived as illegitimate from its inception, and in Hungary the Party came to power after a period of coalition with other political forces but with much less support from the population, in Czechoslovakia the new system originally had a sizable number of supporters. And whereas in both Poland and Hungary anti-Russian and anti-Bolshevik sentiments prevailed, in Czechoslovakia the Party could also draw on attitudes that were basically favorable toward the Russians and, among many groups of the population, were supportive of some form of socialism.

These differences did not, however, lead to any change in the tactics of the Communist Party's leaders in implementing the Communist system in Czechoslovakia. Thus, after a government clearly dominated by the Communist Party took power in February 1948, Klement Gottwald and other Communist leaders moved quickly to change the country's institutions and policies to conform to those that existed in the Soviet Union at the time. In the institutional realm, emulation of the Soviet model involved measures to eliminate the political power and economic base of the regime's opponents, and steps to ensure the Communist Party's monopoly of political power. Party loyalists were brought in to fill government offices, and government organs at all levels were subordinated to Party bodies. Although several other political parties continued to exist, they were clearly subordinated to the Czechoslovak Communist Party. The country's rich web of voluntary associations was simplified, and a system of unified mass organizations was set up to mobilize their members to carry out goals determined by the Communists. A system of censorship was established to control information and to ensure that only those views compatible with the official ideology, Marxism-Leninism, were disseminated in the media and in the arts and culture.

The country's new political leaders also copied Soviet practices in the economic area. Accordingly, they quickly completed the nationalization of economic assets which had been begun between 1945 and 1948 and moved to collectivize agriculture. They also set up the machinery of central planning and a system of five-year plans to guide economic decisions. The country's traditional focus on light industry was replaced by an emphasis on heavy industry, and economic relations were reoriented toward the Soviet Union and other socialist countries.

The leadership took steps to change the political values and attitudes of the population and reorganize the social structure. Wage policies that gave preference to manual labor were accompanied by propaganda campaigns and educational policies that gave preference to children of working-class and agricultural backgrounds. Antireligion campaigns were supplemented by efforts to inculcate Marxism-Leninism as the new value system. In line with these efforts, Communist leaders attempted to politicize all areas of life, including education, culture, and leisure. They also adopted policies that dramatically changed the social structure of the country.

A final element of the Soviet model of economic development, social transformation, and political change was the subordination of the country's foreign policy to that of the Soviet Union. In line with this objective, the country's traditionally warm relations with the West European countries and the United States were replaced by a web of relationships with other East European Communist countries and the Soviet Union.

Given the magnitude of the changes involved and the fact that they were not chosen by the population but rather were imposed from above, it is not surprising that coercion came to play an increasingly important role. As the Stalinist system was consolidated, the secret police came to be important actors. Perhaps in an effort to overcome the influence of the country's democratic past, Czechoslovakia's Communist leaders took very harsh measures against their opponents after February 1948. The purges were also among the most severe in the region, and resulted in the imprisonment or death of many Communist Party leaders who had a base of support within the country, as well as of Jewish leaders and members of other minorities.[2]

As a result of these excesses, the Party lost much of the support that it had at the outset of the Communist era. As in other countries in the region, the policies and institutions associated with the Stalinist model developed in Russia did not work well when transposed to a very different society and culture. However, although the Communist system in Czechoslovakia caused many of the same difficulties that it did elsewhere in the region, the system weathered the death of Stalin quite well. Workers' unrest in Plzeň in 1953 was quickly suppressed by the regime, and the Czechoslovak leadership, headed by Antonín Novotný after the death of Klement Gottwald in 1953, merely paid lip service to the need to de-Stalinize. The lack of pressure from below, coupled with the Novotný leadership's clear lack of interest in steps that would threaten its position, allowed Czechoslovakia to avoid the stormy developments that rocked Poland in 1956 and led to the Soviet invasion of Hungary the same year.

However, by the early 1960s Czechoslovakia's economy, which had weathered the earlier years of Stalinism fairly well, slowed down markedly. In reaction to these developments, as well as growing Slovak dissatisfaction with the position of Slovakia in the common state and the temporary impact of the twenty-second Party congress in the Soviet Union, Party leaders and intellectuals affiliated with the Party tried to reform the system to make it conform to the needs of a developed, European country. This effort, which came to be known as the effort to create socialism with a human face, began at the elite level in the early and middle 1960s and became a broader movement for political reform in 1968. Under the leadership of Alexander Dubček, Party leaders attempted to remove the distortions that had occurred during the Stalinist period and to create a socialist system that would have genuine legitimacy. After initial skepticism, many groups of the population began to support the reformers. However, the support the reformists gained was soon lost when Soviet-led Warsaw Pact troops invaded the country in August 1968. As a result of the invasion, many citizens developed strong anti-Soviet as well as anti-Communist feelings.[3]

The tight political control exercised by the regime of Gustáv Husák, who replaced Alexander Dubček as head of the Czechoslovak Communist Party in April 1969, kept such sentiments from being openly expressed for much of the rest of the Communist era. With the exception of a small group of independent activists, most notably those centered around Charter 77 (a group of courageous dissidents), the strategy of rule adopted by the Husák leadership was effective for more than two decades. A combination of material rewards and selective doses of coercion succeeded in maintaining stability until outside factors provided the catalyst for the fall of communism in 1989.[4]

The impact of Gorbachev's policies in the Soviet Union, of change in Soviet attitudes toward developments in Eastern Europe, and of the collapse of the hard-line Honecker regime in East Germany undoubtedly played a critical role in bringing about the end of Communist rule in Czechoslovakia as well as elsewhere in the region. However, crucial as these developments outside the country were, the collapse of communism in Czechoslovakia, as elsewhere, reflected the serious and underlying problems the system created within the country. In the Czechoslovak case, these included both economic and political difficulties. Thus, despite the surface stability of political life once the country had been "normalized" after the reforms of 1968, it suffered from many of the same problems that plagued its Communist neighbors. As the sections below discuss in greater detail, the Communist system produced a chronic if not acute economic crisis in Czechoslovakia. Poor economic performance in turn had political repercussions.

The last two years of Communist rule saw important changes within the Party leadership and in the willingness of the population to challenge the regime. The political system remained very tightly controlled until the end of Communist rule. However, the impact of Gorbachev's policies and the coming to power of leaders who were somewhat younger, and both less experienced and less committed to maintaining normalization at all costs, led to the formation of new dissident groups and broader participation in illegal protests and demonstrations.

As the mass demonstrations that toppled the Communist government in November 1989 demonstrated, there was widespread dissatisfaction with the Communist system in Czechoslovakia. Many citizens welcomed the change of regime and supported the effort on the part of the country's new leaders to re-create democratic government and a market economy. However, this process has been more complicated than many anticipated. As the breakup of the Czechoslovak federation in 1993 demonstrates, even in Czechoslovakia, which in many respects had better preconditions for the re-creation of democracy and the market than did any of its post-Communist neighbors, the legacy of more than forty years of Communist rule continues to condition both the options available to political leaders and the responses of citizens.

Economic Legacies

The economic impact of communism in Czechoslovakia in part reflected the way in which the Czechoslovak economy differed from the economies of most other states that became Communist. The economies of the Czech Lands and Slovakia also differed to some degree. Already among the most developed of the countries that became Communist after World War II, Czechoslovakia continued to industrialize after 1948. Because the Czech Lands were already at a high level of development, the change in level of development that occurred under communism was not as great as it was in many other states that were far more agrarian at the outset of the Communist period. Nor was the change as great as it was in Slovakia. In contrast to the situation during the interwar period, when efforts to industrialize Slovakia failed, under Communist rule the development gap between the two regions narrowed considerably. Although the Czech Lands remained somewhat more developed at the end of the Communist period, the difference according to most indicators of development was very small.[5]

Czechoslovakia's standard of living also continued to be higher than that in most other European Communist countries throughout the Communist period. Ownership of consumer durables, including household appliances, and ownership of automobiles increased markedly in the 1970s and 1980s, as did ownership of summer or weekend cottages.[6] As discussed in the section of this chapter that deals with the societal legacies of communism, economic policies adopted under Communist rule also led to continued urbanization, particularly in Slovakia, as well as to increases in the educational and skill levels of the population. Although there is a great need for retraining and improvement of skill levels, in world terms both the Czech Lands and Slovakia have educated, skilled labor forces.

However, the bulk of the economic legacy of communism was negative. Czechoslovakia did not experience the acute economic crises that occurred in Poland during the Communist period. However, despite its more favorable starting point at the outset of the Communist period, its economy suffered from many of the same ills that beset other centrally planned economies. The shortcomings and distortions produced by central planning in Communist countries have been extensively catalogued. Evident in the very poor economic performance that led Czech and Slovak leaders to attempt to implement the economic and political reforms of the 1960s, these problems included low labor productivity, poor labor morale, the production of poor-quality goods, inability to determine the true costs of production, and a lack of incentives for both workers and management. The economy also suffered from structural imbalances, and from the effects of the disruption of its traditional focus on light industry and the reorientation of its trading patterns toward the East. The economic structure and policies adopted by the leadership led to difficulties in fostering innovation, and an inability to compete on the world market. In addition to these problems, which also plagued other centrally planned economies, economic performance in Czechoslovakia was also influenced by factors specific to the country, including labor shortages and the aging of the industrial plant, particularly in Bohemia.[7]

In the 1970s and 1980s, external factors, including the delayed impact of the energy crisis and economic recession in the West and changes in Soviet willingness to supply cheap energy to Eastern Europe, compounded the impact of the structural problems of the economy.[8] Difficulties in the agricultural sector, which was almost entirely in state hands, also had negative repercussions for economic performance.[9]

The shortcomings and problems created by Communist economic policies were reflected in the growth of the second, or unofficial, economy. Although far less has been written about this subject in Czechoslovakia than in other Communist states such as Poland or Hungary, unofficial economic activity also was pervasive in Czechoslovakia during the

Communist period. Estimates by officials of the State Planning Commission in the late 1980s indicated that such activity amounted to at least 1 billion to 1.3 billion U.S. dollars in the late 1980s.[10] Average citizens spent an estimated 1 to 10 percent of their work earnings in the second economy. Perhaps the most striking evidence of the extent to which participating in the second economy had become commonplace is provided by the results of an April 1988 survey conducted by the Economic Research Institute. Only six of the two hundred respondents claimed that they had never used a bribe or another unofficial method to obtain what they needed in some area.[11] Experts' disagreements over the best way to handle illegal economic activities and their contribution to the economy was related to broader differences of opinion concerning economic reform in the last two years of Communist rule.[12]

Czech and Slovak Party leaders made several attempts to deal with these problems. The most radical of these were the proposals by Ota Šik and other Party-affiliated experts in the mid-1960s to introduce into the economy certain elements of the market.[13] After the forcible end of the reform, fear of a repetition of the events of 1968 led to a ban on all discussion of serious economic reform for nearly twenty years. The leadership enacted several programs to attempt to improve economic performance. However, these were based on increased centralization and closer economic links to the country's Communist neighbors, and thus did little to achieve the desired goals.[14]

It was only in January 1987, in response to Gorbachev's policies in the Soviet Union and continued economic difficulties, that Czechoslovak leaders adopted a new approach to economic reform. For the first time since the 1960s, they acknowledged the need to decentralize and to introduce elements of the market. The program also called for price reform and change in the country's foreign trade. The principles adopted by the Party were very general, and the timetable for introducing the reforms was very gradual. Critics of the proposals also argued that they did not go far enough in attacking the root of the country's economic problems, and that they could not succeed because they were not coupled with serious political reform.[15] Many of those who argued for the introduction of market principles and the country's reintegration into the world economy would later emerge as officials in the country's non-Communist government. Although economic grievances were secondary in bringing about the end of the Communist system in 1989, the poor performance of the economy helped to erode popular support for the government during the Communist period.

The impact of more than four decades of experience in a centrally planned economy continued to be felt in the post-Communist period. The extent of this impact, however, varied. The imprint of Communist economic policies and organization has proved most enduring in the structure of the economy and in the attitudes of many individuals toward work and their own economic roles. It has been less difficult to overcome in the ownership of economic assets and in trading patterns. In all of these areas, the impact of Communist rule continues to be felt to a greater extent in Slovakia than in the Czech Lands. As a result, the economic legacy of communism was one of the primary factors that contributed to the demise of the Czechoslovak federation in 1993.

At the outset of the post-Communist era, Czechoslovakia differed significantly from its immediate neighbors, both economically and politically. Unlike the leaders of the former German Democratic Republic, where economic organization and the political regime were similar to those of Czechoslovakia prior to the end of Communist rule, Czech and Slovak leaders had to find their way to democracy and the market, and back to Europe, on their own. Conditions in Czechoslovakia at the outset of the post-Communist period also differed from those found in Poland and Hungary. Whereas in Poland agriculture had largely reverted to private hands after 1956, and many small-scale businesses, especially in the service sector, continued to be privately owned, and in Hungary market elements were gradually introduced after 1968, in Czechoslovakia the effort to re-create the market had to begin from practically zero after 1989. Owing to the thoroughness of the nationalization of industry and the collectivization of agriculture, privately owned businesses and farms accounted for less than 1 percent of all those employed during most of the Communist period.[16]

The forced end of the 1968 reforms as a result of the Warsaw Pact invasion also produced an enduring economic legacy, for it led to the purge of those reformers who had experience in and contacts with Western economies, and resulted in the isolation of most Czech and Slovak experts and intellectuals for nearly twenty years. As a result, those experts and officials did not have the broad range of contacts with the West that their Hungarian and Polish counterparts did. The fact that Czechoslovakia's trade relationships were largely with the Soviet Union and other

Communist countries, a situation that persisted until the end of Communist rule,[17] also contributed to cutting Czechoslovakia off from contacts with the West.

Somewhat surprisingly, neither of these factors has made as much difference as might have been expected in the post-Communist period, particularly in the Czech Lands. The passage of laws creating the legal basis for private ownership of economic assets in 1990 was followed very quickly by a relatively high degree of privatization. As in neighboring countries, much of this occurred as the result of the formation of new (and in many cases small) private businesses. The introduction of the originally controversial "voucher," or "coupon," privatization plan, and more traditional methods, including foreign investment and joint ventures, succeeded in privatizing a large number of existing enterprises, although many of the larger industrial enterprises remain in state hands.[18] As a result of these programs, the private sector share of GDP in the Czech Lands grew from 10 percent in 1991 to 20 percent in 1992, and to 44 percent by the end of the third quarter of 1993. In Slovakia, the private sector accounted for approximately 4 percent in 1991, 20 percent in 1992, and 36 percent at the end of the third quarter of 1993.[19]

A further legacy of Communist economic policies evident in the immediate post-Communist period, the country's high level of trade with the Soviet Union and other formerly Communist countries, has also proved to be short-lived. Whereas in Poland and Hungary in the 1970s and 1980s there was a development of greater economic ties to the West and a diversification of trade, Czechoslovakia's trade remained highly concentrated on the countries of the Council for Mutual Economic Assistance (CMEA) throughout the Communist period. The last two years of Communist rule saw a slight increase in trade with developed, non-Communist European countries, but the Soviet Union still accounted for the large majority of the country's exports and imports.[20] By 1991, Germany replaced the Soviet Union as Czechoslovakia's main trading partner. Germany continues to be second-largest trading partner of both the Czech Republic and Slovakia (each republic is the other's largest trading partner), followed by Austria and Hungary.[21] The demise of the CMEA and the break-up of the Soviet Union contributed to this rapid change in the flow of trade. However, it is striking that the forty-year hiatus in both countries' trade with the West, and the low level of contacts between economic and political officials in both the Czech Lands and Slovakia and their European counterparts, were such limited impediments to the rapid reorientation of trading patterns that occurred.

Similarly, the lack of previous experience with Western firms and corporations does not seem to have deterred foreign investors, particularly in the Czech Lands. Despite the fact that there were relatively few experts or officials who had extensive experience in dealing with Western businesspeople or knowledge of the workings of market economies, foreign investment in the Czech Lands grew very rapidly once legal and financial impediments were removed. Investors from abroad have been far less eager to invest in Slovakia, both before and after independence.[22]

At the same time, the impact of the isolation of Czechoslovakia's economics experts and decision makers during the Communist period did affect economic developments immediately after the fall of communism. As in the case of many of the other economic legacies discussed, this impact was greater in Slovakia than in the Czech Lands. Although Czech economists associated with the reforms of the 1960s were purged from their academic and research positions as well as their public positions, several were able to find work in research institutes such as the Prognostics Institute of the Academy of Sciences in Prague in the later years of Communist rule. As the result of the greater opportunities for travel and study abroad available in the late 1960s, a number of students (including a future minister of the economy of the Czech Republic, Karel Dyba) were able to study economics in the West. In Slovakia, by way of contrast, the reforms of the 1960s focused far more on national than on economic issues. Slovakia therefore entered the post-Communist period without the resource that the above group of experts, small though it was, represented in the Czech Lands.

The reluctance of Czechoslovakia's leaders to develop economic contacts with the West prior to 1989 deprived the economy of links that could have fostered technological modernization and innovation. At the same time, this hesitation proved to have certain advantages, because it allowed the country's new non-Communist leaders to pursue stabilization policies without the need to repay or renegotiate massive hard-currency debts.

In contrast to the relatively short-lived impact of the economic legacies discussed above, several features of the economic organization and policies of the Communist era have had a more lasting effect on economic performance in the post-Communist period. These include the concentration of the labor force in particular sectors, and the distorted development patterns that resulted from the emphasis on heavy industry which prevailed for much of the Communist period. As a result, Czechoslovakia entered the post-Communist era with an economy that differed significantly in structural terms from those of developed Western states. One of the most noticeable of these differences was the much lower level of development of the service sector. While the proportion of the population engaged in agriculture continued to decrease throughout the Communist period in both the Czech Lands and Slovakia, the service sector grew very slowly. In the years since the end of Communist rule, both foreign and domestic entrepreneurs have moved to create the financial and other services needed for market economies to function. Many new small businesses have also sprung up to provide personal services of all kinds. However, the service sector still remains less developed than it is in Western countries.

The concentration of the labor force in large, inefficient industries, particularly in heavy industries such as steel, machine manufacturing, and mining, in which the Czech and Slovak republics have little chance of being competitive in the world market, is another enduring legacy of the Communist period. This legacy has been particularly damaging in Slovakia, where a large part of the country's sizable arms industry is concentrated. But it is also important in Bohemia and Moravia, where the closing of unprofitable, ecologically damaging mining concerns and other industrial enterprises has led to unemployment rates that have reached 15 percent in the regions involved. Other areas of the Czech Lands, which were shielded from large-scale closings of unprofitable enterprises by the fact that the law on bankruptcies had not been passed, are also likely to feel the impact of this factor in the future.

The final area in which Communist economic policies have left a lasting legacy is in attitudes toward work, and the willingness of the population to take risks and be innovative. In this area as in the others discussed, there are important differences in the attitudes of Czechs and Slovaks. There are also important differences in the attitudes of younger and older people. Survey research conducted in early 1990 found a great deal of support in the abstract for the principle of re-creating a market economy. However, important differences existed at that time, and increased over the next several years, in the willingness of Czechs and Slovaks to suffer the inevitable consequences of this shift, such as an increase in unemployment, the possibility of losing one's own job, and a decrease in the standard of living. Early surveys indicated that Czechs and Slovaks were approximately equally likely to say that they would like to start a private business or work in the private sector. However, support for privatization of both large- and small-scale enterprises was consistently much higher in the Czech Lands than in Slovakia, as was agreement with the statement that there was a need to re-create a market economy quickly, even if increased unemployment were to result.[23] Dissatisfaction with political developments and leaders as a result of decreases in the standard of living was also much greater in Slovakia than in the Czech Lands prior to the break-up of the federation.

However, despite the fact that Czechs were far more supportive of the move to the market, many Czechs also appear to have difficulty adapting to the new economic demands they face. Thus, the need to take personal responsibility for one's work product, to arrive at work on time and remain until the end of the workday, to deal with increased competition, and, in many areas, to adopt a new attitude toward customers and business associates has created new strains for many workers and employees in the Czech Lands as well as in Slovakia.

The economic legacies of communism also include environmental problems. In both the Czech Lands and Slovakia, the strategy of development that prevailed during the Communist period led to a near-complete disregard of the ecological consequences of economic activities. As the result of measures adopted in the 1970s, economic decision makers were required to take environmental considerations into account in drawing up or modifying economic plans. However, there was virtually no enforcement of these regulations, and they were widely ignored by enterprise directors, economic officials, and territorial and economic planners, who gave priority to other issues.[24] As a result, the post-Communist leaders of Czechoslovakia and the current leaders of the Czech Republic and Slovakia face serious environmental problems but have very few resources with which to address them.

Communist economic policies also contributed in an important way to the break-up of the Czechoslovak federation. Owing to different levels of industrialization and timing of industrialization in the two parts of the country, the impact of the move to the market was much harsher in Slovakia. Because much of Slovakia's industrialization took place during the Communist period, the economic structure of the region reflected the inefficiencies and distortions associated with that model to a greater extent than did the economy of the Czech Lands. Owing to the concentration of the arms industry and also of many of the largest, least profitable industries in Slovakia, the reduction of state subsidies and the introduction of considerations of profitability led to far greater economic disruption and hardship in Slovakia than in the Czech Lands. The impact of this factor was evident in unemployment rates in Slovakia, which were three times higher than those in the Czech Lands; it was also seen in the rapid growth in the numbers of households in poverty in Slovakia.

Differences related to the structure and fate of industry in the two parts of the country were reflected in different perceptions on the part of citizens and leaders in the Czech Lands and Slovakia concerning the value of economic reform and the acceptability of unemployment, as noted above. Economic hardship related to the introduction of the market also provided ready recruits for political forces (including the Slovak National Party and the Movement for a Democratic Slovakia, which was led by former prime minister Vladimír Mečiar) that called for a redefinition of Slovakia's relationship to the Czech Lands, if not the dissolution of the federation. As I have argued in other contexts,[25] the break-up of the federation had its roots in historical factors and also reflected the impact that the strains of the economic and political transitions created for individuals and their families. However, these were conditioned by the economic and political legacies of Communist rule.

Political Legacies

As in the economic area, so too in the political area there were certain positive legacies of Communist rule in Czechoslovakia. Perhaps the most significant of these was the fact that all citizens, with the exception of the Gypsy, or Romani, population, became aware of being members of a common political state, owing to the politicization of many areas of life and the intensity of political propaganda campaigns. The impact of this change was greatest in the most rural areas of the country, such as eastern Slovakia, where levels of illiteracy had been highest and the isolation of peasants from the rest of the country greatest in the interwar period. However, because of the already substantial level of economic development of the country prior to World War II, this benefit was not nearly as great in Czechoslovakia as it was in less developed areas such as parts of Yugoslavia, Bulgaria, Albania, and Romania. It was also far outweighed by the many negative legacies of the kinds of political organization and political change that occurred under communism.

The political legacies of communism in Czechoslovakia are also similar in many respects to those of such rule elsewhere. But there are certain distinctive features that reflect the particular form of Communist rule that prevailed in Czechoslovakia. Among the most important of these is the fact that, with the exception of a short period in the middle to late 1960s, the political system remained highly centralized and tightly controlled. In contrast to the situation in Poland and Hungary, where Communist leaders attempted to come to some sort of accommodation with the population and eventually negotiated themselves out of power, the Husák regime and later the Jakeš regime clung to the use of material incentives and the selective use of coercion, coupled with the backing of the Soviet Union, to stay in power.

As a result, political and ideological considerations continued to be more important in many areas of life than was the case in Poland and Hungary, and independent groups and movements, part of what came to be called "civil society" in those countries, were slow to develop. The small dissident groups that had existed since the late 1970s, most notably Charter 77, provided an important counterweight to the general pattern of political conformity and apathy. But their numbers were small, and their influence on the general population minimal. The numbers of groups and individuals involved in independent activities increased in the last years of Communist rule. However, whereas millions of Poles participated in the activities of Solidarity in Poland in the early 1980s, and dissidents in Hungary were relatively free to propagate their ideas, few of the citizens of Czechoslovakia had any experience with such activities. Further, open dissent was concentrated largely in the Czech Lands. Numerous intellectuals and specialists in Slovakia made use of official organizations such as the Defenders of Nature to engage in what has been termed "creative deviance,"[26] but their numbers were far smaller than the numbers of their counterparts in Prague, and their connections to broader groups of the population were even more tenuous.

To perhaps a greater extent than the economic legacies, the political legacies of communism have been compounded by the impact of the transition to democracy and the reintroduction of the market. As Ivan Volgyes notes in the introduction to this volume, it is often difficult to determine whether particular attitudes and behaviors reflect the legacy of the Communist past or reactions to the uncertainties and difficulties of the transition. In many cases, citizens' political attitudes, values, and behaviors undoubtedly reflect the impact of both factors. The political culture that is emerging in post-Communist states appears to be an amalgam of values and attitudes that reflects each country's pre-Communist past, the results of Communist leaders' efforts to inculcate certain values and attitudes, and the values and attitudes that in effect developed as by-products of living in Communist systems, as well as the particular characteristics of the transition.[27] However, although we cannot weigh the impact of the Communist system alone in any rigorous way, there are a number of areas in which the imprint of the Communist past appears to be clear.

The legacies of the one-party rule, elimination of political opposition, simplification of the country's associational life, and censorship of information which prevailed under communism had an important impact on the development of the party system, citizens' political values and attitudes, and patterns of mass-elite relations once the Communist system was ousted. They also continue to influence the operation of the bureaucracy. The excesses and injustices of the Communist past also created the need to come to terms with individuals' past actions and relationships to the old regime.

One of the clearest legacies of a political system in which one political party controlled political life is the difficulty that Czech and Slovak leaders have experienced in creating a stable party system. The current multiparty system reflects Czechoslovakia's interwar tradition. However, in contrast to the interwar period, when a coalition of five parties ruled for all but a few years, coalitions in post-Communist Czechoslovakia have generally been fleeting. As in many other areas discussed, the impact of this legacy has been clearest in Slovakia, where the break-up of Public Against Violence, the umbrella organization that led the revolution of 1989, has been followed by difficulties in maintaining the government coalition between Mečiar's Movement for a Democratic Slovakia and other parties.

The suspicion that many citizens feel toward political parties contributes to this situation. Noting that they are no longer required to be Party members to advance in their careers or improve their standard of living, many citizens refuse to join political parties. Many also share the view that strong political parties are not as necessary as strong leaders in a democratic political system.[28] The fact that these attitudes, which are particularly strong in Slovakia, also are expressed by sizable groups of citizens in the Czech Lands attests to the impact of communism on popular attitudes toward and perceptions of politics. The low levels of party identification that result from these views in turn mean that many citizens do not have the benefit of a tool that helps to structure political choices and to moderate political conflict in more established democracies. This situation contributed to the fluidity evident in the political situation in the first four years after November 1989, for citizens who are not formally attached to political parties are more likely to change their political preferences; they are also more readily available to be mobilized by extremist movements and parties than are citizens in systems with higher levels of party membership. Political leaders are also less constrained by mass preferences in such a situation.

Public opinion surveys conducted in the Czech Republic indicate that as the post-Communist transition progressed, support for individual parties has fluctuated less than it did in the period immediately after November 1989. The high degree of support for Miroslav Sladek's extreme right-wing Republican Party in parts of Northern Bohemia, however, demonstrates the vulnerability of at least certain groups in the Czech Republic to mobilization by extremist groups. In Slovakia, as the sharp decrease in support for Mečiar's Movement for a Democratic Slovakia after independence illustrates, political preferences are still quite volatile.

The development of a stable party system has also been inhibited by the need to rebuild the network of autonomous interest groups and voluntary associations found in other democratic states, and in Czechoslovakia during the interwar period. The results of efforts to diversify the country's associational life have been mixed. On the one hand, the end of Communist rule was followed by an almost immediate repluralization of political life in Czechoslovakia. Interest groups and voluntary organizations proliferated as citizens took advantage of the new opportunity to form groups to define and articulate their interests. However, many of these groups remain very small, and few have networks that reach to the local level. There are also few links between such organizations and political parties.[29]

Part of the difficulty of resurrecting autonomous citizen organizations can be traced to the impact of the Communist experience on citizens' perceptions of their own roles in politics, on their attitudes toward political authorities, and on their expectations of government. In the political area as in the economic one, however, the country's pre-Communist experiences also appear to have influenced the attitudes and values of citizens. The impact of Czechoslovakia's interwar political traditions has been reflected in a political culture, particularly in the Czech Lands, that differs in important respects from those found in neighboring post-Communist states. Respondents in the Czech Lands, for example, are much less likely than those in Hungary, Poland, and Slovakia, to harbor anti-Semitic views; they are also more likely to favor compromise to solve political issues.[30] However, although citizens rejected much of the value system promoted by the Communist regime, many of them internalized certain of the values propagated by the Communist leadership which are problematic from the perspective of creating a stable democratic political system. Other values and beliefs that continue to influence perceptions of politics were not fostered by the Communist leadership, but rather grew out of the experience of living under Communist rule. These values and attitudes include high levels of cynicism about public affairs and alienation from the political system, as well as distrust of public officials and institutions. They also include a strong belief in wage egalitarianism, and citizens' expectations that their government will continue to provide a high degree of security.

In the initial months after November 1989, levels of citizens' interest in politics and participation in public affairs were very high in Czechoslovakia. The turnout for the country's first post-Communist elections was also very high, as 95 percent of eligible citizens voted. Most citizens indicated that they supported the political changes taking place, and most supported President Havel and the new government. However, after the initial euphoria that accompanied the sudden and unexpected end of the Communist regime subsided, citizens' attitudes changed markedly. Conditioned by their experiences with Communist rule and frustrated by the complexity of the transition and the uncertainty it created, many citizens lapsed once again into political apathy. By October 1990, for example, only 4 percent of those surveyed indicated that they were involved in politics.[31] Levels of dissatisfaction rose sharply, and optimism concerning future political developments decreased.[32]

Citizens' attitudes toward governmental institutions and leaders also became very negative once again. Approximately 88 percent of those surveyed in February 1990 trusted the president, and between 76 percent and 83 percent trusted the federal government, the Federal Assembly, and the governments of the Czech or Slovak republic, for example.[33] By 1992, public attitudes had changed markedly. A sizable portion (78%) of the public in the Czech republic still trusted Václav Havel, but support for Havel was much lower (52%) in Slovakia. Support for other governmental institutions was much lower in the Czech Lands, where 46 percent trusted the federal government and 25 percent the Federal Assembly, and it was lower still in Slovakia, where 26 percent trusted the federal government and 26 percent the Federal Assembly.[34]

Many citizens appear to have reverted to attitudes prevalent during the Communist era, when large numbers felt that politics was not the business of ordinary people, and few felt any responsibility to take action to solve communal problems. The view that it was the state's responsibility, rather than the citizen's, to deal with public problems has been accompanied by the desire of many citizens to see a strong leader emerge to deal with current difficulties.[35]

At the same time, citizens continued to expect the state to provide a high level of material security and social welfare guarantees. These expectations have been particularly pronounced in Slovakia and were one of the differences in political preferences that contributed to the break-up of the state. However, many citizens in the Czech Lands also want the government to provide substantial levels of social security. Although Czechs were far more likely to want to see the government's role in guaranteeing employment and in the running of the economy decrease, many also wanted the state to provide basic health care and pensions.[36]

These attitudes are also coupled with a strong belief in wage egalitarianism, particularly in Slovakia. Such attitudes in part reflect the fact that Czechoslovakia was one of the most egalitarian of the Communist states in terms of wage scales and incomes, but they also may be influenced by the egalitarian tendencies that existed in the interwar period.

The separation many citizens felt from political leaders and the tendency to divide the world into camps (the "us/them" split) that the Communist system produced also appear to shape citizens' attitudes about politics in the post-Communist period. In the immediate period after the fall of the Communist system, this legacy often found expression in the view that a new Mafia (this time one composed of dissidents and intellectuals) had taken over from the old one. With the ouster of intellectuals associated with Public Against Violence from public life in Slovakia after the June 1992 elections, and the emergence of a more professional group of politicians and experts in the Czech republic after the break-up of Civic Forum in 1991, this variant of the critique is less often heard. However, the tendency to divide the world into friendly and hostile groups (be they one's own ethnic group and others, or one's own political persuasion and all others) and the view that political leaders work not for the advantage of citizens but for their own benefit continue to be widespread.

The Communist period has also left its imprint on the country's new political elite. This impact has been evident in the area of elite recruitment when it has been necessary to replace large numbers of officials, and has been seen in the behavior and leadership styles of many new leaders. In the first area, it has been difficult to find enough candidates with appropriate credentials who are willing to serve as government officials, particularly at the local level. Thus, while the lack of any previous government experience during the Communist period was an important political asset for candidates for national office in the first elections in both Slovakia and the Czech Lands and in the 1992 elections in the Czech Lands, at the lower levels there were many holdovers from the Communist era. Many of these officials continue to hold the same attitudes toward citizen input into government decision making which they held during the Communist era. The legacy of the Communist past is similarly alive in the bureaucracies at higher levels, where it also proved to be impractical to replace large numbers of individuals. The continuity of personnel has in many cases resulted in a continuation of the style of operation that prevailed during the Communist era, and there is still a need to reorient many bureaucrats' and officials' style of work and attitude toward citizens.

Many elected officials, particularly in the Czech Lands, did not have any experience with official politics during the Communist era. However, neither those who were former dissidents nor those who are entirely new to politics have had any experience with democratic politics. Patterns of interactions both within the elite and between members of the elite and citizens reflect this fact. Thus, most political leaders have little understanding of the need to accommodate the interests of opponents or to compromise with others whose views differ on key issues. Many tend to elevate differences in priorities to irreconcilable political conflicts, and to put personal issues and ambitions above those of their parties or their country. As in many of the areas discussed above, these patterns are reinforced by the nature of the politics of transition. An electoral system based on proportional representation provides little incentive for representatives to meet with citizens or to be attentive to citizens' demands; lack of resources to visit constituencies or stay in touch with citizens also inhibits contact between members of the political elite and ordinary citizens. The tendency of many new political leaders to focus on high-level politics to the neglect of social or local issues further complicates the relationship between leaders and the led, and reinforces the negative images of politicians and political institutions discussed earlier.

Finally, the political legacies of communism also contributed to the increase in the political salience of ethnicity in post-Communist Czechoslovakia and to the break-up of the Czechoslovak federation. Thus, by preventing any open discussion of the grievances of the Slovaks or any open airing of the Czechs' and Slovaks' true perceptions of each other for much of the Communist period, the Communist system did not allow political and other tensions between the two groups to be worked out within a common framework. The primary step taken to accommodate the different perspectives of each group, the creation of a federal state after 1969, in fact did not reduce the importance of ethnicity as a factor of political division but reinforced it. As in the Soviet Union, where the central government retained most control, the federal system nonetheless provided resources for political leaders at the republic level to organize. The existence of the federal system also set the framework for the debate about the proper form of the state in the post-Communist period and, because the republic-level governments were already established, provided a relatively easily available alternative to the existing federation. Ironically, the success of Communist economic policies in closing the development gap between the Czech Lands and Slovakia also contributed to the increased salience of ethnicity, for it provided new economic and human resources that ethnic leaders could mobilize around ethnic aims.[37]

As in many of the areas discussed above, the impact of transition politics compounded the impact of the political legacy of communism in this area. A poorly developed party system, the fluidity of citizens' preferences, the inexperience of new political leaders, and citizens' distrust of politics all contributed to the fragility of the country's newly re-created democratic political institutions and their inability to resolve the issues that separated Czech and Slovak leaders within the framework of the existing federation.

Societal Legacies

The economic policies discussed earlier, as well as policies explicitly designed to promote social change which were adopted during the Communist era, left their imprint on the structure of Czech and Slovak society. They also led to a number of social problems. Many of these were similar to those that exist in other developed societies; however, in many cases, the way in which social problems presented themselves, or the extent of those problems, was influenced by the nature of the economic and political system. As in the other areas discussed, the impact of the transition has exacerbated many of these and has added new social pathologies to those that already existed.

Although Czechoslovakia's level of economic development changed less than that of many other European Communist states, Communist policies had a major impact on the country's social structure. Continued modernization increased the proportion of the population working in industry and living in urban areas and decreased the numbers of those who made their living in agriculture. The impact of this shift from the countryside to towns and cities was most noticeable in Slovakia, where prior to the institution of a Communist system development levels were significantly lower than those in the Czech Lands. However, the Czech Lands, which before World War II had a social structure similar to those of other developed European countries, also became more urbanized.

The impact of the elimination of almost all forms of private property and the placement of severe restrictions on inheritance had an impact that was perhaps more important than the changes produced by continued economic development. Owing to the elimination of most inheritance rights, the nationalization of industries, and collectivization, most private property was eliminated. As a result of these policies, the structure of society changed markedly. Almost all owners of private businesses and farms were dispossessed, and most professionals, artisans, and craftspeople were forced to join cooperatives or to become state employees.[38] As part of the effort to continue to industrialize, Communist elites expanded educational opportunities. Educational levels increased substantially, particularly in Slovakia. There was also a sizable increase in the number of people with higher technical training. However, the priority given to heavy industry and the neglect of the service sector meant that many occupations frequently found in Western societies were very small at the outset of the effort to re-create the market. Efforts to change the status of social groups also led to changes in the stratification hierarchy, and to a very low degree of differentiation in incomes.

Communist leaders also adopted policies designed to promote change in women's roles. Women's equality was never a high-priority goal, and policies toward women were often determined by their relationship to other, higher-priority goals. As a result, women's roles changed in uneven ways. Change was greatest in the areas of women's employment outside the home and women's access to education. There was far less change in women's participation in the exercise of political or economic power or in the division of labor within the home. As a result of this pattern, and the fact that gender equality as a goal came to be associated with the Communist regime, there has been a significant backlash against the whole idea in the post-Communist period. As a result, women are facing more open discrimination, and it is very difficult for women's activists or legislators to get issues related to women's situation onto the political agenda. At the same time, many of the changes that occurred during the Communist period are likely to persist. Thus, while there is a widespread belief in these societies that levels of women's employment are too high, most women must try to remain in the labor force to maintain their family's standard of living. The pattern of increased educational access for women is also likely to persist. Unfortunately, so is the belief, which prevailed during the Communist period despite official policy to the contrary, that politics is not an appropriate area of activity for women and that women politicians are somehow "funny." The approach of the leadership to women's issues and policies adopted during the Communist period, then, makes it difficult to raise problematic issues. As in many of the areas discussed above, the difficulties posed by the legacy of communism in this area are compounded by the characteristics of transition politics discussed earlier.[39]

The social legacies of communism also include a host of other unresolved social issues, including the situation of the Gypsies, or Roma, the difficult situation and disaffection of many young people, and a number of other serious social problems. The latter include high rates of alcoholism as well as violence against women and children. Because such problems could not be discussed openly under communism, their true extent has become evident only after the collapse of the Communist system. As in many of the other areas discussed, these legacies have been compounded by the indirect legacies of communism, including the impact of the transition from Communist rule. Thus, the opening of borders, and the sudden decrease in police control and in the capacities of the police, have led to increases in prostitution, drug abuse and drug traffic, and other forms of social deviance.[40] The uncertainty and disruption associated with the changes that have attended the end of Communist rule have also contributed to these and other social problems.

The impact of these legacies has also been compounded by the psychological cost of the transition. The need to come to terms with a high degree of uncertainty and change in many areas of life has taken a predictable psychological toll on individuals and their families.[41] This impact of the transition in turn has both economic and political implications.

The Communist legacy in what was Czechoslovakia also has a moral dimension. As Václav Havel has argued perhaps most eloquently, no one escaped the impact of living under communism. With the exception of a few courageous individuals, most citizens had to make some compromise with the regime in order to survive. The impact of living with the falsehoods embedded in the system, of dealing on a daily basis with the contrast between the official version of reality and reality itself, and of witnessing the compromises and betrayals of colleagues and friends was felt by all who lived under the system. In addition to creating the need to come to terms with the question of moral culpability or responsibility, which Havel has claimed must be shared by all who lived in these societies, these experiences have had a profound impact on the moral fabric of society and on citizens' perceptions of each other, their levels of trust of others, and their ability to take others at their word. As Havel and others have argued, it will be some time before these legacies of Communist rule fade.

Conclusion

As the pages above have demonstrated, the legacies of communism are evident in many areas of life in the Czech Republic and Slovakia. In some areas, the impact of four decades of Communist rule continues to be felt very strongly. In others, this impact, although significant immediately after the end of Communist rule, has proved to be of short duration. As the favorable trends in the Czech Republic's economic performance and in the trade patterns of both the Czech Lands and Slovakia illustrate, the choices political leaders make in deciding how to deal with these legacies can be an important factor in determining how long-lasting the legacies will be. However, as the differing impact of the introduction of the market in the two regions has demonstrated, the ability of leaders to make certain choices and the likelihood that such choices will be successful are also conditioned by the nature and significance of particular aspects of the

legacies of communism. Thus, differences in current developments in the
Czech Lands and Slovakia also reflect the fact that the legacy of communism was somewhat different in each.

In a recent article in *Foreign Affairs*, Václav Havel questioned the
value of the label "postcommunist." Noting the long ties of many of
the post-Communist states to Western culture and values, he argued that
the continued description of these states with the label "postcommunist"
was akin to describing the United States as a "former British colony."[42]
Havel's argument is important, for it highlights the danger of assuming
that all negative phenomena in these states are different in a fundamental
way from similar phenomena in other states that have never been Communist. It also sensitizes us to the fact that the legacy of communism is
likely to become less important, either as a factor that conditions the
actions of leaders and citizens or as a justification for certain developments, as time passes. At the moment, however, the legacy of communism, coupled with the impact of the transitions under way, still colors
many aspects of life in important ways.

Havel's article, which argues that the non-post-Communist West
must realize the connection between developments in Eastern Europe
and the former Soviet Union and its own fate, also highlights another
important aspect of this question, the role and responsibility of outside
actors. Although it is clear that the basic task of coming to terms with and
overcoming the many negative legacies of communism falls to leaders and
citizens within the region, the speed with which and the extent to which
this past is overcome will also depend on the actions and the support of
leaders of other states. The impact of this factor is especially clear in
regard to the economic legacies. But continued interest and support by
leaders and citizens in more established democracies is also important if
the political and social legacies of Communist rule — and, as Havel argues,
the label "postcommunist" itself — are to become things of the past.

10

Hungary

Zoltan Barany

What will remain of socialism? All these socialist realist people. They are socialists because they have lived with the socialist reality for forty years; the majority for most of their lives. The lessons, traits, style, morality, and logic of these forty years cannot be dropped in the waste basket.

György Konrád

All historical periods leave legacies that affect subsequent eras. In this century Hungary, along with its East European neighbors, has been the setting for several momentous sociopolitical and economic transformations. It is enough to recall the disintegration of the Habsburg Empire, further complicated by the short-lived dictatorship of the Hungarian Communists in 1919. The end of the Horthy era's authoritarian rule and the beginning of Soviet-imposed communism brought even more comprehensive changes, similar in their magnitude to the current transition. These distinct historical periods have left behind diverse heritages that were of crucial significance to the further development of Hungary's political and economic life, social affairs, and physical environment. While the conditions of present-day Hungary are in many ways the result of four decades of communism, it is often difficult to distinguish between legacies clearly created by the Communist era and those of a thousand-year cultural, social, economic, and political journey. Thus, it is important to be aware of the various facets of the country's political and socioeconomic traditions which were not significantly altered by the Communist period.[1]

This chapter will examine the legacies of communism in Hungary in four areas: politics, economics, social affairs, and the physical landscape and the environment. Each of these substantive sections will address three concerns: the manner in which Communist policies in the given area developed, the legacy the Communists left behind, and the post-

Communist government's first efforts to deal with the situation as it presented itself in 1989–90.

Political Legacies

As it did in the other East European states, the Communist Party established its position as the monopolist of political power in Hungary by 1948. In the Stalinist period (1945–56) the Party was a ruthless executor of the Kremlin's will in Hungary as it persecuted large segments of the population through uncommonly brutal practices. The Party was ruled by a quadrumvirate whose most powerful member, Mátyás Rákosi, fancied being called "Stalin's best East European disciple." Following the ill-fated popular revolution of 1956, the Party renamed itself the Hungarian Socialist Workers' Party (HSWP) and in a few years began a cautious but longstanding and gradual domestic liberalization program. This process, with few and relatively brief interruptions, lasted until 1989 and afforded Hungarians a more pleasant life, higher living standards, and more personal liberties than were enjoyed by their neighbors in Eastern Europe. Indeed, in the post-1956 period the Hungarian style of communism was often depicted as "goulash communism" (to suggest the relatively ready availability of consumer goods), and as "the merriest barrack in the bloc" (to convey such factors as the permission to visit the West with only a few restrictions, the lack of widespread police brutality, and a generally much higher level of cultural freedom than existed elsewhere in the region).

These *relatively* liberal traits were not the result of Hungarian leaders' being more reluctant allies of Moscow than were their colleagues elsewhere in the region; rather, after the 1956 uprising Hungarian leaders appeared to have realized that a more pragmatic and less confrontational approach to a manifestly anti-Communist society might yield considerable benefits. Indeed, the quarter century of post-1960 Hungarian "liberal" communism may be envisioned as the consequence of implicit contracts on two levels: (1) a social contract between the Budapest Communist leadership and Hungarian society in which the leaders agreed to pursue relatively liberal domestic policies as long as the population did not explicitly oppose the regime; and (2) an elite contract between Soviet and Hungarian Communists in which the Kremlin leaders acquiesced to a considerably reduced Soviet role in Hungarian internal affairs as long as their Hungarian colleagues could ensure domestic stability, and full cooperation in and support of Soviet foreign policies.

Although most of the Kádár era was remarkable for its political stability (János Kádár was the HSWP's leader in 1956–88), by the early
1980s the regime was compelled to launch a few limited political reforms
to counter popular dissatisfaction with deteriorating economic conditions
and the rise of a small but increasingly energetic dissident movement.
These reforms (such as the introduction of multicandidate elections in
1985) were not effective, however, for they did not alter the HSWP's
political monopoly. Only in early 1989 did some reform-minded Communist leaders entertain publicly the possibility of a multiparty pluralist
political system; and at that point, owing to the swift radicalization of the
political spectrum, their views and actions were quickly superseded by
those of genuine reformers.

The erasure of the Communist political institutional structure has
proceeded in Hungary with an ease that is remarkable, especially when
one considers other aspects of the Communist legacy. This is quite logical. After all, it is far more difficult to change long-entrenched social
attitudes or to privatize economic sectors than to form political parties or
abolish organizations. The attitudinal political legacies of communism,
which include a distrust of politics and politicians in general and of institutions in particular, widespread apathy and pessimism concerning the
individual's power to influence political outcomes, and cynicism surrounding representatives of the state, are far less simple to overcome.

The institutional legacy of communism should be examined with
reference to institutions in which a large degree of continuity had prevailed, institutions that had changed, and institutions that had to be developed following the demise of communism. The most important political
institution of the past, the HSWP, essentially collapsed during its thirteenth congress in late 1989. In the aftermath of the congress, a much
smaller HSWP emerged, embracing the forces of old-style orthodox
Communists. A new Hungarian Socialist Party (HSP), led by reform-
Communists, also emerged and gradually established itself as a Western-
type social democratic party. The HSWP's local organizations disappeared in relatively short order. The Communist Party, which held a
monopoly of political power in late 1989, became irrelevant in a matter of
months, as in the March–April 1990 elections it was unable to garner 4
percent of the votes necessary for parliamentary representation. In addition, other Communist or Communist-sponsored organizations, such as
the Communist Youth League, the Workers' Guard, and the Patriotic

People's Front, entirely disappeared. The HSP had renounced its HSWP heritage and did much better at the polls, receiving 8.55 percent of the votes and acquiring thirty-three seats in parliament.

Perhaps the most important institutional survivor of the Communist era is the former official trade union, renamed the National Council of Hungarian Trade Unions (MSzOSz). Operating under its Communist-appointed chairman, Sándor Nagy, the MSzOSz impaired the democratic development of labor unions. There are many reasons for the durability of the MSzOSz. In contrast with Poland, no significant independent labor organizations were formed in Communist Hungary, a fact that allowed the official trade union to remain politically powerful and financially strong. The independent unions of the post-Communist era do not have enough members and sufficient financial resources to compete with the mammoth MSzOSz. In order to create equality in the operations of the various trade unions, parliament passed laws calling for the registration of union assets and the deduction of union dues (for all unions, not only the MSzOSz) from payrolls. Some local organizations of the 1.7-million-member MSzOSz refused to comply with the law, and their defiance has been a potential threat to the political transition.

Obviously, Hungary's Communist constitution (dating from 1949 and fashioned after the 1936 Soviet "Stalin" Constitution) could not be adopted by the post-Communist regime. Although a new constitution has yet to be passed by the legislature, the current basic law is essentially a patchwork of amendments passed by parliament in 1989 and 1990. In the latter year, a Constitutional Court was established which has assumed the functions of a supreme court and has become a relatively strong, independent political body. Partly because Hungary has not had such an institution in the past, and partly because of how vaguely the Constitutional Court's powers were defined, many pertinent legal questions were left unanswered during the first few years of its existence. Since the court is empowered by the Constitution to review both laws still under consideration and laws already passed by parliament, the ten-member body is not only a powerful legal instrument but also a policy-making body, whose sphere of influence can extend to the legislative process. Owing to its broad prerogatives, some feared that the Constitutional Court would damage the principle of the separation of powers, although in most cases the judges displayed an awareness of this danger and refrained from abusing their office. By 1992 several thousand cases had already been submitted by individuals to the court for judicial review.

Another institution that has gained a great deal of political clout is the presidency. As a result of a political deal struck between the victor of the 1990 elections (the Hungarian Democratic Forum [HDF]) and the runner-up (the Alliance of Free Democrats [AFD], the main opposition party), the president was elected by parliament and not by popular vote (as elsewhere in the region). The HDF and its governing coalition, on the one hand, and the AFD, on the other, agreed that the latter's candidate, Árpád Göncz, would be elected. An esteemed playwright, translator, and dissident with impeccable anti-Communist credentials, Göncz has tried to be more than a figurehead president, and in doing so has clashed repeatedly with former prime minister József Antall and his government. At the end of September 1991 the Constitutional Court ruled in favor of limiting presidential powers. It found, for instance, that Göncz, while formally commander-in-chief of the armed forces, had to restrict himself to giving guidelines to the army and could not interfere in its day-to-day operations. A more recent issue has been Göncz's postponement of his countersigning of the appointments of the six vice-chairmen of the state-owned Hungarian Radio and Television whom Antall had nominated; Göncz noted that the Constitution set no time limit on approving such appointments. The court ruled that the president had to approve government-nominated candidates unless their appointment endangered the democratic functioning of the institutions concerned.[2]

The problems surrounding the office of the president point to a troubling political legacy of communism. During the Communist era, constitutionalism and legality were not taken seriously, for they were considered formalities that could only restrict the decision-making powers of the rulers. In fact, to allow more elbow room to Communist leaders, the regime was characterized by a complete lack of legal norms regulating a host of important political and societal relationships and rights. This negative legacy explains the current shortcomings of Hungary's legal edifice regulating political institutions: namely, clear boundaries of jurisdiction and responsibility have not yet been drawn. Both the Constitution and individual bills leave many pertinent areas gray or ambiguous, if not ignored. Consequently, the Constitutional Court must take on far more cases than it is able to promptly attend. This legacy can be expected to be eradicated in a few years as constitutional norms and new laws continue to be established.

Another negative political legacy of communism is twofold: (1) the selection of state officials and employees on the basis of ideological conformity and connections rather than merit; and (2) the presence of a large state bureaucracy connected to the Communist era whose members cannot be easily replaced owing to their expertise and personal networks. In the post-Communist era, too, proximity to government and party leaders has time and again proved to be a more reliable indicator of successful political careers than has talent. The dearth of qualified decision makers has been clearly demonstrated by the government's indecisiveness and hesitation in many instances. Although the lack of qualifications of many bureaucrats is less conspicuous than under the former regime, grade school teachers have nonetheless been selected for ambassadorships, and university professors for ministerships, solely on the basis of their political affiliations.

A disturbing political legacy of the Communist regime is the survival of its *nomenklatura* in the administrative and economic spheres. Particularly among the middle-ranking echelons of political officialdom, thousands of former Communist bureaucrats remain, partly owing to their dexterity in holding onto power and partly because there are few qualified to replace them. This point is especially germane to exclusive organizations in which HSWP membership was quasi-mandatory, such as the military and the police forces. Thousands of former officials, enterprise directors, and higher- and middle-level cadres and comrades have been able to transform their political strength into economic muscle. Their superior vantage points allowed them to take advantage of rare entrepreneurial opportunities and maintain their privileged status.

Political culture is another area in which the Communist regime left a troubling legacy. Especially in the post-1956 period, the regime attempted to placate the public with material rewards and cultural liberalization while effectively discouraging political activism. In the post-Communist era many Hungarians have remained politically passive, distrustful of politicians and of politics in general. Until the 1994 national elections, voter participation has been very low by any standard, for several reasons. First, people often lack the political maturity to understand the weight and possible consequences of many issues. Second, they frequently do not see any difference between the contending parties, and therefore encounter difficulties making choices. Third, a substantial proportion of constituents refuse to believe that they can influence political outcomes by participating in politics. Fourth, election dates have been set unwisely on a number of occasions (for instance on summer holidays and weekends). Fifth, greater liberalism in Hungary (and Poland) in the late 1980s may have produced a premature "electoral burnout" in the post-Communist period.

A good example of voter apathy is the case of the by-elections for a parliamentary seat (Kisbér district, Komárom-Esztergom County) left vacant by the death of its occupant in 1990. Three successive two-round elections were declared invalid because of low voter turnout. In June 1992, elections were called for the fourth time, and even though voter participation did not exceed 27 percent the leading candidate finally managed to garner a majority of the votes. It is fair to say that citizens have been distrustful of politicians and have on occasion even openly supported acts of civil disobedience (as during the October 1990 taxi drivers' strike that paralyzed ground transportation for days). The reason behind such acts is the feeling of many that even though a certain measure (in this case, drastic price increases for fuel) may hurt their interests, there are no legal channels by which to remedy the situation.[3] A particularly telling illustration of the general absence of political maturity was the televised debate between two prominent politicians in November 1991. The demeanor of the predominantly urban, middle-class audience—intolerant, discourteous, and boorish—was far more telling than what the debaters had to say.[4]

The single-party system arrested the development of political parties and other organizations. Consequently, another political legacy of communism is the fact that most Hungarians (and, by extension, most East Europeans) do not have a clear sense of how parties operate, organize, and behave in various political arenas and circumstances. In the first few years of the post-Communist era, political parties did not become full-fledged parties in the Western sense. Most of them are broadly based, catch-all parties with little or no ideological core. The gap between voters and the parties has grown, and party membership has shown a declining trend. For instance, the largest opposition party, the Alliance of Free Democrats, lost more than one-third of its members in 1991. The dozen or so competitive parties were able to recruit less than 250,000 members altogether (whereas the HSWP had almost 900,000 registered members in its heyday). Most parties have had problems maintaining party unity, given the diverse viewpoints and political orientations within their ranks. The center-right HDF, for example, comprises at least three definable factions (populist, liberal, and Christian-democratic); and in the summer of 1993 — with the departure of the right-wing populist István Csurka and his associates — it finally proved unable to integrate these diverse forces into the party.

"Party discipline" has evident negative overtones in a post-Communist system, and now many deputies cannot easily accept that the party leader's decisions should not be ignored. It appears that in their efforts to shake off the legacy of the Communist modus operandi, according to which the Party membership's stance had to be identical to the leadership's position, Hungarian politicians of the new era are approaching the other extreme by often disregarding their parties' positions. As a result, the party allegiances of numerous deputies have changed, although parliament has not addressed the numerous defections and changing alliances.

The working class was only nominally involved in Communist politics. This state of affairs has not changed appreciably during the post-Communist era. In fact, politics seems to have become the exclusive bailiwick of the intelligentsia, especially when one looks at the composition of political organizations. This notion should not be considered a legacy of communism, however, for the working class and even a large part of the intelligentsia were squeezed out of politics in earlier eras as well. Even though several parties have reportedly aimed to enroll blue-collar workers as members, politicians have been unable to find the proper tone in addressing them. As a result, workers and peasants have been isolated from politics and have turned their attention to economic concerns instead. Consequently, the political behavior of large segments of the population may be characterized as passive and even apathetic.

At the same time, in the area of civil society the legacies of communism appear to have been overcome to a large extent. Those organizations that make up civil society and were not affiliated with the Party-state were nearly totally obliterated in the Communist period. In the post-1989 era they have made a vigorous comeback. There are more than ten thousand political, social, cultural, and religious associations, all of them fully protected by law. In 1992, 923 groups asked for government aid, and 276 applications received approval. Not surprisingly, the issue of which organizations become the recipients of such assistance is hotly debated between the government and the opposition.[5] One of the most interesting

political organizations is the so-called Democratic Charter. Founded by
intellectuals in September 1991 to counter the increasing strength of
conservative-nationalist forces, the Charter has attracted members such
as the president of the International Pen Club, György Konrád, and the
mayor of Budapest, Gábor Demszky. Its goal is to support the rule of law
and to prevent the government from filling important positions in the
economy, the media, and the judiciary with its own appointees.

In the post-Communist era the traditional conflict between populists
and liberals returned, along with its negative side effects. This attitudinal
polarity dates not from the Communist period but from the late nineteenth century, and assumed great importance during the cultural and
political debates of the interwar period. The populists, a conservative
force with a rural social base, advocated the return to national and Christian roots and opposed many of the sociopolitical and economic changes
coming from the cities, perceived as the domain of the cosmopolitan
Jewish intelligentsia. The liberals, in contrast, urged social, cultural, and
economic progress, and emulation of the ways of the advanced European
countries. In the aftermath of communism the increasing stress that right-
wing political forces have put on "Christian-Hungarian" values, in contrast to supposedly non-Christian, cosmopolitan values, has been a troubling political trend. This crude differentiation has not only served to
divide the electorate but has also fueled anti-Semitic and anti-urban sentiments. The populist-urbanist split of the political scene has underlined
several significant policy debates, on topics ranging from religious education to the control of the media.

Foreign policy is one of the few areas in which the Communist legacy
has been primarily positive. The initially cautious opening to the West
began in the early 1980s and had become increasingly bold by the end of
the decade. Since 1989, drawing on the successes of the late-Communist
period, Hungary has successfully reoriented its foreign policies and foreign trade to Western Europe while maintaining cordial ties with its erstwhile East European allies, particularly the Czech Republic and Poland.
With the demise of the Council for Mutual Economic Assistance (CMEA)
and the Warsaw Treaty Organization, Hungary has managed to establish and improve relations both with the European Union and with NATO
and has been an enthusiastic participant in the Central European Initiative, the Visegrád Triangle, and other regional and international organizations. Budapest has been generally prudent in its relations with its prob-

lematic neighbors to the south and southeast, although the resolution of longstanding animosities with Slovakia and, especially, Romania — animosities resulting from the treatment of sizable Hungarian minorities there — seems as elusive as ever.

Economic Legacies

The relative backwardness of the Hungarian economy is in large part a legacy of the Communist era. It is important to note, however, that the country's economy has traditionally been underdeveloped owing to a host of historical reasons (e.g., its position as the bread-basket of the Habsburg Empire and later of the Austro-Hungarian Monarchy) and socioeconomic reasons (e.g., late modernization, urbanization, and industrialization), and to its lack of natural resources. Still, because of the economic practices of the Communist period, Hungary's economic potential was not utilized and its development was further retarded. As a result, the post-Communist government inherited an economy whose performance placed it decidedly in the lowest third of Europe's economies.

The Communists took over a backward and predominantly agrarian economy, partially destroyed in the war and burdened by considerable reparations payments. Once in power, they enthusiastically adopted the Soviet model of a centrally planned economy — marked by heavy industrialization and collectivization — the applicability of which to Hungarian conditions was left unquestioned. By the early 1950s, despite the immense sacrifices of the population, living standards had decreased precipitously as the flaws of the economic system had become apparent. Starting with the mid-1960s, significant long-term economic changes were implemented, marked by the reevaluation of earlier priorities. Light industry and consumer satisfaction received more attention, while the emphasis on economic growth and investment in mammoth industrial projects continued with less fervor.

The introduction of the New Economic Mechanism (NEM) in 1968 signaled the political elite's realization that the centrally planned economy was not doing for Hungary what it was purported to do. The NEM created a second economy and allowed restrictions caused by central planning to be reduced, fiddled with the market, and cut subsidies, particularly on luxury items. In the mid-1970s, a Soviet- and CMEA-induced retrenchment, driven by political and ideological considerations, made the economy's problems worse instead of solving them. In the late 1970s the regime, now with Moscow's tacit approval, set out once again on the path of reform. Owing mostly to external factors, the timing was less favorable than in 1968, because Hungary's products had become less competitive in Western markets, leading to ever-increasing trade deficits. At the same time, growing inflation, accumulating foreign debts, and budget deficits emerged as serious problems that led to the introduction of income taxes and value-added taxes, along with steep price hikes and austerity measures, in 1988.

To alleviate the economic crisis, the HSWP's 1988 economic program aimed to reduce state subsidies for unprofitable enterprises, devalue the currency (the forint), ease foreign trade regulations, and implement a comprehensive price and wage reform. Moreover, a new corporate law enabled private enterprises to employ up to five hundred people, and permitted foreign companies to buy 100 percent of the stock in Hungarian firms. Nonetheless, most of the new measures were peppered with "weasel clauses" demonstrating the government's resolve to maintain as much economic control as possible and overriding its concern with extricating the country from its economic crisis. Still, these late-Communist developments eased Hungary's economic transformation and made the country more hospitable to foreign firms. At the same time, the new government also inherited an external debt in excess of $20 billion, the largest per capita foreign debt in Europe.

A further negative economic legacy of Hungarian communism may be found in the area of human resources and attitudes. The centralized and paternalistic Communist economic system impeded entrepreneurial spirit, retarded modernization and creativity, and eradicated the notion of economic responsibility. Moreover, in light of state ownership of the means of production, guaranteed employment, and the rigid remuneration system, few incentives remained for improved labor performance and productivity. The workers' morale had plummeted, as shown by widespread absenteeism and theft from the workplace.

The economic programs of the major parties competing in the 1990 elections were short on specific remedies for Hungary's economic ills. Since then, the HDF-led coalition has faced many trying economic challenges, such as high inflation, low productivity, and a declining rate of growth, for which no easy or swift remedy could be found. Clearly, erasing the economic legacy of communism will take decades. There has been some improvement as a result of changes in the economy's institutional structure, such as the abolition of some institutions, such as the National Planning Office; the reorganization of existing structures, such as branch ministries; and the creation of other structures, such as the National Accounting Office. Decision making and responsibility for economic actions have begun to be shifted back to the proper levels. At the same time, Hungarian industry, with its antiquated infrastructure and equipment park, is hard pressed to compete in foreign markets. Along with the other East European states, the country missed out on the post–World War II technological revolution, and catching up in this regard appears to be a formidable task. In spite of vigorous criticism, the new regime has thus far opted for incremental changes rather than "shock treatment," in order to keep unemployment rates as low as possible and to retain control over inflation.

Surely, there is plenty of economic discomfort and uncertainty in post-Communist Hungary. Industrial production has declined by about a third, and unemployment had risen to 10 percent by late 1992. Hungary's foreign debt has also continued to cast a shadow over the country's economic future. The decline in living standards has not been reversed, and income distribution has become more uneven, with poverty rising alongside conspicuous consumption by the nouveaux riches. All of this is taking place in spite of the fact that the International Monetary Fund poured $970 million into Hungary in 1991 alone.

Other important Communist legacies are a lack of qualified decision makers who are not connected with past economic practices, and a widespread aversion to risk taking. Although Communist Hungary's foreign trade was more diversified than that of its neighbors, the collapse of trade with the Soviet Union and other former CMEA states in the aftermath of the revolutions spelled dire consequences to the rigid Hungarian economy and caused much of the growing unemployment. And yet, while Hungary's road of organic economic transformation may seem slow and sluggish compared to the shock therapy administered in Poland and East Germany, this approach has succeeded in preventing hyperinflation and even larger-scale unemployment. Moreover, owing to the persistent tinkering with economic reform during the preceding two decades, Hungary's economy was far more integrated into the economies of Western Europe, and this afforded better access to Western capital and credit markets. Thus, Hungary could avoid large-scale economic dislocations and has received the lion's share of foreign capital invested in the region. The private sector's portion in the economy has risen dramatically, as have Hungary's exports to Western Europe.

There are several conflicting views on the contemporary Hungarian economy. Domestic opinion is dissatisfied and feels a steady decline, whereas many economists and financial analysts abroad consider Hungary a good paradigm for the region. The press has carried many articles on the state of families reduced to poverty, on the dwindling of cash incomes, and on the imminence of economic collapse. Reports are published daily on how privatization is making little headway, but the fact is that by the fall of 1992, 10 percent of state enterprises were in private hands and a further 20 percent were owned by associations. Although privatization did not start from zero, as it did in some of the neighboring states (Czechoslovakia, Romania), it was clear that it would surely take at least several years to accomplish.[6] In 1991, the State Property Agency approved the privatization of 189 state firms with a capital value of 418 billion forints, and early that year the transformation and sale of another 307 firms was in progress. By comparison, the privatization programs of most of the developing countries covered no more than 20 enterprises, and in the highly acknowledged Turkish privatization a total of 48 state-owned firms were transferred to private ownership between 1986 and 1991.[7]

In many respects Hungary's economic performance since 1989 has been one of the best in Eastern Europe. Inflation, which ran at 36 percent during the first three quarters of 1991, stood at 23 percent in late 1992, the lowest in Eastern Europe. No less than 195 billion forints, that is, almost one-quarter of the population's total savings, was accumulated in a single year, 1991. Hungary's trade with the West has expanded dramatically, signifying a crucial reorientation away from the Soviet Union.[8] In the first quarter of 1992 alone, foreign trade surplus amounted to $400 million, although by 1994 this surplus had greatly diminished.[9]

Hungary has been able to attract a large number of investors, who had established approximately eight thousand joint ventures by 1991, and invested $2 billion in the same year. The Budapest stock market, which opened in June 1990, has the largest trade volumes in the region. The influx of foreign capital, the country's progress in developing the institutional infrastructure of a capitalist economy, its relatively low rates of inflation, and its political stability have helped the government promote

Hungary as the "commercial hub of Eastern Europe." The country's leadership hopes that Hungary will be able to join the European Union by the end of the century.

Societal Legacies

The societal legacy that communism left behind in Hungary is in many respects negative, yet some of the adverse phenomena of the present are not necessarily the results of communism. Hungary was a relatively poor and backward country even before 1945, and Hungarians then as now were leading in statistics of suicide and alcoholism. The changes in the country's social fabric were partly the consequence of dislocations following World War II, when large segments of the former ruling elites and bourgeoisie left the country.

In the area of social affairs communism bequeathed some very positive legacies as well as negative ones. In stark contrast with the interwar regime, the Communist leadership had from the beginning paid a great deal of attention to education and culture. By the end of the Communist period, universal literacy was firmly established, and attendance at educational institutions had increased dramatically on all levels, from primary school to university. Not only was education free but in some areas, particularly the natural sciences, music, and physical education, it approached world-class standards. Cultural products (books, exhibitions, and concerts) were generally of high quality and affordable to most. Theoretically, at least, health care was also provided free of charge during the Communist period, although in practice patients were required to offer substantial payments to health care workers, whose salaries were inexplicably low.

The Soviet model that East European leaders adopted and emulated had important ramifications for Hungarian society. The main elements of this approach included the creation of an industrial working class; the transformation of rural society; and the creation of a loyal, white-collar nomenklatura class, along with a technical intelligentsia.

Owing to the postwar heavy industrialization campaign, along with the collectivization of agriculture, the size of the industrial proletariat had grown very rapidly. By the 1970s, the industrial labor force reached its peak: more than 45 percent of those who were actively employed worked in industry. This social class consisted of a more established stratum of industrial workers, who had different values regarding work and politics than did the predominantly unskilled workers recruited from the peasantry. Members of the former group were politically more self-conscious and generally supportive of the new regime, and took pride in their skills and labor. Initially, at least, many of them believed that they were going to be beneficiaries of the Communist regime, whose antipeasant and antibourgeois sentiments they shared.

Communism created a different type of industrial working class as well, a subclass of hundreds of thousands (usually men), who maintained their rural residences but commuted weekly to large cities where most lived in primitive dormitory-style facilities. Their families, left behind in the countryside, often suffered psychological and emotional hardships as their traditional way of life was destroyed. True to their rural backgrounds, many of these new workers remained religious and resentful of the Communists. Their silent opposition to the regime was reflected by widespread absenteeism, alcoholism, and erratic work habits. These industrial workers retained their rural roots for two primary reasons: they could supplement their incomes at home in their small private plots, and housing costs remained lower in rural areas than in the cities. Especially after the mid-1960s, the Hungarian peasantry had a greater chance for economic advancement than did members of the peasantry elsewhere in the region, because of the regime's increased tolerance of private economic activities.

The Communist regime also developed its own elites. The new members of the political elite initially came from the working class, and were quickly set apart from the toiling masses by the privileges they were allotted. As time progressed, however, social mobility had become more and more limited. By the 1970s the proportion of white-collar workers and intellectuals gaining positions in the political and economic leadership had grown considerably. Education had increasingly become an important criterion for advancement, and therefore the proportion of working-class individuals in the higher echelons of power had diminished.

Starting in the early 1970s the distribution of wealth became progressively more unequal. The opportunities for career advancement and the acquisition of material rewards increasingly favored members of the political, intellectual, and social elites and left behind those, particularly the industrial proletariat, living on fixed incomes. By the early 1980s a growing segment of the Hungarian population had become a permanent underclass, mostly unskilled workers, who had little hope of emerging from their misery. According to official sources, in 1987 more than 6 percent of the population lived below the officially set subsistence level.

At the end of the Communist era there were few social problems that did not affect Hungarian society. The educational and health care systems suffered from a chronic shortage of funds. The HSWP and the government were unable to come up with a comprehensive youth policy that could reverse the widening trend of alienation and pessimism among young people. A problem that failed to evaporate, and the government treatment of which was notoriously inadequate, was the lack of housing. More than 20 percent of young families did not live independently five years after their weddings. The lack of affordable housing, in turn, was one of the main causes of Hungary's serious demographic problems. Since 1980 the population had decreased by more than 90,000, and the number of those under age thirty had decreased by more than 360,000. At the same time the number of divorces had rapidly increased, while the number of marriages had dropped.[10]

Every era conserves and creates moral-ethical values; and the legacy of communism in this regard appears to be the denial of the Communist period, the attitude that "it was all a waste," the rejection of everything connected to the preceding forty years. This questioning of the past, the disparagement of the labors of generations, is also a sign of an unhealthy moral transition. The reappearance of the denunciations, and the abandonment of old friends for reasons of political convenience, is reminiscent of Stalinism.[11]

In the meantime, Hungarian society has become less kind to the old and the downtrodden, and often intolerant of national and ethnic diversity. Anti-Semitism, Gypsy bashing, vandalism, and violent attacks against foreign students and workers have become the trademarks of youth gangs. The fact that a large number of uneducated (and increasingly, educated) youths have encountered difficulties in finding employment intensifies their problems. The ensuing economic problems have negative effects on the socialized health care system and continue to force a large proportion of the adult population to hold down two jobs in order to make ends meet. As a result of these and other related phenomena, the average life span of Hungarian men fell from 66.8 years to 65.6 years in the last decade and a half of Communist rule. Moreover, Hungary has been cursed with the highest suicide rate in the world (thirty-six per hundred thousand in 1978, forty-six per hundred thousand in 1988).

Thus, the new post-Communist government has not been in an enviable position. Some of these problems could be at least partially remedied with monies that the state does not have. The government has tried to improve the situation and prevent some problems from getting worse, but with little apparent success. In fact, many social problems have been aggravated since 1989 for a variety of reasons, most of which can be traced back to the economic situation. Crimes and violence have increased perceptibly, yet there is no improvement in sight because the regime cannot afford more and better-equipped policemen. The number of those living in dire poverty has grown owing to increasing unemployment. The education and health care systems have not improved because there are no funds for modernization. Furthermore, owing especially to the high inflation rate, the economic situation of the growing number of pensioners, particularly those who are single, has drastically deteriorated, as has the situation of those living on fixed incomes. In a well-publicized case, the former president Pál Losonczi said that he intended to sell his Communist medals to augment his pension.[12]

At the same time, some sociologists and poll takers insist that the situation is not as hopeless as journalists suggest. Tamás Kolosi, a noted sociologist and the director of an institute for social research, contends, for instance, that while people certainly do not live well, they live better than they think they do.[13] Kolosi argues that in Hungary there exists an artificially created perception that the economic situation is on the brink of an imminent disaster, that living standards are in free fall, and that impoverishment is incredibly widespread.

An average day, they say in Budapest, is worse than yesterday but better than tomorrow. Pessimism and apathy, trademarks of the Hungarian national character at the best of times, have become perhaps the most conspicuous features of post-Communist Hungary. The majority of the population is clearly dissatisfied with their elected leaders' ability to get the country out of its economic predicament and to supplant the thousands of members of the former nomenklatura who managed to hang on to their economic positions if not their political prowess. The public mood is dark, even though most foreign observers contend that Hungary appears to be in a far better situation than most of its neighbors.

Environmental and Urban Development Legacies

The Communist regime inherited from its predecessors a predominantly rural country with many cities and villages largely destroyed by the war. Budapest had been devastated by prolonged fighting; its bridges lay in the Danube, and many of its famed monuments and buildings had been mutilated by extensive bombing. Although the postwar renovations proceeded relatively rapidly, the new planners, at least in the beginning, were rarely concerned with re-creating the prewar cityscapes or maintaining traditional architectural forms. As a result, in many Hungarian cities and towns medieval buildings are now interspersed with functionalist blunders that disrupt long-established architectural harmony and insult the eye. To be sure, as time progressed Communist city planners, too, had become more aware of and concerned with preserving old city centers and historic buildings. The joy of citizens over the renovation of their cities has frequently been ephemeral, however, owing to the poor quality of the materials used and the absence of proper and regular maintenance.

The heavy industrialization campaign led to large-scale urbanization, and the construction industry hurriedly established factories for the building of mass housing projects. By the mid-1950s huge block houses were mushrooming on the outskirts of virtually every city. Propaganda films heralded the construction of these human beehives as a major achievement of the new regime which provided "civilized" dwellings for the growing urban proletariat. The outside appearance of the housing estates differed from one period to the next.[14] In the 1950s the block houses were shoddily built four- or five-story structures housing one- or two-room apartments, occasionally with communal bathrooms, and almost invariably without elevators. In the 1960s and 1970s the buildings had grown in size, frequently rising to twelve to fifteen stories; and although their quality had scarcely improved, the individual dwellings were now somewhat more spacious. In the 1980s the apartment blocs had become more appealing but their numbers had greatly diminished, as the regime was no longer able to spend large amounts on public housing.[15]

By the late 1980s the conditions in the housing projects had drastically deteriorated. Built without much concern for human scale and the environment, the projects have also contributed to many social ills. Hungary's economic difficulties have affected the tenants of these projects more adversely than others. Because the projects are far from city centers and from most places of employment, the swiftly increasing price of mass transportation especially hurts these people. Furthermore, the operating costs of these apartments are so high, following the repeated increases in energy prices, that the apartments' value has plummeted on the housing market.

The new government is cognizant of these problems and has attempted to cushion the financial blow on the population by promising delays of utility price rises and granting various forms of social assistance to the most desperate. Still, even though the problems are acknowledged and plans to alleviate them (e.g., by instituting some form of state support for dwelling maintenance) have been proposed, the real question is where the money will come from.[16] In the future these problems will likely become even more serious if local authorities do not gain the right to manage their income, and whatever state support they may be allotted, as they see fit.

Although Hungary seems to be in a better environmental situation than its neighbors, the former regime's neglect of the physical environment resulted in major problems that will haunt generations to come.[17] Until the 1970s the Communist regime paid relatively little attention to environmental deterioration due to heavy industrialization, the extensive use of fertilizers in the agricultural sector, and the noise and air pollution caused especially by industry and transportation. The environment only became an issue temporarily, owing to well-publicized scandals such as the revelation of massive air pollution near the coal mines of Dorog and Tata and in major cities, the mercury poisoning in Miskolc, or the lead poisoning in Nagytétény.[18] Still, the regime appeared to be somewhat more concerned about the environment than did other regimes in the region. For instance, beginning in the 1970s large sums were spent on the prevention of environmental problems in certain areas — especially centers of tourism, such as the surroundings of Lakes Balaton and Velence.[19] Some guidelines concerning industrial pollution were established in the 1970s, and an environmental education network was established in 1983, but environmentalists continued to wage a quixotic war against contaminators, as compliance was optional and violators were rarely held responsible.

The protection of urban environments remained a low priority for the regime. By the late 1980s the emission of pollutants into the atmosphere reached more than two hundred kilotons. About 8 percent of Hungary's territory is affected by air pollution, but more than 40 percent of the population lives in these areas, which include Budapest and eleven other cities.[20] The main sources of pollution remain transportation and the oil industry, together with other branches of heavy industry. Until January 1992, Hungary did not impose any emission standards on vehicles. The continued importation of relatively cheap — but all the more contaminating — East German automobiles (Trabants and Wartburgs) equipped with two-stroke engines, and the vastly inadequate maintenance of buses and trucks powered by inefficient diesel motors, have contributed most obtrusively to pollution.

Water pollution is a similarly pressing issue, as water consumption doubled between 1970 and 1985 but the development of sewage treatment facilities did not keep pace. The drinking water of more than one thousand of the thirty-two hundred Hungarian communities has been contaminated by nitrates.[21] Urban garbage disposal is generally of an acceptable quality, but there are twenty-five hundred village dumps that conform neither to environmental nor to public health regulations.[22] The countryside, particularly Hungary's relatively sparse forests, has also seen a great deal of devastation owing to myopic forest management, public neglect, and the flagrant disregard of the military (especially the Soviet occupying forces) for their surroundings.

The issue that galvanized the antiregime democratic opposition in the early 1980s was the 1977 Hungarian-Czechoslovak intergovernmental agreement over the building of a hydroelectric dam on the Danube. The ill-conceived nature and the potentially disastrous direct and indirect environmental effects of the project were publicly revealed by experts and scientists, yet the government decided to push on. Bowing to mounting public pressure, Hungary's last (reform-)Communist government, that of Miklós Németh, unilaterally stopped construction on the Hungarian site in November 1989. (The Slovak government has not halted the project.)

Environmental protection figured prominently in virtually every party's electoral campaign in 1990, although the programs were long on rhetoric and short on substance. The new government has taken the environment far more seriously than did its predecessor, but its policies have not been as effective as environmentalists had hoped. The main concerns of the new Ministry for Environmental Protection are air pollution in the major cities and industrial areas and the deteriorating state of the groundwater. Nevertheless, because of the government's limited resources and other priorities, the possibilities for investments in environmental protection are very limited. To offset this problem, the price of electricity and of water services was increased considerably (the cost of water services by approximately 350 percent in 1990 alone) in order to reduce consumption and to shift the burden from the state to consumers. Penalties for contaminators have been increased, and a monitoring system to identify polluters has been put in place. More importantly, steps have been taken to decentralize environmental management. Consequently, the accountability of regional and local administrative bodies has increased.

Conclusion

In spite of its many difficulties, it appears that thus far Hungary has been making slow but steady progress in political democratization and economic transformation. Many of the country's current problems are direct consequences of four decades of Communist rule. Others are due to a variety of factors, such as the region's long history of relative socioeconomic backwardness and the current international economic climate. At the same time, however incomplete and often half-hearted, the long-standing reform efforts of the reform-Communists should not be overlooked, for in 1989 Hungary was much better prepared for political and economic changes than its neighbors. The country faces further challenges and obstacles on the road to full-fledged democracy and economic prosperity. Still, one finds it difficult not to be optimistic about Hungary's chances in the long-term future. Particularly by contrast with some of its former partners in the Communist bloc, Hungary appears to have a realistic chance of alleviating the impact of communism's negative legacies.

11

Romania

Daniel N. Nelson

This chapter portrays Romania's condition in the years immediately prior to the revolt in December 1989, which ended decades of tyranny. It is a story of national disaster. To speak of a Romanian disaster implies, certainly, a calamity and its tragic consequences. Yet the concept contained in the etymology of the term *disaster* also applies — that is, the notion that calamity is brought about by an evil influence. Implicit in the discussion that follows is a view, shared by most Romanians, that the Ceauşescu clan had a pernicious and sinister effect on the nation's society and culture. The Ceauşescu regime, as well, mortgaged the country's considerable national wealth, leading to economic ruin and wasted international respect.

Romania's Communist regime lasted for almost forty-five years, and was led during the last quarter century by one man, Nicolae Ceauşescu. Two generations grew to adulthood during that time, and in December 1989 the Romanian population was composed principally of people without any memory of a different political system. Part of the difficulty confronting Romania's escape from tyranny is the absence of any experience whatsoever with an open, competitive society governed by the rule of law.

This chapter does not reflect changes after December 1989. There are reasons for this. The agony that was Romania prior to the end of Ceauşescu's rule should not be set aside for the sake of current events; there was pain and desperation behind the sacrifices made in December 1989 and thereafter. Further, to know how extraordinarily difficult it will be for Romania to achieve a smooth transition to something close to democracy, one has to hear about the depths to which conditions had fallen.

The Economic and Environmental Disaster

In 1965, the year Ceauşescu became first secretary of the Romanian Communist Party (RCP), a British guidebook described Romania as "making rapid strides towards the luxurious living of the twentieth century. Politics apart, you just have to admire this traditionally poor Latin race which is now realizing that it can become rich by its own efforts and is performing an economic miracle as miraculous as the much-vaunted Italian and German efforts."[1] Even for a touristic guidebook, such effusive praise seems now to have been absurdly premature. Yet there were many scholars who agreed with that assessment. Indeed, Romania was thought to be on an "inexorable march . . . toward modernity";[2] it was characterized principally as "a developing socialist state" as late as the early 1980s.[3]

Economic data do not belie these portrayals of Romania in the 1960s and 1970s. During an extended period — for almost two decades — the socioeconomic indicators usually selected to gauge "development" and "modernization" showed that Romania was rapidly becoming industrialized, urbanized, better educated, and healthier.[4] Although the changes had begun in the late 1940s, as an emphasis on extensive development and the Soviet economic model were solidified, the most rapid transformations occurred in the 1960s and 1970s. Romania's average annual real growth in GNP per capita was higher than that of all other European countries except Bulgaria during the 1960s, and from 1971 to 1975 it was the highest in Europe (5.7% per annum).[5] Moreover, during 1971–75 Romania's industrial output increased faster than that of any other member state of the Council for Mutual Economic Assistance (CMEA), and far more rapidly than that of European Community members.[6] Although there was some slowdown evident already in 1976–80, Romanian growth remained among the highest in Europe, and was substantially greater (at 3%) than that of any other Communist state.

Other standard indicators likewise show that socioeconomic transformations were occurring at breakneck speed. Between 1960 and 1970, for instance, Romania's urban population jumped from 15 percent to 25 percent, and the proportion of the country's gross domestic product (GDP) derived from industry doubled between 1960 and the late 1970s (to 58% in 1978).[7] The agricultural sector, which before World War II had employed more than 80 percent of all working Romanians, accounted for only 28.6 percent by 1981.[8] The most rapid decline in agricultural employment, however, took place in the fifteen years between 1965 and 1980, when the percentage of the workforce employed in agriculture dropped from 56.5 percent to 29.4 percent.

Western images of these changes were, by and large, positive. Not only was Romania forging ahead at an extremely rapid pace, but it was doing so while adopting a stance that appeared to vex Soviet leaders. The oft-cited 1964 declaration of the Romanian Communist Party, stating its intention to pursue an independent path of development, was seized upon by Western observers as part of a national deviation from communism. In that regard, Ceauşescu's autarkic policies were thought to be rooted in a foreign policy independence from the Soviet Union, an independence Ceauşescu sought to spotlight for domestic and Western consumption.

Prognoses for ongoing development, however, were always clouded by the inefficiencies of Party control, central planning, and bureaucracy.[9] Economic plans during the first decade and a half of Communist rule concentrated on recovery from the war, and the completion of collectivization. The centralization of decision making and the emphasis on extensive growth, however, expanded greatly after 1960, and particularly during Ceauşescu's years (the years after 1965). As late as 1960, for example, the mean number of employees per enterprise was 747; by 1982, enterprises averaged 1,830 employees apiece.[10] Pushed by the notion that "the leading sector in the socialist economy is industry, with strong emphasis in heavy industry,"[11] the Ceauşescu regime expanded the sheer volume of industrial output, and imported a great deal of foreign technology at considerable cost, without considering the need for such production.

The built-in irrationality of Stalinist economics eventually caught up with the Romanian Communist Party. The overbuilding of productive capacity in the heavy industries (especially the machine building, petrochemical, and steel industries) was a direct consequence of the centrally planned investments and output targets that were decided without any understanding of the market. Romania was the world's tenth-largest producer of machine tools, for example, and huge Romanian factories (employing on average three thousand workers apiece) turned out vast quantities of "goods . . . below international standards."[12] In 1986 Romania produced, in fact, two and a half times the number of metal-cutting machine tool units produced by the United States. Without markets abroad in which to sell Romanian machinery, chemicals, steel, and the like, however, the loans used to buy the technology with which to expand capacity could not be repaid. Efforts to export Romanian goods within the third world, or to dump substandard machine tools, textiles, and other items in the West, did not resolve the mounting dilemma. The accumulated debt of Romania grew rapidly in the late 1970s, and the debt service ratio reached more than 33 percent by 1981. This is not huge when compared to Poland's debt at that time, but it is still above acceptable norms. In 1981 and 1982, Romania sought and received rescheduled payments on outstanding loans that, by then, had reached more than $10 billion.[13]

Simultaneously, the agricultural sector of Romania's economy, which had been the economy's strongest component before and after World War II, began to disintegrate. As rural areas were depleted of younger generations because of both collectivization (declared to be complete in early 1962) and the labor demands of urban-based industry, the entire agricultural economy was derationalized through the imposition of central planning. Rather than planting what was in demand domestically, and harvesting at optimal times, collectivized Romanian agriculture (which by the early 1960s controlled more than 90% of all agricultural land area) was told to produce for export, and was given a planned timetable for all of the critical steps in food production.

Agricultural products of all kinds were seen by Romanian central planners as a means to obtain hard currency, especially from Western Europe. The Ceauşescu regime attempted to divert as much of the country's grain, fruits, vegetables, and livestock to export as possible, in an effort to earn foreign currency with which to buy Western machines and technologies.[14] Such a politically induced decision, however, placed a premium on raising the output of agriculture at any cost—and the costs included heightened inefficiency in the use of manpower and materials, soil depletion (as the same or similar crops were planted year after year in the same fields), and many other damaging practices. Further compounding Romania's agricultural plight were centrally decreed investment and trade decisions that bought, for example, far more irrigation equipment than could profitably be used, while importing grains (which Romania had the potential to produce in abundance) in exchange for Romanian-made fertilizer (which Romania needed to keep for itself to have more plentiful grain harvests).[15] Regarding agricultural policies, as well as industrial policies, it seems clear that a commitment to private agriculture would have had better results than did enforced collectivization and subsequent central planning. Michael Shafir has noted, for example, that Romanian data reveal the much higher productivity of the tiny proportion of all agricultural land which was in private hands. Private agriculture and private gardens accounted, in 1981, for 60 percent of all potatoes produced, "over 40 per cent of the vegetables, [and] virtually 60 per cent of the milk and eggs."[16]

Policies in support of rigidly enforced, centrally planned extensive growth led Romania relentlessly into a pervasive economic malaise. Virtually every datum available indicates that a plateau was reached in Romanian economic growth in the mid-1970s, and that there was a decided downturn in the late 1970s and early 1980s, with modest and spotty recovery by the mid-1980s. This "recovery," however, was neither substantial nor broad, and many sectors of the economy were unaffected. Measures of Romanian economic performance, almost without exception, reveal that glaring difficulties became apparent in 1979–82. Thad Alton's estimate of East European GNPs shows a stagnant and falling growth rate in those years, with the construction and industry sectors faring the worst in terms of average annual growth in the early 1980s.[17] Labor productivity exhibited poor growth in most sectors; it plummeted in the industrial sector in 1981.[18]

Romania's primary energy production, gauged in thousands of barrels per day of oil equivalent (including coal, crude oil, gas, natural gas liquids, and hydroelectric power), increased 45 percent between 1960 and 1970, and by 20 percent between 1970 and 1980, but only by 7 percent from 1980 through 1986. This basic indicator suggests that Romanian economic expansion had ground to a halt by the early 1980s.[19] From 1979 through 1984, energy consumption, also measured in thousands of barrels per day of oil equivalent, remained almost static, after having risen rapidly in the 1960s and 1970s. Also in the period 1979–84, many indicators of commerce failed to increase, or declined. From 1980 through 1985, the quantities of goods transported by rail and by motor vehicle, for example, failed to grow.[20]

Apart from industry and commerce, however, Romania's economic disaster had ramifications that permeated all aspects of the country's welfare. One compilation of socioeconomic data reports that Romania's per capita GNP, which ranked thirty-seventh in the world in 1977, had fallen to forty-fourth place by 1984. Using a combination of indicators, the same analyst found that Romania's overall socioeconomic ranking among all nation-states, which had been thirty-first in 1977, fell to forty-fifth in 1984.[21]

A country that had once seemed to be on "an inexorable march" toward a rapid expansion of its economic capacity and social complexity — relying almost entirely on the continued growth of industry, subsidized by investment funds accumulated through agricultural exports — began to see the dream of development rapidly unravel.

Pronouncements by the regime, however, continued to speak of "multilateral development" as being imminent, notwithstanding the many signs that the regime's policies had brought the economy to the brink of collapse. The language of delayed gratification was used by Ceauşescu and other high-ranking officials to justify privations imposed on the population. Romania would, it was promised, enter the ranks of developed states by 1990.[22]

The pursuit of "multilateral development," and the "impetuous" development of the forces of production, including both industrialization and agricultural modernization, were part of Ceauşescu's vocabulary for years.[23] But because an extremely large proportion of the national income (35–40% during the 1970s) was to be plowed back into industry as investments, consumption was deferred until some unspecified future time.[24] At the same time, the proportion of the net material product (NMP) used for consumption (both personal and collective) dropped from 75.7 percent in 1961 to 63.7 percent in 1980. Romania had the dubious distinction of being the "leader" in the decline of personal consumption as a proportion of NMP among East European countries.[25]

Development did not imply, then, that Romanian citizens would share much, if at all, in economic advances. Although there were improvements in key measures of social welfare (the number of hospital beds per thousand inhabitants, the percentage of the population enrolled in higher education, the infant mortality rate), these trends did not parallel the rapid urban-industrial expansion described earlier.[26] Most important, many of these improvements in living standards were lost in the 1980s as a host of economic ills befell Ceauşescu's Romania.

When it began to dawn on the regime that a crisis loomed, both problems and their solutions were identified in a manner that was certain to have traumatic consequences for the Romanian population. To Ceauşescu, it appeared that the principal difficulty had nothing to do with his policies. Instead, the foreign debt — in fact, a consequence of failed policies — was seen as the villain. He proceeded to attack the debt with a vengeance, relying entirely on domestic austerity to produce results.

By mid-1989, in fact, the hard currency debt had been erased, and the regime trumpeted its paying off the debt as a great achievement. Nevertheless, Ceauşescu pressed on, greatly limiting imports, while selling everything available for hard currency. After the mid-1980s, Romania had a trade surplus of $2 to $3 billion, almost all of which was quickly allocated for debt repayment.[27] Even after all creditors were paid off, investments as a proportion of national income remained exceedingly high. The Ceauşescu regime, in other words, squeezed the Romanian population to pay for its own policy blunders. Bearing the brunt of mismanagement, corruption, and rigidity meant, for the Romanian population, that they were forced to work harder for less. Wages were lowered, nutritional intake fell, heat and lighting were drastically reduced, and a nation that had been told that it was to enter the ranks of developed states by 1990 instead neared the level of underdevelopment. One report on an International Monetary Fund (IMF) assessment of Romanian economic conditions suggested a 40-percent drop in the standard of living (the total value of goods and services consumed per capita) between the late 1970s and the late 1980s.[28]

Such a colossal failure of a government's economic policies was never acknowledged by Ceauşescu. Subordinates (ministers, local leaders, and so on) were blamed, relieved from duty, and reassigned. Rotation (*rotatie*) of cadres, especially in and out of ministries, was an omnipresent part of Ceauşescu's rule, but it was particularly prevalent among the economic ministries of the government after the late 1970s. Although I will return to the matter of Romania's political disaster during the late Ceauşescu period, it is important to underscore here that the economic disaster, even as Ceauşescu noted that planned targets were not met year after year,[29] did not make the regime culpable in its own eyes. Annual economic plans continued to set unobtainable targets, and ministers and their deputies continued to move in and out of posts as inevitable failures were announced.

At a time when every other European Communist Party-state adopted some measure of economic reform — ranging from muddled face-saving steps in Bulgaria, Czechoslovakia, and the German Democratic Republic, to far-reaching efforts in Yugoslavia, Hungary, and Poland — Ceauşescu's Romania rejected any notion of undoing centralization. A worsening of the disaster described above, then, was far more likely than any positive trend.

With Romania's economic deterioration came yet more egregious environmental ruin. All Communist states paid scant attention to the environment because the key to their economic strategy was extensive growth — bigger, not better, via the consumption of ever-larger inputs of manpower and material. But in Romania, where there was never an opportunity to address even the most rudimentary ecological trade-offs implicit in extensive growth, the Ceauşescu regime produced environmental tragedies on a grand scale.

Entire towns and cities are devastated because of air pollution, including contaminants released through unfiltered smokestacks, and because of groundwater poisoning from innumerable sites where contaminated waste was discarded on a factory's premises. The Romanian town of Copsa Mica reached the front cover of *National Geographic* only because its children ran through the streets blackened by falling pollutants from factory emissions. Meanwhile, Turda residents in Judetul Cluj cope with thick, chalky dust from their cement factories, which causes what one local physician told me were "an unending series of respiratory problems," and cancers of suspicious origin.

Deforestation, topsoil erosion and loss, wetlands drainage, and other phenomena also were accelerated if not created by the political system that ruled Romania for so long. Inadvisable and wasteful practices of strip logging became more common in Ceauşescu's regime because only one thing counted — exports to reduce debt and ensure autarky. A now-retired forestry manager in Transylvania spoke to me about the unrelenting orders he received to produce more output from smaller and smaller forested regions. In the Danube Delta, notwithstanding the assiduous efforts of many international ecologists, drainage of wetlands accelerated during the 1970s and 1980s, altering forever a delicate habitat, and threatening species native to that region.

In all of this, there was a painful lesson emerging which Ceauşescu was unable or unwilling to recognize — namely, that extensive growth consumes at an ever-increasing rate the very resources on which such growth is predicated. Eventually, the lines intersect, and an economy begins to suffer because of the harm it had earlier inflicted on the workforce and the naturally occurring resources of the country.

The Sociocultural Disaster

Often in the name of modernization, but frequently without any rationale at all, the Ceauşescu government inaugurated policies the consequences of which have been calamitous for Romanian society and culture. A quarter century of Ceauşescu's brand of Communist rule had been socially divisive, exacerbating tensions between Romanians and ethnic minorities living within the Romanian state, and creating cleavages between segments and strata of society. At the same time, the destruction of cultural artifacts and the repression of artistic and literary creativity "progressed" further in Romania than it did in most other Communist states, save for China during its Cultural Revolution.

Ethnic Hungarians who are Romanian citizens number between 1.6 and 2.1 million, depending on whose estimate is used. They are the largest minority within Romania, and constitute from 7 to 9 percent of the entire population. Ethnic Germans number only one hundred thousand, and thus comprise less than 1 percent of the country's population. Both Hungarians and Germans, but particularly the latter, have held disproportionately high numbers of managerial and intellectual jobs, and many of the most highly developed cities and areas are in the Banat and in Transylvania, where both nationalities have been concentrated.

During the early years of his regime, it appeared that Ceauşescu was making some effort to placate Hungarians, Germans, and other ethnic minorities. There were many visits to minority counties in the late 1960s, and slogans that underscored the shared labors of "coinhabiting nationalities." In that regard, it appeared that Ceauşescu was reversing some of the overt discrimination against minorities practiced by his predecessor Gheorghe Gheorghiu-Dej, who, when Hungarian-speaking students supported the revolution in Hungary in 1956, closed down an autonomous Hungarian university in Cluj, and implemented other repressive measures.[30]

Ceauşescu's relative tolerance, however, was couched in vague rhetoric. In substance, there was nothing that minorities (especially Hungarians) could applaud. In the 1968–69 reorganization of local government, the thirty-nine (now forty) new *judete* (counties) were gerrymandered so that "Hungarian political 'clout' [was] constrained by the community's division into several counties, and the greatest density of Hungarians combined in a county with a substantial Romanian-speaking population."[31]

Further, Ceauşescu's policies in the 1970s and 1980s made it abundantly clear that the judete in which Hungarians and Germans live — those of Transylvania and the Banat — were to be substantially disadvantaged when it came to investment policies. Quite literally, the distribution of resources was determined by the accumulation of "fixed assets" in Romania's forty judete and thus created "winners" and "losers" during the

Ceauşescu era. Counties in historically Romanian provinces (Walachia and Moldavia) were overwhelming winners, gaining far more fixed assets than counties in Transylvania and the Banat.[32]

Being denied their fair share of political and economic resources is only part of the story, as it were, for Hungarians and members of other minorities in Romania. Although Cluj (Kolozsvár), Timişoara (Temesvár), Hunedoara, Braşov, and other cities of Transylvania and the Banat had been long ago developed as centers of industry and commerce, not only were they denied resources with which to continue that growth but, in fact, they also suffered more than other regions during the austerity of the 1980s. Their higher levels of socioeconomic development were sacrificed, one might say, at a faster pace than were levels of development in regions where evidence of extensive growth was primarily seen in the massive enterprises of the late 1960s and 1970s.

One sign—and a dramatic one—of ethnic Hungarian frustration with Ceauşescu's policies was a large flow of refugees across the border into Hungary in the late 1980s. The number of Romanian citizens, primarily of Hungarian origin, who fled is unclear, but estimates of between twelve thousand and fifteen thousand in the period from January 1988 through June 1989 are plausible. Hungary, in the same period, had granted some five thousand the right to settle permanently in that country, and at a rate of between two hundred fifty and three hundred a week, thousands more were processed by the end of 1989.[33] Some of these were Romanian tourists, students, scholars, and so on who forgot the way home. Most, however, fled in a manner fraught with risk—at night, overland, leaving behind almost all possessions. Relatives left behind were subjected to a variety of harassments and threats to convince others that emigrating would be costly for family and friends.[34]

Prominent Hungarians in Romania became increasingly strident in their criticism of Ceauşescu because of socioeconomic and political injustices. On several occasions, Károly Király, a one-time member of the Political Executive Committee (PEC, the Romanian equivalent of the Politburo), leveled attacks on the regime through public letters. Király, who was part of the highest levels of Party and state in the late 1960s and early 1970s, resigned because of the antiminority policies of the Ceauşescu regime. By the late 1980s, Király's censure of Ceauşescu had been joined by others who had parted ways with the regime earlier, most notably the former premier Ion Gheorghe Maurer.[35] Underground Hungarian-language publications began to circulate within Transylvania, as well, reporting on human rights limitations, and cultural and educational repression.

Policies harmful to Hungarians in Ceauşescu's Romania enflamed old disputes about Transylvania. During the middle and late 1980s, fusillades of articles and books, usually couched in academic terms, were hurled from both Romania and Hungary concerning the history of Transylvania. Briefly, the debate turned on the issue of who first settled in that region and the validity of the evidence marshaled by both sides in that dispute. This issue was important not so much because boundaries could have been redrawn or populations resettled in the political environment of Communist Europe; rather, what one believes about historic claims to Transylvania (whether Romanians settled there after Magyars, or were there continuously since Roman times) has a great deal to do with how legitimate one considers the absorption of ethnic Hungarians into today's Romanian state. Consequently, the debate affected the degree to which one criticized Ceauşescu's policies — sociocultural, economic, and political — toward Transylvanian Magyars, Germans, and other minorities of Romania. For both the Hungarian and Romanian governments, of course, the acrimony may have been an effort to deflect attention from domestic problems. The Romanian efforts seemed to be louder and more orchestrated, however, and included a late-1987 issue of the military history journal *Lupta Intregului Popor*, in which General Ilie Ceauşescu, brother of the late Romanian leader, joined several other authors in condemning Hungarian "falsifications" of history.[36]

By 1989, Hungarian complaints at meetings of the Conference on Security and Cooperation in Europe (CSCE) and other human rights forums, and the involvement of the UN high commissioner for refugees in the matter of ethnic Magyars leaving Transylvania, paralleled further ominous Romanian protests. Once again, military journals took the lead in venting Romanian vitriol; *Viata Militara*, a journal aimed at military officers, was used as a forum for Ilie Ceauşescu and others to lambast Hungary's allowing of anti-Romanian, pro–human rights speeches and demonstrations in Budapest, especially during the politically charged re-burial of Imre Nagy. Hungary's defense ministry at that time, acknowledging the deteriorating Hungarian-Romanian relations, noted that in Hungarian defense thinking there was a shift toward identifying the principal threats as being to the east (i.e., Romania).[37]

The Romanian societal disaster due to Ceauşescu's communism may

yet prove to be worse than anyone could have imagined earlier. Although
its rural population has diminished significantly, Romania is still a country
where more than 45 percent of the population lives outside urban areas.
Among urban dwellers, moreover, a large proportion (perhaps a third) are
people who are first-generation residents of towns and cities. Certainly all
of these people, and many others, have close ties to their families' villages.
In such a social milieu, Ceaușescu tried to push forward a plan to demolish
thousands of villages in the guise of "systematization" *(sistematizare)*. As
long ago as 1972, the Romanian Communist Party Conference set forth a
program to raze villages that were considered "less developed" and to
resettle people in other locales where housing and population density
would be optimal. Opposition to this idea, said all along to be Ceaușescu's
brainchild, was substantial. Resentment and anger toward Bucharest was a
natural consequence among those people whose lives would have been
disrupted, and local leaders were quoted in the Party daily, *Scinteia*, as
having said that a natural death for villages was far preferable to the policy
of "sistematizare."[38] Indeed, the opposition was sufficient, and the delays
so prolonged, that some observers were led to conclude that this program
had been set aside.[39]

In June 1986, however, at the Central Committee Plenum, and a year
later at the Plenum of June 1987, Ceaușescu's emphasis on his bizarre plan
was once again evident.[40] By the spring of 1988, the extent of the destruction and upheaval that would be created by sistematizare became known.
The December 1987 RCP Conference, and subsequent action by the
Central Committee, apparently created a timetable "for the destruction
of rural villages and their replacement by communal dwellings. By the
year 2000, two-thirds of all villages [were] due to have been destroyed."[41]
The scope of this plan, which Ceaușescu discussed in May 1988, exceeds
the magnitude that I had foreseen in 1987 when I estimated that "a couple
thousand of Romania's 13,100 villages *(sate)*" would be razed.[42] It now
appears, amazingly, that the Ceaușescu regime envisioned "modernizing"
seven thousand villages,[43] that is, destroying more than half of the existing
sate, and moving the inhabitants to concentrate these people in more than
five hundred agroindustrial centers where communal housing was to be
built. Even if all of the villages scheduled to be razed were those that
were the least heavily populated, several million people would have been
uprooted.

By mid-1989, the available evidence suggested that the pace of implementing sistematizare was slowed, owing to world condemnation, but certainly not abandoned. Around Bucharest, villages were indeed bulldozed, and the rising number of towns (orase) reported in Romanian statistics suggested that rural modernization, including the forced urbanization scheme of sistematizare, was beginning to have the effect of concentrating populations in agroindustrial complexes.[44]

Why did Ceauşescu insist on this policy? His official rationale was that more farmland was needed to heighten agricultural output, and that in large, urban agroindustrial centers the productivity of agriculture would be maximized. Yet there would have been at least a temporary loss of production from the uprooted people, and an accumulation of hostility toward Ceauşescu and the authorities who implemented his plan. Private plots, which had been responsible for a disproportionate share of produce and livestock, would also have been lost. Further, there seems to have been no consideration of the difficulties likely to be encountered when lands used for human habitation over the course of centuries were suddenly converted to agricultural use. The economics of Ceauşescu's plan, then, were very wrong.

The political rationale may have been far more compelling to Ceauşescu. One clear consequence of this scheme would have been a substantial decline in the number of sate where ethnically homogeneous minority communities resided. In cities, even those such as Cluj, all nationalities mix, and Romanian is the language of most government and commerce. But village life has enabled Hungarians in Transylvania (and Turks and other minorities elsewhere in the country) to retain their language and culture. These would have been seriously endangered in Ceauşescu's plan for rural resettlement, and such a diminution of cultural autonomy was no doubt one of Ceauşescu's goals. The remaining villages — perhaps six thousand — would have been enlarged by communal housing, and the several hundred agroindustrial complexes would have been the cornerstone of the entire project.[45]

From the standpoint of the regime, this may have enabled greater control over mass disaffection. Yet the social consequences of this plan would certainly have been tragic. Part of the tragedy, immediately clear to Hungarians, would have been the effect on Hungarian culture: "When they bulldoze cemeteries and churches, they will bulldoze the entire Hungarian historical heritage."[46] Protests in Budapest against the Romanian rural policy were mounted in the summer of 1988.[47]

The regime's harsh policies toward minorities — policies that enflame ethnic conflict — and the social dislocation certain to follow from any large-scale effort to destroy villages are but two prominent themes within the larger societal disaster wrought in Ceauşescu's era. One could also point to other misfortunes that threatened almost every segment and stratum of Romanian society. Ceauşescu's notions of societal perfection, especially during times of self-imposed, severe austerity, involved harmful policies and practices. He advocated the mass relocation of pensioners to the countryside, where they would have been added to the agricultural labor force, and he often repeated his contention that caloric intake could be reduced because Romanians did not eat scientifically.[48] These and other insights into Ceauşescu's social views reveal a man out of touch with the needs — often the desperate needs — of the people he ruled.

Within Romanian society, the culture — the products of human creativity and intellect in the Romanian population, especially in this century — suffered grievously during the latter half of the Ceauşescu era. It is important to distinguish periods within Ceauşescu's rule because, at least until 1971 (and in some artistic and scholarly endeavors until a few years later) Romanian creativity and learning temporarily gained some latitude. In the social sciences, for example, there was a temporary expansion of research into topics and methodologies (e.g., survey research) that had been repressed since the 1940s.[49]

However, the door closed quickly thereafter. Indeed, one can say with certainty that after the mid-1970s Romanian artists and scholars had to exist within the most constrained environment in Eastern Europe. Individual cases, were there space to describe them here, could provide an evocative account of Ceauşescu's offensive against any creative and intellectual person or group that dared to deviate in word or action from regime-dictated norms. In the West, we came to know best the mathematician Mihai Botez (now Romania's ambassador to the United Nations), the poet and journalist Dorin Tudoran, and the writer Paul Goma. In 1988–89 other intellectual dissidents who remained in Romania (such as Doina Cornea) surfaced, as their courageous personal endeavors to communicate about Romania's conditions precipitated further repression.[50] These intellectual dissidents (Goma was in the West for more than a decade prior to 1989) made the cause of those Romanians who were opposed to Ceauşescu's chaotic autocracy a matter of concern in Western Europe and the United States.[51]

In the 1980s, other Romanians joined the list of dissenters — individuals holding relatively pro-Marxist political views but sharing a common antagonism toward the cultural deprivations being suffered by their country. In late 1987 and early 1988, after the severe disturbances in Braşov on 15 November and a host of other protests and strikes during 1987, the security forces began to incarcerate intellectuals who had expressed criticism of Ceauşescu in the past. Few if any had anything to do with Braşov per se, but all critics were apparently seen with equal suspicion by the regime. Radio Free Europe reported this sweep to arrest prominent dissidents, and noted that among those under house arrest was the former Romanian ambassador to the United States, Silviu Brucan.[52]

Individual cases, however, do not by themselves convey the overriding cultural malaise produced by the long-term suppression of creativity and scholarship, which even in authoritarian systems are usually far less under government attack than was the case in Ceauşescu's Romania. Ceauşescu's offensive was broad and indiscriminate.

To supporters of the Ceauşescu regime, a socialist culture always must be a form of revolutionary action "led and guided by the party."[53] The rigid insistence on the RCP's leading role throughout the cultural sphere was longstanding in Ceauşescu's era. In June 1978, for example, Ceauşescu convened a "Fine Arts Conference" at which he insisted that artists exhibit "a stronger commitment to [the] Party's needs and goals."[54] Cultural control was further emphasized at the Second Congress of Political Education and Socialist Culture in June 1982.[55] The May 1988 appointment of General Constantin Olteanu, former minister of defense, as the Central Committee's secretary for propaganda, and therefore of media and culture, implied that the screws were to be turned even more tightly. In fact, 1988–89 saw heightened rigidity within the media, art, and education.

As the tension, frustration, and desperation of creative or scholarly individuals in Romania surfaced, the regime's efforts to direct cultural activity were redoubled. One can (as did many of their colleagues) criticize Romanian intellectuals for their silence and acquiescence. There was, however, the ominous presence of the Securitate (the security police) in every university, institute, and enterprise; and fear operated daily to immobilize even the most alienated person. The Party's "guidance" and "leadership" in cultural matters was, then, ensured via fear — "paralyzing fear."[56]

The cultural tragedy was, finally, extended beyond treatment of individuals and groups, and entered a phase in which the regime tried to eliminate the physical vestiges of Romanian culture which might serve as alternative symbols for allegiances. Throughout Romania, but particularly in Bucharest itself, older neighborhoods and the churches that formed their core were demolished during the 1980s. Hardest hit were certain central areas of the capital city, although other cities suffered through "modernization" plans. In Bucharest, however, the ostensible purpose of the massive demolition was to create space for a complex of massive Party and government buildings, a "Palace of the People," to serve as a physical monument to Nicolae Ceauşescu. The outcry about the bulldozing of historic churches slowed the process,[57] but it continued into the late 1980s.

The sociocultural consequences of Ceauşescu's quarter century were grave. The combined effects of social tension and conflict, intellectual repression, and irreparable cultural losses would have been astounding to contemplate in 1965 at the outset of the Ceauşescu era. The policies and actions taken by the Ceauşescu regime were calamitous, and may be impossible to repair in the short term.

The Political Disaster

During the 1980s, and arguably as early as the late 1970s, Romania lost diplomatic credibility and aroused considerable enmity in international relations. Domestically, the Romanian Communist Party acquiesced in the chaotic policies and autocratic populism of Nicolae Ceauşescu and his family, thereby forfeiting any legitimacy the system may have gained through the extensive growth that began during the 1950s and continued through the 1970s, or through the anti-Russian tone used by Gheorghiu-Dej in 1964 and enhanced by Ceauşescu in 1968. Romania's political tale from the late 1970s to the late 1980s, then, was a tale of heavy losses on all fronts.

In its foreign policy, the Ceauşescu regime had one consistent strategy with several component themes: it portrayed itself as independent within the Warsaw Pact, as a "developing socialist state" tied to the nations of Africa and Asia, and as a bridge between East and West. The strategy of cultivating worldwide contacts and maintaining a high international profile from a position of uniqueness within the Warsaw Pact was successful for a decade and a half. At least through the 1970s, Ceauşescu was seen as an important actor in East-West affairs, arranging diplomatic initiatives in the Middle East and helping to inaugurate some of the initial U.S.-Chinese meetings in the Nixon administration. During the 1970s, both President Nixon and President Ford visited Bucharest in recognition of the perceived independent role that Ceauşescu had established for himself in world politics, while Western governments and banks made relatively easy credit available and opened their domestic markets to Romanian goods. The United States, for example, granted "most favored nation" (MFN) status to Bucharest, and repeatedly extended it despite mounting reports of human rights abuses. American efforts to support differentiation within Eastern Europe while indicating disfavor with Romanian actions against religious practice, artistic diversity, and political dissent took the form of visits in the mid-1980s by top administration officials including Vice-President Bush, Secretary of State George Shultz,[58] Assistant Secretary of State John Whitehead, and many congressional delegations. These visits produced little in the way of compromise with Ceauşescu.

Romania's international role had become more limited by 1980–81, to such an extent that in a 1981 assessment of the country's prognosis for the rest of the decade I concluded that "the 1980s will see more internal and external constraints. . . . The latitude available for military and foreign policy deviation, already limited, will decline as will Romania's ability to pursue economic plans independent from world markets and energy supplies. . . . Romania's ability to 'go it alone' will decline."[59] Additionally, it was clear at the outset of the 1980s that the domestic political legitimacy Ceauşescu may have gained from his careful confrontation with Soviet hegemony appeared "to have less credibility as time goes on, particularly in light of constraints being imposed on Romanian foreign policy latitude."[60] All of this, of course, was written a number of years prior to the selection of Mikhail Gorbachev as general secretary of the Communist Party of the Soviet Union (CPSU).

From Western perspectives, Ceauşescu's star began to fade because of high levels of debt and the diminished utility of Romanian contacts. When total debt reached more than $10 billion in 1981, and Bucharest renegotiated outstanding loans with a consortium of Western banks, it became clear that Romania was an investment fraught with considerable risk. Ceauşescu, to make matters worse, was not at all forthcoming when IMF officials sought information about Romania's economy. Continued

Romanian obstinacy in dealing with the international financial community was apparent in the December 1987 decision to end payments to the International Bank for Reconstruction and Development.[61] Understandably, no Western firm or financial institution offered new long-term credits to Ceauşescu's Romania, although a couple of small short-term loans (of a few hundred million dollars or less) were granted by consortia of Western banks.[62]

Western governments and institutions were further encouraged to dissociate themselves from this bad risk by the establishment of alternative or permanent channels of communication in the Middle East, and between Washington and Beijing. These two arenas, in which Ceauşescu had exhibited his usefulness in the early and middle 1970s, no longer presented any opportunities for Romanian diplomacy. This did not stop Ceauşescu from continuing his globe-trotting activities. Indeed, even at the age of seventy, in 1987–88, Ceauşescu made several international tours. In the spring of 1988 alone, Nicolae and Elena Ceauşescu (with an accompanying entourage) went on wide-ranging tours to West Africa (7–15 March) and Asia (a two-week excursion in April 1988). Although trade was on Ceauşescu's agenda in all of the countries he visited, it is clear that repair of his erstwhile high international profile was also a principal purpose of the trips. It appears, however, that the trips resulted neither in significant new trade agreements nor in heightened prestige.[63]

In the late 1970s and early 1980s, Western indifference and suspicion toward Ceauşescu emerged owing to the combined effects of human rights abuses in Romania and the regime's espionage activities abroad. In the former arena, the accumulation of individual cases provided a portrait of systematic intimidation, incarceration, and torture of persons suspected of advocating alternative political views, that is, those critical of Ceauşescu. For people who sought to propagate a religious faith, there was danger as well, and priests, ministers, and ordinary believers were often subject to police harassment and arrest. Perhaps the best-known of these cases was that of the Romanian Orthodox priest Gheorghe Calciu,[64] who after spending over two decades in custody was freed in 1984 and allowed to emigrate in 1985. Many other Lutheran, Baptist, and Islamic clergy and believers were persecuted as well.[65]

The Securitate, the Romanian secret police, which implemented most of the repression against "enemies of the state," became far better known in the West with the defection of Ion Pacepa in 1978. Pacepa's revelations, made first to the CIA and other Western intelligence agencies, and later published in a mass-market book, revealed Securitate operations to assassinate Romanian dissidents living abroad, and the existence of a huge and pervasive network of informants within Romania. Although the Securitate was generally thought to operate independently of the KGB,[66] Pacepa's account tied in all too well with the events in Europe during the 1980s. The "Tanase affair" in France involved a Romanian agent (Mihai Haidacu) sent to assassinate a well-known dissident émigré (Tanase); the agent turned himself in to French authorities and became a double agent, feigning a successful assassination of the Romanian dissident in order to pinpoint a network of Romanian agents within France.[67] As the French uncovered additional Romanian spies, and plots to kidnap or kill other Romanian exiles,[68] even the longstanding mutual affinity between Paris and Bucharest soured considerably. In West Germany, plots by Romanian agents posted at the Romanian Embassy were reported by *Die Welt* in 1984.[69]

Domestic repression, coupled with the activities of the Securitate abroad which were obviously unacceptable, alienated Western governments from any close association with Ceauşescu. The bizarre lengths to which Ceauşescu's personality cult (discussed further below) was being carried in the 1980s made a strongly negative impression in the West as well.[70] Without the support and the financial largesse of European Community members and the United States, Romania's economic independence from the Soviet Union was tenuous. And without the diplomatic attention of NATO members, it is doubtful that a Romanian regime could utilize anti-Russian sentiments as a ploy to gain domestic legitimacy. American criticism of Romania's economic policies and human rights record, which because of the Jackson-Vanik amendment were always brought into the limelight when the renewal of MFN status (the benefits of which included lower tariffs and American government credits) was debated in the U.S. Congress, led the Romanians in February 1988 to renounce this arrangement.

If all of this were not enough bad news for Ceauşescu's foreign policy, one must consider that the elevation of Mikhail Gorbachev to the post of CPSU general secretary led to a geometric expansion of Romania's political distance from Moscow. Whereas during the Brezhnev era Romania was merely a "deviant" in some aspects of foreign policy, Ceauşescu's regime was detrimental to Gorbachev's efforts to reinvigorate Communist Party-states through far-reaching economic and political reform. Ceaușescu's repeated insistence that he would have nothing to do with decentralization, much less the injection of competition into economic or political spheres, placed him squarely in opposition to Gorbachev's notions of *perestroika* and *demokratizatsiya*. The Romanian leader made it abundantly clear, only eight months after Gorbachev took office, that Bucharest would, as it were, "stay the course" of state socialism.[71] Gorbachev's visit to Romania in 1987 underscored these deep-seated differences, which later became even larger. By the spring of 1988, the Romanian leader was speaking of "rightist deviation" as the "principal danger" to socialism just prior to a formal state visit by USSR president Andrei Gromyko,[72] and in 1989 the strident tone was even more audible. Ceaușescu's offenses, from Moscow's perspective, included not only his aberrant positions in international politics, at CSCE meetings, at the United Nations, and in other forums, but most particularly his rejection of economic transformation and domestic openness.[73]

Within the ranks of East European Communist states, Romania's human rights record became scandalous even among regimes that "lived in glass houses." From the standpoint of other Warsaw Pact members, the unrest among Romania's Hungarian minority, which had begun to generate a large exodus (as discussed above), was another of Ceaușescu's offenses. Indeed, the flight of ethnic Hungarians from Transylvania into Hungary escalated into an "explosive political problem" for several reasons. First, the notion that the ethnic minorities of one Communist country would escape to another Communist state flew in the face of both the internationalism of Marxism (according to which class identity should transcend international boundaries) and Lenin's view that an end to capitalism would see the disappearance of nationalism.[74] More important than ideology, however, was Hungary's decision, at an early 1988 CSCE follow-up meeting in Vienna, and again at the 1989 Paris CSCE session, to support a Western condemnation of the Romanian government's human rights record. Károly Grósz, who became the leader of the Hungarian Socialist Workers' Party in the spring of 1988, sought further international pressure on Romania and tried to use the nationalistic issue of Transylvania to add to his own legitimacy. Grósz's own political weaknesses, and his failure to lead reform within Hungary, enabled other politicians to pick up the anti-Romanian banner in 1989. This intra–Warsaw Pact tension was, at the least, counterproductive for Moscow and the other regimes, all of which were confronting ample domestic socioeconomic and political difficulties.

Nor could the Romanians offer much more to Gorbachev's foreign policy. Whereas for twenty years Romania's role in the Warsaw Pact had enabled Ceauşescu to act as an intermediary between Moscow and some of the USSR's adversaries, most notably China and Israel, other East European leaders, as well as the Soviets themselves, began to act in the same venues.[75] Several leaders of Communist Europe visited Beijing between 1986 and 1989, including Wojciech Jaruzelski and Miloš Jakeš, before Mikhail Gorbachev's own path-breaking trip in May 1989. Soviet and Israeli contacts also progressed toward a renewal of diplomatic relations. In such an environment, there was little room for Ceauşescu to play the role of facilitator. Not only did Ceauşescu offend the sensibilities of the new Soviet leadership; he also could not even ingratiate himself with Gorbachev as he had been able to do with previous Soviet leaders during a period when Soviet policies toward the United States, Israel, China, and other states were frozen in a hostile view of the world.

It is at home, however, that the political disaster of the Ceauşescu era was most evident and most foreboding. The loss of credibility and the growth of suspicion abroad pales in comparison to the chaotic policies and autocratic populism that Ceauşescu pursued.

Far from being merely a matter of economics, the manner in which Ceauşescu distributed resources reflects the chaotic decision-making processes that appear to have dominated the Romanian government for some time. I examined data regarding the distribution of fixed assets among Romania's forty judete over a fourteen-year period, 1970–1983. Such fixed assets, excluding roads and bridges, provided a measure of centrally determined investments over a critical time span in Ceauşescu's lengthy rule. I found that ethnic biases and familial ties were the strongest explanations for patterns of gains and losses in counties' proportion of national fixed assets. Transylvanian judete suffered bigger drops in their national standing than did counties in traditionally Romanian provinces. The counties in the Olt Valley from which the Ceauşescu clan hailed gained greatly in fixed assets.[76]

Multilateral development thus connoted nothing more or less than a continuation of old-style politics—not surprising, but politically devastating in a country where the leadership demanded more and more of the population while continuing to impose economic privations and severe constraints on personal freedoms. The transparent biases of Ceauşescu's resource distribution schemes would have been politically disruptive for any system. In a country where minority nationalities already mistrusted Ceauşescu, and where the popular image of the Ceauşescu clan went from bad to worse, no amount of rhetorical obfuscation could help.

In the late 1960s, and most evidently in 1968, Ceauşescu commanded widespread popular approval in Romania. The principal component of this appeal was a populist, pseudo-charismatic identity strongly colored by anti-Soviet sentiments. For a brief moment, Ceauşescu became a national hero when he both condemned the Soviet–Warsaw Pact invasion of Czechoslovakia and inaugurated a new defensive doctrine of a "struggle of the entire people" *(lupta intregului popor)* when Soviet military action against Romania seemed imminent.

A populist image with an emphasis on Ceauşescu's charisma wore thin in the 1970s. By 1971, when Ceauşescu returned from a trip to China and instituted a mini–Cultural Revolution in Romania, it was clear that the country's future would not be one of intimacy between ruler and masses. Ceauşescu's resolute pursuit of a Stalinist economic model, and his repression of religion, minority rights, and dissent while causing irreparable injury to Romania's social and cultural heritage, weakened incrementally his base of popular support. Not until the unrelenting austerity of the 1980s — when Ceauşescu made the Romanian population pay for his mistakes of economic and social policy — did the bottom fall out of the regime's support by the public.

We have very few data regarding public opinion in Romania in those years, and almost none that gauge political opinions longitudinally. Radio Free Europe (RFE), however, had enlisted the services of well-known polling firms in Europe (such as Gallup International) to interview East Europeans who were traveling in the West. Using continuous sampling techniques over two-year spans, the pollsters gained a large ersatz national sample of individuals to whom a number of standardized questions were posed. Although there were substantial problems with this methodology which should cause us to question exact measurements, large trends can be discerned by these sampling techniques.[77]

The RFE data include responses to several questions asked consistently over a lengthy period of time. One revealing question — "How does socialism work out in practice in your country?" — taps public evaluations of the Communist system's performance. In that regard, Romanian respondents were rather positive in the middle to late 1970s. Indeed, between interviews in 1975–76 and another series of interviews in 1979–80, the Romanian sample registered a positive trend; specifically, the percentage responding that socialism was working out well or very well increased by 7 percent, while the percentage answering that it was working out badly or very badly decreased by 6 percent.[78]

A comparison of the 1979–80 survey conducted for RFE with data collected in 1984–85, however, demonstrates the severity of the Ceauşescu regime's political decline among the people it ruled. Among five East European states (Czechoslovakia, Hungary, Poland, Bulgaria, and Romania), Ceauşescu's Romania suffered the largest negative shift of public attitudes in the early 1980s. Positive evaluations of the performance of Romanian socialism dropped by 24 percent, while negative answers increased by 25 percent. This very large movement toward nonsupportive responses was almost 50 percent greater than the negative shift in responses to the same question among Polish nationals.[79]

Prior to the late 1980s, attitudinal antagonism toward Ceauşescu was largely individual or local. Rarely, in the first decade and a half of this regime, did strikes or protests erupt which could be visible beyond the immediate environs. Not only were police (*militia*) and the Securitate effective in controlling the situation; people were also not as certain before the 1980s that they would be affected personally by Ceauşescu's chaotic autocracy, and they probably hoped that something would happen to remove him. The repression and austerity of the 1980s, however, removed any hope that Romanians had retained. In the late 1980s, then, one began to see more than the sporadic strikes (e.g., the strike among miners) seen in the late 1970s.

Throughout 1987, disturbances erupted in cities across Romania. Workers and students demonstrated in Iaşi in February 1987, and by that summer, industrial actions were reported at a number of locales. These included violent protests and repression by the authorities in Turda, in Judetul Cluj. Student protests at universities in Cluj and Timişoara are known to have occurred in the fall, while rumors of fire-bombings in Bucharest near the end of 1987 cannot be discounted. The most noted instance of unrest in 1987, however, took place in the large city of Braşov, where workers at the Steagul Rosu (Red Flag) Truck Factory walked out on 15 November. Marching from the industrial outskirts of Braşov toward the town center, the workers were joined by thousands of other citizens protesting additional restrictions on heat, light, and other essentials announced on 10 November. Some demonstrators, however, chanted for the removal of Ceauşescu and a return to democracy. At the old-town square, some twenty thousand protesters invaded the city's Party headquarters and destroyed furnishings and records before the army and the Securitate intervened in force, arresting hundreds. So severe was the Braşov rioting that a Romanian Communist Party conference, scheduled to begin in November, was delayed until December.

Having alienated the West and the Soviets, Ceauşescu lost as well the acceptance of his population. How, then, did he stay in power during the 1980s? Some of the principal reasons for Ceauşescu's longevity as Romanian leader qua dictator are embedded in Romanian culture and history. In Romania there have been few instances of large-scale popular revolt against authorities, and the most recent — the 1907 peasant rebellion — is a dubious example for contemporary Romania. There is no independent church to provide the nucleus around which a dissident movement could develop, as the Roman Catholic Church did in Poland; and there is very little contact between intellectuals and workers (which was so important for Solidarity's origins).

However, one must credit Ceauşescu with tenacity and resourcefulness. He surely understood how to discourage political opposition and how to disrupt it in its nascent stages. The tools he used, unfortunately for Romania, extended his regime at extraordinary political cost to the country he ruled.

The personality cult of Nicolae Ceauşescu, which spread to encompass his entire family during the latter half of his rule, must be given credit in any effort to explain Ceauşescu's ability to retain power in spite of failed policies and popular antagonism. Yet we need to be more precise when speaking of a personality cult in conditions of rigid authoritarianism. The leader who tries to gain or maintain legitimate authority via a personality cult tries to base his appeal and popular allegiance on two planes — that of adulation and that of coercion. In an earlier examination of leadership strategies in Communist states, I referred to a leader who used such a combination as an autocratic populist — that is, a ruler who sought to ensure his authority by enforcing adulation.[80] Ceauşescu implemented such an awkward strategy by speaking of himself as a man opposed to bureaucracy, as one who had struggled, and — early in his rule, particularly — as a leader who would be seen and heard throughout the country.

Simultaneously, the Securitate was an omnipresent tool of oppression. The absurd lengths to which the Ceauşescu cult went in the 1970s and 1980s, however, exceeded the credulity of Romanians of all strata. Consequently, the Securitate — the coercive component of Ceauşescu's cult — was heard from more and more.

Although other writers have detailed the specific development and forms of Ceauşescu's autocratic populism,[81] this phenomenon nevertheless merits emphasis here in light of recent events. In the world of literature, Ceauşescu's cult long ago reached incredible proportions, and novelists, poets, and critics carefully infused their works with allusions to the crazed routine of adulation devoted to the leader and his family. Poems, hymns, articles, books, speeches, and media "documentaries" provided overflowing glorification of Nicolae *and* Elena's genius and bravery. Beginning in the late 1970s to celebrate her sixtieth birthday, and accelerating thereafter, "cultism" was extended to Elena Ceauşescu and to Nicu, their youngest son (born in 1951). In January 1988, another of Elena's birthdays produced yet more extreme examples of her own well-established autocratic populism, including a number of vapid "poems" that overflow with praise for her alleged brilliance, achievements, devotion, and so on.[82]

Personality cults became a hindrance to regime legitimacy within Romania, and damaged the overall acceptance of a socialist system. And yet, until the system's performance began demonstrably to fail, there is some evidence that the projection of strength, and the image of leadership, was a viable substitute for management skills and charisma, and that Ceauşescu's own persona added to the level of popular support for the Communist regime and the socialist system. "As an idol," Mary Ellen Fischer wrote, Ceauşescu "does play an important role. . . . of a royal personage and, as such, satisfies the instinctive needs of the Romanian 'masses' for a strong monarch."[83] That usefulness waned, both because of policy failures and because of the cult's excesses. Yet the leadership strategy of autocratic populism was, for many years, a key element in Ceauşescu's political position.

Rotatie (literally, rotation) was the practice of moving party cadres in and out of posts in the *nomenklatura*, never allowing one individual to remain at one job long enough to develop loyalties or to establish patron-client relationships. This built-in insecurity among cadres was a vital tool for Ceauşescu. It may never be known, of course, whether or not Ceauşescu, Elena, or other close associates decided specifically to inaugurate such a practice. Instead, rotatie may have been less a planned tactic to interrupt the formation of political opposition than a consequence of Ceauşescu's own well-earned political insecurity. There is no question, however, that the turnover rate of personnel in ministerial-level posts (e.g., the positions of the premier, the deputy premier, ministers, and chairmen of state commissions and councils) was extraordinarily high.

During the 1970s and 1980s (through the end of 1987), the mean annual turnover rate of those in ministerial-level (as defined above) governmental positions was higher in Romania than in any other member state of the Warsaw Pact. Although there were short periods — for example, 1985 and 1986 — when Bulgaria had a turnover rate among its top state posts of 33 percent, whereas Romania's rate was 29 percent, the Romanian rate was still higher than that of Poland, Hungary, and Czechoslovakia. From 1970 through 1987, almost a quarter of Romania's highest state posts changed hands every year at the behest of Ceauşescu: this mean turnover rate exceeded that of every other country in the region by a substantial margin.[84] A different set of political elites, but one that is nevertheless intertwined with ministerial-level posts, was the stratum of county first secretaries. During the 1980s, between four and ten of the first secretaries of the judete were replaced each year. Even lower-level Party cadres were rotated frequently, a policy that Ceauşescu asserted would "improve the competence" of Party elites.[85]

Thus, one can attribute Ceauşescu's political survival in part to his assiduous use of his control of the nomenklatura. Judete and local officials, as well as ministers and the chairmen of state councils, all of whom were simultaneously important Party cadres, were targets of the wrath of Nicolae and/or Elena when anything did not go well. Since nothing was going well, dismissals occurred entirely without reason — except when they resulted from the politically astute tactic of keeping one's opposition from coalescing around particular people or specific ministries, or in certain locales.

There were no advantages to be gained for Romania, however, from Ceauşescu's successful manipulation of the nomenklatura. Indeed, the single most egregious characteristic of domestic politics in Ceauşescu's era may have been the graft and pervasive corruption that his leadership infused into the country. Corruption was not new to Romania, but it became endemic during the 1980s. By 1989, in fact, few of the well-intentioned, honest Party cadres I first met in Romania in the early 1970s remained both involved in positions of responsibility, and honest. By the late 1980s, for example, the income of local leaders was tied to the production of the units for which they had responsibility. To survive in a system where administrative irrationality dominated, and where they certainly had no control over how much the local unit produced, occupants of the two hundred thousand local leadership posts had little alternative but to participate in falsified reporting of output. With insecurity a constant in their lives, they resorted to whatever means were available to insulate themselves from the leadership's displeasure. They could not, however, eliminate from their lives a persistent fear of either being "precipitated downward or . . . being sucked upward."[86]

The institutions that protected Ceauşescu from his own people — the Securitate and the military — are yet additional aspects of Romania's political disaster. As discussed earlier, the Securitate became the constant companion, although not an entirely trusted ally, of Ceauşescu. The fear wrought by the Securitate was debilitating to Romanian society, and the Securitate's extensive penetration of social and cultural organizations was certainly a costly endeavor. The fact that Ceauşescu needed a secret police to survive, and depended on their repressive "services," was a political tragedy for Romania and a severe loss for the country's international respectability.

Ceauşescu's relations with the Romanian military lost him the support of an institution that was viewed with some respect among the masses, and weakened severely the Romanian Army's potential to play a positive role in the country's development. The military as a whole, and particularly the army, suffered reduced allocations and a diminished role in defending the nation (because patriotic guards were to be crucial in a "struggle of the entire people"), and resented its forced participation in the economy to offset shortages of civilian labor, particularly in construction and in "militarized" sectors of the economy.[87] At the same time, an increased political reliance on the army and the Securitate is evident as generals or former generals moved into a number of high-level RCP posts. When the regime's need for a heavy military and security involvement in the Party and the state is viewed in light of the diminished resources and professionalism of the military and security establishments, it seems clear that civil-military relations could no longer be satisfactory.

Across the spectrum of political issues, then, a point was reached at which Ceauşescu's Romania was spurned by the West and looked upon as an embarrassment by the Gorbachev leadership in Moscow. Domestically, irrational policies and a personal style out of touch with popular needs had led to a drastic reversal of public evaluations, and created a highly alienated population. Ceauşescu's means of survival — manipulation of the nomenklatura — may have been his life raft, but it succeeded only in making central and local administration more difficult and filled with corrupt practices. Further, Ceauşescu's reliance on the Securitate and the alienation of the military are "accomplishments" that exacerbated the political disaster and make the country's future particularly difficult.

Conclusion

Nation-states perennially experience crises of varying duration which evoke high levels of tension and uncertainty, sometimes coupled with the threat of violence. Catastrophic events likewise befall political systems owing to the deaths of charismatic leaders or other shocks to the national psyche. Few countries, however, must endure prolonged abuse from their own rulers. When that has happened — and has been accompanied by massive violence, as in Stalin's purges, China's Cultural Revolution, Idi Amin's Uganda, or Pol Pot's Khmer Rouge regime — there has been worldwide revulsion and condemnation.

In Romania, especially since the mid-1970s, a tragedy unfolded, albeit not one in which physical violence caused the death of thousands. But systematically imposed harm to a nation may be defined more broadly, and in that regard the last decade and a half of Romania's was extraordinarily damaging. The regime of Nicolae Ceauşescu was Romania's disaster, in the oldest sense of that word, because malevolent intentions penetrated formal institutions in a manner that endangered the economy, the environment, society, culture, and the political order. In the foregoing pages, I have tried to portray the condition of Romania as the fourth decade of the Communist regime ended. It is a portrait of a country deeply wounded by austerity and repression, but with the added twist that such wounds were imposed with exceptional violence. Many of the policies, domestic and foreign, described above had no rational foundation and no sensible explanation, except for the desire of a family and its sycophants to maintain their power.

One Romanian novelist, Augustin Buzura, expressed this condition through a character in his novel *The Wall of Death:*

I have a feeling of being on a planet where only amateurs and dilettantes are accepted . . . where people have to beg for what they are entitled to . . . where they only wish to survive. It is an absurd world full of miracles, of — idiots holding professors' chairs and of wise people exiled in caves, a world in which reality is one thing and opinions about reality another . . . a world of the devil, in which the devil is gaining the upper hand.[88]

In a novelist's portrait of insanity, then, we find one image of Romania circa 1989. And even were we to rely on a more empirical assessment of Romanian reality in the late 1980s, we would doubtless be equally grim. Romania waited for the passing of Nicolae Ceauşescu, and hoped that Elena and/or Nicu could be moved aside prior to their consolidation of power. These hopes were, in part, fulfilled. But there was ample time for Romania's disaster to extend further before that leadership transition took place.

12

Bulgaria

Luan Troxel

The most vivid symbol of the Romanian uprising in December 1989 was the sight of the Romanian flag with its Leninist center ripped out. Eastern Europe in 1990 and 1991 [or 1992 and beyond, for that matter] is like the Romanian flag: its Leninist center has been removed, but a good deal of its institutional and cultural inheritance is still in place.

Kenneth Jowitt, *New World Disorder*

Discussing the legacies of communism in Eastern Europe is fundamentally important for assessing the obstacles to implementing liberal democracy and capitalism in the region. While it is perfectly clear and logical that there should be some legacies of communism in the region (after all, a whole generation of young people grew up under Communist regimes), it is nonetheless difficult to determine just what those legacies are. At times it is difficult to distinguish between that which is a legacy of communism, and that which is a legacy of the pre-Communist past. At other times, it becomes clear that certain characteristics that we are inclined to term "legacies of communism" do not flow directly from the nature of communism, but rather might have come from any modernizing regime after World War II. Of course, it would be quite simple to identify negative characteristics of East European politics, economics, and society and attribute their existence to the former Communist regimes. However, we should instead set up standards for the categorization of legacies of communism and for their evaluation.

Ideally, an objective determination of the legacies of communism would require a systematic comparison of Eastern Europe before and after communism, and a consideration of which currently existing characteristics are a result of the passage of time or were likely to come about even in the absence of Communist regimes. Those characteristics would be eliminated from our category of legacies of communism, while other existing characteristics might be included. Such a review would be rather arduous and perhaps even impossible to carry out. For that reason, in my discussion of the legacies of communism in Bulgaria I will instead discuss those characteristics of the former regimes which most aptly described the essential nature of "real existing socialism" or communism. Having done that, I will point out a number of outcomes which flow directly from the essential nature of communism, for those outcomes, in my view, can most adequately be labeled the legacies of communism.

After the Bulgarian Communist Party (BCP) took power in Bulgaria after World War II, it attempted to transform Bulgarian politics, economics, and society along ideologically preconceived lines. Bulgaria was to become a socialist state through rapid industrialization (which would lead to a rapid rise in living standards), egalitarianism (which would be imposed from above through the development of an extensive welfare state), and transformation of the agrarian society to an urban and industrial one. The truly defining characteristic of Bulgarian communism, then — the essential nature of the regime — could be found in the hypercentralization necessary to make such a rapid and radical transformation possible. Not only was the political system to be centralized under the political control of the BCP, but the entire economic structure would be centrally planned, and even the structure of society would be determined from above. The outcomes and consequences of the centralization of the three realms — political, economic, and social — constitute the legacies of communism in Bulgaria.

Political Legacies

Political centralization had as its central tenet the ideological goal of the dictatorship of the proletariat. In more practical terms, the secondary goal was to forestall alternative power structures from emerging. Hence, anyone who wanted to be involved in politics had to be so involved within the Party apparatus. While the secondary goal of centralization was not achieved in Poland, Hungary, and Czechoslovakia (as we know from dissident activities in those countries), it seemed to have been fairly well achieved in Bulgaria. First, dissident-type organizations appeared very late in the Communist period in Bulgaria. Second, even when such organizations appeared, they were not especially dissident in their intentions. Finally, the Party was fairly successful at disbanding such organizations, lest they become more dissident.

The first dissident-type group to make a deep impression in Bulgaria was the Club for Glasnost and Perestroika, which was founded in 1988 by a number of professors — including the future president of Bulgaria, Zhelyu Zhelev — from Sofia University. The group was not dissident in its intentions. Rather, its purpose was to bring Gorbachevist openness to intellectual discussions in Bulgaria. Nonetheless, in early 1989 several of its student members were expelled from the university, and a number of its activists who were also members of the BCP were expelled from the Party.

Another such group, which gained wide publicity during the upheaval in Bulgaria in the fall of 1989, was Ecoglasnost. It grew out of a local environmental movement known as the Ruse Committee. Ecoglasnost was founded in 1989 by a group of citizens concerned with the environment, generally, and with the BCP's hydroelectric projects in the Rila Mountains. Although at the outset it had no explicitly stated political aims, it challenged the legitimacy of the regime insofar as it set itself up as a necessary alternative to the official Committee for the Defense of the Environment.

Neither of these organizations could serve the purpose served by dissident organizations elsewhere in Eastern Europe, however. Neither was set up to explicitly challenge the rule of the Party. In fact, a number of members of the Club for Glasnost and Perestroika had been Party members. And in a 1989 interview Peter Beron (then head of Ecoglasnost) pointed out that Ecoglasnost's members, too, were very much tied to the Communist power structure: "Most of our members are well-known figures who have a high position in the social hierarchy. We are not an anti-state or anti-party organization."[1]

The Party generally used two methods to ensure that dissident groups failed to gain wide allegiance. First, it would usually catch on to a group's existence early, and disband the group or decapitate it by arresting the leadership. The second method that the Party used was to preemptively attack potential sources of organization — specifically, intellectuals banding together with workers. This was a tactic that Party leaders all over Eastern Europe tried in the postwar period, but the Bulgarian leaders appeared to be the most successful.[2] While Party leaders in Poland were unable to divide KOR (the Committee for the Defense of the Workers) from Solidarity, leaders in Bulgaria successfully maintained the separation between the workplace and academia. Even after the 1989 fall of Todor Zhivkov, the BCP's leader since 1954, Party leaders were in Sofia and the provinces constantly meeting with workers, lest the workers be tempted by the same forces that had created the intellectual ferment in the capital.[3]

The late and almost nonexistent formation of dissident groups in Bulgaria, as well as the all-encompassing nature of the Party, meant that there were really only two forums for political ideas in Bulgaria: the Party, where alternative ideas could be moderated, and the kitchen table, where most alternative ideas were expressed only to family members and were thereafter confined to the kitchen.

There are several legacies, then, of this hypercentralization of political power. First, alternative power sources did not exist, and hence, opposition groups in the immediate aftermath of the 1989 "revolution" had little organizational and political experience. They also had few potential leaders along the lines of Václav Havel or Lech Wałęsa to lead their movements. Moreover, they barely had movements, as they were unaccustomed to organizing and carrying on a political struggle. Thus the Bulgarian Socialist Party (BSP, formerly the BCP) argued in its 1990 election campaign that the opposition was made up of inexperienced and naïve individuals who would bring the nation to the brink of an economic catastrophe.[4]

A second legacy of the hypercentralization of political power was the fact that many talented and reformist individuals remained within the Communist Party apparatus. Since Bulgaria did not experience the split that occurred in other East European Communist parties in the wake of 1968, the reformers, who in other countries opted out of the Party and became dissidents, remained largely within the BCP. This explains why dissident organizations in Bulgaria were weaker and later in appearing. But it also meant that the Party was able to continue along a somewhat reformist pathway, which secured greater mass trust and satisfaction. And when the time came for Party reassessment in 1989, there were still reformers within the Party who could legitimately claim to carry out change.

A third legacy of political centralization was the fact that the society that emerged from the system breakdown in 1989 and 1990 constituted a weak, uninformed, and ill-prepared electorate. A newly created electorate must be convinced to rationally participate in the political arena through party structures and voting. Bulgarians, however, had rarely had the experience of participation (as opposed to mobilized activity).[5] For that reason, they could hardly be expected to make wise political choices, particularly in the first free election in 1990.

It is partly as a result of these legacies of communism—the inexperience of the opposition, the reformist elements within the Party, and an ill-prepared electorate—that Bulgarian voters have continued to give a great deal of electoral support to the BSP in the free elections since 1989.

Societal Legacies

Just as the BCP created a hypercentralized political system after World War II, it tried similarly to control society through hypercentralization. The first centralized attempt at control was through socialization. The Party would dictate the characteristics and ideals of the "new socialist man," to which society was expected to conform. In other words, the Party would control society by making it internally uniform. Once the new socialist men were successfully socialized to the norms and values of the Party, behavioral control would have been established through political obedience.

Of course, it would be simple to argue that the Party was successful in socializing the Bulgarians, who for that reason remained relatively nondissident throughout the postwar period. Such an assertion would be highly contentious, however, as certain events even prior to 1989 showed the scant extent to which the new socialist man had been created. Dissident-type elements could at times be found, and social upheaval took place at various points; moreover, materialism seemed to run rampant in the 1980s.

When the Party failed to achieve control through socialization, it tried another method: creating fear. The Party, being all-powerful, could do to nonconformists nearly anything it wanted to do. It could punish the offenders by sending them to hard labor camps, by excluding them from higher education and desirable jobs, or by harassment. The problem for most Bulgarians was not that they feared being sent to a prison camp, per se, but that whereas they knew that the Party had a variety of unpleasant options to which it could resort should it wish, they did not know exactly what punishment would be meted out for which crime. In essence, Bulgarians became fearful of the unknowns of what might happen to them should they not conform. In this way, the Party used the fear of punishment to enforce compliance to its norms. If the masses were not successfully socialized, at least they would behave as though they were.

Punishment was not enough, however; one can fear punishment, but its use as a method of control is much more likely to be successful in a paranoid environment. The Party, therefore, created such an environment by forging divisions within society by means of the process of "atomization," and by playing on preexisting societal divisions. As a result, the level of trust between members of society was very low, because every "new socialist man" was aware that one possible consequence of noncompliance with the regime was to be informed upon by other "socialist men," and perhaps, eventually, to be sent to a hard labor camp (the last of which closed in the 1960s). Being unable to weigh the costs versus the benefits of acting in a particular way immobilized the Bulgarian populace. Hence, society became controlled through a paranoid environment that fed Bulgarians' fear of the unknown.

Fear is not in itself an inherently bad legacy of communism. Fear often motivates positive action. In the Bulgarian case, however, this fear of the unknown spawned two other more serious legacies of communism: the lack of societal trust, and ethnic tensions.

Fear of the unknown was fundamentally based on societal divisions. People feared their neighbors, their colleagues, and sometimes even members of their own families. A level of societal distrust as high as the level found in Bulgaria can offer little hope for the prospects of stable democracy in the near future. Indeed, we see societal distrust demonstrated in the large number of parties competing in elections (thirty-seven parties participated in the 1991 election). Although this in itself is not representative of a high propensity for instability, the fact that few parties have actually achieved representation in the parliament (three did so in 1991) indicates that there is a high level of effective disenfranchisement in Bulgaria, which also points to further instability in the near future.[6]

Moreover, the Party played upon societal divisions in its campaign against Bulgaria's ethnic Turkish minority. While the Turks and the Bulgarians have apparently lived together peacefully for much of the postwar period, tensions between them flared up in the winter of 1984–85, when the BCP initiated a campaign of "Bulgarizing" the Turks by banning the use of Turkish in public, instituting forced name changing, and closing many mosques. Though ethnic tensions appeared to die down between 1987 and 1988, they reappeared with the mass exodus and forced expulsion of many Turks in 1989.[7] The Party ensured support for its policies toward the Turks by creating fears among the Bulgarians that the Turkish minority would want cultural autonomy, and after that, political autonomy, perhaps leading to the establishment of the "Turkish Yoke" in Bulgaria once again.[8]

The Bulgarians were still quite concerned with this problem in January 1990, when many of them came from the provinces to the parliament to protest the planned restoration of some of the Turkish minority's rights.[9] This fear continued through the elections in the summer of 1990. The BSP invoked nationalist slogans, thereby giving itself the image of a national, Bulgarian party. This image, along with the BSP's relative unity, gave voters a view of the BSP as a stable and secure choice for the future. As a relatively united party, led by familiar faces, which now promised protection in the face of ethnic tension, the BSP managed to win the elections in 1990.

So, just as the political legacies of communism have helped to maintain the BSP's power since 1989, the societal legacies of communism have done the same. The Party rode to power in 1990 largely on a wave of ethnic fear. Furthermore, it managed to maintain the fear of what the Turks might demand in the elections in 1991.

Economic Legacies

Just as the BCP transformed Bulgaria's society and polity through centralization, it also rapidly transformed the economy in the same way. The centralization and ensuing transformation of the economy were meant to rapidly industrialize the country, creating the conditions for the implementation of an advanced welfare state, and the creation of a prosperous proletariat. Although the country rapidly industrialized, that industrialization had a number of unintended side-effects that may be termed the economic legacies of communism: distorted growth (both demographically and industrially), heavy dependence on the Soviet Union, external debt, and environmental degradation. In addition, the failed attempts at creating an advanced welfare state and a prosperous working class led to rising expectations that could be met neither by the old regime, as the period of rapid development passed, nor by the new elites who took power in 1989 and have taken power since then.

Rapid Transformation of the Demographic Structure

The first side-effect of the centralized economy was the rapid transformation of the demographic structure. Although most Bulgarians had been

TABLE 6. Goods per One Hundred Households in Bulgaria

	1965	1970	1975	1980	1985
Radio	59	62	76	88	97
Television	8	42	66	75	93
Washing Machine	23	50	59	71	89
Refrigerator	5	29	59	76	94
Automobile	2	6	15	29	37
Telephone	—	7	12	24	42

Sources: Data from Robert McIntyre, *Bulgaria* (London: Pinter, 1988), 124; John Lampe, *The Bulgarian Economy in the Twentieth Century* (London: Croom Helm, 1986), 194; *Statisticheski spravochnik* (Sofia: Tsentralno Statistichesko Upravlenie, 1986), 226.

small landholders prior to World War II, rapid industrialization witnessed a massive exodus from the countryside to the cities. Indeed, whereas the rural proportion of the population in 1939 was 77.3 percent, by 1956 it had dropped to 66.4 percent; and by 1965 the urban proportion had surpassed the rural.[10] In some ways, the rapid transformation of the countryside and the urban areas must have been a source of great pride for Bulgarians. After all, it ensured that a number of children from peasant families would move up the social hierarchy to become manual workers, or even university-educated white-collar workers.[11] Indeed, intergenerational data from 1967 showed that 49.8 percent of the peasant fathers' offspring who were surveyed became workers. Although the offspring of fathers working manual jobs did not fare as well in their move to nonmanual labor, the 13.5 percent who did make the jump showed that there was movement in the system.[12]

There were other outcomes of the demographic shift. One such outcome was the new physical layout of the cities. Sofia, like other cities in Eastern Europe, had to expand rapidly to accommodate the influx of new residents. Hence, the capital's old center was retained, but surrounded by a mass of new buildings ranging from moderately sized cooperative apartment buildings to massive apartment complexes, of which the best known is Mladost.

Along with the new residents came a modern welfare state with all the necessary buildings to house it: a shopping complex (Tsentralen Universalen Magazin) and many health clinics, hospitals, and schools. In short, Bulgaria modernized. Of course, its health and sanitary standards might not have been what the capitalist West would expect, and the new build-

TABLE 7. Food Consumption in Bulgaria
(kilograms per capita)

	1956	1960	1970	1975	1980	1985
Meat	26.6	29.1	41.4	58	61.2	71.3
Fish	1.1	2.2	5.5	6.2	6.9	8.3
Milk	81	92	117	143	169	191
Eggs	69	84	122	197	204	239
Grain	257	261	239	218	216	197

Sources: Data from McIntyre, Bulgaria, 24; Statisticheski spravochnik (1986), 121–22; Statisticheski godishnik (Sofia: Central Statistical Office, 1974), 73.

ings were not especially aesthetically pleasing, but the new Bulgaria was a far cry from the prewar one, in which most Bulgarians lived out their lives in rural settings, fewer than 10 percent of the villages had electricity, and agronomic technology was extremely primitive.[13]

In this sense, there is most likely a legacy of pride for those Bulgarians who witnessed the transformation. Indeed, evidence of this comes from election polls in 1990 and 1991. Although there is little survey evidence from Bulgaria across the postwar period to support the contention that Bulgarians derived pride from their economic development, there is much evidence to support the notion that Bulgarians had good reason to be satisfied. Both availability of consumer goods and food consumption increased dramatically in the postwar period. Washing machines and refrigerators, for instance, were found in a vast majority of Bulgarian homes by the mid-1980s (see table 6). For a population the overwhelming majority of whose members had lived in villages without electricity and running water prior to World War II, such change was significant.[14] In addition, the consumption of most food products increased greatly between the late 1950s and the end of the 1980s (see table 7). A notable exception is the consumption of grains, which declined over the same period. That, too, however, was a sign of success, since it indicated that bread consumption was declining, with a concomitant increase in other food consumption.

Indeed, more broadly based indexes of personal consumption per capita showed a relatively constant increase for Bulgaria throughout the 1970s (table 8). Perhaps even more telling, however, is the fact that although Bulgaria started out in 1960 at a lower base than the other countries of Eastern Europe, by 1978 it had achieved a level of consumption virtually equal to that of the German Democratic Republic and Hungary,

TABLE 8. Index of Personal Consumption per Capita

	1960	1965	1970	1975	1978
Bulgaria	82.5	100	118.2	138.8	146.5
Czechoslovakia	96.5	100	111.5	123.2	130.3
East Germany	93.5	100	112.2	137.4	146.8
Hungary	92.4	100	118	136	146.5
Poland	89.6	100	116.4	145.7	157.5

Source: Thad Alton, "Research Project on National Income in East Central Europe," Columbia University Occasional Paper 57, 1979, 16.

and it had surpassed Czechoslovakia's consumption level. It did not reach Poland's level of consumption, but as we now know, that level was artificially inflated through the use of Western loans. Bulgarians, it seems, had good reason to be satisfied with postwar changes in their domestic situation.

The extent to which these changes could evoke pride in individual Bulgarians, however, is dependent upon the perspective of the individuals in question. As already mentioned, older Bulgarians who witnessed the transformation and who experienced the changed living circumstances might well count this among the positive legacies of communism in Bulgaria. Indeed, the election results from 1990, in particular, seem to bear this out. In that election, there was a direct link between age and party preference. In fact, more than half of those who voted for the BSP in 1990 were older than forty-five years of age.[15]

Young people, however, had a broader geographical perspective. They compared Bulgaria's level of development not to its past level of development, but to the level of development of other states. As one former Central Committee member attested in 1989: "The new generation wants theoretical socialism. They're maximalists.... They don't care how far Bulgaria has come. They want to be like Switzerland, like Austria. It's not that way. They are more critical than the older generation."[16] As might be expected, then, the youth tended to vote more heavily in favor of the main opposition, the Union of Democratic Forces (UDF), than for the BSP. Approximately 50 percent of the youth (defined as those twenty-nine years of age and under) voted for the UDF, whereas 35 percent voted for the BSP.[17]

The youth's critical view of Bulgaria is a very deep-rooted legacy of communism. Indeed, hopes and expectations soared in the period immediately following the overthrow of Zhivkov in November 1989. As reality has not met these expectations, demonstrations have erupted, a significant portion of the youth has emigrated (this will be discussed in the next section), and general political instability has ensued (as demonstrated by the rapid turnover in governments).

Labor Policy and Demographic Changes

The demographic shift that brought masses of Bulgarians to urban centers was coupled with the labor policy shift toward full employment of the adult population: women, too, were to become full, active members of the workforce. While the ideological goal of this policy was to create equality among men and women (something that should have been one of the more positive legacies of communism), in practical terms it wreaked havoc on families in Eastern Europe, as it was accompanied by a radical decline in birth rates.

At the end of World War II, education was made compulsory for Bulgarians through age seventeen. The intention was to expand the educated workforce for the eventual new economy. As a result of the expansion of education and the BCP's labor policy, by the early 1970s the proportions of women and men were roughly equal at all educational levels; by the end of the 1980s women made up half of the overall workforce.[18] Although the stated rationale for employing men and women equally was to increase gender equality, the ultimate outcome was not always so clearly egalitarian. Women appeared in greater numbers in jobs that were lower paying and less prestigious.[19] Not only was there a disparity between the stated ideological goals and the actual outcome of women's participation in the labor force, but the BCP's labor policy apparently also affected birth rates. Although the BCP, like its counterparts elsewhere in Eastern Europe, tried to maintain the "woman as mother," as well as the "woman as worker," by instituting a system of monetary supports, paid maternity leaves, and daycare centers, birth rates dropped precipitously in Bulgaria in the postwar period. In 1985, the natural rate of population increase was 1.3 per thousand.[20] In consequence, Bulgaria's population structure is heavily weighted toward the elderly. Indeed, women aged sixty and over make up 21 percent of Bulgaria's population.[21] By comparison, women sixty-five and over make up 8.2 percent of the population in France, 9.7 percent in West Germany, 10.4 percent in Sweden, and 9.3 percent in the United Kingdom.[22] In addition, the retired labor force in Bulgaria is more than 2.3 million, whereas the total population is only about 9 million.[23]

As a legacy of communism, this distorted demographic structure has significant ramifications. In the short run, the lack of employable youth may well have been a boon for Bulgaria as the economy collapsed in 1990. While unemployment reached 13 percent by September 1992, it would have been higher had the demographic structure been more equally weighted.[24] However, the pensioners in Bulgaria are creating significant problems for the state. Although they are not economically productive, they demand much from the state in the form of pensions, health care, and the like. In the long run, then, the distorted economic structure is likely to affect negatively the structural changes taking place in the economy. This problem is compounded by the significant outflow of youth in 1989, which can also be considered a legacy of communism.[25]

Industrial Distortions and Economic Dependence

Bulgaria's industrialization had several other intertwined consequences. One was that industrial development was distorted by Bulgaria's inclusion in the Council for Mutual Economic Assistance. Rather than developing those sectors of the economy in which it might have had a natural strength, Bulgaria was forced to develop in a manner dictated by the needs of the common socialist market. A second consequence was a heavy dependence on the Soviet Union, which provided everything from guidance on sectoral development to energy aid. A third consequence, which derives directly from Bulgaria's having been dependent on the Soviet Union, even as the Soviet Union was in a steep economic decline, is Bulgaria's rather large foreign debt.

In 1990 many members of Bulgaria's new elites, both individuals from the opposition camp and those from the socialist camp, pointed to economic growth and a generally increasing standard of living as primary explanations for political quiescence in Bulgaria throughout the postwar period and for continued support for the BSP in the first post-Communist elections.[26] Bulgaria's long-term economic growth and the increase in living standards came from two sources: the implementation of a policy of rapid industrialization (as discussed above) and an advantageous trade relationship with the Soviet Union.

In the 1970s, Bulgaria, like other states in Eastern Europe, began to

TABLE 9. Energy Dependence: Net Imports of
Total Energy from the USSR as a Percentage of
Total Energy Imports

	1960	1970	1980
Bulgaria	73	86	96
Czechoslovakia	68	79	92
East Germany	57	66	78
Hungary	53	70	84
Poland	73	88	78
Romania	50	15	17

Source: William Reisinger, Energy and the Soviet Bloc
(Ithaca, N.Y.: Cornell University Press, 1992), 18, 74,
81–82.

grapple with debt problems. Unlike other states of Eastern Europe, however, Bulgaria did not face a *severe* debt crisis until the late 1980s. Bulgaria
was not plagued by the debt crisis in the earlier years primarily because the
Soviet Union gave it special economic help and because Bulgarian trade
was export-oriented. Bulgaria's first debts, in the late 1960s, were paid off
by the Soviet Union.[27] This economic aid was in addition to the 4.4 billion
rubles that the Soviet Union gave to Bulgaria between 1947 and 1975 as
heavy industry credits.[28] Throughout the 1970s, Bulgaria's debt remained
manageable. Although Bulgaria was becoming increasingly dependent
on foreign imports of energy, by 1980 virtually all of its imports came
from the Soviet Union, and at such low prices that Bulgaria, along with
Czechoslovakia and East Germany received the highest amount of implicit fuel subsidization in the bloc (see table 9).[29]

Bulgaria did its part, too, in avoiding a debt crisis. It increased the
export component of its net material product from 15 percent in 1960 to
50 percent by 1983.[30] It was able to do so partly because, unlike other East
European countries, it was able to feed itself and export foodstuffs, and
partly because it increasingly developed its electronics sector. By the early
1980s, the agricultural and electronics sectors accounted for about 70
percent of Bulgarian exports.[31]

By 1985, Bulgaria had the lowest per capita net debt of all the states of
Eastern Europe. The practical consequence of this was that the Party
could partially insulate the domestic economy from external effects.
Granted, Bulgaria did run up a foreign debt and by 1986 had even moved
into the third position in Eastern Europe for per capita net debt. None-

TABLE 10. Per Capita Net Debt (in dollars)

	1985	1986
Bulgaria	120	389
Czechoslovakia	182	209
Hungary	836	1,133
Poland	729	836
Romania	267	239

Source: Data from U.S. Bureau of the Census, *Statistical Abstracts of the United States, 1988* (Washington, D.C.: U.S. Government Printing Office), 823, cited in Joan Spero, *Politics of International Economic Relations,* 4th ed. (New York: St. Martin's, 1990), 329.

theless, the country was able to stave off its crisis until the late 1980s, and even then the debt did not reach the huge proportions of the Hungarian or Polish debts (see table 10).

While Bulgaria was rather successful in staving off crisis during the Communist period, its success was predicated on its dependence on and allegiance to the Soviet Union. When the Soviet Union cut off preferential trade relations with Bulgaria, the latter was left with whole sectors of the economy which had been designed around trade with the Soviet Union, a heavy foreign debt (reaching $12.2 billion by mid-1992),[32] and nowhere else to turn. The economic aid provided to Bulgaria by the International Monetary Fund and the World Bank has been comparatively little.[33] And the Russians are apparently no longer concerned about their former ally. Indeed, a Russian parliamentarian, Andronik Migranyan, said on a visit to Sofia, "Recently Bulgaria has been content to show Russia only its behind and there is nothing for Russia to do with this behind but kick it. . . . For the first time in more than 100 years Bulgaria will have to find its own place in the Balkans and in Europe without counting on Russian support."[34]

Environmental Legacies

The environment was another area affected by a centralized industrial policy. The advanced industrial states now carry out cost-benefit analyses to determine how much environmental cost should be tolerated per unit of economic gain.[35] Poor and industrializing countries, however, simply cannot afford the luxury of considering such costs. So, during the process of rapid industrialization everywhere in Eastern Europe, concern about the environment tended to be subordinated to the goals of creating an industrial capacity.[36]

The environment was further ignored, however, not only in the pursuit of rapid industrialization, but also because it was possible to ignore environmental costs that were not easily seen, since centralization allows for a high level of secrecy. After all, in the advanced industrial states the governments formulate environmental policy, which private industry must either follow or be fined for not following. Since industry in Eastern Europe was government owned, the governments in the region were unlikely to formulate legislation that was not in industry's short-term interest. Likewise, governments were unlikely to impose fines on themselves for environmental damage.

The environmental legacy of communism may be the most damaging legacy of all. Sulfur dioxide emission per head averaged 150 kilograms in Eastern Europe in 1984, whereas it was 61 kilograms per head in the states of the European Community.[37] More specifically, in what appears to be Bulgaria's most polluted city, Ruse, the incidence of lung disease in 1975 was 969 per hundred thousand inhabitants. By 1985, that figure had jumped to 17,386 per hundred thousand.[38] In 1986, the number of children hospitalized in Ruse for lung ailments was 2,924, and the number of adults hospitalized for that reason was 1,546. Moreover, about 86,000 children and 62,000 adults were treated on an out-patient basis.[39] This seems exceedingly high for a city with a population of 170,594.[40]

A potentially even greater environmental catastrophe that is a direct legacy of the Communists' industrialization policy could come from Bulgaria's nuclear power plant, Kozlodui. Kozlodui's reactors are old and apparently are not well maintained. Indeed, some Western engineers consider Kozlodui the most dangerous nuclear power plant in the world.[41] A Bulgarian government commission estimated that the chance of an accident in one of Kozlodui's reactors over the course of a year was 1 in 550.[42] This is not surprising given the large number of fires that have taken place at Kozlodui in the late 1980s and early 1990s. Should there be a more dangerous fire (one that affects the reactors) or some other such accident, the outcome would be disastrous — as nuclear accidents are wont to be — and the disaster would be particularly great as the plant is less than one hundred miles from the capital. Even if another fire does not take place, Kozlodui has already caused contamination of groundwater around the plant, and 217 workers have already suffered excessive exposure to radiation.[43] The International Atomic Energy Agency has concluded that the contamination was the result of "several serious accidents" that have already taken place.[44]

To its credit, the European Community has given $13 million in aid to modernize the oldest of Kozlodui's reactors,[45] but such modernization may not be possible at that cost. One engineering company has estimated the cost of bringing the reactors up to safety standards at $30 million each. But even if the reactors can be modernized, and even if the money can be found, this is money that could have been put to more productive use had the condition of Bulgaria's nuclear reactors not been so poor.

In short, then, this legacy of communism has been quite costly to Bulgaria and is likely to continue to be so. It is costly not only in terms of the diversion of scarce financial resources from investment to repair but also in terms of the foreign investment that is forgone. Western firms are so put off by the potential environmental damage that East European governments have to reduce the asking prices for businesses; and even at that, the Western firms sometimes pull out in the middle of deals if they find environmental damage.[46]

Concluding Thoughts on Democracy and Capitalism

As stated at the outset, assessing the legacies of communism is important, in part, for determining the prospects for democracy and capitalism in Eastern Europe. It should not be surprising, then, that the spring and summer of 1990 found many Bulgarians discussing the legacies of communism. In this period, prior to the first free Bulgarian parliamentary elections, the main question for most Bulgarians was, What has my country done for (or to) me, and what might it do for (or to) me in the future? The BSP addressed this question in its election campaign. Its answer was clear and unequivocal: The Bulgarian Communist Party had erred in the past, but these errors were attributable to certain individuals who had overstepped the bounds of power. Otherwise, the Bulgarian Communist Party had industrialized a primarily peasant country, and had given the populace free and universal health care and education; an economic system wherein one might not get rich, but in which one could get by; and stability, despite the potential for instability created by Bulgaria's sizable Turkish minority. In the future, the population could expect continued civil peace and a slow transformation of the economy which would ensure economic stability. In short, the BSP argued that the legacies of communism were primarily positive.

Opposition candidates, too, were concerned with the legacies of communism. They argued that the Communists had offered the country little but economic ruin and civil strife and were likely to offer more of the same in the future. The extent to which the Communists had created civil peace was in direct proportion to the number of hard-labor camps in Bulgaria over time. Indeed, after these camps began to disappear in the 1960s civil strife emerged as a result of the BCP's policies toward the ethnic Turks. And although Bulgaria had certainly been industrialized under the Communists, the costs were high: a distorted economy, heavily dependent upon Soviet aid and markets; a degraded environment; and a formerly bustling agricultural sector that could now barely support the needs of the country. The opposition, then, primarily evaluated the legacies of the Communist past in a negative light.

In the end, the BSP won the 1990 elections on political, social, and economic grounds. A majority of Bulgarians had apparently accepted the BSP's vision of the past. In this way, the legacies of communism were instrumental in securing the BSP victory.

Some might argue that the BSP triumph in itself demonstrated the lack of democracy in the country in 1990. This is truly an untenable position, however, as the elections were declared free and fair by international observers. The BSP victory did inhibit the growth of stable democracy, nonetheless, insofar as international institutions were more reluctant to give Bulgaria aid partly on these grounds. Without aid, then, Bulgaria immediately spiraled into economic chaos that made stability all the more impossible to maintain.

By the fall of 1990, people were waiting in food lines for hours for such common items as milk, bread, cheese, flour, sugar, and meat. Even when rationing was implemented, the lines did not subside. Since people's expectations as to what might await them in their capitalist future had soared, the economic crash came as quite a shock. Not surprisingly, protests and demonstrations broke out, and continued until the BSP government resigned under tremendous popular pressure.

When the BSP lost the 1991 elections, some observers were inclined to interpret this as a wholesale rejection of the Communist past and as a re-evaluation of the legacies of communism. While the latter explanation is most likely correct, the more extreme, former position, expounded by Lawrence Eagleburger, then U.S. deputy secretary of state, is most certainly overstated: "Bulgaria . . . has not only overcome the legacy of communism, it is in the process of overcoming the legacy of history."[47]

What Eagleburger failed to recognize is that a legacy cannot disappear overnight, nor can one that was forged over the course of nearly forty-five years disappear in one year. When an heir receives a particularly extensive inheritance, that inheritance is difficult to squander in a short period of time. Likewise, the legacies of communism remain — from the continuing weak state of the economy to the dead forests. The question is, what effect will these legacies have on democracy and capitalism in Bulgaria? In the first free election, they enhanced the electoral strength of the BSP. And although the BSP lost the second election, much of its strength still derived from the positive evaluation of these legacies. It is likely, then, that in the future the BSP will continue to be a political force (although perhaps a declining one) because of these legacies. That may, however, be detrimental to democracy and capitalism in Bulgaria — not because the BSP has refused to play the parliamentary game fairly, but because international aid seems to be contingent upon the BSP being weak.

Democracy, capitalism, and the future of Bulgaria hang in the balance. In which direction the balance tips is partly dependent upon Bulgaria's economic standing, which is largely dependent on foreign aid and investment. The extent to which foreign aid and investment are tied to the continued existence of the legacies of communism may have already predetermined Bulgaria's future. For, the words of Eagleburger notwithstanding, the words of Tennyson are more appropriate here: "Though much is taken, much abides."

13

Albania

Elez Biberaj

Albania has had the misfortune of being ruled by one of the most repressive Communist regimes in the world, and for a longer period than any other East European state. Enver Hoxha, a founding member of the Albanian Communist Party, ruled the country with an iron hand from the end of World War II until his demise in 1985. He was succeeded by his protégé Ramiz Alia, who pursued less repressive policies but refused to end the Communist monopoly on power until student demonstrations in December 1990 forced him to sanction the creation of opposition parties. According to a study by the U.S. Commission on Security and Cooperation in Europe, "the degree of brutality and inhumanity which existed in the policies and practices of the Hoxha and Alia regimes is almost impossible to comprehend."[1] The last East European state to get rid of Communist rule, Albania is arguably the most underdeveloped country in Europe. Sali Berisha, who succeeded Alia as president after his Democratic Party swept the Communists out of power in the March 1992 elections, has inherited a country devastated by forty-seven years of Communist rule. The old Communist infrastructure has collapsed, and a new system is struggling to emerge. The misguided policy of self-reliance, pursued for many years by the Communists, has resulted in the impoverished country's having become totally dependent on foreign aid to feed its population. The specific conditions in which the Communists left Albania are likely to make its transition from totalitarian rule to democracy and a market economy the most difficult in the region. While most of the obstacles to Albania's democratization are the direct result of Hoxha's rule, some are deeply rooted in the country's history and political culture.

The author's views do not necessarily reflect those of the Voice of America or of the U.S. government.

The Historical Background

Albania started the transition process with a historical legacy that includes lengthy foreign occupation and domination, and the lack of a democratic tradition. Its political growth and nation building had been inhibited by close to five centuries of Ottoman occupation and by territorial encroachments by contiguous neighbors, as well as by economic and social backwardness, and regional, tribal, and religious differences. The Albanians are divided into two subgroups: the Gegs in the north and the Tosks in the south. Their different historical experiences and levels of economic development had resulted in divergent political cultures, both of which were inhospitable to liberal democracy. The Gegs were organized according to tribal groups, with the *bajraktar* (clan chieftain) playing a dominant role. The Tosks lived in a semifeudal society, with a small group of large landowners controlling about two-thirds of the land. Because of prolonged periods of foreign occupation and domination, Albanians in general came to view central authorities with great distrust, essentially considering them as foreign.

For centuries, Albania served as a battleground between the Roman Catholic Church, the Orthodox Church, and Islam. The great religious schism of 1054 resulted in the split of Albania into a Catholic north and an Orthodox south. Islam was introduced into Albania following the region's conquest by the Turks in the fourteenth century. By the end of the seventeenth century, the majority of the population had converted to Islam. While there were several factors that influenced the conversion, political and economic motives were the most decisive. During the long Ottoman rule, many Albanians rose to leading positions in the empire. Albania is Europe's only predominantly Muslim country. At the end of World War II, some 70 percent of the population was Muslim, 20 percent was Orthodox, and 10 percent was Roman Catholic.[2] While generally most observers use the same figures with regard to the current religious composition of the Albanian population, some take exception, arguing that as a result of the Communist regime's antireligious policies a large percentage of Albanians are atheist.[3] The Albanians have traditionally displayed a high degree of religious tolerance. The motto of the founding fathers of modern Albania was "The religion of the Albanians is Albanianism." While for the Albanians the main identification was to be ethnonational rather than religious, some observers have insisted (as did Hoxha when justifying the outlawing of religion in 1967), that multiconfessionalism had undermined Albania's national union. Kiço Blushi, a prominent writer, has argued that Albanians have "never" been able to present a unified position on the national question because of their religious differences. According to Blushi, Communist attempts to create "the new man" have resulted in a "homo Albanicus" who can easily be manipulated by foreigners because his spiritual structure is "half Christian, half Islamic, half religious, half atheist."[4] In a spirited critique of Blushi's argument, Abdi Baleta, a member of the legislature, has maintained that Albanians have survived foreign attempts at assimilation thanks to their multiconfessionalism.[5]

Albania was the last Balkan country to organize a national movement and gain its independence from the Turkish empire, which it did in 1912; but large Albanian-inhabited territories—Kosovo and Çamëria—remained under Serbian and Greek occupation, respectively. Although its independence was recognized and guaranteed by the Great Powers, Albania's existence as an independent entity was not readily accepted by its more powerful neighbors. During World War I, the country was occupied by a half dozen foreign armies; and at the end of the war Serbia, Greece, and Italy made efforts to further partition it. Albania's independence was preserved largely thanks to President Wilson's support at the Paris Peace Conference and the inability of neighboring states to agree on how to divide the tiny Balkan state.

Faced with an extremely hostile external environment, the political groups, forces, and parties that emerged in Albania in the postindependence period were oriented toward ensuring the nation's sovereignty and independence and recovering lost territories. Their programs on the internal organization of the Albanian polity were less clear. Western political ideas were slow to penetrate the country, as few Albanians had been educated in the West. Albania lacked a well-developed middle class imbued with democratic ideals, and most of the members of the emerging political, cultural, and military elites had been educated in Turkey, a country that also lacked a democratic political tradition. The semifeudal Albanian clan society was characterized by widespread authoritarian tendencies, and apparently there were strong sentiments for the selection of a strong leader in the mold of Gjergj Kastrioti Skënderbeu (Scanderbeg), the legendary fifteenth-century leader who successfully fought the Turks for a quarter of a century.

The first Albanian political parties, in the Western sense of the term, appeared in the early 1920s. The two most important political groups were the People's Party, led by Fan S. Noli, a Harvard-educated Eastern Orthodox clergyman who served briefly as prime minister in 1924, and the Progressive Party, led by Ahmet Zogu, a chieftain from Mati. But Albania's experiment with political pluralism was short lived: the main political parties engaged in endless feuding, the parliament was ineffective, and the country was plagued by political instability. Order was restored following Zogu's accession to power in December 1924, and three years later he proclaimed himself the king of the Albanians. King Zog proceeded to establish an authoritarian monarchy, which prevented the development of a genuine multiparty system. But despite Zog's dictatorship, Albania under his rule was by far a much freer society than it was to be under the subsequent Communist rule of Enver Hoxha. Zog succeeded in laying the foundations of a modern state and carried out significant cultural and economic reforms.

Predominantly a backward agrarian society with no tradition of a working class, Albania was less suited for communism than any other nation in Eastern Europe. Although small Communist groups began to appear in the major cities in the 1920s and the 1930s, the Albanian Communist Party (ACP) was established only in 1941, with the direct assistance of Yugoslav Communists. By claiming to be fighting for the national liberation of their country, the Communists were able to attract significant popular and Allied support during World War II. By the end of the war, the ACP had overpowered its weaker, poorly organized opponents and proceeded to establish a single-party state in the Soviet mold.

Between 1945 and 1948, Albania was under heavy Yugoslav influence and came close to being absorbed by its more powerful northern neighbor. Albania's new political, economic, and cultural institutions were modeled closely after those of Yugoslavia. The private property of wealthy Albanians was confiscated without compensation, all industrial plants and mines were nationalized, and agrarian reform was instituted. Hoxha embarked on a highly repressive domestic policy, crushing the opposition through a campaign of terror and intimidation. With the intensification of the East-West conflict, Hoxha's regime allied itself closely with the Soviet bloc, to the detriment of relations with Western countries, including such neighboring countries as Greece and Italy.

Hoxha further consolidated his power following the break with Yugoslavia in 1948. Through a series of show trials, he eliminated real and potential opponents within and outside the ACP, which at its first congress in 1948 changed its name to the Albanian Party of Labor (APL). Moscow, which during the period 1945–48 had practically given Yugoslavia a free hand in Albania, offered Tirana substantial economic and military assistance as Albania came to play a critical role in Stalin's strategy of exerting pressure on Yugoslavia. With the assistance of Soviet and East European advisers, the Albanian government launched an ambitious program of economic development with the aim of transforming the country into what the official propaganda termed an agrarian-industrial state. Albania adopted the Soviet system of centralized economic planning, emphasizing the rapid development of heavy industry. Its external interactions were almost totally restricted to the Soviet bloc, as political and economic relations with the West remained frozen. Albania also joined the Council for Mutual Economic Assistance and became a founding member of the Warsaw Treaty Organization, although the Soviet Union never signed a defense treaty with its small ally.

By the mid-1950s, Hoxha's government had earned the reputation of being the most Stalinist regime in Eastern Europe. It was not surprising, therefore, that Albanian Communist leaders would oppose Soviet leader Nikita S. Khrushchev's de-Stalinization campaign. Hoxha's opposition to Khrushchev was conditioned primarily by his well-founded fear that de-Stalinization would result in his own replacement as Party and state leader; but Moscow's rapprochement in 1955 with Belgrade also played a role, as Albania feared renewed Yugoslav domination.

By the end of the 1950s, relations between Tirana and Moscow had reached a critical point. Meanwhile, the Albanians had begun to forge an alliance with the Chinese Communists, who also objected to Khrushchev's domestic and foreign policies. Albania's 1961 break with the Soviet Union and the USSR's East European allies and Tirana's alliance with China were monumental developments in the country's post–World War II history. While Soviet bloc members moved toward improving political and economic ties with the West, relaxing Communist Party control over the society, and experimenting with limited economic reforms, Albania moved in the opposite direction. It became almost totally isolated, developing relations only with China and selected third world countries. Domestically, Hoxha increased the repression and attempted to extend the Party's control over all aspects of life. The Tirana regime went even further than Beijing in abolishing the private sector, fully collectivizing agriculture, and outlawing religion. The loss of Soviet bloc economic assistance also retarded Albania's economic development, as distant China was unable to meet Albanian requests fully because of its own domestic problems; nevertheless, the Chinese did provide Albania with several billion dollars in economic and military assistance, thus ensuring the existence of Hoxha's repressive regime.[6]

Albania's alliance with China did not last long. Following the Sino-American rapprochement in the early 1970s, Tirana publicly accused China of betraying its Marxist-Leninist principles. Hoxha could not follow his Chinese allies in improving ties with the West because he feared the possible repercussions that such a development would have for Albania's domestic policies. Indeed, despite increased centralization and repression, Hoxha's policies were encountering considerable domestic opposition as younger technocrats questioned the course the Party was pursuing both internally and externally. Hoxha responded by carrying out a series of bloody purges which by the mid-1970s had resulted in the demise of a number of senior officials, including the minister of defense, Beqir Balluku. On the eve of the break with China, the Albanian parliament approved a new constitution (1976), which embodied Hoxha's views on major policy issues. The document sanctioned the one-party system, abolished private property, prohibited the government from seeking foreign credits or forming joint enterprises with foreign companies or countries, and reaffirmed the regime's 1967 decision to abolish institutionalized religion, thus making Albania the world's only atheist state.

The break with China, which removed the last and only source of foreign assistance, placed Albania in a precarious position. Rather than opening up the country to the West and to its former Soviet bloc allies, Hoxha's regime turned further inward, self-reliance having become the main element in Albania's economic development. The disastrous consequences of Hoxha's policies became evident within a few years, as the economy entered a phase of rapid decline. Nevertheless, the regime stayed the course.

Hoxha's death in April 1985 raised hope that Albania would finally follow the example of other Communist countries, end its international isolation, and initiate much-needed political, economic, and social reforms. Alia, who became Hoxha's successor almost by default because other potential successors had either been eliminated by the dictator or had died, attempted to tinker with reform, but without changing the main tenets of his mentor's policies. Meanwhile the economy continued to deteriorate. Alia did not begin to consider making serious economic reforms and opening the country up until 1990, after the demise of communism in other East European countries. But by this time it was too late. Opposition to Communist rule had become widespread, especially among workers and the youth. Student demonstrations at Tirana University in December 1990 finally convinced the regime to end its monopoly on political power and permit the establishment of opposition parties. During the next two years, Albania would witness unprecedented political turmoil. In the 22 March 1992 elections, the Communists, who only a year earlier had won a landslide election victory mainly thanks to support from the countryside, suffered a humiliating defeat, as the Democratic Party, the first opposition party in the post-1945 period, captured 92 seats in the 140-seat parliament. Alia resigned, paving the way for Berisha to become Albania's first post-Communist president.

There is general agreement among observers that no other East European country suffered more under communism than did Albania. For close to half a century, Albania was isolated from the outside world and from democratic values and principles; and this isolation, combined with a lack of democratic traditions, inculcated and reinforced a set of values and behaviors not particularly hospitable to the development of democracy. Multiple political, social, and economic legacies of Communist misrule will constitute serious constraints on Albania's transition to democracy. President Berisha, who has appealed to the West to treat his country as a special case, meriting closer attention and extensive aid, has said that it will take at least a generation to establish a genuine pluralistic democracy in Albania.[7]

Political Legacies

Unlike communism in other East European countries, communism in Albania was homegrown, and therefore eradicating its legacies will be much more difficult. The Albanian Communists were not installed in power by an outside force but won on their own, admittedly with some assistance from Yugoslav Communists and, in the final stages of World War II, the Allies. Albanian Communists enjoyed a higher degree of legitimacy than did their colleagues in other East European states, who, with the notable exception of the Yugoslav Communists, were installed in power by the Soviets. This factor made it possible for Hoxha to impose upon his people one of the most repressive regimes the world has known.

The Communist regime engaged in gross violations of human and political rights and relied upon a well-coordinated process of political socialization to ensure the population's obedience. Relying on the military, the secret police, and mass organizations, the APL attempted to exercise total control over all aspects of life, and held an unchallenged monopoly over political power. The ruling party prohibited the creation of any group or organization outside its control, ensured that political behavior was overtly conformist, and left no avenues for public participation in the decision-making process. Elections were a facade, their only purpose being to legitimize the ruling party. Almost always, the authorities claimed unanimous popular support. In the last election for the People's Assembly before the legalization of opposition, the Central Election Commission announced a voter turnout of 100 percent. It said that all had voted for the official candidates, with only one ballot in the entire country found to be void.[8] No other regime could claim such "widespread" support.

The People's Assembly played a minor role, if any, in Albanian politics. It met only twice a year and approved decisions already made by the Party leadership. Members of the parliament had no opportunity to express independent views or to criticize government policy. Communists controlled all leading positions, and members of the Politburo were usually in charge of senior government posts, including the highest post in the Council of Ministers (the post of prime minister) and the highest posts in ministries dealing with defense and economic matters. The position of the chair of the Presidium, the titular head of state, was largely a ceremonial position.

Under the Communist reign, the rule of law was alien to Albania. During the so-called Cultural Revolution in the mid-1960s, the government went so far as to abolish altogether the Ministry of Justice and to prohibit the practice of law. The Communist Party's supremacy was enshrined in the constitution. Even when ruling Communist parties in other East European countries experimented with limited political reforms, expanded the possibilities for political participation, and tolerated the creation of dissident groups and organizations, the APL did not stray from its Stalinist policy. Even after Hoxha's death, the APL continued to hold a tight grip over the society. It was only after the downfall of communism in other East European countries that Alia began to contemplate the possibility of real changes. But even then he was not willing to give up the APL's monopoly on power and permit the creation of other political parties. He accepted demands for political pluralism in December 1990 in the face of a real danger of a popular revolt similar to the uprising that resulted in the violent downfall of Nicolae Ceaușescu's regime in Romania.

Albania's Communist regime had succeeded in totally suppressing the opposition. On the eve of the sanctioning of political pluralism, no dissident community existed. Whereas in other East European countries dissident communities had emerged, the development of a democratic elite in Albania and the emergence of an "Albanian Havel" were impossible. The non-Communist elite had long ago been obliterated, while prominent intellectuals, including the country's best-known writer, Ismail Kadare, were too closely identified with the regime.

The lack of a well-developed liberal elite is perhaps the greatest political legacy of communism and at the same time the greatest obstacle to the development of democratic institutions. With very few exceptions, leaders of the new parties, most of them former APL members, display a nascent understanding of democracy. And the population at large, at last free of Communist shackles, shows a remarkable ignorance of the responsibilities of democracy, and limited tolerance for diverse points of view.

Another political legacy of communism is the deep gulf between the government and the people. Although, as mentioned earlier, the Communist regime in Albania was homegrown, it was viewed by many as a "foreign" government. Despite the change in regimes, many Albanians display little trust in the government and see their society as divided into "us" and "them." There appears to be a widespread perception that all government officials are corrupt and that they are only interested in looking after their selfish interests and the interests of their families and clans.

The development of a democratic culture is hindered by a lack of a sense of personal responsibility and accountability, a widespread apathy, and a deeply rooted expectation that others — the new government or foreigners — would simply step in and solve the country's problems. According to a 1991 public opinion survey, although the overwhelming majority (90%) of Albanians favored a market economy, only a third believed that individuals should take more responsibility for themselves. More than half of the respondents expressed the view that the state should take more responsibility for providing for everyone.[9]

The emerging political parties have not had sufficient time to develop into viable political entities, and the party system remains volatile and party identification weak. Political participation outside the realm of political parties remains limited. Clear rules for the political game have yet to be established. The parliament, with no tradition of a loyal opposition and composed largely of inexperienced members, has become obstructive. Nevertheless, the country's new political elite seems determined to build a civil society based on the rule of law. The Albanians are in the process of drafting a new constitution, which will contain clear provisions limiting government discretion. After long debates on the form of government, Berisha surprised his opponents, who had accused him of authoritarian tendencies, and came out publicly in favor of a parliamentary system. Berisha said that against the historical background of seventy-five years of dictatorial rule, the Albanians needed to reject "the notion of a country dominated by a single person." He argued that the future of democracy in Albania depends to a great extent on the development of a parliamentary tradition.[10]

With its arbitrary use of power, the Communist regime left a legacy of popular conformism and apathy which has become a serious obstacle to the development of a civil society. Albanians are wrestling with the question of why they tolerated Hoxha's dictatorship for so long. Some observers have suggested that unless Albanians acknowledge their collective responsibility for the Communist devastation of their country, they will not be able to build a new and better society.[11] Berisha has said that "it is not only the dictator who is to blame for a dictatorship,"[12] adding that all Albanians share responsibility for what happened to their country under Hoxha's rule.[13] Teodor Keko, a member of the legislature, deploring the fact that the Albanians had resigned themselves to Communist rule and did not organize even one revolt against Hoxha's dictatorship, has called upon his fellow citizens to ask for "Albania's forgiveness." He has thus expressed what has troubled many Albanians: "We preserved our lives but gave up Albania's life."[14]

Economic Legacies

Hoxha's Albania went further than any other East European country in attempts to copy the Stalinist model of economic development.[15] The model "represented an extreme form of centralism and autarky and perpetuated a stagnant economy caught in a low-level productivity trap."[16]

Its main aspects included the adaptation of a highly centralized planning system, the complete abolition of private property and private economic activity, and heavy industrialization. All decisions regarding investments and allocation of resources were made at the very top level of the decision-making process. In setting the nation's economic priorities, Communist leaders were driven by their desire to make Albania economically self-sufficient. By the late 1960s, agriculture was fully collectivized and private property prohibited. After the break with the Soviet Union in the early 1960s, Albania confined its external economic transactions primarily to China. In the wake of the deterioration of ties with Beijing in the mid-1970s, and the subsequent break-up of the alliance with China, Albania adopted a policy of almost total self-reliance. The Communist regime took the unprecedented step of constitutionally constraining its actions by prohibiting foreign credits and investments — the first, and probably the only, country in the world to take such an extreme course of action. The self-reliance policy had devastating implications for the country's development.

With its heavy emphasis on the rapid industrialization of the country, the Communist regime pursued a policy that neglected other sectors of the economy. But perhaps more importantly, the highly rigid system left no room for initiative and destroyed the work ethic. Moreover, because of the lack of accountability on the part of decision makers, the system was characterized by massive waste and mismanagement of national resources. Enterprises, heavily subsidized by the state, had no initiative to improve their efficiency. By isolating the country and pursuing a policy of self-reliance, the Communist regime delayed the implementation of fundamental economic reforms. Even when it became quite obvious that the system had retarded the country's economic development, the authorities were not willing to initiate meaningful reforms. By the mid-1980s, the economy began to register negative growth. Alia responded by initiating a partial decentralization of the economic decision-making process and increasing external interactions. However, he did not accept suggestions that would have permitted competition between economic units and the development of markets. He was also adamant in opposing the legalization of private property, insisting that the APL would make no concession on such a crucial issue.[17]

Alia began to seriously contemplate the introduction of economic reforms only after the downfall of communism in other East European countries, which was accompanied by increased labor unrest in Albania and outright internal opposition to the Tirana regime. But Alia's measures were too little and too late. Within months of the end of the Communist monopoly on power and the subsequent political upheaval, the centralized economic system collapsed, and there was no mechanism to replace it. The lack of raw materials forced the shutdown of most enterprises, and the peasants forcibly disbanded agricultural cooperatives. Only rapid intervention by the international community prevented famine. The coalition government, formed in June 1991, was unable to effect any changes, and the economic situation continued to deteriorate.

The Democratic Party inherited a country in the midst of a severe economic crisis. It is estimated that economic output declined by as much as 60 percent between 1990 and 1992. The gross domestic product per capita in 1992 was estimated at less than four hundred dollars, while inflation exceeded 300 percent annually. At least 50 percent of the urban labor force was unemployed.[18] The democratic government moved boldly and steadfastly to rectify the situation. It repealed the rule that provided that workers be paid 80 percent of their wages when enterprises were forced to shut down their operations because of lack of raw materials; it liberalized prices; it slashed the explosive growth of the money supply; it ended most subsidies; and it launched a far-reaching program of privatization. By the end of 1992, the government claimed that economic decline had been arrested, that the Albanian currency, the *lek*, had been stabilized, and that most of the agricultural sector had been privatized. The government, however, encountered serious difficulties in privatizing the large industrial sector, since Albanian citizens did not have the necessary capital or access to credits, while foreign investors were wary of buying unprofitable enterprises. The government was also forced to modify some aspects of the reform program in order to lessen its impact on the poorest sectors of the society.

Albania will face immense difficulties in establishing a free-market economy. The Communists destroyed the small class of private entrepreneurs that had existed when they took power. Moreover, they had prevented the emergence of a managerial class. Thus, with the collapse of central planning in 1991, Albania lacked qualified decision makers who could supervise the transition to a market economy.

Perhaps one of the most lingering legacies of communism is the issue of the ownership of land and property. The Communists had nationalized the land and property without compensation. The land law, approved by the parliament in the summer of 1991, does not recognize original ownership rights but provides for the distribution of land free of charge to peasants who will farm it. Article 8 of the law states: "Neither former ownership nor the amount or boundaries of land owned before collectivization are recognized in the granting of land as the property of or for the use of physical or juridical persons."[19] By the end of 1993, the government claimed that more than 90 percent of the land had been reprivatized on the basis of the land law; however, in many parts of the country conflicting claims to the same land have caused increased social tensions. Moreover, the law does not permit the sale of land. Although the Democratic Party promised during the election campaign to resolve land disputes, the law has yet to be amended. The government is also faced with increasing demands for compensation for property seized by the Communists. Some sixty thousand Albanians whose property was expropriated in 1946 have created an association, and through various means, including demonstrations, this group has pressured the government and the parliament to provide compensation for property taken by the Communists. In July 1992 the parliament approved a compensation bill, but it fell short of what the former proprietors had demanded.

Societal Legacies

Under Communist rule, Albania underwent a comprehensive social transformation. Whereas at the end of World War II it had been a predominantly agrarian society, by 1990 the Communist regime had forged a significant working class. In addition, it had transformed rural society from its traditional peasant base to a more working-class one, in the process having totally collectivized agriculture and prohibited private ownership. Hoxha launched an all-out, violent assault on the peasantry, pushing it into a state of extreme impoverishment by the time of his death. Even in the most remote, mountainous areas, land was taken away from peasants, and they were prohibited from raising livestock outside collective cooperatives.

The Communists created an elaborate social welfare system, which guaranteed Albanian citizens job security, price stability, and free education and medical care. Moreover, through a concerted policy of reducing wage differentials, the Communists ensured that social and economic differentiation was kept at a low level.

The APL carried out perhaps the greatest social experimentation in Eastern Europe, imposing its total control over all aspects of life, with the aim of perpetuating its rule. No room was left for any sort of activity outside Party control, not even the intimate details of family life. Through an extensive spy network, supported by the all-encompassing police and military establishment, the ruling party controlled popular demands for greater freedoms and ensured the population's continued conformity with its policies. The objective of the police state was to prevent the rise of alternative power centers that might potentially threaten or undermine APL control over Albanian society.

The regime devoted tremendous resources to nation building and modernization, with the goal of instilling in the population appropriate Marxist-Leninist values. To this end, the population, beginning in the mid-1960s, was subjected to a relentless campaign of Communist education, which climaxed in 1967 with the official banning of religion and the shutdown of all religious institutions. This was accompanied by a well-coordinated campaign of ideological struggle against what the ruling elite described as alien manifestations and influence. Albania's "new" socialist man was expected to be imbued with appropriate Communist traits, morality, and atheistic ideas, and to be free of any past "bourgeois" cultural traits. The authorities pursued a merciless struggle against "class enemies," and the effects of that struggle will be felt for years if not decades to come. Real and potential enemies of the regime were executed, imprisoned, or sent into internal exile. Their innocent families and relatives often met the same fate. Education and social advancement were strictly controlled, and those people who did not have a "good" biography could not climb the social ladder. The class struggle was not aimed solely at anti-Communist foes but also engulfed the ruling Communist elite. Indeed, in the last decades of Communist rule the class struggle was heavily concentrated on members of the Party who either questioned the Party's policies or were disenchanted with communism. Purges, especially at the highest level, became a way of life under Hoxha's rule. The most prominent victims of these purges were members of the Party's Politburo and Central Committee. Mehmet Shehu, who for close to three decades had served as the country's prime minister, allegedly committed suicide in 1981 rather than face public disgrace. Other senior officials, including ministers of defense, internal affairs, foreign affairs, and the economy, were either executed or sentenced to long prison terms.

While most Albanians suffered under Communist rule, the regime pursued especially repressive policies in the north, where it continued to encounter armed opposition until the early 1950s. During the interwar years the northerners had dominated Albanian politics (King Zog was a Geg), but the Communists had their main base of support in the south, and the Communist *nomenklatura* was overwhelmingly Tosk. Hoxha also attempted to forcefully "southernize" the entire country, placing Tosk officials in leading positions in the north and imposing a standard literary language, heavily based on the Tosk dialect. Hoxha's policies had the effect of increasing regional differences, as reflected by increased friction between north and south in the post-Communist era.

Through brute force and an extensive system of privileges, Hoxha succeeded in creating a loyal nomenklatura class. But the nomenklatura did not include the nation's best and brightest; instead, it was composed of a small group of idealists, mostly veterans of World War II, who evidently believed in communism; and an overwhelming majority who blindly carried out orders from above. Even those who eventually made it to the top echelons of Party and state bureaucracies were mediocre people, rewarded not for their abilities but for loyalty to the system and its leaders. The nomenklatura, especially members of the Politburo and the Central Committee, enjoyed extensive privileges. In the wake of the end of Communist monopoly on power, the Albanian press gave a detailed picture of the privileges, abuses, and corruption of Politburo members. While the majority of the population had lived at the level of mere subsistence, senior Party officials had amassed enormous wealth, and enjoyed luxurious living quarters for themselves and their families, villas in resort areas, fancy cars, travel and medical treatment in the West, study abroad, special stores, and unlimited access to imported goods. The highest members of the leadership lived in a special housing compound, totally isolated from the citizenry. It was disclosed that the Hoxhas lived in a house with twenty-five refrigerators, twenty-eight color televisions, and nineteen telephone lines.[20]

The intelligentsia was used by the Communists to ensure Communist political control. Because of severe restrictions, intellectuals were unable to publicly defy the Party, let alone offer organized opposition or provide leadership to other groups that potentially could have opposed the Communists. The regime dealt very severely with dissidents, while it generously rewarded conformist behavior. Yet, once dissidence emerged openly, it was the intellectuals who provided the leadership for opposition parties and groups.

By 1990, Communist rule had taken a heavy toll on the Albanian population, who were by now highly dispirited and apathetic. There was widespread alienation, and disillusionment with Communist rule; social malaise had become pervasive; and there were disturbing signs of increased disintegration of social controls and self-discipline, resulting in a significant increase in social pathologies.

Perhaps one of the greatest challenges facing Albania's post-Communist leaders is the pervasive moral and spiritual crisis, a direct legacy of the previous regime. Large segments of the population appear simply to have lost confidence in themselves, in their country, and in their government and institutions. Many see no future in their own country. Several hundred thousand Albanians have fled their country, most of them illegally, since 1990. Among those who have fled are many members of the technical intelligentsia. This brain drain will have a devastating impact on Albania.

Many Albanian analysts insist that the biggest damage that communism did to Albania is not the country's economic devastation but the destruction of Albanians' national traits and dignity. These analysts are concerned not with the rise of nationalism but with the lack of what they term "Albanianism." There appears to have been a widespread decline of national pride and civic morale. Some Albanians have gone so far as to adopt foreign names and even change their religion in an attempt to gain permission to settle in other countries. Observers have decried the de-nationalization, and de-Albanianization that occurred under communism.[21] As Dritero Agolli, a leading writer and member of the Socialist Party's leadership, has put it: "In Albania everything has to be revived: thought and philosophy, family and morality, religion and spirituality, science and art, justice and patriotism, the army and the economy, the city and the village."[22]

Albanians seem ill-prepared for the painful transition to a market economy. Things are very likely to get much worse before they get better. In the near term Albanians will likely see their standard of living, already the lowest in Europe, decline still further. The dismantling of the Communist social welfare system, combined with the swelling of the ranks of the unemployed, put many citizens in a precarious position. The state simply has no resources with which to alleviate the social burden of new reforms.

The population in general is not familiar with the workings of a market economy. Few people are willing to take the risk involved in engaging in private initiative; the majority of those who do are former members of the Communist nomenklatura — people who studied or traveled abroad, and thus established contacts that later helped them raise the necessary capital to go into private business. This development has given rise to complaints by many people that although the Communists have lost political power at the national level they continue to control the economy. There also seems to be a widespread perception that the private businessmen who have opened shops have done so as a result of having engaged in corrupt practices. Such beliefs are reinforced by rampant official corruption, which increased dramatically during the political upheaval in 1991–92. During the coalition government, growing official corruption was blamed for impairing international relief efforts. It was believed that humanitarian supplies were diverted into the black market or into private repositories for the bureaucrats. President Berisha has said that corruption is "the first peril and enemy of democracy in Albania. It is one of our most bitter legacies from the Communist regime."[23]

The societal legacy of communism also includes the problem of reintegrating into society the massive number of former political prisoners and other people uprooted by the former government. It is estimated that as many as several hundred thousand people were sent into internal exile. Many of these people demand to return to their original places of residence and to reclaim the houses and other property that the Communists expropriated without compensation. The reintegration of such a large segment of society would represent a formidable challenge for any government, but might turn out to be an impossible task for a government with very limited resources at its disposal. The issue of former political prisoners also raises the sensitive question of what action, if any, ought to be taken against former officials, particularly members of the dreadful secret police, Sigurimi.[24] Berisha has appealed for reconciliation, saying, "If all those who are guilty were to be punished, then Albania would have to be turned into one gigantic concentration camp."[25] He has opposed the opening of secret police files, saying that this would likely have a traumatic effect on the society, because it would be revealed that people had spied even on their families and close relatives. It is said that one in four Albanians was a police informer. Berisha has urged, however, that the files of politicians be opened, and the parliament is considering the issue.

With the downfall of communism, Albania has witnessed the resurgence of regional tensions. On the one hand, Gegs are resentful at what they see as Hoxha's deliberate policy of subduing the north politically, economically, and culturally. Some have gone so far as to accuse the Communists of having pursued a policy of internal colonialism.[26] On the other hand, there appears to be resentment in some parts of southern Albania that a northerner is now president (Berisha comes from the northern district of Tropojë). With an increasing number of northerners occupying senior positions in the post-Communist government, the Tosks apparently fear Geg political domination. While regional conflict does not currently seem to be severe enough to present a threat to the country's stability, the authorities cannot afford to ignore it.

Physical and Environmental Legacies

No doubt the most observable inheritance of Hoxha's Communist rule is the country's physical landscape. Thousands of bunkers, a testimony to the Communist leadership's siege mentality, stand all over Albania. These ugly structures can be found in the plains, on the coast, on the mountains, in school backyards, and even in urban areas. Not only are these bunkers of no value from a defense point of view, but they represent a monument to the immense waste of resources under Communist rule. Albanian officials estimate that the average cost of one bunker was equal to the cost of a two-room apartment. The bunkers also occupy significant amounts of arable land, and the costs of removing them are, at least for now, prohibitive. Had Communist authorities invested in the housing sector the enormous resources and labor used to build the bunkers, Albania would have long ago solved its critical housing shortage. Instead, most Albanians live in overcrowded apartments, and there are reportedly fifty thousand homeless.[27] It is not unusual for a couple and their children to live in the same cramped apartment as their in-laws. Communist decision makers paid little attention to housing maintenance, and as a result the vast majority of apartment complexes are in a debilitated state, with little chance of repair in the near future. Although Berisha's government has launched a drive to privatize the housing sector and encourage private construction companies, it will probably take Albania many years to alleviate the housing shortage. Indeed, the housing problem is likely to be exacerbated in the near term by an increasing influx of people from rural to urban areas. The Communists strictly controlled the movement of people from villages to the cities, and in 1992 two-thirds of the population still lived in the countryside. But with the lifting of restrictions on free movement, and the growing desperation in the countryside, Albania is likely to witness a significant shift in the population from rural to urban areas, with an accompanying increase in social tensions at a time of severely diminished resources and greater competition for scarce jobs. By 1992 Tirana had already been encircled by settlements of thousands of villagers who took over, and constructed illegal housing on, land formerly owned by the state. Tirana authorities are confronted with growing friction between the newcomers and city dwellers.

With its policies of uneven economic development, and its emphasis on the development of heavy industry, the Communist regime neglected the development of infrastructure, an omission that now is complicating the country's economic recovery. The road system is insufficient for Albania's rapidly growing needs. Until 1991 private vehicles were banned, and in the entire country there were no more than several hundred cars, all belonging to Party and government officials. With the introduction of market economic reforms, the number of private vehicles has steadily increased, and the current road network is not designed to handle the heavy traffic. Moreover, there has been a dramatic increase in the number of motor vehicle accidents.

Another serious problem area for the post-Communist government is the underdevelopment of communications. The Communist regime was obsessed with exercising total control over the population and preventing unauthorized contacts between the population and outsiders. The number of telephones was limited, and telephones were reserved for the privileged members of the nomenklatura. Direct links with other countries were established as recently as the spring of 1990. The lack of a modern, well-developed communications network is discouraging foreign businessmen from conducting business in Albania. Albanian authorities are now engaged in discussions with several international companies regarding modernization of the communications network.

In their attempt to rapidly industrialize the country, the Communists pursued policies that tremendously damaged the environment. With foreign assistance, first from the Soviet Union and then from China, the government constructed large steel, coal, and petrochemical projects, with the aim of ensuring the country's economic independence. The emphasis was on large-scale production, and no attention was devoted to the protection of the environment. Albania's rivers, lakes, and coastal areas, and the air in the major industrial centers, were heavily polluted as a result of the use of antiquated machinery and technology in mining, the metallurgical industry, light industry, and thermal energy production. The emission of highly toxic gases and dust into the atmosphere has become a serious problem. A case in point is the gigantic steel mill in the industrial city Elbasan, built in the mid-1970s with Chinese assistance. Described by Albanian leaders at the time as "the second liberation of Albania," the steel combine was built with outdated machinery and technology and was not fitted out with adequate equipment to control or minimize air pollution. The plant emits a range of poisonous gases, including carbon monoxide, phenol, cyanic acid, and ammonia, and represents a serious health hazard for the population in Elbasan and surrounding areas. Although the steel mill has apparently been operating for years at an annual loss of up to $100 million, its complete shutdown will be politically unacceptable; in the late 1980s the complex employed more than ten thousand people.

In most industrial areas, the burning of fuel oil and coal, without any measures to protect the environment, has caused serious air pollution. Crude oil floats freely from some oil fields into rivers and lakes owing to the lack of appropriate equipment to adequately separate oil from water.

The Communist government's campaign in the 1960s to open virgin lands, and the accompanying massive deforestation, have caused significant damage to the fauna. According to a joint World Bank–European Community report, the overexploitation of forests, especially overcutting for fuelwood, the main source of heating, is endangering natural regeneration and is leading to further problems. The report suggested that the government close or rebuild the mills that were the worst polluters.[28] As a result of inappropriate agricultural practices, the countryside already shows signs of serious environmental degradation.

By the early 1990s, the state, having become totally dependent on foreign aid, had no funds to allocate to the protection of the environment or to attempts to correct the problems caused by misguided policies. The neglect of the environment has had serious repercussions not only for the management of natural resources but also for the health care system. The continuous deterioration of the environment has been accompanied by a significant incidence of respiratory, eye, and skin diseases. Liver ailments and intestinal illnesses such as dysentery have spread, largely because of water pollution and the poor maintenance of water purification systems. The government is now unable to adequately fund health care services or to take any meaningful measures to deal with environmental problems. For years to come, Albanians will continue to pay a heavy price for the Communist regime's environmentally unsound policies.

Conclusion

Since December 1990, when the Communists were forced under popular pressure to sanction the creation of opposition parties, Albania has witnessed astounding revolutionary changes. The transfer of power from the Communist regime to a democratically elected government has been accomplished with a relatively low level of violence. But the majority of Albania's population has known only Hoxha's regime and therefore has no experience with pluralistic democracy. The lack of a well-developed liberal elite is a great obstacle to the development of democratic institutions. Nevertheless, President Berisha seems committed to the establishment of a pluralistic democracy based on the rule of law. In the two years since he assumed power, his government, despite formidable challenges, has achieved impressive results. Law and order were restored, and at the beginning of 1994 Albania was probably the most stable country in the Balkans. The human rights situation has improved dramatically, and Albania is in the process of building a truly independent judiciary. For the first time since World War II, Albanian citizens enjoy full democratic freedoms and liberties. The independent news media, although they have a long way to go in becoming truly objective in their reporting, are recognized as an indispensable element of the emerging pluralistic system. A comprehensive reform program, aimed at creating a market economy, is well under way. The agricultural sector has been almost totally privatized; prices have been liberalized; new businesses are emerging; and new legislation has been approved to encourage foreign investment. With the assistance of Western legal experts, Albanians are working on the establishment of a legal and tax structure and on the development of environmental regulations to ensure stability for foreign investments.

Despite these initial encouraging signs, however, Albania is grappling with formidable challenges in building a democratic society and making the transition from a highly centralized Communist economic system to a free-market economy. The economic reforms that the government is committed to implementing are likely to take a heavy social toll and could lead to a disenchantment with democracy, most graphically expressed in the Communist resurgence in the local elections in July 1992.

The prospects of Albania's fledgling democracy are heavily dependent on continued and increased Western assistance. With a relatively modest amount of aid, the West can make the difference. For the next three to four years, Albania will need food assistance and help with the implementation of agricultural reforms. With an increased allocation of resources, Albanian agriculture has good prospects for a speedy recovery. Albania has an urgent need for continual technical assistance programs in all fields, and for foreign advisers to different government ministries and institutions. Without the know-how and seed capital, individual entrepreneurs will find it almost impossible to establish small and medium-sized enterprises. Albania also desperately needs foreign assistance to develop its badly neglected infrastructure.

Albania is a small country, with a population of 3.2 million. But it is endowed with substantial resources and represents a growing market for Western goods and services. With modest Western assistance, Albania's prospects for establishing a genuine, pluralistic democracy and a market economy would be perhaps the best in the Balkans. Within a relatively short period of time, Albania could become a showcase throughout Eastern Europe and the former Soviet Union. And a viable democratic Albania would go a long way in contributing toward the reestablishment of stability in the volatile Balkans.

14

The Collapse
of the Yugoslav Alternative

Robin Alison Remington

By the winter of 1994, the civil war that had begun in the former Communist Yugoslavia following the June 1991 declarations of independence by Slovenia and Croatia had made the former Yugoslavia the Lebanon of the New Europe.[1] There is no accurate body count. As the year ended, the fighting in Bosnia and Herzegovina had claimed more than 200,000 lives, and displaced more than 2.5 million refugees.[2]

Faced with international outrage over conditions in Serbian "detention centers," and the human consequences of policies of "ethnic cleansing," the United Nations tightened sanctions on Serbia and Montenegro.[3] In the summer of 1993 Washington warned that sanctions may be applied to Croatia as well if the fighting in Central Bosnia between Croatian forces and Bosnian Muslims does not stop.[4] Since September 1992 the Federal Republic of Yugoslavia (now consisting of Serbia and Montenegro) has been barred from participating in the work of the United Nations.[5] Forces from NATO member countries have been authorized to join UN peacekeepers attempting to deliver humanitarian aid to besieged cities in Bosnia and Herzegovina; the UN Security Council's "no-fly zone" over Bosnia has been in place since October 1992.

Why? Whatever happened to the Yugoslav federation of south Slav nations, comprising multiple nationalities in six republics and two once-autonomous provinces (see table 11)? Pundits and politicians are divided between blaming historic Balkan tribalism and the belief that somehow communism is the culprit. Lord David Owen, the European Union (EU) co-chair of the Geneva International Peace Conference on Yugoslavia, goes so far as to link communism to negotiating strategies: "I've been struck by this feature of Communist societies — it does corrupt values. . . . We have to face up to the lying factor. They will look you straight in the face and they lie. And you know it, and they know you know it."[6]

The question of the role played by the legacies of communism on the

TABLE 11. Percentage Distribution of Ethnic Groups
in Yugoslav Successor States

Slovenia		*Federal Republic of Yugoslavia*	
(UN 22 May 1992)		(Not recognized as of	
Slovene	91	November 1992)	
Croats	3	*Montenegro*	
Serbs	2	Montenegrins	6.8
Other	4	Muslims	14.6
Croatia		Serbs	9.3
(UN 22 May 1992)		Albanians	6.6
Croats	77.9	Yugoslavs	4.0
Serbs	12.2	Other	2.7
Yugoslavs	2.2	*Serbia*[b]	
Muslims	1.0	Serbs	85
Other	6.7	Yugoslavs	5
Bosnia and Herzegovina		Muslims	3
(UN 22 May 1992)		Montenegrins	2
Muslims	43.7	Romanies	2
Serbs	31.4	Other	3
Croats	17.3	Vojvodina	
Yugoslavs	5.5	Serbs	65
Other	2.1	Hungarians	20
Macedonia		Croats	5
(UN 7 April 1993)		Romanian	2
Macedonians	64.6	Other	4
Albanians	21.0	Kosovo	
Turks	4.8	Albanians	82
Romanies (Gypsies)	2.7	Serbs	10
Serbs	2.2	Muslims	3
Others	4.7	Romanies	2
		Other	3

Sources: Ruza Petrovic, "The National Composition of Yugoslavia's
Population, 1991," *Yugoslav Survey* 33, no. 1 (1992), based on 1991
census data. Since the Petrovic article does not give a breakdown of
Serbia proper, Vojvodina, and Kosovo, the figures for those areas are
taken from Central Intelligence Agency, *The Former Yugoslavia: A Map
Folio* (Washington, D.C.: CIA, 1992). Official Yugoslav figures. Kosovar
Albanians boycotted the 1991 census.
Note: Parenthetical notations beginning with "UN" are dates of UN
membership.

Yugoslav road to civil war is important for the policy makers of other
multiethnic societies, post-Communist and non-Communist alike. It is
crucial for the would-be architects of the New Europe; and essential for
evaluating Europe's institutional infrastructure (the EU, NATO, the
Western European Union, and the Conference on Security and Coopera-

tion in Europe), which must undergo its own restructuring to meet the challenges of any "new world order" that comes to replace the "cold war order" that dominated the international system from 1946 until 1991. It is a significant, researchable question.

In the search for preliminary answers, this analysis rejects the ethno-historical determinism at the heart of the "Balkan tribalism" explanation as parochial and self-serving. Croats, Serbs, and Bosnian Muslims are not engaged in the tragic war that is savaging Bosnia and Herzegovina be-cause of centuries of ethnic hatred,[7] or by virtue of a historic curse, any more than Germans were destined to be Nazis or are destined to be neo-Nazis. Rather, this chapter starts with the assumption that — notwith-standing the negative consequences for the Serbian psyche of five hun-dred years under the Turks, and the consequences of Croat experiences in the Austro-Hungarian empire — the tragedy of Bosnia and Herzegovina is a manmade disaster.

If we assume that civil war in the former Yugoslavia was not inevita-ble, the long-term causes of the Yugoslav wars of succession must be investigated. Along with the legacies of communism, some other likely candidates include historically conflicting conceptions of the basis of the Yugoslav state, flawed post-Tito political institutions, and the unintended consequences of the hard-currency debt incurred in the 1970s. There is also a long list of short-term precipitants to be examined: sectarian poli-tics, the criminal irresponsibility of Yugoslav republic politicians, the pol-iticization of the armed forces, and gridlock within the European Com-munity (EC) in the face of German demands to control the timetable for recognition of Croatia and Slovenia.

To understand how the legacies of communism fit into this complex set of causes and/or precipitants of war requires establishing the conse-quences of the failure of the first Yugoslav state (1918–41), and the nature of the Yugoslav alternative to the Soviet model — nonaligned, socialist self-management.

The Collapse of Interwar Yugoslavia

Twice since 1918 a south Slav state has collapsed in interethnic violence. The Kingdom of Serbs, Croats, and Slovenes (1918–41) and Communist Yugoslavia (1945–91) both sought and failed to integrate the conflicting political cultures of the Serbs and the Croats into a stable federal union. Journalistic accounts that see the new Europe as a revival of the Austro-

Hungarian Empire assume a superficial cultural determinism.[8] Such an interpretation ignores the conflicting agendas that emerged with the origin of the first Yugoslav state. The founders of the interwar Yugoslavia clearly came together on the basis of a fundamental misunderstanding. That misunderstanding continued to shape the relationship of these nations throughout the second Yugoslavia and is at the heart of the 1991 collapse into civil war.[9]

Having willingly accepted the Hungarian king in exchange for what became an increasingly token autonomy following the 1102 Treaty of Zagreb, Croats had a keen awareness of the pitfalls of unequal relationships. Hence the Council of Croats and Slovenes wanted a confederal Yugoslavia, a partnership of equals. For Serbs, the new Yugoslavia was confused with longings for the restoration of the golden age of Tsar Dusan's medieval Serbian empire. In terms of the 1990s, this translated into two very different visions of the relationship between the post-Communist Yugoslav republics. Slovenia and Croatia favored a confederative community of nations (akin to the consociational model), while the Serbs insisted upon an integrated federation in which the Serbian population advantage (the Serbs comprised roughly 9 million out of a total of 23 million) would translate into political advantage (federative in form, but "greater Serbia" in substance model).

In the Kingdom of Serbs, Croats, and Slovenes, the tensions between these two visions were sharpened by dysfunctional behaviors developed to preserve the Serb, Croat, and Slovene nations trapped within the competing Habsburg and Ottoman empires. The lack of shared historical myth exacerbated the tensions created by Serbian centralizing tendencies and the Croats' use of political obstructionism to protect or expand their rights. There were no parties based on cross-cutting cleavages operating throughout the kingdom, and a lack of experience in operating the machinery of parliamentary government was an additional problem.

When the leader of the Croatian Peasant Party, Stjepan Radić, was shot in parliament following an argument with a Montenegrin deputy, King Alexander first asked the Slovenes to form another government; when that failed he declared the dictatorship in 1929. What the Serbian king may well have perceived as a problem of law and order during a time-out to construct viable political parties, many Croatians experienced as martial law amounting to Serbian colonization. In response, Croatian militants established a violent resistance movement, the Ustashi.

The Ustashi were among the terrorist groups that assassinated King Alexander in 1934. Still more importantly, when Hitler's war machine dismembered the first Yugoslav state in 1941, Ante Pavelić, who was the leader of the Ustashi, returned as head of the so-called Independent Kingdom of Croatia. Hundreds of thousands of Serbs, Jews, Gypsies, and Croatians who resisted the slaughter died in concentration camps at the hands of Croatian fanatics.[10] Jasenovac, the Ustasha extermination camp, has been poignantly described as "the Serbian Babi Yar, a piercing wound in the heart."[11] Serbs fought back. Atrocities were committed in retaliation.

In short, Communist Yugoslavia inherited a legacy of national and communal hatred stemming from the failed experiment with integration in interwar Yugoslavia and the horrifying experience with Ustasha fascism in World War II. One might compare the second Yugoslavia to a politically arranged marriage contracted in hopes of bringing peace to the region.

Communist Yugoslavia: The Yugoslav Alternative

Notwithstanding Allied aid and belated Soviet assistance, the Communist-led partisan army essentially won the national liberation struggle itself.[12] Along the way, the Yugoslav Communist Party transformed itself from a small underground revolutionary organization of about 12,000 members to a ruling party of some 140,000.[13] Its leadership was by far the most consolidated in Eastern Europe. Securely allied to Moscow within the mainstream international Communist movement, Yugoslav Communists had what they thought was a sure thing in the Soviet model of socialist development. There was even talk of becoming a Soviet republic.

That was not to be. The break with the Soviet Union in 1948 forced Tito's supporters to detour from the Soviet road to socialism. Yugoslav theorists turned to the young Marx, looked to the experience of the Paris Commune of 1871, and studied Fabian socialism with G.D.H. Cole. They came up with the idea of a participatory, self-managing socialism which was formally accepted at the Sixth Congress of the Communist Party of Yugoslavia in 1952; thereby providing Yugoslav and Western academics alike with a virtual cottage industry focused on the Yugoslav alternative of socialist self-management, nonaligned between East and West.

The heart of this idea involved a fourfold reordering of relationships between Party, state, and society: democratization, decentralization, de-bureaucratization, and de-etatization (i.e., taking the state out of the business of managing enterprises and public services). In principle this was designed to prevent a concentration of power and ensure equal access to the political process. Internally, it legitimized socialist pluralism in what Kardelj came to call the "pluralism of self-managing interests."[14]

In practice the move to self-managing socialism, symbolized by the Party's changing its name to the League of Communists of Yugoslavia (LCY), substantially restructured the Party's "leading role." Emphasis shifted to the Party's ideological and educational mission. Now Party members were supposed to persuade both local government bodies and self-managing organizations in the economy of the merits of Party policies. Commands were out of order. Thus, the LCY gave up its monopoly over political life, while retaining its monopoly on party organization.[15] This redefined the function and tactics of the Party, reorganized its relationship to society, and substantially weakened Party coherence by introducing ambiguity into the rules of the political game.

With respect to national and territorial bureaucratic politics, the results were certainly not what the architects of this brave new world had in mind. From the beginning, the Yugoslav Communist Party saw south Slav nationalism as the number-one enemy of Party unity.[16] Yugoslav communism required restraining Serbian nationalism and replacing the Serbian historic vision of greater Serbia with a south Slav federation in which the smaller nations and nationalities had some incentive to buy in instead of opting out. Initially, it was assumed that wartime partisan solidarity, reinforced by a formal commitment to multinational federalism, would buy time while the socialist revolution redirected nationalist passions into class identity.[17] The policy implications of Yugoslav history and the bloody national and communal saga during World War II were submerged in postwar revolutionary euphoria.

The break with Moscow added new, complex dimensions to the Yugoslav national question. The Yugoslav Communist Party's insistence on its own national road to socialism within the international Communist movement had unintended consequences for center-republic relations at home. The political outcome of a League of Communists of Yugoslavia was to strengthen regional Party organizations vis-à-vis the federal Party. Self-management was equated with decentralization, which in turn became an expansion of the autonomy of the republics and provinces. Since the republics and provinces were largely synonymous with national identities, this reopened the Pandora's box of ethnic politics.

Some scholars argue that Yugoslav political leaders set out to achieve socialist pluralism via social fragmentation; to institutionalize local, communal interests in an elaborate system of checks and balances so as to contain national and ethnic conflicts.[18] If so, the founders of Yugoslav self-management could be seen as forerunners and practitioners of Arend Lijphart's consociational democracy.[19]

However, whatever the intent, by the 1960s the ideological propositions of nonalignment combined with the campaign for market socialism to divide republic and provincial Party organizations along territorial, bureaucratic lines, thereby creating regional political actors motivated by acceptable, in-system economic nationalism. Meanwhile, foreign policy goals led to support for Macedonian nationalism as an instrument in Yugoslav-Bulgarian relations;[20] and to acceptance of the Bosnian Muslim campaign for national status as a component of Yugoslav influence building among Muslim countries in the Middle East and North Africa.[21] In short, domestic and foreign policy imperatives alike obscured the differences between good and bad nationalism in the Yugoslav context. There followed cycles of centralization-decentralization. But notwithstanding the attempt to reconstruct the center in the wake of the rise of the Croatian mass national movement in 1970–71, the balance of power between the republics and the federal Party steadily shifted in the direction of the regional parties.

For our purposes there were four consequences of Yugoslav non-aligned self-management which become factors in understanding the collapse into civil war: (1) a permanent identity crisis of the LCY which restricted Party adaptability, undermined coherence, and essentially substituted Tito's charismatic authority for political institutionalization; (2) a security situation in which external threat functioned to repress differences rather than to resolve them; (3) the resulting elevation of the Yugoslav National Army (JNA) to a privileged economic and political position within Yugoslav society; and (4) the de facto association of territorial and bureaucratic politics with national and communal political agendas.

Dilemmas of the Titoist Solution

Meanwhile, Tito's efforts to stage-manage his own succession via the Constitution of 1974 became part of the problem. What was known as the

Titoist solution created a complex, cumbersome political machine.[22] This was an elaborate Party-state collective leadership based on the diffusion of power by means of four key elements: (1) the federalization of the Party into nine parts (the regional parties plus the Party organization in the Yugoslav armed forces); (2) the use of interrepublic and/or provincial consensus as the standard decision-making procedure; (3) the use of territorial/ethnic quotas for political jobs at all levels; and (4) the use of rotation schedules that incorporated the principle of de-professionalization of politics in theory, and prevented any vestige of cadre job security in practice.

Officially, the federal government retained responsibility for foreign policy, defense, and a "united market." The result was what critics attacked as the "parcelization of power."[23] This strengthened regional politicians, and expanded the number of unofficial political actors in the interrepublic and center-regional political tug-of-war. Thus the federal Party was rapidly reduced to mediating between powerful republic and/or provincial competitors for declining resources.[24]

To govern, all politicians crave and need legitimacy. In this regard, Tito's successors suffered under numerous handicaps. As godfather of Yugoslavia, Tito was a hard act to follow. The political merry-go-round of collective leadership prevented his successors from achieving name recognition. Worse still, Tito's own reluctance to make the hard choices when it came to the economy had left his successors with a $20-billion hard-currency debt, subject to continual International Monetary Fund (IMF) demands that the Yugoslav population live within a tight budget that required steadily declining standards of living. Clearly, legitimacy via economic performance was not in the cards. In these circumstance, appeals to the nation became the only truly political game in town. Faced with a persistent shortage of bread, republic and provincial politicians turned to national, ethnic, and communal circuses.

The Serbian president Slobodan Milošević rode to power on his pledge to protect Kosovar Serbs and reintegrate Kosovo into Serbia proper. His populist street politics threatened the Slovenes, who identified with the Albanian majority population in Kosovo. There was nationalist backlash in Croatia. By the autumn of 1988, a pervasive sense of systemic crisis had become the central reality uniting politicians, workers, and housewives. There was general agreement that the economy, the political system, and the League of Communists itself were in crisis.

"New Thinking" in Moscow: The Gorbachev Factor

These crises were intensified by Mikhail Gorbachev's "new political thinking" for his country and the world.[25] When Gorbachev took over as head of the Communist Party of the Soviet Union in March 1985, he set out to overhaul the staggering Soviet command economy: to make socialism competitive in the twenty-first century. Along the way, Eastern Europe became a liability to the foreign policy imperatives of perestroika. Gorbachev renounced the Brezhnev Doctrine,[26] thereby removing the Soviet military threat to democratizing countries in the bloc and setting off a hurricane of political change throughout Communist Eastern Europe. In Poland, the Solidarity prime minister Tadeusz Mazowiecki took over as head of the first non-Communist coalition government since 1945. The Berlin Wall came down, and once-hegemonic Communist parties were reduced to minor or drastically recast roles in the political drama of democratic transition.

After Communism

With the violent overthrow of Ceaușescu's dictatorial "socialism in one family," the LCY saw the handwriting on the wall. The Party gave up its formal monopoly on power at its January 1990 Fourteenth Extraordinary Congress but was unable to make the functional transition to the role of a united player in the new political environment of multiparty politics.

Multiparty Politics from Below

Essentially, the LCY congress deadlocked over conflicting visions: the vision of Yugoslavia as a community of equal nations (the EC model), and the vision of Yugoslavia as an integrated federal system in which Serbian numbers would add up to political advantage (a "greater Serbia" model). When Milošević supporters blocked Slovene proposals for reforming the LCY itself, Slovene delegates walked out. The Serbian delegation wanted to continue the congress but could not get enough votes to do so. Therefore, the delegates went home with the understanding that the congress would be reconvened. However, as there was no agreement as to how to break the political gridlock, the congress could not reconvene, and the LCY went into terminal decline.

Throughout 1990, multiparty elections within the republics produced a new array of political actors whose interests and constituents openly clashed over political and economic reform agendas. Center-right parties came to power in Croatia and Slovenia, as did nationalist coalitions in Bosnia and Herzegovina, and in Macedonia. Milošević kept his job as president of Serbia. His restyled Socialist Party of Serbia retained control of the Serbian parliament, and predictably allied itself with the winning Communist Party of Montenegro, headed by Momir Bulatović. The most serious loser was Prime Minister Ante Marković. Despite the prime minister's favorable rating in the polls,[27] his government party, the Alliance of Reform Forces, was unable to establish a major foothold in any of the six republics.

Throughout 1989, intra-republic clashes had had an almost operatic quality, and were part of a choreography of political struggle. However, the dynamics of that struggle changed with the electoral victory of Franjo Tudjman's Croatian Democratic Union in the spring of 1990. As nationalist euphoria swept through Croatia, the new president responded to pressure from his Croatian constituents to make Croatia the republic of Croatians. The flag of the interwar Kingdom of Croatia — under which Hitler's puppet Croatian fascist government had massacred Serbs living in Croatia — was everywhere, even on packets of sugar in Zagreb cafes. The rewritten republic constitution dropped its reference to the political rights of the six hundred thousand members of the Serbian minority.

The "revitalized belief system" built on the myth of partisan solidarity which had served as the cornerstone of ethnic harmony in Communist Yugoslavia could not survive in the face of Croatian fears of Serbian hegemonic ambitions, and the searing memories of what had happened to the Serbian minority in the last independent Croatia.[28] Amid talk of Croatian "sovereignty" — well short of independence — Serbs in Knin, the heart of the Krajina region, declared that they were not about to live in an independent Croatia outside of Yugoslavia. If Croats insisted on an independent state, they would join Serbia. Tensions rose when the Serbian militants chose to demonstrate this self-proclaimed sovereignty by harassing tourists and blockading the main road from Zagreb to the Adriatic coast, thereby cutting the artery of Croatian tourism. When Tudjman responded to these tactics as a problem of law and order and established an ethnically pure Croatian paramilitary police, Krajina Serbs called on Serbia and the federal army for protection.

During this prelude to civil war, the Croatian elimination of the Serbian minority's political rights in the new Croatian constitution threatened the political and economic status of Serbs in Croatia. Local Serbian militants flouted the political authority of the Croatian government, threatening the economic security of Croatia and Yugoslavia alike. This became an internal security problem for the Zagreb government. Members of the Serbian minority, in turn, saw Croatian paramilitary force as a threat to their physical security. In Serbia, the safety of Serbs living in Croatia was seen by extension as a security concern of Serbia proper. The scandal surrounding the Croatian defense minister's alleged purchase of Hungarian arms and the army's abortive efforts to arrest him underlined the external security dimension of rising Croatian nationalism. Serbs saw this as a threat to the survival of the Yugoslav state.

Milošević caused an escalation of tensions by declaring the right of all Serbs to live within Serbia. He warned that if Croatia became independent he would open the question of borders, and this was perceived in Zagreb as a Serbian land-grab. This suspicion was reinforced by Milošević's attempt to strengthen his hand vis-à-vis Croatia and to deal with his Serbian internal opposition by giving the army emergency powers. When the Serbian resolution delegating those powers was voted down by one vote, Borisav Jović, Serbia's representative on the Yugoslav collective presidency, resigned. Milošević refused to recognize the authority of the presidency;[29] thereby proving that he himself was as unwilling to accept federal authority as were those he accused of attempting to destroy Yugoslavia.

Because the "sovereign" republics of Slovenia and Croatia suddenly reversed themselves to come to the defense of the federation, it seems reasonable to assume that all parties were still engaged in a struggle over determining the parameters of a shared future within some kind of Yugoslavia. However, this brief window of opportunity disappeared with the successful Serbian and Montenegrin maneuver to prevent the Croatian representative Stjepan Mešić from taking over as president of the Yugoslav presidency in mid-May 1991, as mandated by the normal rotation schedule. Although Mešić would have been the first non-Communist president of Yugoslavia, in my view he was not rejected primarily on ideological grounds, notwithstanding the charges of Bolshevism, and Milošević's own socialist rhetoric.

On the contrary, as Milošević and Tudjman alike assumed the roles of national and ethnic gladiators, any meaningful differences between left and right disappeared. In short, although the differences between Franjo

Tudjman's Croatian Democratic Union and Slobodan Milošević's Socialist Party of Serbia are sometimes cast in terms of the struggle between
democratic and Communist agendas, both of these leaders are first and
foremost nationalists who, for national goals, are willing to sacrifice economic infrastructure, impoverish their people, and force draft-age young
men to kill, hide, or live in exile.[30]

Tudjman struggled to consolidate his power. Milošević needed to
hold on to his. Rising criticism of the Serbian president's authoritarian
style, as well as visible economic mismanagement and Serbia's growing
isolation at home and abroad increasingly tarnished his image as the "sav-
ior" of Serbia.[31]

The Internationalization of the Yugoslav Crisis

In this struggle for power and political survival, EC promises to make a
$1.1-billion loan to underwrite Yugoslav unity, as well as to open negotia-
tions on associate membership for that united Yugoslavia within the EC
itself, were tempting; but they were not tempting enough to change the
dynamic of confrontation. Equally, President Bush's assurance to Prime
Minister Ante Marković that the United States would not "encourage or
reward those striving to disrupt the country" had little impact.[32] While
there is no evidence to confirm the popular rumor that U.S. Secretary of
State James A. Baker III, during his June 1991 visit to Yugoslavia, encouraged Marković to use military means to hold the country together,[33]
Washington's efforts to calm the emerging crisis appear to have been
largely ineffectual.

In the events following the Slovene and Croatian declarations of
"independence" at the end of June, the Slovene decision to renege on an
agreement to allow joint customs presence on Slovenia's borders during
ongoing negotiations with the federal government played a much more
catalytic role than is generally realized.[34] When the Ljubljana government
attempted to achieve a *fait accompli* by forcing out federal customs agents
and unilaterally moving Slovenia's border with the rest of Yugoslavia to
the former dividing line with Croatia, the Yugoslav Army went in to reestablish a federal customs presence. Meanwhile, the Slovene defense minister escalated by proclaiming that the army had "declared war" against
Slovenia.[35]

Once the shooting started, control over the Slovene political spectrum was no longer in the hands of policy makers who saw the declaration

of independence as part of the ongoing jockeying for position in the struggle for a confederal Yugoslavia; control was now in the hands of those who equated independence with separation. For the army and the federal government, what had begun as a show of force to demonstrate federal authority became a fateful misstep on the road to civil war.[36]

Although the European Community was able to broker a cease-fire monitored by EC observers in Slovenia, the damage to the fabric of civil-military relations and the corporate identity of the JNA was done. As one colleague told me in early July, as we watched a defensive JNA press conference on Belgrade television, "This is our most dangerous time. The army is unpredictable; a wounded animal."

In the wake of the Slovene fiasco, moderates in the JNA lost ground. Local Serbian authorities in the self-proclaimed autonomous region of Krajina went on the initiative to declare that they were uniting with Bosanka Krajina in Bosnia and Herzegovina to form "a greater Serbian community." Violence escalated rapidly. Hardliners within the armed forces more and more openly supported Serbian irregulars who were battling Croatian militia, occupying territory well beyond the lands where Serbs were in the majority. Political dialogue among republic leaders collapsed into polarized confrontation. Meanwhile, the Serbian agenda openly shifted to the creation of a rump Yugoslavia minus Slovenia and Croatia.[37] By September Macedonia held its own independence referendum, confirming that Macedonians did not want any part of this reduced "greater Serbia."

The German Solution Backfires

German threats to recognize Croatia if the federal army did not exercise restraint were seen in Serbia as confirmation of the "Fourth Reich" theory,[38] in which Tudjman, like the leader of the wartime Kingdom of Croatia before him, was considered a German pawn. One does not have to agree with all of these accusations of German-Austrian expansionism to accept the reality of the consequences of Bonn's strategy. What in fairness Chancellor Helmut Kohl of Germany may have seen as a policy of deterrence only shifted the violence into high gear.[39]

A divided Croatian leadership blockaded JNA garrisons in Croatia, and then attacked them in a desperate attempt to provoke Germany into following through on what Zagreb saw as promises of recognition if Serbian insurgents and their JNA supporters continued bombarding Cro-

atian cities.[40] Once the UN arms embargo was declared, cease-fires bro-
kered by the European Community and the United Nations became a
revolving door to more determined fighting. Serbs kept pushing to occupy more territory before the fighting stopped. Croats openly violated
the cease-fire agreements in search of weapons. According to one Croatian official, who acknowledged that their forces had captured sixty army
garrisons and begun fighting in several others, including one at Varaždin,
north of Zagreb, "We had some work to finish up."[41]

In this manner, the Croatian government deliberately increased the
punishment inflicted on Croatian cities and civilians in the name of independence. For the sake of gaining territory, the Serbian leadership accepted steadily increased risk to the lives and fortunes of the Serbian
minority in the proliferating, self-proclaimed autonomous regions and
throughout Croatia.[42]

Creeping Coup: The JNA

Still more predictably, the role of the army in the civil war was no longer
that of an instrument of Yugoslav or even Serbian political goals. With
twenty-five thousand soldiers and their families hostage, the conflict became a war of the army against Croatia. Army leaders warned that it would
be an eye for an eye: one structure of vital importance for Croatia would
be destroyed for each army installation destroyed.[43] As this battle raged,
the federal government faded away. Prime Minister Marković was no
longer reported as a party to the perpetual cease-fire agreements. His
demand for the resignation of Defense Minister Kadijević and other high-
ranking military leaders fell on deaf ears.

In October, the collective state presidency fell victim to a de facto
coup d'état conducted by Serbia and supported by the Montenegrin vice-
president Branko Kostić, and representatives from the once-autonomous
provinces Vojvodina and Kosovo. Kostić announced that he and his supporters in the presidency were assuming the powers of parliament.[44] In an
effort to avoid being sucked into the whirlpool of civil war, the parliament
in Bosnia and Herzegovina predictably declared its independence from
any such rump Yugoslavia.[45]

Notwithstanding the virtual lack of international reaction — which
was perhaps a result of the somewhat "Alice-in-Wonderland" manner in
which all four of the objecting republics insisted that they were members
in good standing of the Yugoslav state presidency, and also independent —

academically speaking, this was an attempted civilian coup. The nature and extent of military support was unclear. Indeed what was under way might best be described as a "creeping coup";[46] a tacit alliance between Milošević and the eroding federal army which definitively cut the former federal government out of the loop. In December, Marković resigned in protest of a federal budget that gave 80 percent of available resources to keep the now essentially Serbian army fighting.

War Clouds over Bosnia and Herzegovina

In Croatia, a UN special envoy, the former American secretary of state Cyrus Vance, negotiated a shaky fifteenth cease-fire. Some fourteen thousand UN peacekeepers went in to try to ensure that the cease-fire stayed firm enough to allow the UN "inkblot" deployment that Vance recommended to pacify the most violent areas.

However, the European Community's divided agendas and UN foot-dragging directly contributed to pushing Bosnia and Herzegovina off the tightrope of negotiated solutions into civil war. Vance and President Alija Izetbegović alike warned the EC that this ethnically entangled republic — according to the April 1991 census, 43.7 percent Muslim, 31.3 percent Serb, and 17.3 percent Croat[47] — would pay the price of giving in to pressure from Bonn for recognition of Croatia and Slovenia by the arbitrary 15 January deadline. To no avail the Bosnian president appealed to the United Nations for assistance to prevent rising violence in response to the republic's declaration of sovereignty, and the subsequent demand for constitutional independence by the parliament of Bosnian Serbs.[48]

The EC's 27 May rationale for stepped-up economic sanctions against Serbia rested on an assessment that Serbia was particularly responsible for the violence in Bosnia and Herzegovina because it controlled the JNA and Serbian irregular forces. Whether or not the nature of that control can be disputed, Belgrade has undeniably been the supplier and patron of such Serbian forces. Yet it is also hard not to agree with those who argue that by recognizing Bosnia and Herzegovina as a sovereign and independent state "before the three national parties, which had won the parliamentary elections, managed to reach a mutual agreement on the internal political structure, the EC has virtually given the go ahead signal for the outbreak of the war."[49]

Repercussions of the EC's demand that any former Yugoslav republic seeking recognition must request it by 23 December 1991 continue to un-

fold:[50] rising body counts, untold wounded, and the millions of refugees
created by policies of ethnic cleansing.[51] German exhortations that Croatia must not jeopardize the peace process, attempts by the Yugoslav
prime minister Milan Panić and the Bosnian Serb leader Radovan Karadzić to disassociate themselves from military excesses by Serbian irregulars or the army of Bosnian Serbs, and the inspection or opening of "detention camps" are Band-Aids on the mutilated body of a once-peaceful
multiethnic society.

Legacies of Communist Rule

Having established this context, it becomes possible to draw some tenta-
tive conclusions about the relationship of the bloody collapse of the Yugoslav alternative to the legacies of communism. But first it is essential to be
more precise about what we mean by communism.

Communism is a transnational political movement that first emerged
in an organizational form when Karl Marx was commissioned to write the
founding document for the League of Communists in 1847. This document was a dual-strategy attempt to change the balance of power between
workers and owners on a country-specific level, and to thereby challenge
the dominance of capitalism as the engine of the international political
economy. With the consolidation of Bolshevik power in the Russian revolution of 1917, that transnational movement became an instrument of
Soviet foreign policy. Thereby, on a country-specific level, communism
became the ideological foundation of a competing model of one-party
hegemonic rule and command economy.

On the level of the international system, a Communist subsystem of
ruling and nonruling parties became a strategic threat to the political and
economic dominance of non-Communist countries. Within this subsystem, ruling Communist parties were divided primarily on the basis of
whether they followed the Soviet or the Chinese model, with the Yugoslav
self-managing alternative having its primary influence on nonruling parties that came to be known as Eurocommunists, which in fact frequently
did not acknowledge this influence for domestic or interparty reasons.

So what do we mean by the legacy of communism in nonaligned,
socialist Yugoslavia? Ideologically, we mean the belief in participatory
socialism as the integrating glue for a multinational society still burdened
with bad memories of former associations between its component parts.
Economically, we mean the belief in a socialist market economy as some-

thing more than a contradiction in terms. Politically, we mean an official commitment to the League of Communists of Yugoslavia, which was considered to be the best navigator around for a leaky ship of state. Seen in this light, what legacies of communism were related to the collapse into civil war in 1991?

Conclusions Regarding Root Causes

First among the root causes of the collapse of the Yugoslav alternative were clashing conceptions of the nature of the state (the EC model versus the greater Serbia model). This factor predated Communist Yugoslavia.

Second was stunted institutional development and the subsequent withering away of the federal center. Tito had hoped that a united LCY would provide coherence for a post-Tito system that had a great deal more in common with Western theories of consociational democracy than with Marxism-Leninism.[52]

However, Tito was the godfather of Communist Yugoslavia. His cult of charismatic authority can be seen, in part, as a consequence of the failure of the utopian aspects of socialist self-management to replace historic national identities with a class identity. Still more important, the post-Tito solution to the containment of nationalism turned the ethnic key into the key to power. There were no political posts reserved for "Yugoslavs" on the carousel of collective leadership.

The third root cause was the unintended consequences of hard-currency debt. Given the problems that developing and Communist countries alike have in dealing with IMF prescriptions for economic health, I do not think we can say that the cycle of export-driven dependency is a legacy of communism. In principle, all of the Yugoslav republics were committed to the market. In fact, the war of economic and political reform in 1988–90 essentially replayed the 1965 struggle over market socialism with much the same political lineup. Now, however, ideological objections were no longer openly acceptable, and the constitution of 1974 had removed an important range of political cleavages, thereby hardening the position of less-developed regions that were expected to pay the bill for change.

There remains the underresearched area of bureaucratic infrastructure. Where in these bureaucratic channels were economic reforms aborted? What of Communist bureaucrats who remained on the job? Here, I believe it is safe to assume that those who benefited most from

the command economy were not necessarily enthusiastic about dismantling it.[53]

Conclusions Regarding Short-Term Precipitants

First, there does appear to be a direct connection between precipitants of
Yugoslavia's disintegration and sectarian politics. The political socialization and professional experience of former Communist cadres were poor
qualifications for the job of making the transformation to multiparty politics. Of the key players on the road to civil war, only the leader of the
Bosnian Muslims, Alija Izetbegović, had never been a member of the
LCY.

Notwithstanding the break with Moscow, Yugoslav Communists
were a part of a political subculture that believed that there was a "right"
course at any given time. The strength of Leninist organizational theory
was intraparty coherence in the name of democratic centralism. I believe
that the periodic paralysis of the LCY was to a substantial degree a result of failure to reconcile these norms with Kardelj's "pluralism of self-
managing interests." For Milošević — or, for that matter, Tudjman — to
accept the inevitability of opposition parties did not necessarily mean that
he was willing or able to play by the democratic rules of the game, or
tolerant of political pluralism, or skillful at compromise and negotiated
settlement.

We can also say that part of the problem was the failure of socialist
self-management and the campaign for market socialism to reverse the de
facto social contract that — in a manner typical of Communist populations
throughout Eastern Europe — guaranteed political support in return for
economic security. In this relationship between the regime and society,
the Marxist myth of a future utopian society had considerably less drawing
power than did a job virtually impossible to lose, subsidized food, an
apartment, medicine, and education.

Tito's golden age of ethnic harmony had steadily increased economic
expectations and had politicized workers, students, and housewives. Yet
even here a more definitive judgment must wait until our colleagues in
social psychology begin serious cross-system comparisons. For example,
how greatly does the underlying attitude described here differ from that
of those who expect American presidents to control the deficit with "no
new taxes"?

A second short-term cause of Yugoslavia's collapse was the criminal irresponsibility of republic-level political leadership: power lust is a political pathology that goes deeper than the ideological or political-economic-organizational aspects of Communist political systems. If anything, this factor, like the criminal-terrorist activity of Serbian irregulars such as Vojislav Seselj's Chetniks, and of the Croatian neofascist successors of the World War II Ustashi, is a legacy of the dark side of nationalism, not communism.

A third short-term cause was the role of the JNA. Yugoslav armed forces were never typical of the Communist penetration model of civilian control.[54] And notwithstanding the fact that the military leadership in many ways provided the backbone of the staggering LCY during the post-Tito period of attacks on the federal Party, there is considerable evidence that the military establishment was in the process of adjusting to the shift to a multiparty political environment.[55] Along the way, military spokesmen showed by far more flexibility than did Milošević.

If one goes back to the nature of the clashes between the Slovenes and the army which factored into the Slovene humiliation of the armed forces during the failure of the military's show of force following Ljubljana's declaration of independence, there may be a connection to the Communist self-image of the military leaders involved. Still, legacies of communism appear to have less explanatory value than does the literature on civil-military relations for understanding the JNA response to hemorrhaging civilian legitimacy, increasingly fragmented boundaries between the Yugoslav armed forces and an anarchic society that functioned as a counterpart of John Herz's "security dilemma,"[56] and the army's corporate visceral reaction to the Croatian strategy of blockading and attacking army garrisons.

Once the guarantor of Yugoslav brotherhood and unity, the JNA became the engine of mass destruction. There can be no doubt that the JNA was a corporate entity in a race for its own survival.[57] With the collapse of Yugoslavia, that survival depended on what appears to have been a tension-ridden Serbian civil-military coalition. Reportedly, Milošević charged the army with not doing its job, and the army attacked him for abandoning Yugoslavia.[58] Given the 1 June 1993 dismissal of the federal president Dobrica Ćosić on charges of playing politics with supporters in the army, and the subsequent firing of the chief of staff, Života Panić, this appears to be at best a stressful partnership with minimal ideological content.

A fourth short-term cause was the revival of ethnonationalism in post-Tito Yugoslavia. Politically, opening the Pandora's box of national and ethnic grievances had much more to do with the consociational aspects of the Constitution of 1974 than with the legacy of socialist self-management. However, one can say that to the extent that the state sector of the economy failed to meet the demands of IMF austerity prescriptions for economic health, this was also a legacy of communism.

A fifth short-term cause was the internationalization of the Yugoslav crisis: As the EC debated whether to give Greece a copyright on the name "Macedonia," and the Bush administration quibbled about the cost of UN peacekeepers, the war clouds broke over Bosnia and Herzegovina. One-third of Croatian territory is occupied. Vukovar has been flattened and Dubrovnik scarred by the fighting in Croatia. The four-century-old Mostar bridge has destroyed by Croatian mortars. Sarajevo, city of sorrows, still suffers from Serb shelling and from Serb and Muslim snipers. The Serbian economy is exhausted.[59] Serbia has become an outcast from Europe — the unrecognized third Yugoslavia, suspended from the United Nations and facing the prospect of a war-crimes investigation.

Germany played a documented role in spreading the war to Bosnia and Herzegovina and appears to have successfully lobbied against applying EC or UN sanctions to Croatia for atrocities in Central Bosnia. And lest Americans be too self-righteous, it should not be forgotten that the Bush administration played a direct role in aborting the February 1992 Lisbon agreement for an ethnic division of Bosnia and Herzegovina which would have given Bosnian Muslims 44 percent of the territory, and control over all but 18 percent of the Muslim population.[60] As for the Clinton foreign policy team, the former American ambassador Warren Zimmerman was the fifth professional foreign service officer to resign from the State Department in protest at American policy toward Bosnia.[61]

The Balance Sheet

With respect to long-term causes, my research leans toward the conclusion that the collapse of Communist Yugoslavia into civil war was not a legacy of Yugoslav-style communism. The issue is much more ambiguous with regard to short-term precipitants. Here, certainly, the political socialization of what might be considered a Communist mind-set regarding conflict resolution played its role, as did the ability of those who would pay the bill for economic reform to abort the long-term stabilization program. Nonetheless, on balance, this analysis concludes that the failure of market socialism in the 1960s and 1970s, the legacy of Tito's personality cult, and the flawed political machinery put in place by his attempt to stage-manage his own succession had substantially more to do with the collapse into civil war than did any legacy of the Yugoslav alternative of nonaligned socialist self-management.

Whereas it is fair to say that the Serbian parliament's decision to print money to keep state enterprises afloat, which contributed to the Slovene and Croatian decision that sovereignty required separatism, had something to do with the legacy of attitudes stemming from four decades of a predominantly command economy, the effort to portray the conflict between Croatia and Serbia as a morality play of democracy versus communism distorts reality. Serbian president Milošević's statement that he would accept Croatian independence only if the borders were changed to allow Serbs living in the Krajina region to join Serbia was made because Milošević *is* a nationalist, not because he *was* a Communist. Croatia's willingness to carve up Bosnia and Herzegovina, Zagreb's scorched-earth policy in the Medak region, and the destruction of the homes of Serbs living in Croatia and of Croats who have opposed government policies undermine Tudjman's democratic credentials.[62] This is not a war over ideology, class, or economic organization. It is a war for territory, fueled by ethnonationalist ambitions and fears, which is not to say that those ambitions and fears inevitably added up to war.

The failure of the European Community to put the containment of the Yugoslav crisis above the appearance of unity within the EC itself is a product of the complex political dynamic flowing from the unification of Germany, the community's attempt to stay the course of European integration scheduled for 1992, and the inability of existing European — indeed, international — institutions to cope with the "new world disorder" that has emerged in the wake of the collapse of the Soviet empire and the end of the cold war international system.[63] The counterproductive policy of the Bush and Clinton administrations reflected a mix of election pressures and domestic imperatives. Policy makers in New York, Brussels, and Washington cannot sidestep responsibility for widening the Yugoslav wars of succession or for the rising level of violence. It would be more accurate to say that the legacy of communism contributed to the civil war in Croatia, German arrogance unleashed the dogs of war in Bosnia, and European-American cold war economic and security strategies have made it impossible to recapture them.

My analysis disagrees with Lord Owen's view that the "lying factor" is somehow unique to Communist societies. Rather, there is the as-yet-unexplored question as to what extent four decades of confronting the Communist ideological and strategic threat created a shared "the-ends-justify-the-means" mentality in the West and East alike. In high school I asked my teacher how real people could lose real jobs because "we lost China," when China had never been ours. He told me not to ask "dangerous" questions.

The Communist enemy became a significant other justifying the unthinkable; creating the witch-hunt mentality of the former House Committee on Un-American Activities. How else can we explain purges of the State Department, the blacklisting of Hollywood actors, censorship, invasions of privacy, and unexcusable experiments exposing retarded children and others to nuclear radiation without their knowledge — all in the name of national security?

In my view, it is the specter of World War I, not the legacy of communism, that is haunting the New Europe. Meanwhile, the need to create an enemy in the name of unity haunts Europeans and Americans alike.

Patterns, Lessons, and Implications: In Lieu of a Conclusion

Zoltan Barany

The purpose of this book is to offer the reader a comprehensive analysis of the conditions that prevailed in Eastern Europe at the end of four decades of communism, undoubtedly the most ambitious sociopolitical and economic experiment of our century. On the most fundamental level, communism's aim is to radically alter the world. Seen in this light, the operation was successful but the patient's condition deteriorated, for in the period 1945–90 Eastern Europe's polities, societies, and economies experienced more drastic and rapid changes than ever before, though it would be difficult to dispute that the overall impact — the political and socioeconomic "bottom line" — of communism was overwhelmingly negative.

The twentieth century has been a particularly eventful one for this region, with the collapse of the empires after World War I, the tumultuous interwar period, the tragedy of Nazism and World War II, the decades of communism, and finally, the current era of democratization, which has been concomitant with a new age of nationalism in several areas. Thus, although it was undeniably communism that had shaped the post–World War II fate of this region, the contributors to this book tried to stress that a variety of problems originated in the pre-Communist eras. In the aftermath of the 1989 revolutions, it has been customary to focus on the negative consequences of Communist rule and neglect the legacies of the Communist systems that did accelerate progress in a number of areas. Therefore, the contributors made an effort to point out the positive aspects of the socialist heritage as well.

Many people in the West are still oblivious to the immense diversities within this region and consider the East European states fairly similar to each other. In fact, Albania and Poland are no more alike than Portugal and Sweden are. The people of this region possess widely different cultures, traditions, histories, levels of economic development, and patterns of social relations. In the interwar period, for instance, Czechoslovakia was a modern, democratic, and economically advanced European state that was seemingly centuries ahead of Bulgaria in most indicators of socioeconomic development. When studying the heritage of the Communist period, it is also important to remember where the individual countries of the region started from at the time of the Communist takeovers. Obviously, a relatively well developed state such as Czechoslovakia had far more to lose than did its less advanced neighbors.

To be sure, in good measure communism did act as an "equalizer" for this region, owing to the fact that it initially imposed nearly identical (i.e., Stalinist) political, economic, and sociocultural systems on the region. The Soviet-Yugoslav break in 1948, the demise of the Stalinist variety of totalitarian system, and the cautious emergence of "national" communism in the 1950s suggested at first subtle but increasingly unmistakable diversity in the region. With the passing of time, the East European states' domestic politics, economic practices, and social affairs had become more and more dissimilar even in the Communist era. These variations, in turn, had signified far-reaching consequences for the post-Communist age. For example, owing to its longstanding experimentation with economic reforms and its established Western contacts, Hungary was far better prepared for the post-Communist age than was Albania, a country whose leaders maintained their Stalinist policies with remarkable obstinacy and virtually isolated it from the outside world for decades.

Ultimately, however, none of the East European countries was well equipped to face a democratic and market-capitalist era, for communism not only retarded the few positive political and socioeconomic trends that emerged in the interwar period but in many ways confirmed and reinforced traditional backwardness everywhere.[1] The Communist parties enjoyed a virtual political monopoly throughout the region and managed to render other political and social organizations either inconsequential (as were the "fellow traveler" parties, where they existed) or totally dependent on its patronage (as were umbrella organizations such as "popular fronts"). Political participation, particularly voting, was strictly a pro forma affair, the only important reason for holding elections at all being the ruling elites' attempt to gain "legitimacy" from those they ruled and oppressed.

Another Communist heritage is the disproportionately large state bureaucracies whose reduction is made difficult by the dearth of qualified decision makers unaffiliated with the former regimes. Replacing the

Communist nomenklatura has proved to be an arduous task in the region, for the new political elites are numerically weak and ill-equipped to govern. Partly as a result of the absence of genuine opposition parties during the Communist period, the development of ideologically and programmatically distinctive political parties has been slow and uneven in the region.

For the most part, the Communist systems managed to destroy the feeble civil societies originating from the interwar period and were quite successful in suppressing real and imagined opposition of any sort. Poland's Solidarity movement, in my view, is the glorious exception to the rule of generally weak, poorly organized, fragmented, and ineffectual dissident groups (certainly not "movements") in the region.[2] Dissidence was the bailiwick of marginalized intellectuals who were unable to reach even their peers, let alone other social strata, with their messages. Most dissidents, as Jane Curry notes, habitually limited themselves to describing the adversities of the Communist system (adversities with which most of their fellow citizens were already intimately familiar) without setting their sights on the future or pointing out potential remedies and solutions.

Although the Communist political institutions have been discarded with remarkable ease in the majority of East European states, the legacy that appears to be the most difficult to overcome is attitudinal rather than institutional or structural. A regionwide political legacy of communism is the population's general political apathy and withdrawal, its low level of political sophistication, and its backward political culture. Communism had promoted some values, such as egalitarianism and security (in employment, social welfare, and the like), that were to a large extent internalized by the population and now make the transition process all the more difficult to bear. However, other attitudes that impede the development of a politically active citizenry — such as cynicism about public affairs, skepticism regarding the individual's political efficacy, alienation from the political system, and distrust of public institutions and officials — had also been formed during or reinforced by Communist rule. Furthermore, communism also appears to have enhanced the intolerance toward opposing views that was traditional among the region's contending political and social forces.

The pervasive skepticism and mistrust in politics is also reflected in other areas, for example, in mass-elite relations and in relations between dominant and minority ethnic groups. A host of other deeply held values and attitudes fostered by the everyday reality of the Communist system now frustrate the processes of transition. The post-Communist leaders, most of whom tend to be intellectuals with few ties to and little understanding of the working classes, often lack the ability to talk to "the people," thereby inadvertently giving nationalist demagogues the chance to manipulate and exploit popular sentiments.[3] Elez Biberaj, in chapter 13, calls attention to the widespread decline of national pride and, more generally, civic morale in Albania, an observation that rings true for most of the region. At the workplace, most workers did not have much incentive to work hard and efficiently, and generations had grown up with what Andrzej Korbonski, in chapter 8, aptly calls a "distorted popular attitude to work."

The forty-odd years of Communist rule had drastically transformed the generally rather backward societies of this region. The policies of heavy industrialization, urbanization, forced collectivization, and gradual mechanization of agriculture had been largely successful, in that in every East European state they created a relatively large urban working class drawn mostly from the rural population. The Communist regimes promised social mobility to the working class, but starting with the late 1960s that social mobility had increasingly remained no more than a promise. With decelerating economic growth and, in several states, growing reliance on the political and economic input of the intelligentsia, the working class had become stabilized, and its members had fewer opportunities for upward mobility. The peasantry was clearly the victim of Communist social engineering. Driven by the goals of industrial development, the Communist states were unwilling to invest in the rural sphere. The countryside had remained socioeconomically deprived, and tensions between the industrial working class and the peasantry had increased in many areas.

Although these were to be egalitarian societies, the privileges and lavish lifestyle of the political, economic, and sociocultural elites had contrasted sharply with the relatively modest living standards — and among some groups (Albanians, Gypsies, and unskilled laborers) dire poverty — of the general population. By the late 1970s, in some of the region's countries, a growing and seemingly permanent underclass had developed, with little hope for substantial improvement in sight. Still, the socioeconomic conditions of the vast majority of the population were generally quite uniform, and income disparities were lower than in the West. In the post-Communist period, in turn, the egalitarian values that many in Eastern Europe had come to share often elicit hostility toward those who have become successful.

The social problems that Communist propaganda assigned to the West nonetheless did not spare these societies. Particularly toward the end of the Communist period, more and more of these problems presented serious dilemmas in a growing number of East European states. Housing remained a problem that few of the regimes — with the notable exception of East Germany — were able to alleviate, let alone resolve. Crime, alcohol abuse (and by the 1980s, drug abuse), and a variety of health problems were also on the increase by the 1970s, although reliable statistics were seldom published. With the limited liberalization policies of some of these states in the 1980s came increased access to uncensored information (particularly from and about the West), which contributed to the growing disenchantment of youth with the hypocritical and repressive system. In addition, public services, such as education and health care, had suffered increasingly from chronic financial problems.

The inadequacies of the centrally planned economic system had become clear in most East European states by the 1950s and 1960s, but for political and ideological reasons few regimes had attempted more than the introduction of piecemeal reforms. As Ivan Volgyes suggests, the economic system imposed on the region by the Soviet Union had retarded balanced economic development, ignored market conditions, and operated on untenable economic assumptions. As a result, the region's economies had experienced decreasing rates of productivity and had become less and less competitive even when contrasted with the economies of a growing number of developing states. Institutionalized impediments to technological advancement, and myopic investment policies, ensured that the region missed out on the post-1945 technological revolution. The irrational but enduring policy of heavy industrialization had caused tremendous damage to these countries, depleting their scarce natural resources and devastating their environment. The central planners' longstanding neglect of infrastructure and physical plants puts the new economic and political elites in an unenviable situation. Furthermore, serious debt burdens dating from the Communist period had restricted the economic options of several East European countries (Hungary and Poland, in particular) in the post-Communist period.

In the international sphere, it was obviously the Soviet Union that to a large extent determined the fate of the region during the Communist era. The Soviet bloc's international organizations, in which membership was quasi-mandatory, not only limited the sovereignty of the East European states (as outlined in the Brezhnev Doctrine) but also required those states to forgo the option of economic integration with the developed West.[4] Even so, there was little real integration either in the Warsaw Pact or in the Council for Mutual Economic Assistance, and those organizations ensured the institutionalized isolation of their member states from the West. In essence, both of these organizations were grossly asymmetrical "alliances," and arguably the only country aside from the USSR which derived a "net benefit" from them was Bulgaria. Moscow's domination of the region secured East European dependence on the Soviet Union both in the economic realm (particularly with respect to Soviet energy and raw material deliveries, and the large Soviet market that was willing to absorb substandard East European goods) and in the security arena (especially with respect to air defense).

One of the most important of the few positive legacies of communism is the social welfare system, which included nominally free medical care, education, and universal pension and maternity benefits. All of these achievements had their negative sides, however. For instance, medical care was generally substandard, education on all levels was extensively utilized to indoctrinate its recipients with Marxist-Leninist ideology, and maternity benefits served the regimes' pronatalist objectives. The Communist systems also achieved near-universal literacy, a considerable benefit that indirectly increased the general population's knowledge about their environment. Moreover, newspapers, books, and other cultural goods and services, while seldom free of ideological undertones, were widely available, heavily subsidized, and frequently of high quality. Another positive legacy is the security of guaranteed (and mandatory) employment for all, an ideologically motivated goal that was realized at a tremendous economic cost. At the same time, the Communist electrification campaign that brought electricity to remote areas was an obvious benefit to all. In general, the more backward countries and regions of Eastern Europe derived the most benefits from communism's positive legacies.

One question that is fundamental, albeit often neglected, when appraising the Communist past is the question of what kind of political, social, and economic developments would have taken place in Eastern

Europe had the region somehow escaped communism, and whether the overall consequence of those developments would have been as overwhelmingly negative as those of communism. Obviously, it is impossible to *know* the answer, yet I believe it is fair to say that barring an enduring fascist dictatorship, any other system of government and any other set of economic policies would have held more benefits for the people of this region.

As the foregoing chapters conclusively show, the Communist experiment had devastating effects on Eastern Europe and left the region ill-prepared for a transition to democracy and market capitalism. As Bennett Kovrig argues in chapter 2, the weak states and impoverished societies of this region are a poor foundation for political stability and economic success. Still, overcoming the negative legacies and preserving the few positive ones has been and will be easier for some countries than for others. The pre-Communist legacies of the region also influence the individual states' post-Communist prospects. Unlike the Balkan countries, the East-Central European states enjoyed more favorable socioeconomic conditions and at least some democratic experience before the Communist takeovers; they seem to have maintained their comparative advantages throughout the Communist era. Thus, it appears that the East-Central European states, with the possible exception of Slovakia, are better positioned to clear the obstacles in their quest for prosperity and democracy than are their neighbors in the Balkans.

NOTES

Chapter 1. Ivan Volgyes, The Legacies of Communism

1. See Ivan Volgyes, "Political Socialization in Eastern Europe: A Conceptual Framework," in Ivan Volgyes, ed., *Political Socialization in Eastern Europe* (New York: Praeger, 1975).

2. See Dean S. Rugg, *Eastern Europe* (London: Longman, 1985).

3. The Hungarian economist Eva Ehrlich examined the extent of the backwardness of East European economies and created with Paul Marer an index of change. Her study is adopted and cited in Paul Marer, "The Economies and Trade of Eastern Europe," in William E. Griffith, ed., *Central and Eastern Europe: The Opening Curtain?* (Boulder, Colo.: Westview, 1989).

4. For a good study on the subject, see Bob Deacon, ed., *The New Eastern Europe: Social Policy, Past, Present, and Future* (London: Sage, 1992).

5. For the best analysis of the subject, see Walter D. Connor, *Socialism, Politics, and Equality: Hierarchy and Change in Eastern Europe and the USSR* (New York: Columbia University Press, 1979).

6. For one of the most comprehensible attempts to address the subject, see R. Barry Farrell, ed., *Political Leadership in Eastern Europe and the Soviet Union* (Chicago: Aldine, 1970).

7. David Mason, *Public Opinion and Political Change in Poland* (Cambridge: Cambridge University Press, 1985); and idem, *Revolution in East Central Europe* (Boulder, Colo.: Westview, 1992). See further the series of studies of change in public opinion by the Erasmus Foundation for Democracy, Budapest, Hungary, 1991–94.

8. László Bruszt and János Simon, "Political Culture, Political and Economic Orientations in Central and Eastern Europe during the Transition to Democracy, 1990–1991," Politikatudományi Intézeti Tanulmányok (Budapest, 1993).

9. G. Arriagarda, "Reflections on Recent Elections in Latin America and Eastern and Central Europe," in L. Garber and E. Bjorklund, eds., *The New Democratic Frontier* (Washington, D.C.: National Democratic Institute for International Affairs, 1992).

10. The fact that the turnout in local elections is lower than in national elections, in and of itself, should not be regarded as unusual; the same pattern seems to hold in established democracies as well. The fact that the turnout is so extremely low, however, does cause observers of the political scene in Eastern Europe considerable concern.

Chapter 2. Bennett Kovrig, Marginality Reinforced

1. This essay draws on a research project focusing on European institutions and democratization in Eastern Europe, sponsored by the United States Institute of Peace, Washington, D.C.

2. See Daniel Chirot, ed., *The Origins of Backwardness in Eastern Europe: Economics and Politics from the Middle Ages until the Early Twentieth Century* (Berkeley: University of California Press, 1989); and Andrew C. Janos, *The Politics of Backwardness in Hungary, 1825–1945* (Princeton: Princeton University Press, 1982).

3. E. H. Carr, *Documents on British Foreign Policy*, 1st ser., vol. 10, nos. 505, 581, quoted in Norman Davies, *White Eagle, Red Star: The Polish-Soviet War, 1919–1920* (London: MacDonald, 1972), 105.

4. See George Schöpflin's sober appraisal "The Political Traditions of Eastern Europe," *Daedalus* 119, no. 1 (1990): 55–90.

5. *Foreign Relations of the United States, 1945: The Conferences at Malta and Yalta* (Washington, D.C.: U.S. Department of State, 1955), 103.

6. Quoted in Anne Simonin and Helene Clastres, eds., *Les idées en France, 1945–1988: Une chronologie* (Paris: Gallimard, 1989), 40, 179.

7. See George Schöpflin, "Nationalism and National Minorities in East and Central Europe," *Journal of International Studies* 45, no. 1 (1991): 51–66.

8. Testimony before the Senate Foreign Relations Committee, quoted in *RFE/RL Daily Report*, 17 Oct. 1991. Cf. Gerhard Wettig, "Security in Europe: A Challenging Task," *Aussenpolitik* 43, no. 1 (1992): 4.

9. Charles Gati, "Will Democracy Take Root in East-Central Europe?" in Dick Clark, ed., *United States-Soviet and East European Relations: Building a Congressional Cadre* (Queenstown, Md.: Aspen Institute, 1991), 40.

10. *RFE/RL Daily Report*, 5 Feb. 1992.

11. *Globe and Mail* (Toronto), 5 Mar. 1992.

12. Gallup poll cited by Associated Press, 29 Jan. 1992.

13. *Times Literary Supplement*, 22 May 1992.

14. Council on Foreign Relations, *Documents on American Foreign Relations, 1956* (New York: Harper, 1957), 45.

15. *Economist*, 11 July 1992, 26; ibid., 22 Feb. 1992, 47.

16. *IMF Survey* 21, no. 14 (1992): 210–12.

17. *Economist*, 15 Feb. 1992, 60.

18. See Tibor Palankai, *The European Community and Central European Integration* (New York: Institute for East-West Security Studies, 1991), 4.

19. Gianni Bonvicini et al., *The Community and the Emerging European Democracies: A Joint Policy Report* (London: Royal Institute of International Affairs, 1991), 81–83; Dominique Moisi and Jacques Rupnik, *Le nouveau continent: Plaidoyer pour une Europe renaissante* (Paris: Calmann-Levy, 1991), 162, 174–80.

20. *Le Monde*, 7 Mar. 1992.

Chapter 3. Ivan Volgyes, The Economic Legacies of Communism

1. The summary of many of these early views may be found in Morris Bornstein, ed., *The Soviet Economy* (Boulder, Colo.: Westview, 1981).

2. See Alexander Ehrlich, *The Russian Industrialization Debate* (Cambridge: Harvard University Press, 1960), esp. 145–62.

3. For a cogent summary of the classical model see Richard E. Ericson, "The Classical Soviet-Type Economy: Nature of the System and Implications for Reform," *Journal of Economic Perspectives* 5, no. 4 (1991): 11–29.

4. See János Kornai, *Anti-Equilibrium* (Amsterdam: North Holland, 1971); and idem, *A hiány* (Scarcity) (Budapest: Közgazdasági és Jogi Könyvkiadó, 1982).

5. Though dealing with the subject of forced labor, an early study by Swiniewicz focused first on the dilemmas of labor and forced industrial development. See S. Swiniewicz, *Forced Labor and Economic Development* (London: Oxford University Press, 1963).

6. Michael Kaser, *Comecon*, 2d ed. (London: Oxford University Press, 1967), 23–30.

7. Martin J. Kohn and Nicholas R. Lang, "The Intra-CMEA Foreign Trade System," in U.S. Congress, Joint Economic Committee, *East European Economies* (Washington, D.C.: Government Printing Office, 1982), 141 ff.

8. It is debatable whether eventually the CMEA became a net loss for the USSR or for the East European member states. The most cogent analysis of the subject is contained in Paul Marer, "Has Eastern Europe Become a Liability to the Soviet Union? The Economic Aspect," in Charles Gati, ed., *The International Politics of Eastern Europe* (New York: Praeger, 1976), 104–5.

9. The concept of value in Eastern Europe remains a troublesome issue. In the absence of a real market, "market value," often established by such reputable Western accounting firms as Price Waterhouse or Arthur Anderson, remains an abstract concept. However good a factory or a firm may be, however much of a potential market it may have, its real value equals the amount a potential buyer is willing to offer for it. While in the abstract, again, this may be an economic tautology, as far as the local population of Eastern Europe is concerned the "bargains" snapped up by foreign firms amount to the sale of the "national inheritance."

10. One of the first major studies calling attention to the prospects for and the implications of an ever-increasing national debt among the countries of Eastern Europe is Joan Parpart Zoeter's "Eastern Europe: The Growing Hard Currency Debt," in U.S. Congress, *East European Economies*, 1350–68. For more specific information, see, for instance, Hajna Istvánffy Lőrinc, "Foreign Debt, Debt Management Policy, and Implications for Hungary's Development," *Soviet Studies* 44, no. 6 (1992): 997–1013.

11. For the best summary of the root of the problem, see Walter D. Connor, *Socialism, Politics, and Equality: Hierarchy and Change in Eastern Europe and the USSR* (New York: Columbia University Press, 1979).

Chapter 4. Jane L. Curry, The Sociological Legacies of Communism

1. Ted Gurr, *Political Structures and Regime Change, 1800–1986* (Ann Arbor, Mich.: ICPSR, 1990), 38.

2. This has become increasingly visible to observers concerned with the problems that are evident in the transition. One of the first East European scholars to articulate this was Miroslawa Marody, in her compilation *Co nam zostalo z tych lat . . .* (London: Aneks, 1991). For an early Western analytical warning of the dangers of relying on non–East European models to deal with change in Eastern Europe, see Ken Jowitt, *New World Disorder: The Leninist Extinction* (Berkeley: University of California Press, 1992).

3. Guiseppe DiPalma, in *To Craft Democracies* (Berkeley: University of California Press, 1990), as well as the *Journal of Democracy*, which began to appear just as the Communist regimes fell in Eastern Europe, were pioneers in using the Latin American and South European experiences as models for Eastern Europe.

4. Urie Bronhoffenbrenner, *Two Worlds of Childhood: US and USSR* (New York: Russell Sage Foundation, 1970).

5. Mia Marody, *Polacy, 80* (Warsaw: University of Warsaw, Institute of Sociology, 1981).

6. In the Polish case, for instance, 40 percent of the respondents to a survey done in July 1992 said that delegates to the parliament represented their party's interests, 27 percent said that the delegates represented their own personal interests, 5 percent said that the delegates represented their friends and families, and only 12 percent said either that the delegates represented their voters' interests or that they represented the society's interests. Centrum Bodania Opinii Spolechnych (CBOS), "Opinia publiczna o poslach, radnych, i politykach" (July 1992). In periodic surveys done by CBOS on the population's attitudes toward organs of government, the Sejm and the Senate have fallen, since the first partially free elections, from the top quartile of respected institutions to the bottom quartile, and often rank below the police. The same kind of drop has been seen in other states, where it has been evidenced not only by comparable public opinion data but also by the drop in interest in elections.

7. Judith Pataki, "Hungary: Domestic Political Stalemate," *RFE/RL Research Report* 2, no. 1 (1993): 92.

8. For a full discussion of the mass media, their transformation, and the governments' responses, see "The Media" (special issue), *RFE/RL Research Report* 1, no. 39 (1992).

9. See Jane L. Curry, "Democratization of the Media in Eastern Europe: A Help or Hinderance to Democracy Building" (paper presented to the International Communications Association, Miami, Fla., May 1992).

10. For a discussion of the stages through which the post-Communist elites

have gone, see Thomas Baylis, "Plus Ça Change? Transformation and Continuity among East European Elites" (paper presented to the American Association for the Advancement of Slavic Studies, Phoenix, Ariz., Nov. 1992).

11. For a discussion of the goals and programs of East European dissident groups, see Jane L. Curry, ed., *Dissent in Eastern Europe* (New York: Praeger, 1984).

12. Leszek Balcerowicz, the finance minister of Poland's first two non-Communist governments, is the one person who claims to have worked out a program — however much an economists' exercise it was in the mid-1980s — for how the transition to capitalism would occur. Even so, his group's program was skeletal at best.

13. According to an East European saying that makes this swiftness clear, the "revolution" took six months in Poland, six weeks in East Germany, six days in Czechoslovakia, and six hours in Romania.

14. Bronislaw Geremek, *Rok 1989 Bronisław Geremek opowiada Jacek Zakowski pyta* (Warsaw: Plejada, 1990), 40.

15. Leszek Balcerowicz, *800 Dni* (Warsaw: BGW, 1992), 56–64.

Chapter 5. Barbara Jancar-Webster,
The Environmental Legacies of Communism

1. For an overview of environmental pollution in the former Communist countries, the reader is referred to the reports issued by the respective governments, including Don Hinrichsen and György Enyedi, eds., *State of the Hungarian Environment* (Budapest: Hungarian Academy of Sciences, Ministry for Environment and Water Management and the Hungarian Central Statistical Office, 1990); Bedrich Moldan, ed., *Zivotni prostredi Ceske republiky: Vyvoj a stav do konce roku 1989* (Prague: Academia, 1990); Socialist Republic of Yugoslavia and Republic of Slovenia, Skupscine, "Porocilo o stanju okolya v SR Sloveniji," *Porocevalec* 16, nos. 5/I (20 Feb. 1990), 5/II (20 Feb. 1990), and 7 (8 Mar. 1990); the National Reports of Estonia and Lithuania to United Nations Conference on the Environment and Development (UNCED), 1992; and the unpublished "Report of the USSR to UNCED 1992," ed. N. Voronstov.

2. George R. Davis, "Energy for Planet Earth," *Scientific American* 263, no. 3 (1990): 55–58.

3. H. Brooks, "The Technology of Surprises in Technology, Institutions, and Development," in W. C. Clark and R. E. Munn, eds., *Sustainable Development of the Biosphere* (New York: Cambridge University Press, 1986), 247–56.

4. Ibid., 253.

5. For a development of this thesis, see Barbara Jancar, ed., *New Directions in Environmental Management in Eastern Europe* (Armonk, N.Y.: Sharpe, 1993).

6. Lester R. Milbraith, *Envisioning a Sustainable Society: Learning Our Way Out* (Albany, N.Y.: SUNY Press, 1989).

302   Notes to Pages 88–109

7. Elemér Hankiss, "Reforms and the Conversion of Power," *East European Reporter* 3, no. 4 (1990): 8–9.

8. See Barbara Jancar, *Environmental Management in the Soviet Union and Yugoslavia: Structure and Regulation in Communist Federal States* (Durham, N.C.: Duke University Press, 1989), 213–61. The Czech "Ekologicka sekce Ceskoslovenske biologicke spolecnosti pre CSAV" is a classic case in point.

9. "Annual Report on the Environmental Conditions in Russia in 1991" (submitted to the Supreme Environmental Council of the Russian Parliament, Committee on Ecology and Natural Resources, 7 Oct. 1992).

10. This paragraph is based on author's recollection of oral reports at the Ecological Conference, Moscow State University, Moscow, 5 Oct. 1992.

11. "Chem my dyshim?" (How are we breathing?), *Rossiiskie vesti* (Russian news), 26 Sept. 1992.

12. For a discussion of the evasion of implementation, see Jancar, *Environmental Management in the Soviet Union and Yugoslavia*, chap. 3.

13. The quotation is from Evgenii Schwartz, interview by author, Institute of Geography, Moscow, spring 1992.

14. *Economist*, 13 Nov. 1992.

15. Rose Gutfeld, "Keeping It Green," *Wall Street Journal*, 24 Sept. 1992, R9.

16. For a brief description of the protest movement, see Mike Edwards, "Siberia: In from the Cold," *National Geographic* 177 (Mar. 1990): 2–39.

17. Leonid Leibzon, "Yamal: An Endangered Peninsula," *Moscow News*, no. 45 (8–15 Nov. 1992): 4.

18. Announced by Viktor Danilov-Danilyan at the Moscow State University Ecological Conference, Moscow, 5 Oct. 1992.

Chapter 6. Zoltan Barany, The Military and Security Legacies of Communism

1. Soviet troops were stationed in Czechoslovakia (1968–91), East Germany (1945–94), Hungary (1945–91), Poland (1945–92), and Romania (1945–58).

2. See Zoltan Barany, "Civil-Military Relations in Communist Systems: Western Models Revisited," *Journal of Political and Military Sociology* 19, no. 1 (1991): 75–100.

3. Amos Perlmutter, *The Military and Politics in Modern Times* (New Haven: Yale University Press, 1977), 26.

4. See the discussion of the varieties of civilian control in Samuel P. Huntington, *The Soldier and the State* (Cambridge: Harvard University Press, 1957), 84.

5. On the importance of the Soviet factor, see Dale R. Herspring, "Civil-Military Relations in Post-Communist Eastern Europe: The Potential for Praetorianism," *Studies in Comparative Communism* 25, no. 2 (1992): 103–4.

6. See Samuel P. Huntington, *The Third Wave: Democratization in the Late Twentieth Century* (Norman: University of Oklahoma Press, 1991), 251–53. See

also Augusto Varas, "Civil-Military Relations in a Democratic Framework," in Louis W. Goodman, Johanna S. R. Mendelson, and Juan Rial, eds., *The Military and Democracy: The Future of Civil-Military Relations in Latin America* (Lexington, Mass.: Lexington Books, 1990), 199–218.

7. For the differences in the Communist period, see Ivan Volgyes, "Regional Differences within the Warsaw Pact," *Orbis* 26, no. 3 (1982): 665–79. For differences in the post-Communist period, see Zoltan Barany, "Civil-Military Relations in Comparative Perspective: East-Central and Southeastern Europe," *Political Studies* 41, no. 4 (1993): 594–611.

8. For more comprehensive accounts, see Zoltan Barany, "East European Armed Forces in the Transitions and Beyond," *East European Quarterly* 26, no. 1 (1992): 1–30; and Herspring, "Civil-Military Relations in Post-Communist Eastern Europe," 99–122.

9. See George W. Price, "The Romanian Armed Forces," in Jeffrey Simon, ed., *European Security Policy after the Revolutions of 1989* (Washington, D.C.: National Defense University Press, 1991), 468; and Walter M. Bacon Jr., "Security as Seen from Bucharest," Occasional Paper no. 9111, Center for International Studies, University of Missouri, St. Louis, Mo., Dec. 1991.

10. Vladimir Socor, "Forces of Old Resurface in Romania: The Ethnic Clashes in Tirgu-Mures," *Report on Eastern Europe*, 13 Apr. 1990, 40; *Unirea* (Alba Iulia), 1 Dec. 1990, cited in *Romania Libera*, 5 Dec. 1990, translated in *Foreign Broadcast Information Service — Eastern Europe*, 13 Dec. 1990, 41; *Guardian*, 27 Sept. 1991.

11. Zbigniew Brzezinski, *The Soviet Bloc: Unity and Conflict* (Cambridge: Harvard University Press, 1967), 458–59.

12. See, for instance, Jeffrey Simon, *Warsaw Pact Forces: Problems of Command and Control* (Boulder, Colo.: Westview, 1985); and Teresa Rakowska-Harmstone, *Warsaw Pact Political and Military Integration: A Political Analysis* (Stanford, Calif.: Hoover Institution Press, 1990).

13. Chapter 14 in this volume, by Robin Alison Remington, analyzes the situation in the former Yugoslavia.

14. See Ivan Volgyes, "Military Security in the Post-Communist Age: Reflections on Myths and Realities," *Studies in Comparative Communism* 25, no. 1 (1992): 89–95.

15. See, for instance, Daniel N. Nelson, *Romanian Politics in the Ceausescu Era* (New York: Gordon and Breach, 1988), 175–210.

Chapter 7. Thomas A. Baylis, Eastern Germany

1. In Brandenburg, the PDS took 21.2 percent of the vote, putting it in second place ahead of the Christian Democrats; its candidate for mayor in the city of Potsdam, a man with past Stasi connections, won 45 percent of the vote in that

city but was defeated in a subsequent runoff. See Robert Leicht, "Ein Hauch von roten Socken," *Die Zeit*, 17 Dec. 1993, 1; Joachim Nawrocki, "Die Zeit verwirrt," ibid., 17 Dec. 1993, 4.

2. See, e.g., Richard Hilmer and Rita Müller-Hilmer, "Es wächst zusammen," *Die Zeit*, 8 Oct. 1993, 6–9, reporting on an Infratest survey commissioned by *Die Zeit*. Pluralities of the sample of former East Germans identified twelve "particular strengths" of the GDR (including "social justice," "care of the state for the individual," education, and sexual equality), as opposed to just eight for the Federal Republic (including the political system, consumption opportunities, and personal freedom).

3. See the interesting discussion in Gert-Joachim Glaessner, *The Unification Process in Germany* (New York: St. Martin's, 1992), chaps. 7–8. See also Irma Hanke, *Alltag und Politik: Zur politischen Kultur einer unpolitischen Gesellschaft* (Opladen, Germany: Westdeutscher, 1987).

4. Jürgen Kocka, "Crisis of Unification: How Germany Changes," *Daedalus* 123, no. 1 (1994): 186–87.

5. The allusion here is to former West German permanent representative Günter Gaus's famous characterization of the GDR as a "society of niches" *(Nischengesellschaft)*.

6. See Michael Mertes, "Germany's Social and Political Culture," *Daedalus* 123, no. 1 (1994): 6–10.

7. Here I disagree with the evaluation of Timothy Garton Ash in his otherwise illuminating chapter on inter-German relations in *In Europe's Name* (New York: Random House, 1993), 203–15.

8. It is not widely recognized that significant reform sentiment did emerge within the SED during the last years of the regime, for example at Berlin's Humboldt University, and within the Party's own think tank, the Academy for Society Sciences. Those involved, however, had little contact with dissidents outside the Party. See Henry Krisch, "Delegitimation of the Old Regime: Reforming and Transforming Ideas in the Last Years of the GDR," in M. Donald Hancock and Helga Welsh, eds., *German Unification: Process and Outcome* (Boulder, Colo.: Westview, 1994), 56–61.

9. See Peter H. Merkl, *German Unification in the European Context* (University Park: Pennsylvania State University Press, 1993), 101.

10. The term is a pun on the German word for "recorder," *Blockflöte*.

11. The term *spontaneous revolution* is Sigrid Meuschel's, as cited in Merkl, *German Unification*, 116; it is slightly unfair insofar as it minimizes the quite genuine leadership role performed by the dissidents at a critical moment in the uprising.

12. See Helmut Müller-Enbergs, Marianne Schulz, and Jan Wielgohs, eds., *Von der Illegalität ins Parlament*, 2d ed. (Berlin: Christoph Links, 1992). For back-

ground, see Robert F. Goeckel, *The Lutheran Church and the East German State* (Ithaca: Cornell University Press, 1990).

13. A Stasi report of 1 June 1989 estimated the number of such groups at 160, with a membership of around twenty-five hundred, of whom six hundred were in leadership bodies and sixty constituted a "hard core." See Armin Mitter and Stefan Wolle, eds., *"Ich liebe euch doch alle . . .": Befehle und Lageberichte des MfS* (Berlin: BasisDruck, 1990), 46–71. The actual number of groups seems to have been much higher; in 1988, for example, 325 groups are said to have belonged to an overarching "Concrete for Peace" network. Since the groups had no formal membership, and the boundaries between them were fluid, however, the Stasi's error is perhaps understandable.

It is important to note that loose networks of groups throughout the GDR existed from early in the 1980s. See the informative article by Jan Wielgohs and Marianne Schulz, "Von der 'friedliche Revolution' in die politische Normalität," in Hans Joas and Martin Kohli, eds., *Der Zusammenbruch der DDR* (Frankfurt am Main: Suhrkamp, 1993), esp. 227–30.

14. Ibid., 239.

15. See Garton Ash, *In Europe's Name*, 196.

16. For my own contribution to the overestimation of the GDR's "success," see Thomas A. Baylis, "Explaining the GDR's Economic Strategy," *International Organization* 40 (spring 1986): 381–420.

17. West German government studies indicate that by the mid-1980s East German consumption of food, alcohol, and tobacco was similar to West German patterns; most East German households possessed basic appliances such as refrigerators, washing machines, and television sets, and nearly one-half owned automobiles. Housing, medical care, and public transportation were inexpensive or free, and were probably superior in quality to that in other Communist countries. See *Materialien zum Bericht zur Lage der Nation im geteilten Deutschland 1987* (Bonn: Bundesministerium für innerdeutsche Beziehungen, 1987), 520 ff. A West German sociologist has estimated that the GDR's living standards in 1990 resembled those in the FRG at the beginning of the 1960s. Wolfgang Zapf, "Die DDR 1989/1990 — Zusammenbruch einer Sozialstruktur?" in Joas and Kohli, eds., *Der Zusammenbruch der DDR*, 43.

18. See Carl-Heinz Janson, *Totengräber der DDR* (Düsseldorf: Econ, 1991), 66.

19. Paul Marer, "Economic Policies and Systems in Eastern Europe and Yugoslavia: Commonalities and Differences," in Joint Economic Committee, Congress of the United States, *East European Economies: Slow Growth in the 1980s*, (Washington, D.C.: U.S. Government Printing Office, 1986), 3:613. See also John Garland's detailed account "FRG-GDR Economic Relations," in ibid., 3: 169–206.

20. See Günter Schabowski, *Das Politbüro* (Hamburg: Rowohlt, 1990), 37–41; see also Janson, *Totengräber der DDR*, 104–7.

21. See Hannsjörg F. Buck, "Die Sozialpolitik der SED am Beispiel des Wohnungsbaus," *Deutschland Archiv* 26, no. 4 (Apr. 1993): 507–20, which shows that DDR statistics modestly exaggerated the amount of new housing constructed but drastically overstated the rehabilitation of older housing by treating cosmetic improvements as full-scale "modernization."

22. See the interesting reflections on this issue in Heiner Ganssmann, "Die nichtbeabsichtigten Folgen einer Wirtschaftsplanung," in Joas and Kohli, eds., *Der Zusammenbruch der DDR*, 172–93.

23. See Thomas A. Baylis, "Transforming the East German Economy: Shock without Therapy," in Michael G. Huelshoff, Andrei S. Markovits, and Simon Reich, eds., *From Bundesrepublik to Deutschland: German Politics after Unification* (Ann Arbor: University of Michigan Press, 1993), 77–92.

24. Zapf, "Die DDR 1989/1990," 41.

25. See Mary Fullbrook, "Aspects of Society and Identity in the New Germany," *Daedalus* 123, no. 1 (1994): 219–21.

26. Garton Ash, *In Europe's Name*, 201; Manfred Kuechler, "Political Attitudes and Behavior in Germany," in Huelshoff, Markovits, and Reich, eds., *From Bundesrepublik to Germany*, 44–45.

27. In 1989, for example, 76.6 percent of the emigrants were under the age of forty, and 51.4 percent were single men between eighteen and thirty. Sigrid Meuschel, "Revolution in der DDR: Versuch einer sozialwissenschaftliche Interpretation," in Joas and Kohli, eds., *Der Zusammenbruch der DDR*, 112.

28. See Fullbrook, "Aspects of Society and Identity," 223–25.

29. See the interesting comments of Meuschel, "Revolution in der DDR," 103–4.

30. There is not the space here to examine this bitter controversy in detail. For an intelligent assessment, see Wolfgang Emmerich, "Affirmation — Utopia — Melancholie: Versuch einer Bilanz von vierzig Jahren DDR-Literatur," *German Studies Review* 14 (May 1991): 325–44.

31. The regime seems to have been lulled into complacency by the absence of serious domestic unrest in the first years after the Ostpolitik treaties opened up the GDR to greater Western penetration. Even in retrospect, Honecker told Garton Ash in 1992 that the decision to permit more East-West travel was part of a conscious strategy and was not the result of Western economic dependence. Garton Ash, *In Europe's Name*, 197–98.

32. See Wolfgang Rüddenklau, *Störenfried: DDR-Opposition 1986–1989* (Berlin: BasisDruck, 1992), which includes numerous texts from *Umweltblätter.*

33. Joan DeBardeleben, "'The Future Has Already Begun': Environmental Damage and Protection in the GDR," in Marilyn Rueschemeyer and Christiane

Lemke, eds., *The Quality of Life in the German Democratic Republic* (Armonk, N.Y.: Sharpe, 1989), 157–58.

34. Peter Wensierski, *Von oben nach unten wächst gar nichts: Umweltzerstörung und Protest in der DDR* (Frankfurt am Main: Fischer Taschenbuch, 1986), 19–23.

35. DeBardeleben, " 'The Future Has Already Begun,' " 153–56.

36. Ibid., 145–48.

37. Mike Dennis, *The German Democratic Republic: Politics, Economics, and Society* (London: Pinter, 1988), 181.

38. Gordon A. Craig, "United We Fall," *New York Review of Books*, 13 Jan. 1994, 38, citing Peter Merkl.

39. Wensierski, *Von oben nach unten*, 153–57.

40. See Werner Grühn, "Umweltforschung und Umweltbewusstsein in den neuen Bundesländern," *Deutschland Archiv* 25 (July 1992): 676–78.

41. Kocka, "Crisis of Unification," 188.

42. See Thomas A. Baylis, *The West and Eastern Europe: Economic Statecraft and Political Change* (Westport, Conn.: Praeger, 1994), 199–200.

Chapter 8. Andrzej Korbonski, Poland

1. The argument that follows is taken from Andrzej Korbonski, "Civil Society and Democracy in Poland: Problems and Prospects" (paper presented at a conference on "Civil Society, Political Society, Democracy," Bled, Slovenia, 16–18 Sept. 1993).

2. Grzegorz Ekiert, "Democratization Processes in East Central Europe: A Theoretical Reconsideration," *British Journal of Political Science* 21, no. 3 (1991): 300; Charles Taylor, "Invoking Civil Society," in Greg Urban and Benjamin Leeds, eds., *Working Papers and Proceedings of the Center for Psychological Studies* (Chicago, 1990), 1, as cited in Gail Kligman, "Reclaiming the Publics: A Reflection on Recreating Civil Society in Romania," *East European Politics and Societies* 4, no. 3 (1990): 420.

3. Janina Frentzel-Zagorska, "Civil Society in Poland and Hungary," *Soviet Studies* 42, no. 4 (1990): 759–77; Edward Shils, "The Virtue of Civil Society," *Government and Opposition* 26, no. 1 (1991): 3–20; and Michael Bernhard, "Civil Society and Democratic Transition in East Central Europe," *Political Science Quarterly* 108, no. 2 (1993): 308–9.

4. Aleksander Smolar, "The Polish Opposition," in Ferenc Feher and Andrew Arato, eds., *Crisis and Reform in Eastern Europe* (New Brunswick, N.J.: Transaction, 1991), 176; Elemér Hankiss, "The 'Second Society': Is There an Alternative Model Emerging in Contemporary Hungary?" in ibid., 303–34; Giuseppe di Palma, "Why Democracy Can Work in Eastern Europe," *Journal of Democracy* 2, no. 1 (1991): 28–30; Ekiert, "Democratization Processes in East Central Europe," 300.

5. Andrew Arato, "Civil Society against the State: Poland, 1980–1," *Telos* no.

47 (spring 1981): 23–47; and idem, "Empire and Civil Society," ibid., no. 50 (winter 1981–83): 19–48.

6. See, for example, Z. A. Pelczynski, "Solidarity and the 'Rebirth of Civil Society' in Poland, 1976–1981," in John Keen, ed., *Civil Society and the State* (London: Verso, 1988), 361–80.

7. Ralf Dahrendorf, *Society and Democracy in Germany* (Garden City, N.Y.: Doubleday, 1967), 31, 299–311.

8. For a perceptive discussion, see Piotr Sztompka, "The Intangibles and Imponderables of the Transition to Democracy," *Studies in Comparative Communism* 24, no. 3 (1991).

9. Dahrendorf, *Society and Democracy in Germany*, 331.

10. Kenneth Jowitt, "The Leninist Legacy," in Ivo Banac, ed., *Eastern Europe in Revolution* (Ithaca: Cornell University Press, 1992), 210.

11. George Schöpflin, "The End of Communism in Eastern Europe," *International Affairs* (London), 66, no. 1 (1990): 13.

12. Shils, "Virtues of Civil Society," 12–13.

13. See "Wir haben alles verloren: Die Katastrophe in Mittel und Osteuropa," *Der Spiegel*, no. 50 (10 Dec. 1990).

14. Richard Ackermann, "Environment in Eastern Europe: Despair or Hope?" *Transition* 2, no. 4 (1991): 10.

15. Louisa Vinton, "Assessing Ecological Damage Caused by Soviet Troops," *Report on Eastern Europe* 2, no. 19 (1992): 15–19.

16. Marlise Simons, "Investors Shy Away from Polluted Eastern Europe," *New York Times*, 13 May 1992.

Chapter 9. Sharon L. Wolchik, The Czech Republic and Slovakia

1. See Sharon L. Wolchik, *Czechoslovakia in Transition: Politics, Economics, and Society* (New York: Pinter, 1991), for a more detailed discussion of the Communist period and references to other studies.

2. See Jiří Pelikán, *The Czechoslovak Political Trials, 1950–1954* (Stanford, Calif.: Stanford University Press, 1971); and Gordon Skilling, *Czechoslovakia's Interrupted Revolution* (Princeton: Princeton University Press, 1976).

3. See Skilling, *Czechoslovakia's Interrupted Revolution*; Robin Remington, *Winter in Prague: Documents on Czechoslovak Communism in Crisis* (Cambridge: MIT Press, 1969); and Barbara Jancar, *Czechoslovakia and the Absolute Monopoly of Power: A Study of Political Power in a Communist System* (New York: Praeger, 1971), for a discussion of this period.

4. See Vladimir Kusin, *From Dubček to Charter 77: A Study of 'Normalization' in Czechoslovakia, 1968–1978* (New York: St. Martin's, 1978); Wolchik, *Czechoslovakia in Transition*, chap. 1; and Gordon Skilling, *Charter 77 and Human Rights in Czechoslovakia* (Boston: Allen and Unwin, 1981).

5. See Sharon L. Wolchik, "Regional Inequalities in Czechoslovakia," in Daniel Nelson, ed., *Communism and the Politics of Inequalities* (Lexington, Mass.: Lexington Books, 1983).

6. Ibid.

7. Friedrich Levcik, "The Czechoslovak Economy in the 1980s," in *East European Economies: Slow Growth in the 1980s*, paper prepared for Joint Economic Committee, United States Congress (Washington, D.C.: U.S. Government Printing Office, 1986), 3:85–108; Karel Dyba, "Reforming the Czechoslovak Economy: Past Experiences and Present Dilemmas" (paper presented at Woodrow Wilson International Center for Scholars, Washington, D.C., October 1989); and Josef Brada, "Czechoslovak Economic Performance in the 1980s," in *Pressures for Economic Reform in the East European Economies*, paper prepared for Joint Economic Committee, United States Congress (Washington, D.C.: U.S. Government Printing Office, 1989).

8. See John Hardt, "Soviet Energy Policy in Eastern Europe," in *East European Economic Assessment*, pt. 2, paper prepared for Joint Economic Committee, United States Congress (Washington, D.C.: U.S. Government Printing Office, 1981), 189–220; Jan Vaňous, "East European and Soviet Fuel Trade," in ibid., 541–60; John Kramer, "Soviet-CMEA Energy Ties," in *Problems of Communism* 34, no. 4 (1985): 32–47.

9. See Josef Brada and Arthur King, "Czechoslovak Agriculture: Policies, Performance, and Prospects," in *East European Quarterly* 17, no. 3 (1983): 345–47.

10. Martin Fassmann, "The Shadow Economy's Funds: From Where Are Drawn the Grey Billions on the Market and in Services?" in *Hospodářské noviny*, 9 Dec. 1988, 3, as reported in "Solutions to 'Shadow Economy' Problems Proposed," JPRS-EER-89-035 (31 Mar. 1989).

11. Vladimír Hanzl, Marie Ševerová, Vlasta Štěpová, and Jan Žůrek, "Problém nejen morální, ale i ekonomick," *Hospodářské noviny*, 20 Jan. 1989, 8–9.

12. See Wolchik, *Czechoslovakia in Transition*, 234–39.

13. See Skilling, *Czechoslovakia's Interrupted Revolution*, chap. 14; Martin Myant, *The Czechoslovak Economy, 1948–1988* (Cambridge: Cambridge University Press, 1989); Judy Batt, *Economic Reform and Political Change in Eastern Europe: A Comparison of the Czechoslovak and Hungarian Experiences* (New York: St. Martin's, 1988); and Karel Dyba and Karel Kouba, "Czechoslovak Attempts at Systemic Changes," in *Communist Economies* 1, no. 3 (1989): 313–25.

14. See the sources cited in the previous note; and Sharon L. Wolchik, "Economic Performance and Political Change in Czechoslovakia," in Charles Bukowski and Mark Cichock, eds., *Prospects for Change in Socialist Systems: Challenges and Responses* (New York: Praeger, 1987); and idem, *Czechoslovakia in Transition*, 242–44.

15. See Dyba, "Reforming the Czechoslovak Economy"; Dyba and Kouba, "Czechoslovak Attempts"; and Myant, *Czechoslovak Economy*, 250–52.

16. Federální statistický úřad, Česky statistický úřad, Slovenský statistický úřad, *Statistická ročenka ČSSR* (Prague: SNTL, 1988), 191; and Wolchik, *Czechoslovakia in Transition*, chap. 3.

17. See Wolchik, *Czechoslovakia in Transition*, 257–72.

18. See Kamil Janacek, "Recent Czechoslovak Trends Offer a Mixed Picture," in *RFE/RL Research Report* 1, no. 32 (1992); Ben Slay, ed., "Roundtable: Privatization in Eastern Europe," in ibid., 2, no. 32 (1993).

19. See Janacek, "Recent Czechoslovak Trends"; Slay, ed., "Roundtable: Privatization in Eastern Europe"; and "Slovak Economic Monitor," in *Plan Econ Report* 9, nos. 42–43 (1993), for detailed analyses of these statistics.

20. See Wolchik, *Czechoslovakia in Transition*, 257–66, for further details.

21. "Czech Economic Monitor," in *Plan Econ Report* 9, nos. 26–27 (1993); "Slovak Economic Monitor," in ibid., 9, nos. 42–43 (1993).

22. Foreign investment has dropped further since independence. Total foreign investment in Slovakia for 1992 was U.S.$150 million. By the end of the third quarter of 1993, that figure had dropped to U.S.$86 million. See Economist Intelligence Unit, "Slovakia Invites Western Business, But Is Anyone Listening?" in *Business Eastern Europe*, 15 Mar. 1993; and "Slovak Economic Monitor," in *Plan Econ Report* 9, nos. 42–43 (1993).

23. "Czechs and Slovaks Say Efforts to Split State Are 'Mere Politics,'" USIA Research Memorandum, 20 Dec. 1991, 21–26.

24. See Catherine Albrecht, "Environmental Policies and Politics in Contemporary Czechoslovakia," in *Studies in Comparative Communism* 20 (autumn–winter 1987): 291–302; Sharon L. Wolchik and Jane Curry, "Specialists and Professionals in Policy-Making in Czechoslovakia and Poland," report to the National Council on Soviet and East European Research, Washington, D.C., 1984.

25. See Sharon L. Wolchik, "The Politics of Ethnicity in Post-Communist Czechoslovakia," in *East European Politics and Societies* 8, no. 1 (1994).

26. Martin Butorá, a founder of Public Against Violence, interview with author, Bratislava, Mar. 1990.

27. See Wolchik, *Czechoslovakia in Transition*, chap. 2.

28. See Association for Independent Social Analysis, "Výzkum politickych postojů" (Prague: AISA, 1992).

29. Sharon Wolchik, "The Repluralization of Politics in Czechoslovakia," *Communist and Post-Communist Studies* 26, no. 4 (1993).

30. "Attitudes toward Jews in Poland, Hungary, and Czechoslovakia: A Comparative Survey" (American Jewish Committee and Freedom House, January 1991).

31. lb [pseud.], "Pokles důvěry pokračuje," *Lidové noviny*, 9 Oct. 1990, 1–2.

32. See, for example, Association for Independent Social Analysis, "Výzkum politickych postojů"; and information from Institut pro výzkum veřejného mínění, May 1992.

33. Institut pro výzkum veřejného mínění, "Chances and Expectations: Results of the Survey — Czechoslovakia, May 1990," as reported in "Growing Dissatisfaction with Political Situation," *Foreign Broadcast Information Service — Eastern Europe*, 30 May 1990.

34. See Wolchik, "Politics of Ethnicity."

35. Association for Independent Social Analysis, "Democracy, Economic Reform, and Western Assistance in Czechoslovakia" (Prague: AISA, 1992).

36. See Marek Boguszak and Vladimír Rak, "Czechoslovakia — May 1990 Survey Report" (Prague: AISA, 1990); and idem, "Společně, ale každy jinak," *Lidové noviny*, 21 Dec. 1990.

37. See Wolchik, "Politics of Ethnicity."

38. See Wolchik, *Czechoslovakia in Transition*, chap. 3.

39. See Sharon L. Wolchik, "Women and the Politics of Transition in the Czech and Slovak Republics," in Marilyn Rueschemeyer, ed., *Women in the Politics of Postcommunist Eastern Europe* (London: Sharpe, 1994), 3–28.

40. See John Kramer, "Drug Abuse in Central and Eastern Europe," in James Millar and Sharon Wolchik, eds., *The Social Legacy of Communism* (Cambridge: Cambridge University Press, 1994); and other essays in the present volume.

41. See Valerie Bunce and Maria Csanadi, "Uncertainty in the Transition: Post-Communism in Hungary," *East European Politics and Societies* 7, no. 2 (1993), 240–75.

42. Václav Havel, "A Call for Sacrifice: The Co-Responsibility of the West," *Foreign Affairs* 73, no. 2 (1994): 2–7.

Chapter 10. Zoltan Barany, Hungary

1. An excellent analysis along these lines is Andrew C. Janos, *The Politics of Backwardness in Hungary, 1825–1945* (Princeton: Princeton University Press, 1982).

2. A fine synopsis of the country's road to "the rule of law" is Edith Oltay's "Hungary," *RFE/RL Research Report* 1, no. 27 (1992): 16–24.

3. Ivan Szelényi, "Demokrácia, legitimáció es polgári engedetlenség," *Magyar Hírlap*, 9 Nov. 1990.

4. See the commentary of Mihály Sükösd, "Fekete-fehér, igen-nem," *Népszabadság*, 25 Nov. 1991.

5. See Edith Oltay, "How Civil Groups Adjust to Democracy," *RFE/RL Research Report* 1, no. 32 (1992): 18–20.

6. See, for instance, David Stark, "Privatization in Hungary: From Plan to

Market or from Plan to Clan," *East European Politics and Societies* 4, no. 3 (1990): 351–92; and János Mátyás Kovács, "From Reformation to Transformation: Limits to Liberalism in Hungarian Economic Thought," ibid., 5, no. 1 (1991): 61–72.

7. László Csaba, "A Convalescent Economy," *New Hungarian Quarterly* 33, no. 126 (1992): 3.

8. *Wall Street Journal*, 24 Sept. 1992.

9. In the first quarter of 1992, exports reached $2.4 billion and imports more than $2 billion, a 13-percent increase and a 10-percent decrease, respectively. See "Economic and Business Notes," *RFE/RL Research Report*, 15 May 1992, 14.

10. See Zoltan Barany, "The Bankruptcy of Hungarian Socialism," *Südost-Europa* 38, no. 4 (1989): 209–10.

11. Rózsa H. Varró, "40 év erkölcsi hagyatéka," *Szabadság*, 9 Aug. 1991.

12. AFP news agency (Budapest), 21 Nov. 1991.

13. Katalin Bossányi, "Hogyan élünk? Beszélgetés Kolosi Tamással," *Népszabadság*, 23 Nov. 1991.

14. For an excellent discussion of urban planning under socialism, see György Enyedi and Viktória Szirmai, *Budapest: A Central European Capital* (London: Belhaven Press, 1992), 142–55.

15. Paul G. Hare, "Industrial Development of Hungary since World War II," *Eastern European Politics and Societies* 2, no. 1 (1988): 150.

16. János Dési, "Pusztuló lakótelepek, nyomorgó emberek," *Magyar Hírlap*, 27 Nov. 1991.

17. For a comprehensive account, see Joan DeBardeleben, ed., *To Breathe Free: Eastern Europe's Environmental Crisis* (Baltimore: Johns Hopkins University Press, 1991), especially the chapters dealing with Hungary by Zoltán Király and Miklós Persányi.

18. "Törvénytervezet a környezetről," *Magyar Hírlap*, 9 Nov. 1991.

19. See, for instance, Gábor Falus, "Védeni hosszú távon: A Velencei-tó ma és holnap," *Népszabadság*, 29 Aug. 1987.

20. Hubertus Knabe, "Glasnost' for the Environment: On the State of Environmental Protection in Hungary," *Osteuropa*, no. 7, 1989, cited in Juergen Szalay, "Environmental Management: Current Problems and Prospects," *Report on Eastern Europe*, 5 Oct. 1990, 22.

21. *Kis Újság*, 17 May 1990, 5.

22. Anna Várkonyi, "A Catalogue of Woe: The Environment," *New Hungarian Quarterly* 33, no. 126 (1992): 93.

Chapter 11. Daniel N. Nelson, Romania

1. Ted Appleton, *Your Guide to Rumania* (London: Redman, 1965), 14.

2. Trond Gilberg, *Modernization in Romania since World War II* (New York: Praeger, 1975), 251.

3. Lawrence Graham, *Romania: A Developing Socialist State* (Boulder, Colo.: Westview, 1982).

4. Gilberg, *Modernization in Romania*, 97–206.

5. Central Intelligence Agency, *Handbook of Economic Statistics* (Washington, D.C.: CIA, 1987), 40.

6. *Kraje rwpg, 1960–1975* (Warsaw: Glowny Urzad Statystyczny, 1976), 48.

7. Charles L. Taylor and David A. Jodice, *World Handbook of Political and Social Indicators*, 3d ed. (New Haven: Yale University Press, 1983), 1:204, 220.

8. Nicolas Spulber, *The Economies of Communist Europe* (New York: Wiley, 1957), 5; See also *Anuarul statistic* (Bucuresti: Directia Centrala de Statistica, 1983), 58.

9. Werner Gumpel, "Das Wirtschaftssystem," in Klaus-Detlev Grothusen, ed., *Rumänien: Südosteuropa-Handbuch* (Göttingen: Vandenhoeck and Ruprecht, 1977), 2:293–94.

10. Serban Orescu, "Multilaterally Developed Romania: An Overview," in Vlad Georgescu, ed., *Romania: Forty Years (1944–1984)* (Washington, D.C.: Praeger, for the Center for Strategic and International Studies, 1985), 13.

11. Nicolae Ceauşescu, in *Scinteia*, 2 June 1966.

12. Orescu, "Multilaterally Developed Romania," 13.

13. Wharton Econometrics, *Review of the Second Romanian Economic Memorandum to Western Banks*, pt. 1 (22 and 19 Mar.), pt. 3 (4 Apr.) (Philadelphia: Wharton Econometric Forecasting Associates, 1983), 9.

14. Gerhard Schmutler, "Industrie und Landswirtschaft," in Grothusen, ed., *Rumänien: Südosteuropa-Handbuch*, vol. 2.

15. *Frankfurter Allgemeine Zeitung*, 17 Feb. 1983.

16. Michael Shafir, *Romania: Politics, Economics, and Society* (London: Pinter, 1985), 45.

17. Thad P. Alton, "East European GNPs: Origins of Product, Final Uses, Rates of Growth, and International Comparisons," in Joint Economic Committee of the U.S. Congress, *East European Economies: Slow Growth in the 1980's* (Washington, D.C.: U.S. Government Printing Office, 1985), 110.

18. Ibid., 124.

19. Central Intelligence Agency, *Handbook of Economic Statistics*, 130.

20. Ibid., 212, 214.

21. Ruth Sivard, *World Social and Military Expenditures* (Washington, D.C.: World Priorities, 1980, 1987–88), 24, 46.

22. *Congresul al XI-lea al Partidului Comunist Roman* (Bucharest: Editura Politica, 1974).

23. Nicolae Ceauşescu, "Raport la cel de-al X-lea Congres al Partidul Comunist Roman" (Bucharest: Editura Politica, 1969), 13–15. See also idem, "Raport la

Conferinta Nationala a Partidului Comunist Roman" (Bucharest: Editura Politica, 1972), 98.

24. Marvin Jackson, "Perspectives on Romania's Economic Development in the 1980's," in Daniel N. Nelson, ed., *Romania in the 1980s* (Boulder, Colo.: Westview, 1981), 275.

25. Alton, "East European GNP's," 97–98.

26. *Anuaral Statistic al Republica Socialiste Romania* (Bucharest: Directia Centrala de Statistica, 1972, 1979, 1980); see also *Demographic and Statistical Yearbook of the U.N.* (New York: United Nations, 1950–79).

27. Paul Gafton, "1987 Plan Targets Not Met," *Romanian Situation Report*, no. 3 (Radio Free Europe Research [hereafter "RFER"]), 1987, p. 6.

28. *Frankfurter Allgemeine Zeitung*, 17 Feb. 1983.

29. *Scinteia*, 23 Dec. 1987.

30. Robert King, *Minorities under Communism* (Cambridge: Harvard University Press, 1973), 146–69.

31. Daniel N. Nelson, "Dilemmas of Local Politics," *Journal of Politics* 41 (Feb. 1979): 37.

32. Daniel N. Nelson, *Romanian Politics in the Ceausescu Era* (New York: Gordon and Breach, 1988).

33. See Mary McGrory, "Hungary for Change," *Washington Post National Weekly Edition*, 24–30 July 1989. See also "Give Us Your Tired, Your Poor . . ." *Time*, 4 July 1988, 40.

34. William Echikson, "Hungarian Refugees Spark Rare East-Bloc Row," *Christian Science Monitor*, 13 June 1988.

35. Vladimir Socor, "Dorin Tudoran on the Condition of the Romanian Intellectual," *Romanian Situation Report*, no. 15 (RFER), 1984, pp. 29–31.

36. "The Dispute with Hungary over Transylvania," *Romanian Situation Report*, no. 4 (RFER), 1988, pp. 15–19.

37. See the discussion by Michael Shafir of Ilie Ceauşescu's vituperative remarks in "'Revisionism' under Romanian General's Fire," *RAD Background Report/86* (RFER), 17 May 1989.

38. "Rural Reorganization," *Romanian Situation Report*, no. 7 (RFER), 1987, p. 14.

39. Shafir, "Revisionism," 143.

40. *Scinteia*, 25 June 1986. See also ibid., 25 June 1987, 4.

41. *Eastern Europe Newsletter* 2, no. 7 (1988): 7.

42. Nelson, *Romanian Politics in the Ceausescu Era*.

43. William Echikson, "Hungarians Protest Romanian Plan to Destroy Villages," *Christian Science Monitor*, 27 June 1988.

44. *Scinteia*, 19 Apr. 1989, 1, reports on the law mandating such changes; and further discussion of the distribution of such towns is in ibid., 14 May 1989, 1.

45. Gafton, "1987 Plan Targets Not Met."

46. William Echikson, in *Christian Science Monitor,* June 19, 1988.

47. Ibid.; see also Gafton, "1987 Plan Targets Not Met"; and *Eastern Europe Newsletter* 2, no. 7 (1988).

48. *Scinteia*, 22 Dec. 1987.

49. Daniel N. Nelson, "Romania," in William A. Welsh, ed., *Survey Research and Public Attitudes in the Soviet Union and Eastern Europe* (New York: Pergamon, 1981).

50. The case of Cornea has been widely noted in the Western press. In 1989, however, others, such as Gabriel Andreescu (a scientist in Bucharest), spoke eloquently about their country's plight. See his letter to the Paris CSCE meeting, published in Paris in *Liberation*, 8 June 1989.

51. Socor, "Dorin Tudoran."

52. Vladimir Socor (1988).

53. Elena Zamfir, in *Era Socialista* 10, no. 3 (Feb. 1988).

54. *Scinteia*, 24 June 1978.

55. *Foreign Broadcast Information Service — Eastern Europe*, 24 June 1982.

56. Mihail Sturzda, "Interviews with Romanians Published in Paris," *Romanian Situation Report*, no. 6 (RFER), 1988, p. 17.

57. *New York Times*, 6 Oct. 1985.

58. *New York Times*, 15–16 Dec. 1985.

59. Daniel N. Nelson, "Conclusion: Development, Communism, and Balkan Tradition," in Nelson, ed., *Romania in the 1980s*, 307.

60. Ibid., 311.

61. *Scinteia*, 25 June 1987, 4.

62. *Financial Times*, 19 June 1985.

63. *Scinteia*, 6–16 Mar. 1988; ibid., 6–20 Apr. 1988.

64. *Amnesty International Report* (London: Amnesty International, 1980).

65. *Amnesty International Report* (London: Amnesty International, 1983), 272–73.

66. Ladislav Bittman, *The KGB and Soviet Disinformation* (Washington, D.C.: Pergamon-Brassey, 1985), 32; see also Jeffrey T. Richelson, *Sword and Shield: Soviet Intelligence and Security Apparatus* (Cambridge, Mass.: Ballinger, 1986), 210.

67. Richard F. Starr, *Yearbook on International Communist Affairs* (Stanford: Hoover Institution Press, 1986), 333.

68. *Le Monde*, 11 Feb. 1983.

69. *Die Welt*, 9 Nov. 1984.

70. *New York Times*, 20 Dec. 1985.

71. *Scinteia*, 15 Nov. 1985.

72. *Scinteia*, 4 May 1988.

73. Henry Kamm, "For Bucharest, a Great Leap Backward," *New York Times*, 15 Feb. 1988, 6.

74. Echikson, "Hungarians Protest Romanian Plan."

75. Jackson Diehl, "It's Raining on Ceausescu's Parade," *Washington Post National Weekly Edition*, 10 Nov. 1986, 17.

76. Nelson, *Romanian Politics in the Ceausescu Era*.

77. Daniel N. Nelson, "Non-Supportive Participatory Involvement in Eastern Europe," *Social Science Quarterly* 67, no. 3 (1986).

78. Daniel N. Nelson, "Public Legitimation in European Communist States," in Sabrina Ramet, ed., *Adaptations of Communism* (Bloomington: Indiana University Press, 1993), 18.

79. Nelson, "Romania."

80. Daniel N. Nelson, "Charisma, Control, and Coercion: The Dilemma of Communist Leadership," *Comparative Politics* 16, no. 1 (1984): 1–16.

81. Mary Ellen Fischer, "Idol or Leader? The Origins and Future of the Ceausescu Cult," in Nelson, ed., *Romania in the 1980s*. See also Vladimir Tismaneanu, "Romania," in Richard F. Starr, ed., *Yearbook of International Communist Affairs* (Stanford, Calif.: Hoover Institution Press, 1986); and Shafir, "Revisionism."

82. Dan Ionescu, "Poems for Elena Ceausescu," *Romanian Situation Report*, no. 2 (RFER), 1988.

83. Fischer, "Idol or Leader," 130.

84. Central Intelligence Agency, *Chiefs of State and Cabinet Members of Foreign Governments* (Washington, D.C.: Directorate of Intelligence, CIA, 1970–87).

85. *Scinteia*, 9 Sept. 1979.

86. Sturzda, "Interviews with Romanians."

87. Nelson, *Romanian Politics in the Ceausescu Era*.

88. Augustin Buzura, *The Wall of Death*.

Chapter 12. Luan Troxel, Bulgaria

1. *Zycie Warszawy*, quoted in *Foreign Broadcast Information Service — Eastern Europe*, 21 Nov. 1989, 11.

2. On the Bulgarians' success, see L. P. Morris, *Eastern Europe since 1945* (London: Heinemann, 1984), 57–58.

3. On 20 November, Mladenov met with workers at the Sofia plant Sredets; on 22 November, Atanasov met with other plant workers in Sofia; on 24 November, Lukanov met with workers in Lovech and Pleven, Atanasov with workers in Varna, and Yovchev with workers in Khaskovo. One of the directors of the Trade Union Research Institute pointed out to me that this was a deliberate strategy.

4. Krasimira Ivanova, "Imame silna sotsialna programa," *Sofiiski vesti*, 10 May 1990, 5.

5. The distinction is Jowitt's. See Kenneth Jowitt, "The Leninist Legacy," in

New World Disorder: The Leninist Extinction (Berkeley: University of California Press, 1992).

6. Approximately 25 percent of the vote went to parties that did not gain representation. See Luan Troxel, "Socialist Persistence in the Bulgarian Elections of 1990 and 1991," *East European Quarterly* 26, no. 4 (1993).

7. For the text of Zhivkov's speech to the nation explaining the situation with the Turks in 1989, see "Edinstvoto na bulgarskiya narod e grizha i sudba na vseki grazhdanin na nasheto milo obshtestvo," *Ikonomicheski Zhivot*, 31 May 1989, 1.

8. For a discussion of the rumors that were widespread in Bulgaria concerning this issue, see Jeri Laber, "The Bulgarian Difference," *New York Review of Books*, 17 May 1990, 36.

9. One member of parliament suggested to me in a private interview in December 1990 that this display of nationalism was coordinated by the local Communists in order to mask the weakness of the Bulgarian Communist Party at the time.

10. *Statisticheski spravochnik* (Sofia: Tsentralno Statishtichesko Upravlenie, 1989), 3.

11. There is also countervailing evidence that suggests that this demographic shift actually resulted in the capital's being populated with alienated peasants who were unable to feel any ties to the city. During the 1970s a spate of films were released supporting this notion. Among them were *Selyaninut s koliloto* (The peasant with the bicycle) and *Durvo bez koreni* (A tree without roots).

12. Atanas Atanasov and Aron Mashiakh, *Promeni v sotsialnata prinadlezhnost na zaetite litsa v Bulgaria* (Sofia, 1971), quoted in Walter Connor, "Social Change and Stability in Eastern Europe," *Problems of Communism* 26, no. 6 (Nov.–Dec. 1977): 16–32.

13. Joseph Rothschild, *East Central Europe between the Two World Wars* (Seattle: University of Washington Press, 1974), 333.

14. Ibid., 333.

15. "Nakude sled tumnata staichka," *Kultura*, 17 Aug. 1990, 4.

16. Personal interview with author, October 1989.

17. Mikhail Mirchev, "Chiya e mladezhta," *Debati*, 26 Dec. 1990, 10.

18. On education, see Peter-Emil Mitev, *Youth and Labor* (Sofia: Bulgarian Studies Association, 1983), 191. On the employment rates of men and women, see *Statisticheski spravochnik*, 1989, 65.

19. Compare, for instance, women's rates of participation in positions that are service related (82.5% of those in such positions are women), and those that are management related (30% are women). *Statisticheski spravochnik*, 1989, 65. To compare rates of participation in skilled and unskilled jobs, see Mitev, *Youth and Labor*, 286.

20. Maria Todorova, "Improbable Maverick or Typical Conformist: Seven

Thoughts on the New Bulgaria," in Ivo Banac, ed., *Eastern Europe in Revolution* (Ithaca, N.Y.: Cornell University Press, 1992), 153.

21. *The World's Women, 1970–1990: Trends and Statistics* (New York: United Nations, 1991), 13.

22. M. Donald Hancock et al., *Politics in Western Europe* (Chatham, N.J.: Chatham House 1993), 74.

23. Todorova, "Improbable Maverick or Typical Conformist," 153.

24. Michael Wyzan, "Bulgaria: Shock Therapy Followed by a Steep Recession," *RFE/RL Research Report*, 13 Nov. 1992, 50.

25. On the outflow of youth, see Troxel, "Socialist Persistence."

26. Private interviews carried out by the author in the fall of 1990 with UDF, BSP, and Fatherland Party of Labor members of parliament. Also, interviews with advisers and politicians from the Bulgarian Communist Party in the fall of 1989 pointed to this.

27. John Lampe, *The Bulgarian Economy in the Twentieth Century* (London: Croom Helm, 1986), 191.

28. Ibid., 184–85.

29. William M. Reisinger, *Energy and the Soviet Bloc* (Ithaca, N.Y.: Cornell University Press, 1992), 18, 74, 81–82.

30. Lampe, *Bulgarian Economy in the Twentieth Century*, 178.

31. Ibid., 181.

32. *Financial Times*, 3 July 1992, 6.

33. See *Economist*, 12 Oct. 1991, 43, for comparative figures on aid from the IMF and the World Bank; and Michael Wyzan, "Bulgaria," 51–52, for a discussion of the relative paucity of IMF, World Bank, and European Bank for Reconstruction and Development aid.

34. Slavtcho Petrov, "Embracing Macedonia Too Tightly?" *East European Reporter*, July–Aug. 1992, 31.

35. See, for instance, "Environmentalism Runs Riot," *Economist*, 8 Aug. 1992, 11; and "Abolishing Litter," ibid., 22 Aug. 1992.

36. For a discussion of this problem in Poland, see Piotr Wilczynski, "Environmental Management in Poland," in Denizhan Erocal, ed., *Environmental Management in Developing Countries* (Paris: Development Centre of the Organisation for Economic Co-operation and Development, 1991).

37. *Economist*, 17 Feb. 1990, 56.

38. Richard Crampton, "The Intelligentsia, The Ecology, and Opposition in Bulgaria," *World Today*, 46, no. 2 (1990): 24.

39. Clement Smith, "Bulgaria Chokes Itself to Death," *New Statesman*, 29 Apr. 1988, 17–18.

40. *Contemporary World Atlas* (Chicago: Rand McNally, 1987), 99.

41. *New York Times*, 8 Dec. 1992, A13.

42. John Kramer, "The Nuclear Power Debate in Eastern Europe," *RFE/RL Research Report* 8, no. 35 (1992): 59.
43. *New York Times*, 8 Dec. 1992, A13.
44. Ibid.
45. Kramer, "Nuclear Power Debate in Eastern Europe," 59–60.
46. See, "East European Pollution Blights Investment, Too," *New York Times*, 13 May 1992, A1.
47. Eagleburger is quoted in *International Herald Tribune*, 7–8 Mar. 1992, 2.

Chapter 13. Elez Biberaj, Albania

1. Commission on Security and Cooperation in Europe, *Human Rights and Democratization in Albania* (Washington, D.C.: CSCE, 1993), 10.
2. Stavro Skendi, ed., *Albania* (New York: Praeger, 1956), 57.
3. See Neshat Tozaj, "The Albanian's Religion" (in Albanian), *Populli Po* (Tirana), 31 July 1993, 5.
4. Kiço Blushi, "Who Sows National Discord" (in Albanian), *Tirana* (Tirana), no. 486 (Sept. 1992): 2–3; and idem, "Who Benefits from National Discord" (in Albanian), *Zëri i Rinisë*, 11 Nov. 1992, 3–4.
5. See Abdi Baleta's article in *Patrioti* (Tirana), no. 12 (Oct. 1992): 1–3.
6. Elez Biberaj, *Albania and China: A Study of an Unequal Alliance* (Boulder, Colo.: Westview, 1986).
7. President Berisha, interview by author, conducted by telephone, Washington, D.C., and Tirana, 30 Dec. 1993.
8. *Zëri i Popullit* (Tirana), 3 Feb. 1987, 1.
9. United States Information Agency, *Albanians Speak Out on Political Issues*, M-99-91 (Washington, D.C.: USIA, 1991).
10. Radio Tiranë Network, Albanian-language broadcast at 1830 GMT, 21 Oct. 1992, translated in *Foreign Broadcast Information Service — Eastern Europe* (hereafter *FBIS-EEU*), 22 Oct. 1992, 4.
11. See a series of articles by Betim Muço in *Zëri i Rinisë*, 2, 6, 9, 13, and 16 May 1992.
12. *Der Spiegel* (Hamburg), 30 March 1992, 201–4, translated in *FBIS-EEU*, 7 Apr. 1992, 2–3.
13. *Republika* (Tirana), 18 June 1992, 3.
14. Teodor Keko, "Our Salvation: Intelligence, Realism, and Sincerity" (in Albanian), *Rilindja Demokratike* (Tirana), 7 Mar. 1992, 2.
15. For background see Elez Biberaj, *Albania: A Socialist Maverick* (Boulder, Colo.: Westview, 1990), chap. 5; and Adi Schnytzer, *Stalinist Economic Strategy in Practice: The Case of Albania* (New York: Oxford University Press, 1982).
16. World Bank and European Community, *An Agricultural Strategy for Albania* (Washington, D.C.: World Bank, 1992), 2.

17. Ramiz Alia, *Fjalime e biseda* (Speeches and conversations) (Tirana: "8 Nëntori," 1988), 4:377.

18. World Bank and European Community, *Agricultural Strategy for Albania*, 2.

19. *Zëri i Popullit*, 23 July 1991, 1–2.

20. *Bashkimi* (Tirana), 31 July 1991; and *Zëri i Popullit*, 3 July 1991.

21. Fatos Arapi, "This Is Golgotha" (in Albanian), *Zëri i Rinisë*, 16 Sept. 1992, 3.

22. *Zëri i Popullit*, 1 Dec. 1991, 3.

23. Radio Tiranë Network, Albanian-language broadcast at 2010 GMT, 11 June 1992, translated in *FBIS-EEU*, 12 June 1992, 5.

24. Ten former Politburo members, as well as Hoxha's widow, have been sentenced for abuse of power.

25. *Rzeczpospolita* (Warsaw), 25 Feb. 1992, 6, translated in *FBIS-EEU*, 6 Mar. 1992, 2–3. A day after the Democratic Party's election victory, Berisha said: "In building Albania we need many things, but what we do not need are hatred and revanchism. The Democratic Party invites all the democratic forces in Albania not to waste time in destruction and confusion, but to devote their talents and energies to building the future. It is true that in the past the dictatorship committed ugly deeds, but it is also true that the Albanians as a whole are at the same time the accomplices and fellow victims of the regime under which we lived. Our common responsibility and our common suffering must unite us with the ideals of democracy for the construction of a new Albania." Radio Tiranë Network, broadcast in Albanian at 1310 GMT, 23 Mar. 1992, translated in *FBIS-EEU*, 24 March 1992, 4–5.

26. Abdi Baleta, a member of the parliament, has called for measures to redress what he sees as discriminatory practices against northerners. See *Zëri i Rinisë*, 9 Sept. 1992, 3–4.

27. *Gazeta Shqiptare* (Tirana), 9 Nov. 1993, 1.

28. World Bank and European Community, *Agricultural Strategy for Albania*, 143–50.

Chapter 14. Robin Alison Remington, The Collapse of the Yugoslav Alternative

1. This chapter assesses developments in the former Yugoslavia as they unfolded up until January 1994.

2. *New York Times*, 11 Nov. 1993. That figure included refugees: 700,000 in Croatia; 647,000 in the Federal Republic of Yugoslavia (Serbia and Montenegro); 45,000 in Slovenia, and 27,000 in Macedonia. It did not appear to include nonrefugee Serbs and Montenegrins who were "at risk" as a result of international sanctions that have produced a drastic shortage of food, heat, and medicine in the as-yet-unrecognized rump Yugoslavia.

3. For analysis, see Patrick Moore, "Ethnic Cleansing in Bosnia: Outrage but

Little Action," *RFE/RL Research Report*, 1, no. 34 (1992): 1–7; Roy Gutman, *Witness to Genocide: The 1993 Pulitzer Prize Winning Dispatches of the Ethnic Cleansing of Bosnia* (New York: Macmillan, 1993). According to a UN civil rights investigator for Bosnia, the former Polish prime minister Tadeusz Mazowiecki, in late 1993 up to ten thousand Mostar Muslims were in Croatian detention camps, where conditions are "brutal and degrading." *New York Times*, 8 Sept. 1993. Despite warnings, this did not result in an expansion of UN or U.S. sanctions to include Croatia.

4. *New York Times*, 1 Aug. 1993.

5. Contrary to the impression in the Western media, the United Nations didn't cancel Yugoslav membership outright. See Patrick Moore, "The First Month of the Bosnian Peace Process," *RFE/RL Research Report* 1, no. 40 (1992): 5.

6. *New York Times*, 29 Dec. 1993.

7. For a discussion of the Western "myth" that the Croatian-Serbian conflict is "centuries old," see Sabrina Petra Ramet, "War in the Balkans," *Foreign Affairs* 71, no. 4 (1992): 80.

8. Joseph C. Harsch, "Back to the Future in the Balkans," *Christian Science Monitor*, 29 Jan. 1992.

9. The longevity of this conflict is captured by a June 1971 interview that I conducted with Vlado Benko, a political science professor in Ljubljana. When asked about the rising national tensions swirling around the abortive 1971 constitutional amendments, the professor characterized the 1917 Declaration of Corfu (which accepted the Serbian king, and a much more centralized version of the union than Croat and Slovene negotiators wanted, in order to gain Serbian military support to push back the Italians who had invaded Slovenia) as "the original sin of Yugoslavia."

10. The Serbian author Lazo M. Kostich cites German sources to substantiate his estimate of 750,000. See Lazo M. Kostich, *Holocaust in the Independent State of Croatia* (Chicago: Liberty, 1981), 4. The British historian Fred Singleton puts the figure at 350,000. Fred Singleton, *Twentieth-Century Yugoslavia* (New York: Columbia University Press, 1976), 88.

11. Christopher Hitchens, "Why Bosnia Matters: Appointment in Sarajevo," *Nation*, 14 Sept. 1992, 238.

12. This section draws upon my earlier chapter "Self-Management and Development Strategies in Socialist Yugoslavia," in Gerasimos Augustinos, ed., *Diverse Paths to Modernity in Southeastern Europe: Essays in National Development* (Westport, Conn.: Greenwood, 1991), 57–87.

13. Ivan Avakumovich, *History of the Communist Party of Yugoslavia* (Aberdeen, Scotland: Aberdeen University Press, 1964).

14. Edvard Kardelj, *Self-Management and the Political System* (Belgrade: Socialist Thought and Practice, 1980).

15. Dennison Rusinow, *The Yugoslav Experiment, 1948–1954* (Berkeley and Los Angeles: University of California Press, 1977), 74.

16. Paul Shoup, *Communism and the Yugoslav National Question* (New York: Columbia University Press, 1968); and Christopher Cviic, *Remaking the Balkans* (London: Royal Institute of International Affairs, 1991).

17. Shoup, *Communism and the Yugoslav National Question;* also Walker Connor, *The National Question in Marxist-Leninist Theory and Strategy* (Princeton: Princeton University Press, 1984), 222 ff.

18. See Sabrina P. Ramet, *Nationalism and Federalism in Yugoslavia, 1962–1991*, 2d ed. (Bloomington: Indiana University Press, 1992); also Vojislav Stanovcic, "History and Status of Ethnic Conflicts," in Dennison Rusinow, ed., *Yugoslavia: A Fractured Federalism* (Washington, D.C.: Wilson Center Press, 1988), 34.

19. Arend Lijphart, *Democracy in Plural Societies: A Comparative Exploration* (New Haven: Yale University Press, 1977). On Yugoslavia, see also Jack C. Fisher, *Yugoslavia — Regional Differences and Administrative Responses* (San Francisco: Chandler, 1966); and Pedro Ramet, *Nationalism and Federalism in Yugoslavia, 1963–1983* (Bloomington: Indiana University Press, 1984).

20. Stephen E. Palmer and Robert R. King, *Yugoslav Communism and the Macedonian Question* (Hamden, Conn.: Shoe String, 1971).

21. Dennison I. Rusinow, "Yugoslavia's Muslim Nation," *Universities Field Staff International (UFSI) Reports* (Hanover, N.H.), no. 8 (Europe), 1982.

22. This section expands upon my earlier analysis, Robin Alison Remington, "Nation versus Class in Yugoslavia," *Current History* 86, no. 523 (1987): 365–68, 386–87.

23. Najdan Pasić, open letter to the LCY Presidium, *Politika* (Belgrade), 29 Sept. 1982.

24. In 1986, the thirteenth Party congress of the League of Communists of Yugoslavia recognized and warned against emerging economic and political crises. At that time the crisis was perceived in terms of economic imperatives, the need to address "inadequate mechanisms and methods" of implementing the system, and the search for Party unity and cohesion. *Politika* (Belgrade), 25 June 1986.

25. Mikhail Gorbachev, *Perestroika: New Thinking for Our Country and the World* (New York: Harper and Row, 1987).

26. Mikhail Gorbachev, speech to the Council of Europe at Strasbourg, *Economist*, 15 July 1989.

27. *Borba* (Belgrade), 21 May 1990. Marković was seen as the politician "pulling Yugoslavia forward" by ratings that ranged from 60 percent in Serbia to 92 percent in Bosnia and Herzegovina; above those of Milošević, Tudjman, and Kucan.

28. The quoted phrase is from M. George Zaninovich, *The Development of Socialist Yugoslavia* (Baltimore: Johns Hopkins Press, 1968), 44 ff.

29. An English-language text of Milošević's speech is in *Politika: The International Weekly* (Belgrade), 23–29 Mar. 1991.

30. Increasingly large numbers of Serbs and even Montenegrins are resisting military service under current conditions, as are many of the students who have openly demanded Milošević's resignation.

31. See Stephen Engelberg, "Carving Out a Greater Serbia," *New York Times Magazine*, 1 Sept. 1991. Even if one believes that Engelberg's sources are suspect and had their own agendas, subsequent events support the general thrust of his analysis.

32. Quoted by Milicia Stamatovic, "The Future Lies in Democracy," *Politika: The International Weekly*, 6–12 Apr. 1991, 2.

33. Based on conversations in Belgrade and Zagreb, 23 June–1 July 1991. For a balanced, academic assessment, see Ljubivoje Acimović, "US Policy towards Yugoslavia and Serbia," *Review of International Affairs* 42, nos. 998–1000 (1991): 11–14.

34. Based on conversations with Yugoslav colleagues and with the American ambassador to Yugoslavia, Warren Zimmerman, in Belgrade, 30 June–9 July 1991.

35. The quotation is from a BBC broadcast, 27 June 1991. There is some ambiguity centering on who gave orders for what in this case. Army spokesmen have accused federal politicians of being unwilling to face up to their own responsibility. *Narodna Armija* (Belgrade), 6 July 1991. Former prime minister Ante Marković, who insisted on Belgrade television that he had been left out of the decision-making loop by army commanders at the time of the operation, later charged that the army was acting on its own in Slovenia. *Vreme* (Belgrade), 23 Sept. 1991.

36. Who gave orders to whom, and who was responsible for what, remains very unclear. Prime Minister Marković said flatly on Belgrade television that his order had been exceeded. The army insists that it was acting in accordance with decisions of the government and the presidency, and that politicians must take their share of responsibility. *Narodna Armija* (Belgrade), 6 July 1991. Subsequently, in a closed session of the Federal Executive Council whose proceedings were leaked within days, Marković went on to accuse the army of acting on its own in Slovenia. *Vreme* (Belgrade), 23 Sept. 1991, 5–12.

37. Interviews in Belgrade, 27 June–9 July 1991.

38. In fact, Belgrade BBC had cited this theory from the British press even before it was taken up as a Serbian rallying cry. Belgrade Television, 28 June 1991. In the postmortem of the EC recognition of Croatia and Slovenia, this theory was elaborated: "The united Germany of today is not the same as the West Germany of yesterday. . . . New structures are already operating within the European Community. Actually, Germany and Italy are developing their alliance; on the other

hand, they have brought into accord their interests regarding the division of Yugoslav territory. The same interests and motives are involved as those that brought about the establishment of the Rome-Berlin axis on the eve of World War II." Mirko Ostojić, "Breaking Up of Yugoslavia," *Review of International Affairs* 43, no. 1001 (1992): 7.

39. For a provocative, undoubtedly controversial account, see John Newhouse, "The Diplomatic Round (Yugoslavia)," *New Yorker*, 24 Aug. 1992, 60–71.

40. See German statements regarding the EC peace conference, in *New York Times*, 6 Sept. 1991. Although the statements were presumably intended as deterrence directed against Serbian forces within the federal army, the Croatian leadership seemed to assume that they were not a threat but a promise.

41. *New York Times*, 19 Sept. 1991.

42. Note that only roughly one-fourth of the Serbs living in Croatia are in the Krajina region. See Shoup, *Communism and the Yugoslav National Question*.

43. *Politika: The International Weekly*, 5–11 Oct. 1991.

44. President Stjepan Mešić, supported by the representatives of Slovenia, Macedonia, and Bosnia and Herzegovina, denounced this as a coup against the federal government. *New York Times*, 5 Oct. 1991. For analysis, see Dragan Bujosevic, "Yugoslavia — A Country That No Longer Exists: Drawing New Borders," *Politika: The International Weekly*, 12–18 Oct. 1991.

45. *New York Times*, 16 Oct. 1991.

46. I appreciate the insights of Milan Popović, John Marshall Fellow at the University of Missouri, Columbia, in this regard (personal communication, 2 Oct. 1991). If anything, this would equate with a level of praetorianism that Eric Nordlinger, *Soldiers in Politics: Military Coups and Governments* (Englewood Cliffs, N.J.: Prentice-Hall, 1977), would characterize as that of a moderator attempting to achieve veto power over an unacceptable outcome. This is quite different from the scenario of military takeover considered by Marko Milivojevic, "The Political Role of the Yugoslav People's Army in Contemporary Yugoslavia," in Marko Milivojevic, John B. Allcock, and Pierre Maurer, eds., *Yugoslavia's Security Dilemmas: Armed Forces, National Defence, and Foreign Policy* (Oxford: Berg, 1988), 15–59.

47. See Milan Andrejevic, "Bosnia and Herzegovina: A Precarious Peace," *RFE/RL Research Report* 1, no. 9 (1992): 7.

48. National Public Radio, 28 Mar. 1992. For analysis, see Milan Andrejevich, "More Guns, Less Butter in Bosnia and Herzegovina," *RFE/RL Research Report*, 13 Mar. 1992.

49. Steven Niksic, "Threats and Blackmail," *Politika: The International Weekly* (Belgrade), 16–22 May 1992, 4.

50. Text of EC "Declaration on Yugoslavia" (Brussels, 17 Dec. 1991), in *Review of International Affairs* (Belgrade), 42, nos. 998–1000 (1991): 28. See also Predrag Simic, "Europe and the 'Yugoslav Issue,'" ibid., 43, no. 1001 (1992): 1–5.

51. See Patrick Moore, "Ethnic Cleansing in Bosnia: Outrage but Little Action," *RFE/RL Research Report* 1, no. 34 (1992): 1–7. American officials are reported to have independent confirmation that as many as three thousand may have died in Serb-run camps during May and June 1992. *New York Times*, 26 Sept. 1992.

52. For a thoughtful analysis of consociationalism and its critics, see Paul Brass, *Ethnicity and Nationalism: Theory and Comparison* (New Delhi: Sage, 1991), 333–43.

53. Vojislav Stanovcic, "Bureaucracy and Socialism: The Experience of Yugoslavia," in Jaroslaw Piekalkiewicz and Christopher Hamilton, eds., *Public Bureaucracies between Reform and Resistance* (New York: Berg, 1991), 179–215.

54. See A. Ross Johnson, "The Role of the Military in Yugoslavia: An Historical Sketch," in Roman Kolkowicz and Andrzej Korbonski, eds., *Soldiers, Peasants, and Bureaucrats: Civil-Military Relations in Communist and Modernizing Societies* (London: Allen and Unwin, 1982), 193–97; and Robin Alison Remington, "Civil-Military Relations in Yugoslavia: The Partisan Vanguard," *Studies in Comparative Communism* 11, no. 3 (1978): 250–64.

55. Federal Secretariat of National Defense, statement asserting that all political organizing should be banned from the armed forces, Belgrade Tanjug domestic service, 13 Dec., translated in *Foreign Broadcast Information Service — Eastern Europe*, 14 Dec. 1990; Robin Alison Remington, "Yugoslav Soldiers in Politics: On the Road to Civil War," Occasional Paper no. 9109, University of Missouri–St. Louis Center for International Studies, 1991.

56. Herz describes the response of individuals and groups in an anarchic society as the acquisition of power to avoid threat; that, in turn, "renders others more insecure and compels them to prepare for the worst." John Herz, "The Security Dilemma," *World Politics* 2 (1950): 157.

57. Debate rages over the future of the army, its size, mission, ethnic composition, and political leanings. Milos Vasic, "Sumrak generala" (Eclipse of the generals), *Vreme* (Belgrade), no. 72 (9 Mar. 1992): 18–19.

58. According to the military editor of the independent Belgrade weekly *Vreme*, Milos Vasic, "both sides have a lot to complain about." *New York Times*, 29 Nov. 1991.

59. Official inflation estimates of 1 December 1993 were more than 18 percent per day. *New York Times*, 2 Dec. 1993. By the new year an unofficial estimate was 1 million percent for the month of December 1993.

60. David Binder's analysis in the *New York Times*, 29 Aug. 1993, quotes State Department officials as saying that these days that agreement does not look so bad.

61. *New York Times*, 7 Jan. 1994.

62. *New York Times*, 10 Oct. 1993.

63. For a thoughtful analysis of the need for "new thinking about security," see Charles Gati, "From Sarajevo to Sarajevo," *Foreign Affairs* 71, no. 4 (1992): 76.

Chapter 15. Zoltan Barany, Patterns, Lessons, and Implications

1. On the issue of East European "underdevelopment," see Daniel Chirot, ed., *The Origins of Backwardness in Eastern Europe* (Berkeley: University of California Press, 1989); and George Schöpflin, "The Political Traditions of Eastern Europe," *Daedalus* 119, no. 1 (1990): 55–90.

2. The "proliferation" of putative dissidents is an interesting, albeit hardly new, phenomenon in Eastern Europe. Just as during the Communist period there were many more members of the World War II "partisan associations" than actual partisans, now the number of those who claim to have been dissidents is much greater than the number of actual dissidents. According to a current Czech joke, a person who knows someone who knows someone (and so on) who read a samizdat publication qualifies as a former dissident.

3. Along these lines, see Zoltan Barany, "Mass-Elite Relations and the Resurgence of Nationalism in Eastern Europe," *European Security* 3, no. 1 (1994): 162–81.

4. For excellent studies on Soviet–East European relations, see Zbigniew Brzezinski, *The Soviet Bloc: Unity and Conflict* (Cambridge: Harvard University Press, 1967); Sarah Meiklejohn Terry, ed., *Soviet Policy in Eastern Europe* (New Haven: Yale University Press, 1984); and Glenn R. Chafetz, *Gorbachev, Reform, and the Brezhnev Doctrine* (Westport, Conn.: Praeger, 1993).

CONTRIBUTORS

Zoltan Barany is assistant professor of government at the University of Texas at Austin. He is the author of *Soldiers and Politics in Eastern Europe, 1945–90* (1993) and co-author of the forthcoming *Political Transitions and the Military*. His current research and writing focuses on marginality, ethnopolitics, and the East European Roma (Gypsies).

Thomas A. Baylis is professor of political science at the University of Texas at San Antonio. He is the author of *Governing by Committee* (1989) and *The West and Eastern Europe* (1994). His current research is on the process of elite change in eastern Germany and the former Czechoslovakia and on the shaping of executive authority in the new regimes of East-Central Europe.

Elez Biberaj is chief of the Albanian Service at the Voice of America in Washington, D.C. He received his Ph.D. in political science from Columbia University in 1985 and is the author of *Albania and China: A Study of an Unequal Alliance* (1986) and *Albania: A Socialist Maverick* (1990). He has also contributed articles to *Problems of Communism, Conflict Studies, Survey*, and other journals.

Jane L. Curry is associate professor of government at Colby College, Waterville, Maine. She is the author of *The Black Book of Polish Censorship* (1984) and *Polish Journalists: Politics and Professionalism* (1988), the editor of *Dissent in Eastern Europe* (1984), and the co-editor of *Poland: A State of Crises* (1995). She has written widely on public opinion, the mass media, and pluralism in Eastern Europe.

Barbara Jancar-Webster, professor of political science at the State University of New York at Brockport, is a specialist on the environmental policies and political-economic systems of East-Central Europe and the former Soviet Union. Her recent publications include *Environmental Management in the Soviet Union and Yugoslavia* (1987) and *Environmental Action in Eastern Europe* (1993).

Andrzej Korbonski is professor of political science at the University of California–Los Angeles. He has written widely on East European and Soviet politics, economics, and military affairs. He is currently writing a book on relations between the Roman Catholic Church and the Polish state.

Bennett Kovrig is professor emeritus of political science at the University of Toronto. He has written widely on Hungarian politics and East-West relations and is the author of *The Myth of Liberation: East-Central Europe in U.S. Diplomacy and Politics since 1941* (1973), *Communism in Hungary* (1979), and *Of Walls and Bridges: The United States and Eastern Europe* (1991).

Daniel N. Nelson is director of graduate programs in international studies at Old Dominion University, Norfolk, Virginia. His most recent books are *Security After Hegemony* (1994) and *Romania After Tyranny* (1992) which he edited. He is a member of the Council of Foreign Relations (New York) and the International Institute of Strategic Studies (London), and he is a councillor of the Atlantic Council of the United States.

Robin Alison Remington is professor of political science at the University of Missouri-Columbia. Her field research in the former Yugoslavia began as an exchange scholar at the Institute of International Politics and Economics, Belgrade, in 1970–71. Since then she has published more than thirty articles and chapters on Yugoslav politics, most recently focusing on the consequences of internationalization of the Yugoslav wars of succession.

Luan Troxel is assistant professor of government at Smith College, Northampton, Massachusetts. She received her Ph.D. in political science at the University of Michigan in 1992. She has done extensive field research in Eastern Europe on topics ranging from ethnopolitics and electoral politics to gender politics. She has published various articles and chapters on these topics and is currently working on a book on Bulgarian politics in the postwar period.

Ivan Volgyes is professor of political science at the University of Nebraska–Lincoln. In addition to his academic work he has also been a senior advisor on Eastern Europe to Martin-Lockheed and General Electric corporations. He has written widely on East European, Soviet, and post-Soviet politics and is currently at work on a volume entitled *Politics in Post-Communist Europe*.

Sharon L. Wolchik is director of Russian and East European studies and professor of political science at the George Washington University, Washington, D.C. She is the author of *Czechoslovakia in Transition: Politics, Economics, and Society* (1991), and the co-editor of *The Social Legacy of Communism* (1994) and *Women, State, and Party in Eastern Europe* (1985). Her current research focuses on gender issues and mass-elite relations in post-Communist Eastern Europe.

INDEX

Abgrenzung, 122, 133
Academy of Sciences: Hungary, 89; USSR, 89
Agolli, Dritero, 260
agriculture: in Czechoslovakia, 160; in Eastern Europe, 13, 49; in Romania, 199–201
Albania, 17, 63, 73, 165, 245–66, 289, 290, 292; and China, 249–50, 264; demonstrations, 245, 251; economy, 249, 254–57, 262–63, 265–66; elections, 245, 251, 252; emigration, 260; environment, 262–65; famine, 256; former Communists, 34; and Greece, 246–47; history of, 246–51; industrialization, 254–56, 262–65; inflation, 256; intelligentsia, 259–60; isolation of, 249–51, 253, 263; in Kosovo, 247; opposition, 259–60; People's Assembly, 252; politics, 248–54, 265; prospects, 265–66; reforms, 252–53; regional tensions, 246, 259, 262; religion in, 246, 258; and secret police, 261–62; and Serbia, 247; social welfare, 257–58; society, 257–62; and Soviet Union, 255, 263, 266; and Yugoslavia, 248–49, 251
Albanian Communist Party (ACP), 245, 248–49. *See also* Albanian Party of Labor
Albanian Party of Labor (APL), 249, 253, 255, 258
Albanians, 29, 292
Alexander, King, 270, 271
Alia, Ramiz, 245, 251, 253
Alliance of Free Democrats (AFD), 181, 183
Alliance of Reform Forces, 276
All-Polish Association of Labor Unions (OPZZ), 141–42
Alma-Ata, 90
Alton, Thad, 202
Antall, József, 181
anti-Russian attitudes, 27, 153
Aral Sea, 84
Armenia, 87
Association of Centers of Industrial Production Regions, 53
Austria, 161
Austro-Hungarian Empire, 65, 138, 186, 269–70
authoritarianism, 25, 26, 34

Baker, James A., III, 278
Balcerowicz, Leszek, 76

Balkans, 24, 31, 105, 265, 266, 269, 295; and military, 109, 114, 117; threat of Yugoslav civil war, 40
Balluku, Beqir, 250
Baltic states, 87, 98
Banat, 206–7
banking and finance, 50–51
Belarus, 87
Belgium, 27, 33
Berisha, Sali, 245, 251, 254, 261, 262, 265
Berlin, 23, 121, 132, 133, 147
Berlin Wall, 23, 275
Beron, Peter, 229
Biberaj, Elez, 292
Blushi, Kiço, 247
Bohemia, 23, 24; environment, 84
Bornstein, Morris, 42
Bosnia and Herzegovina, 92, 267–69, 279, 280, 288; census, 281, 287; civil war, 281–82, 286, 287–88; ethnic minorities, 282–87; independence, 280; Muslims in, 267, 269, 273, 281, 284; Serbs in, 281–82
Botez, Mihai, 211
Brezhnev Doctrine, 275, 294
Brezhnev, Leonid I., 86, 275
Brucan, Silviu, 212
Bucharest, 79, 210, 213, 214
Budapest, 185, 189
Bulgaria, 13, 33, 63, 73, 78, 165, 204, 223, 227–44, 290; demographic structure, 233–34, 237; economy, 37, 233–40; education, 237; elections, 232, 236, 243–44; environment, 87, 240–42; ethnic minorities, 232–33, 243; former Communists, 34; indebtedness, 39, 236, 239–40; industrialization, 234–37; living standards, 234–37; military, 105, 117; political opposition, 228, 231; political participation, 230–31; politics, 228–31; reforms, 230–31; repression, 231–32, 243; security, 113–14, 116–17; social welfare, 242–43; society, 231–33; and Soviet Union, 238–40, 294; unemployment, 238; women, 237–38; and Yugoslavia, 273
Bulgarian Communist Party (BCP), 228, 229, 230–32, 236–37; labor policy of, 237–38, 242–44
Bulgarian Socialist Party (BSP), 230–31, 233, 236, 242–44
Bundestag, 131; elections, 123
Bündnis-90, 126

etization, 153–54; State Planning Commission, 159; women, 174; youth, 174
Czechs, 24, 153, 157, 163

Dahrendorf, Ralf, 123, 143, 145
Daladier, Édouard, 25
Danilov-Danilyan, Viktor, 93
Danube, 84, 89, 205; and hydroelectric project on, 89, 196
Danube Circle, 89
Defenders of Nature, 166
Delors, Jacques, 40
democracy, 35, 55, 82–83, 289–90; in West, 35, 83
Democracy Now, 126
Democratic Awakening, 126
Democratic Charter, 185
Democratic Farmers' Party (DBD), 124, 125
Democratic Front of Russia, 91
Democratic Party (Albania), 251, 256
Democratic Party (SD; Poland), 141
Demszky, Gábor, 185
Diósgyőr, 48
dissidents, 32, 67–68, 73–75, 77, 125–26, 141, 166, 211–12, 228–29, 291
Dorog, 195
Dresden, 78
Dubček, Alexander, 156
Dubrovnik, 286
Dulles, John Foster, 36
Dusan, Tsar, 270
Dushanbe, 90
Dyba, Karel, 162
Dzhurov, Dobri, 105

Eagleburger, Lawrence, 244
East European economies, 5–7, 37–38, 42–54, 82, 292–94 (see also specific countries); autarkic development, 46–47; banking and finance, 50–51; central planning, 6, 44–45, 62; and environment, 85–87, 293; and free market, 36, 49–50; industrial development, 5–6, 43–44, 60, 293; and infrastructure, 45, 51; integration of, 46, 48, 87, 98; living standards, 36–37, 45–46, 99; price structure, 50; privatization, 37; shortages, 12, 62; and Soviet model, 43; stagnation of, 47; and state involvement, 6, 38, 44; and unemployment, 16, 17, 52–53, 61, 99, 238
East European societies, 7–13, 55–83, 95,

291–94; anti-Russian attitudes, 27, 153; civil society, 32, 33, 142–45, 184–85; cynicism, 68–70; development options, 80–82; dissidents, 73–75, 125–26, 211–12, 291; divisions ("us" and "them"), 17–18, 67–68; egalitarianism, 70–71; ethnic divisions, 63–64, 67; materialism in, 70–71; and media, 72–73, 132, 293; and military, 102–10; professionals, 75–77; values of, 56–57, 58, 66–73
East Germany. See German Democratic Republic
East-Central Europe, 23, 295; and European Union, 40; and military, 107, 109, 110, 114–15; security, 116–17; Visegrád Four, 40, 114
Eastern Europe: armed forces, 101–17 (see also military, East European); authoritarianism, 25, 26; backwardness, 23, 24, 26, 44, 290; Communist control of, 70–71; constitutional monarchies, 25; democracy in, 35; development options, 80–82; economy (see East European economies); education, 58–60; environment, 2–5, 84–100 (see also specific countries); human rights, 29; image in West, 23; imperial rule in, 24; international security of, 101–17; liberalism, 25; living standards, 36, 45–46; nationalism, 29–30, 113; politics, 14–16, 289–90; and popular disillusionment, 60; regional diversity in, 289–90, 295; regional security of, 110–17; secret police in, 67, 212; societies (see East European societies); sovietization of, 26–29, 139–41; totalitarianism in, 27–28; as distinct from Western Europe, 41; and Western powers, 26, 34–35
Ecoglasnost, 229
Economic Research Institute, 159
Economist (London), 38
education, 58–60, 294; of military, 107–8; political content of, 58–59, 62, 107
egalitarianism, 70–71
elections, 15, 33, 34, 68, 70, 75, 91; in Albania, 245, 251, 252; in Hungary, 34, 179–80, 183; in Poland, 38; popular attitudes toward, 91
elites (Communist), 10, 62–63, 67–69, 71–72, 88–89, 154, 229–30, 290–91; in Albania, 258–60; and economic reforms, 159–60; and environment, 5; and lustration, 33; and privileges, 10; responsibility

elites (Communist) (*cont'd.*)
of, 41; in Romania, 222–24; and Soviet
patronage, 27, 153–54
elites (former Communists), 62, 77–78; in
Albania, 34, 259; in Bulgaria, 34, 229; in
Czech Republic, 77; in Eastern Europe,
34; in Hungary, 77, 182, 190–91; and lustration, 33; in Poland, 77, 149–51; and
power conversion, 36, 77, 88–89, 182; in
Romania, 34; in Serbia, 34; in Slovakia,
167–68; in Yugoslavia, 283–84, 287
elites (post-Communist), 73–74, 99, 292; in
Albania, 259–61; in Czechoslovakia,
167–69; and environment, 88–92; in
Hungary, 182–83; in Poland, 150–
51
elites (pre-Communist), 24
emigration, 65
employment, 45, 52; and labor market, 45,
60–62
entrepreneurs, 62, 77, 147, 163
environment, 2–5, 48, 84–100; drinking
water, 93, 196; in East Germany, 133–37;
and economic development, 85–87; and
health problems, 93; Hungary, 194–97;
information about, 86; organizations,
92–95; Poland, 148–50; protection of, 4–
5, 91–98
"Environmental Library," 133–34
Environmental Protection Act, 92
Environmental Protection Fund, 92
environmental scientists, 89–91, 95, 97
Eppelmann, Rainer, 126
ethnic divisions, 63–64, 67, 82
ethnic minorities, 29–31, 34, 63–64;
Belgium, 30; Bosnia and Herzegovina,
281–82, 287; Bulgaria, 232–33; Canada,
30; Croatia, 276–77, 279; France, 30;
Kosovo, 29, 247, 274; Lithuania, 29; Romania, 186, 206–9, 217; Slovakia, 29,
186; Spain, 30; United Kingdom, 30;
Vojvodina, 29; Yugoslavia, 267, 269, 273,
281–82, 284
European Bank for Reconstruction and Development (EBRD), 98
European Community (EC). *See* European
Union
European Convention on Human Rights,
32
European Union (EU; formerly European
Community), 13, 34, 35, 36, 39–40, 137,
185, 190, 199, 241, 264; protectionism

in, 54; and Yugoslavia, 268, 269, 278–81,
283, 286–87
Europeanization, 64–66, 87–88

Feshbach, Murray, 42
Fischer, Mary Ellen, 222
Foreign Affairs, 176
France, 24, 26, 27, 28, 30, 32, 33, 37, 66, 89,
216, 237
Free Democratic Party, 124
Free German Youth, 123, 131

Gegs, 246, 259, 262
Genscher, Hans-Dietrich, 34
Geremek, Bronislaw, 40
German Democratic Republic (GDR), 28,
63, 112, 121–37, 188, 204, 235, 239; col-
laboration with regime, 124; currency,
133; dissent in, 125–26; economy, 127–
29; elections, 124–25, 135; and environment, 87, 133–35; Evangelical Church
of, 125, 128; fall of communism, 121;
Greens, 135; housing, 128–29, 293; ideological rivalry with FRG, 122; intelligentsia, 130–32; intra-German trade, 128–
29; lustration in, 33; media, 132–33; migration, 133; military, 105, 115; nostalgia
after, 121; political culture of, 122–23;
relations with West Germany, 28, 121–
22, 126–29, 131–34; reunification, 99,
135–36; secret police (Stasi), 124, 133;
society, 130–33; uprising in June 1953,
28; women, 130; workers, 129–31; youth,
131
German influence in Eastern Europe, 65
Germans, 24, 27
Germany, 25, 26, 32, 33, 34, 37
Germany, Federal Republic of (FRG), 28,
66, 81, 121–25, 216, 237; and Czechoslovakia, 161; elections, 124–25; Ministry of
Environmental Protection, 97; relations
with East Germany, 28, 121–22, 126–29,
131–34; reunification, 99, 135–36; and
Yugoslavia, 279–80, 287
Gheorghiu-Dej, Gheorghe, 206, 213
Gierek, Edward, 71
Goga, Octavian, 25
Goma, Paul, 211
Göncz, Árpád, 181
Gorbachev, Mikhail S., 88, 93, 131, 214,
216–17, 218, 225, 229, 275
Gottwald, Klement, 153, 155

Great Britain. *See* United Kingdom
Great Depression, 25
Greece, 36, 37, 114, 286; and Albania, 246, 247, 248; civil war, 27; and Macedonia, 286
Gromyko, Andrei A., 217
Grossman, Gregory, 42
Grósz, Károly, 217
Group of Seven, 97
Gulf of Finland, 96
Gypsies, 63, 165, 174, 192, 271, 292

Habsburg Empire, 177, 186, 270
Haidacu, Mihai, 216
Halle, 134
Hankiss, Elemér, 88
Havel, Václav, 125, 170, 175, 176, 230
Herz, John, 285
Hitler, Adolf, 25, 26, 271, 276
Honecker, Erich, 125, 128–29
Horthy, Admiral Miklós, 177
House Committee on Un-American Activities, 288
housing, 3–4, 67, 128–29, 192, 209, 293
Hoxha, Enver, 245, 248–50, 254, 257–59, 265
human rights, 29, 34
Hungarian Democratic Forum (HDF), 181, 184, 187
Hungarian minority: in Romania, 206–10, 217; in Slovakia, 29; in Vojvodina, 29, 280
Hungarian Radio and Television, 181
Hungarian Socialist Party (HSP), 179
Hungarian Socialist Workers' Party (HSWP), 178, 179, 183, 187, 192, 217
Hungary, 10, 13, 18, 23, 27, 32, 37, 50, 63, 65, 74, 76–78, 123, 136, 153, 160, 161, 166, 177–97, 204, 223, 277, 293; airspace, 112; banking, 51; civil society, 184–85; culture and education, 190–91; economy, 53, 186–90; elections, 34, 91, 183, 187; environment, 84, 194–97; foreign policy, 185–86; GDP, 36–37; government, 187–88; housing, 192, 194; indebtedness, 39, 187; infrastructure, 52; living standards, 182; military, 105, 109; political liberalization in, 178–80; political participation, 15; politics, 178–86; poverty, 192–93; presidential powers, 32, 181; privatization, 49, 189; public dissatisfaction, 35; revolution of 1956, 28, 36,

68, 155; and Romania, 217–18; society, 190–93; Soviet role in, 178; unemployment, 193; Western contacts, 188, 290
Huntington, Samuel P., 108

indebtedness: of Bulgaria, 39; of Hungary, 39, 187–88; of Poland, 39, 147; of Romania, 39, 200
industrial development, 5–7, 9–10, 60–63, 146; and environment, 85–87, 194–96
inflation, 70
infrastructure, in Eastern Europe, 4–5, 45, 51
Institute for Youth Research, 131
intelligentsia, 8–11; in Albania, 259–60; in Czechoslovakia, 162–63; in East Germany, 131–32; technical, 8–11
interest articulation, 45
International Atomic Energy Agency, 242
International Monetary Fund (IMF), 13, 38, 50, 188, 204, 214, 274, 283, 286
international trade, 6, 53, 161
Istanbul, 147
Italy, 25, 26, 27, 28, 33, 127; and Albania, 248
Izetbegović, Alija, 281, 284

Jackson-Vanik Amendment, 216
Jakeš, Miloš, 218
Japan, 86
Jaruzelski, Wojciech, 218
Jews, 24, 63, 64, 155, 185, 271; and anti-Semitism, 169, 185, 192
John Paul II, 142
Jović, Borisav, 277
Jowitt, Kenneth, 145, 227
Jugendweihe, 121

Kádár, János, 10, 71, 179
Kadare, Ismail, 253
Kadijević, Veljko, 280
Karadzić, Radovan, 282
Kardelj, Edvard, 284
Katowice, 149
Keko, Teodor, 254
KGB (Soviet intelligence service), 216
Khrushchev, Nikita S., 249
Király, Károly, 207
Klaus, Václav, 52
Kocka, Jürgen, 122, 136
Kohl, Helmut, 279
Kolosi, Tamás, 193